Spell of Desire

Volume 3

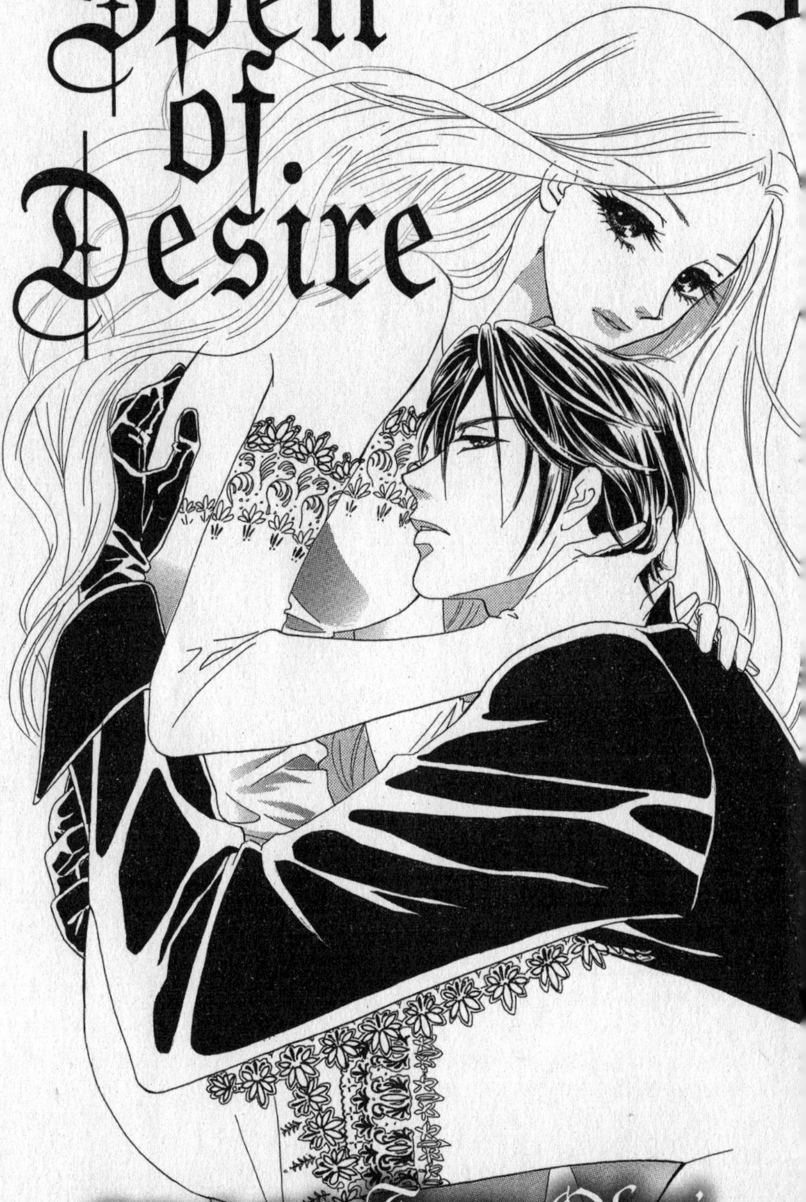

story & art by Tomu Ohmi

Spell of Desire
Volume 3

Contents

story

One day, Kaname, dressed all in black, appears in front of Kaoruko. He tells her that her mother, whom she long thought was dead, is actually alive—and in fact, a Witch Queen. The power of the Witch Queen has been entrusted to Kaoruko's care. Meanwhile, Kaoruko and Kaname find themselves drawn to each other, but nothing can come of it since he is the Witch Queen's knight. Kaoruko is commanded to appear before the Black Witches Coven, and she decides to become a black witch. However, in order for that to happen, a ritual must be performed, in which she will lose her virginity...

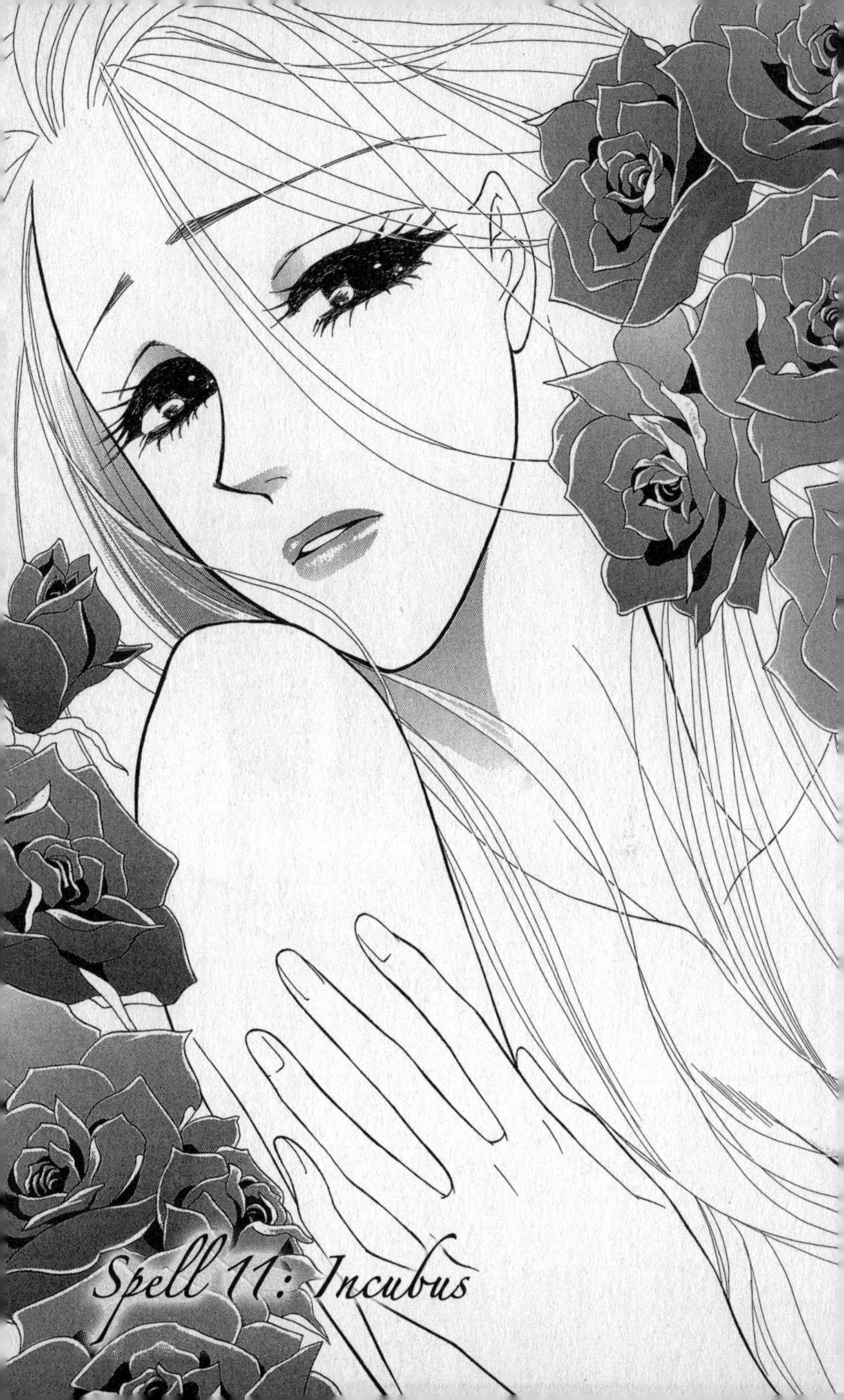
Spell 11: Incubus

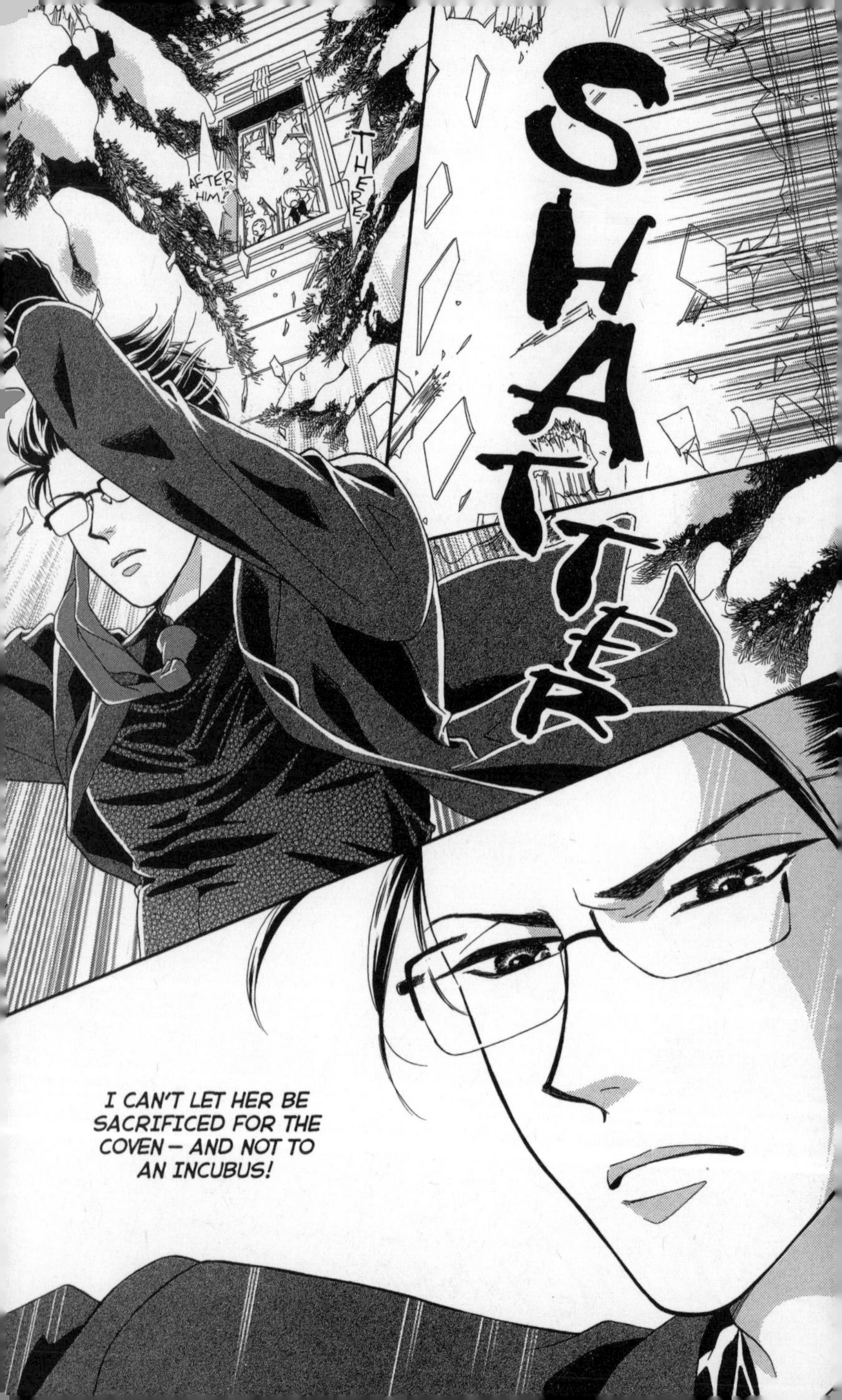
SHATTER
THERE!
AFTER HIM!
I CAN'T LET HER BE SACRIFICED FOR THE COVEN — AND NOT TO AN INCUBUS!

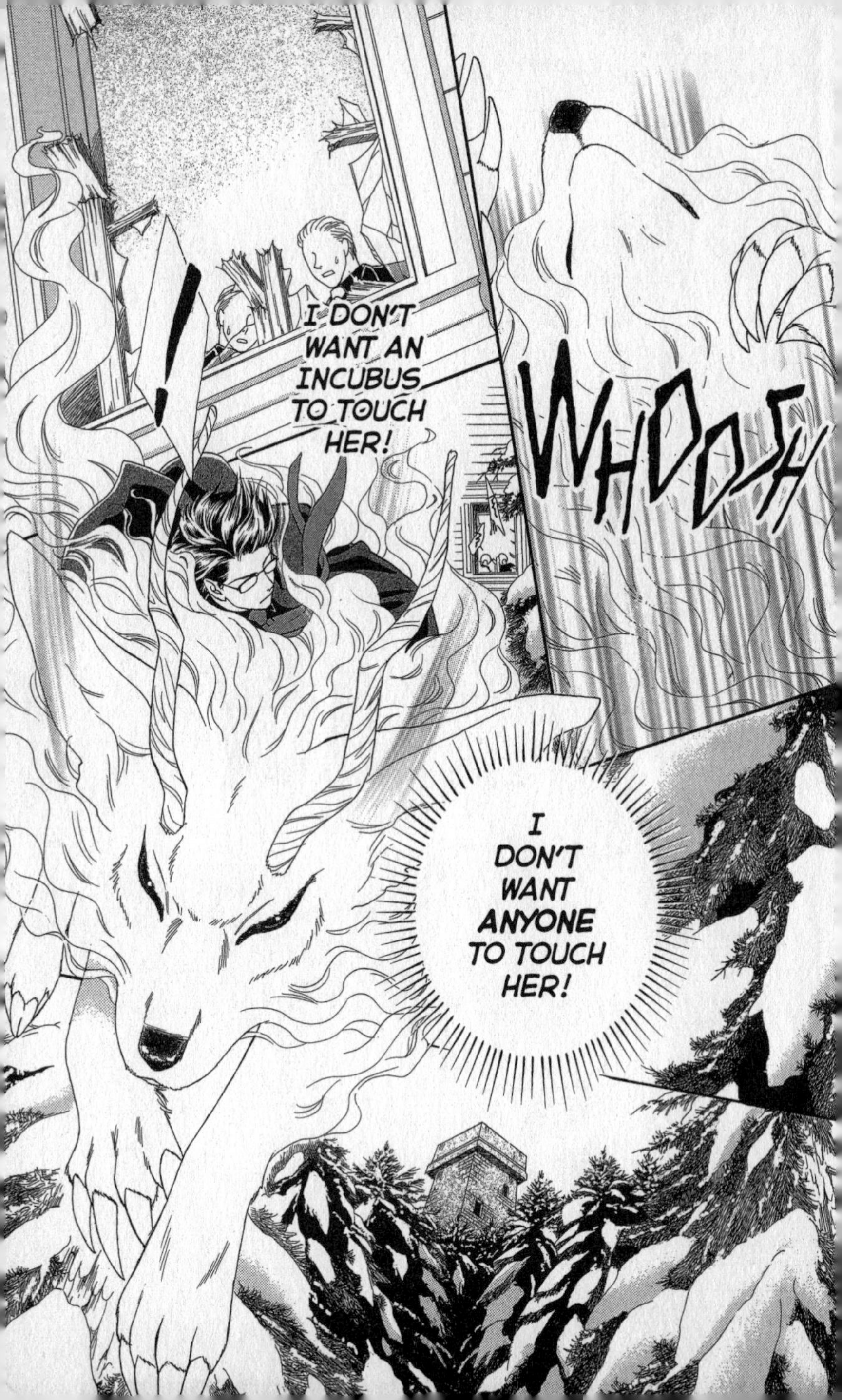
WHOOSH
!
I DON'T WANT AN INCUBUS TO TOUCH HER!
I DON'T WANT ANYONE TO TOUCH HER!

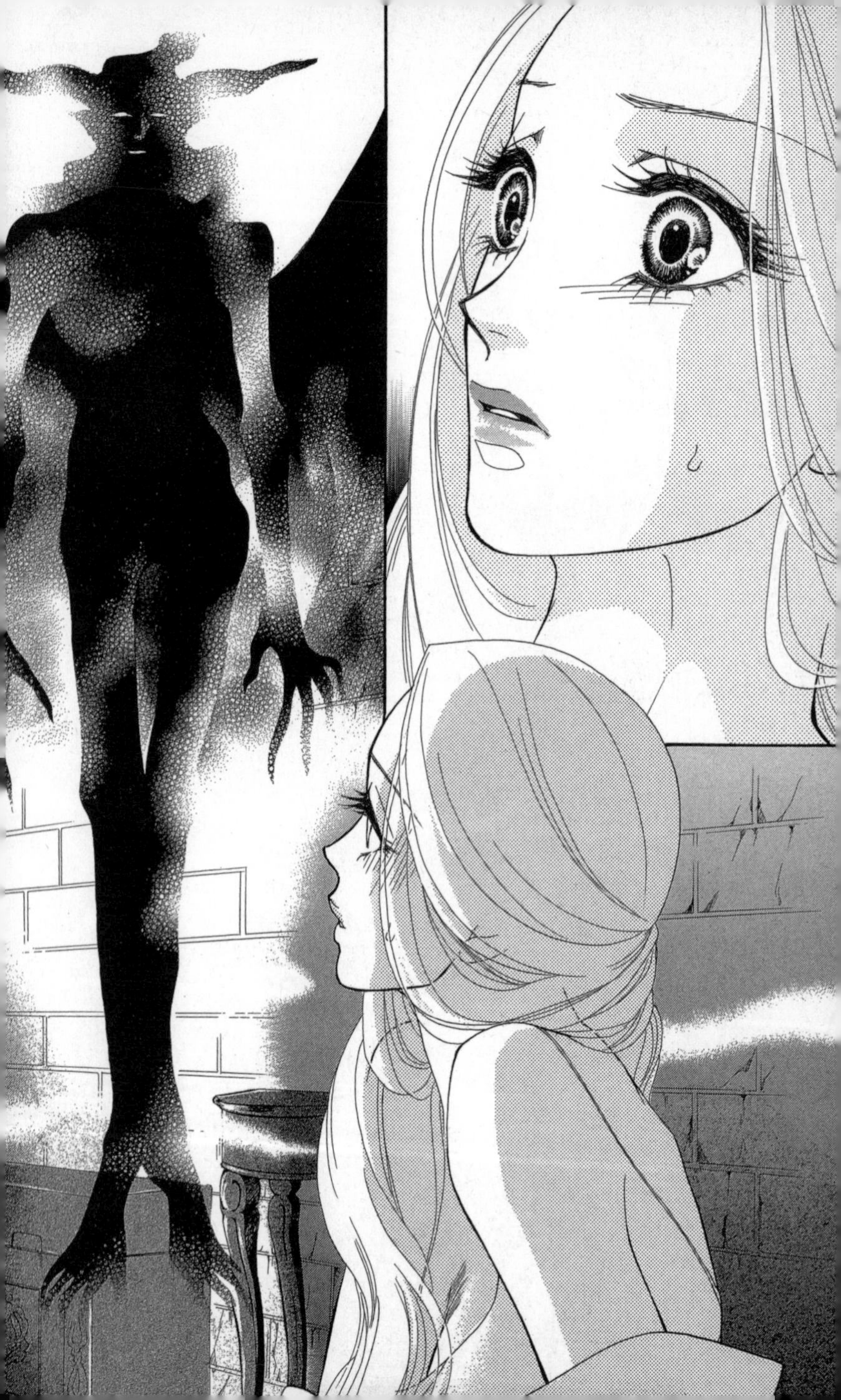

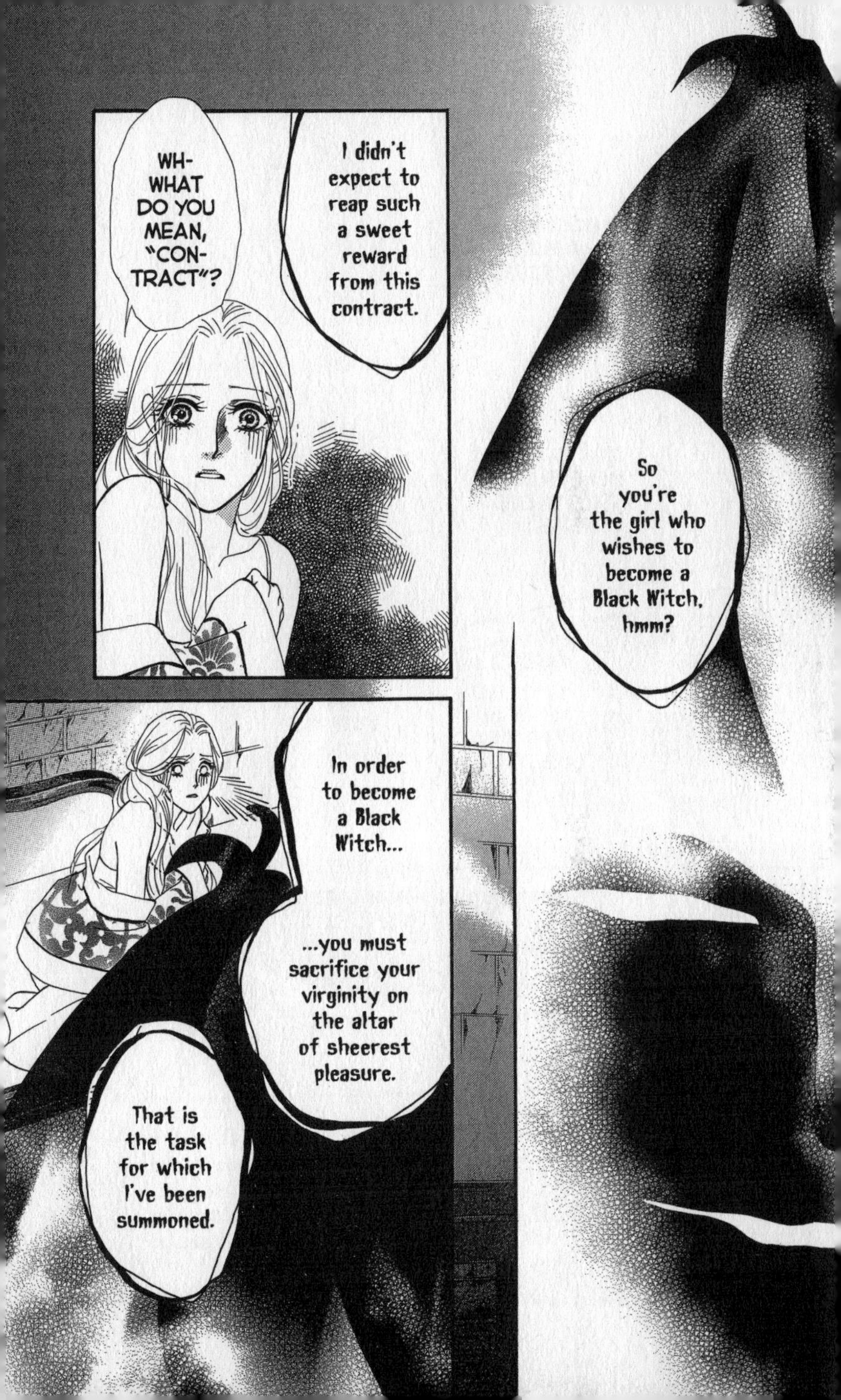
So you're the girl who wishes to become a Black Witch, hmm?
I didn't expect to reap such a sweet reward from this contract.
WH-WHAT DO YOU MEAN, "CON-TRACT"?
In order to become a Black Witch...
...you must sacrifice your virginity on the altar of sheerest pleasure.
That is the task for which I've been summoned.

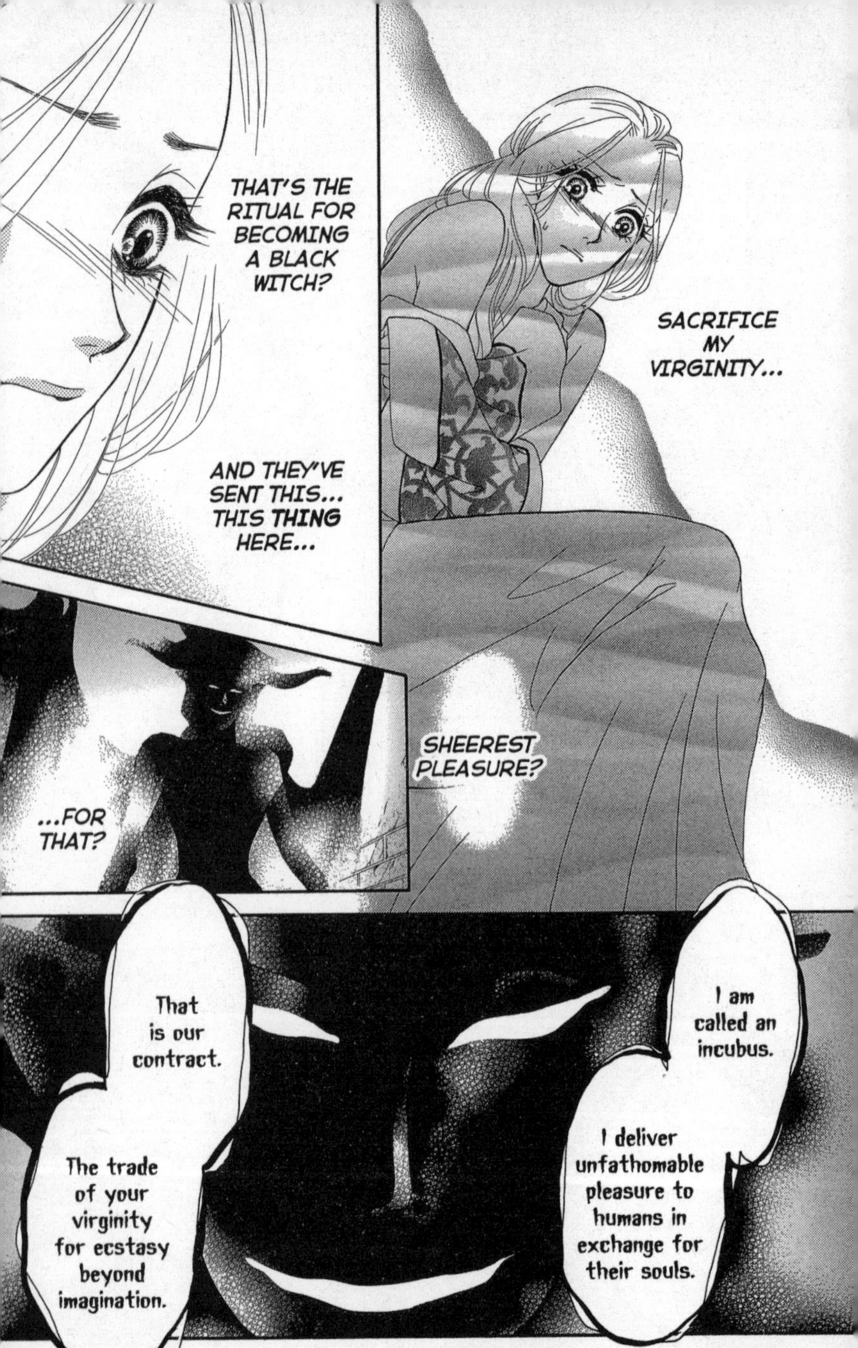

SACRIFICE MY VIRGINITY...
SHEEREST PLEASURE?
THAT'S THE RITUAL FOR BECOMING A BLACK WITCH?
AND THEY'VE SENT THIS... THIS THING HERE...
...FOR THAT?
I am called an incubus.
I deliver unfathomable pleasure to humans in exchange for their souls.
That is our contract.
The trade of your virginity for ecstasy beyond imagination.

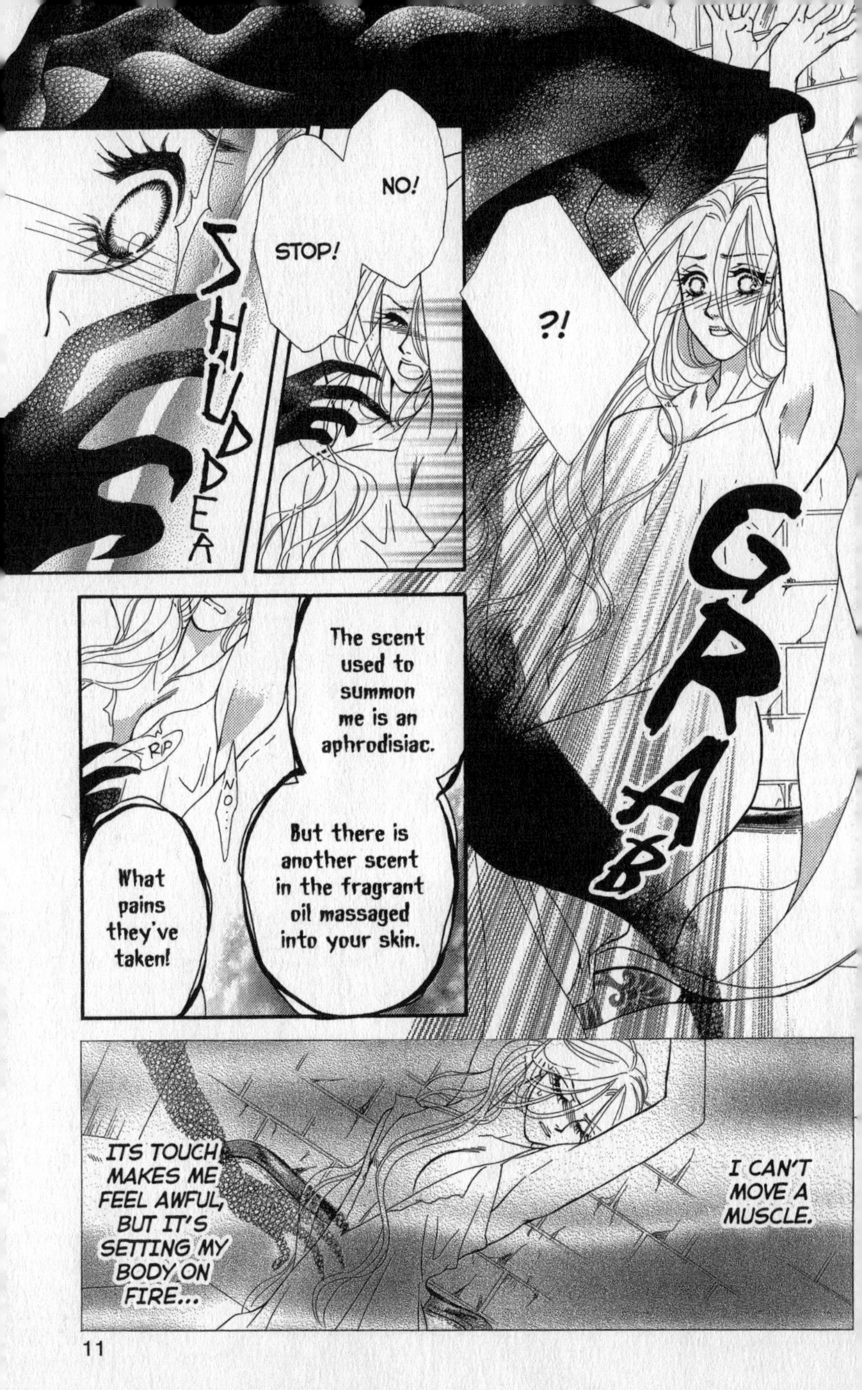
?!
GRAB
NO!
STOP!
SHUDDER
The scent used to summon me is an aphrodisiac.
But there is another scent in the fragrant oil massaged into your skin.
RIP
NO...
What pains they've taken!
I CAN'T MOVE A MUSCLE.
ITS TOUCH MAKES ME FEEL AWFUL, BUT IT'S SETTING MY BODY ON FIRE...

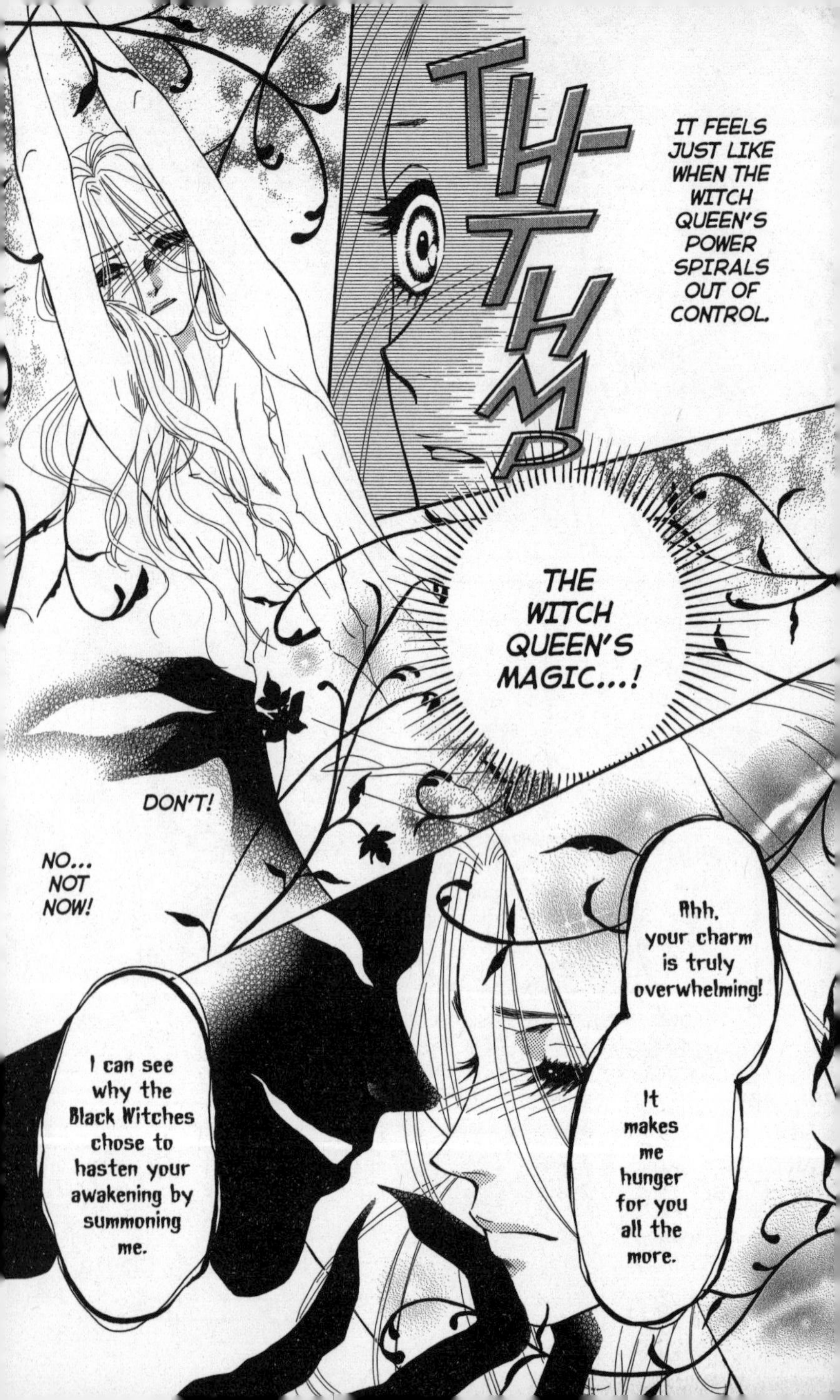
IT FEELS JUST LIKE WHEN THE WITCH QUEEN'S POWER SPIRALS OUT OF CONTROL.
TH-THUMP
THE WITCH QUEEN'S MAGIC...!
DON'T!
NO... NOT NOW!
Ahh, your charm is truly overwhelming!
It makes me hunger for you all the more.
I can see why the Black Witches chose to hasten your awakening by summoning me.

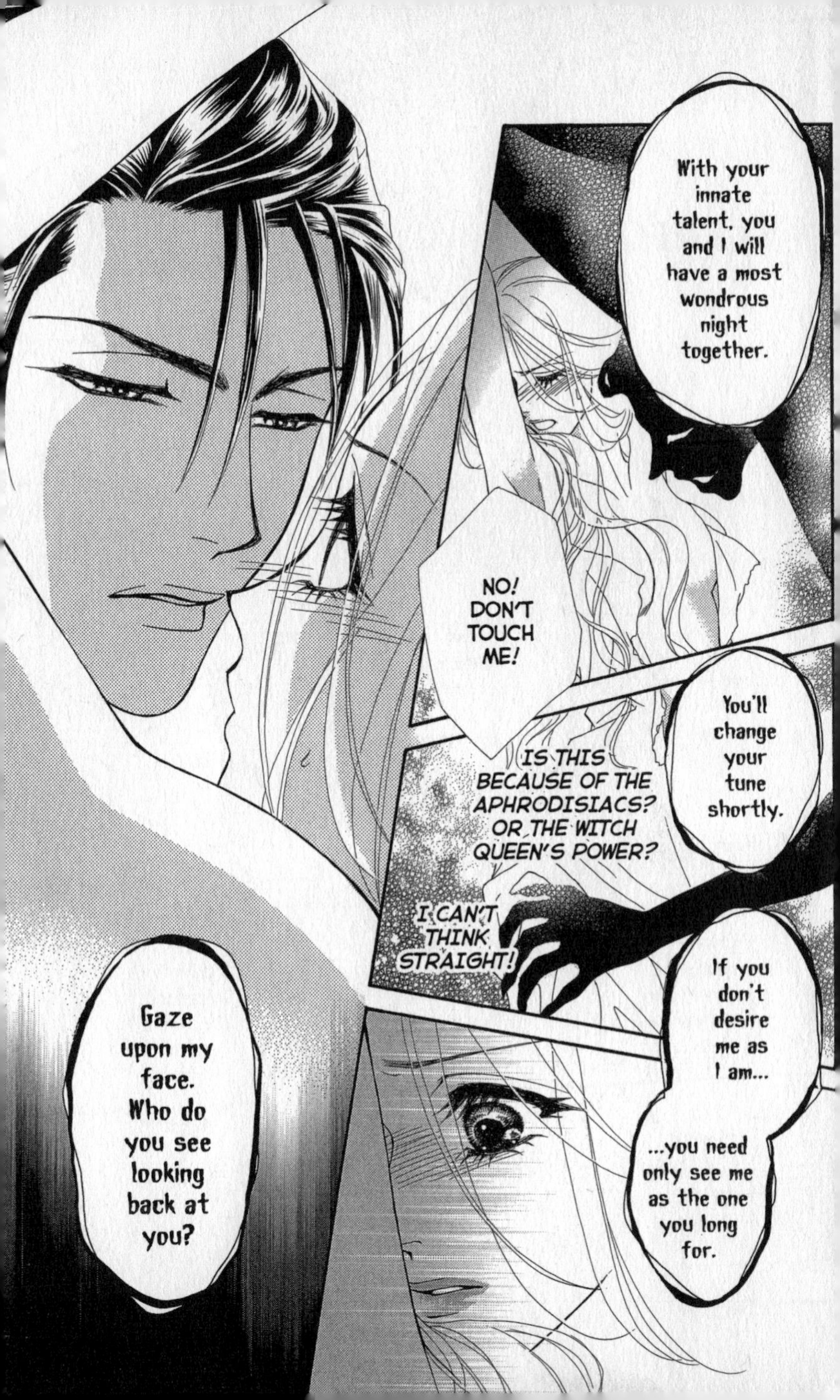
With your innate talent, you and I will have a most wondrous night together.
NO! DON'T TOUCH ME!
You'll change your tune shortly.
IS THIS BECAUSE OF THE APHRODISIACS? OR THE WITCH QUEEN'S POWER?
I CAN'T THINK STRAIGHT!
If you don't desire me as I am...
...you need only see me as the one you long for.
Gaze upon my face. Who do you see looking back at you?

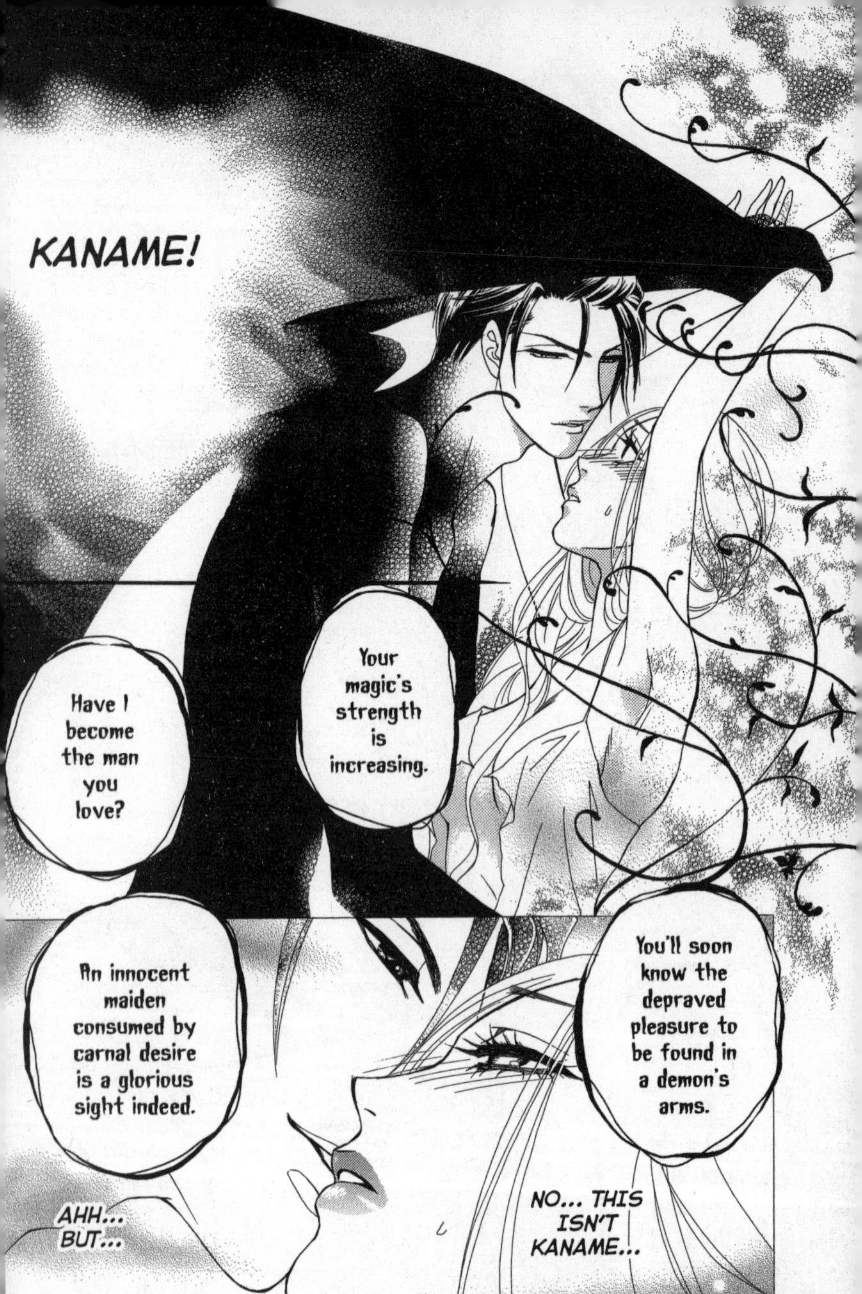
KANAME!
Your magic's strength is increasing.
Have I become the man you love?
You'll soon know the depraved pleasure to be found in a demon's arms.
An innocent maiden consumed by carnal desire is a glorious sight indeed.
NO... THIS ISN'T KANAME...
AHH... BUT...

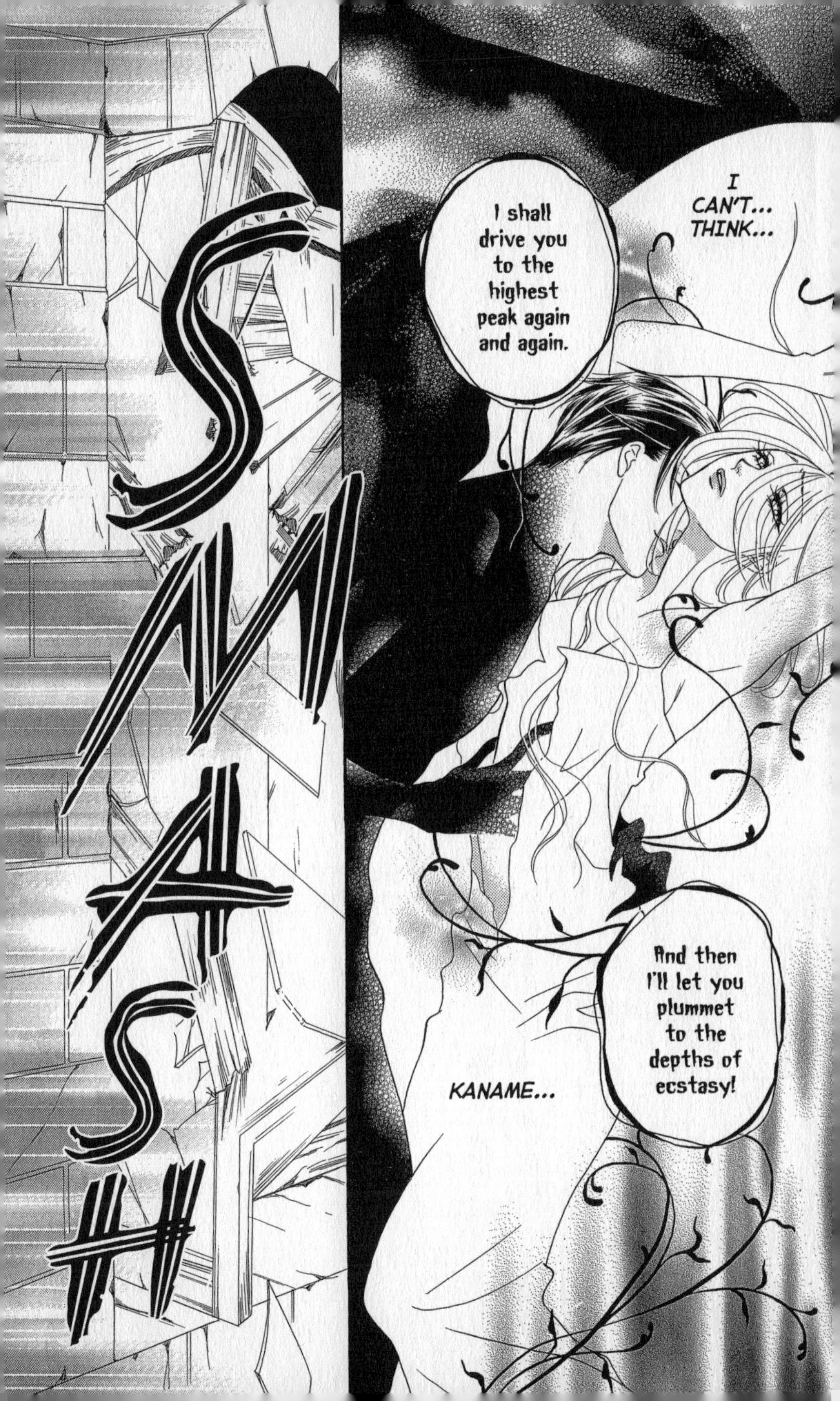
I CAN'T... THINK...
I shall drive you to the highest peak again and again.
And then I'll let you plummet to the depths of ecstasy!
KANAME...
SMASH

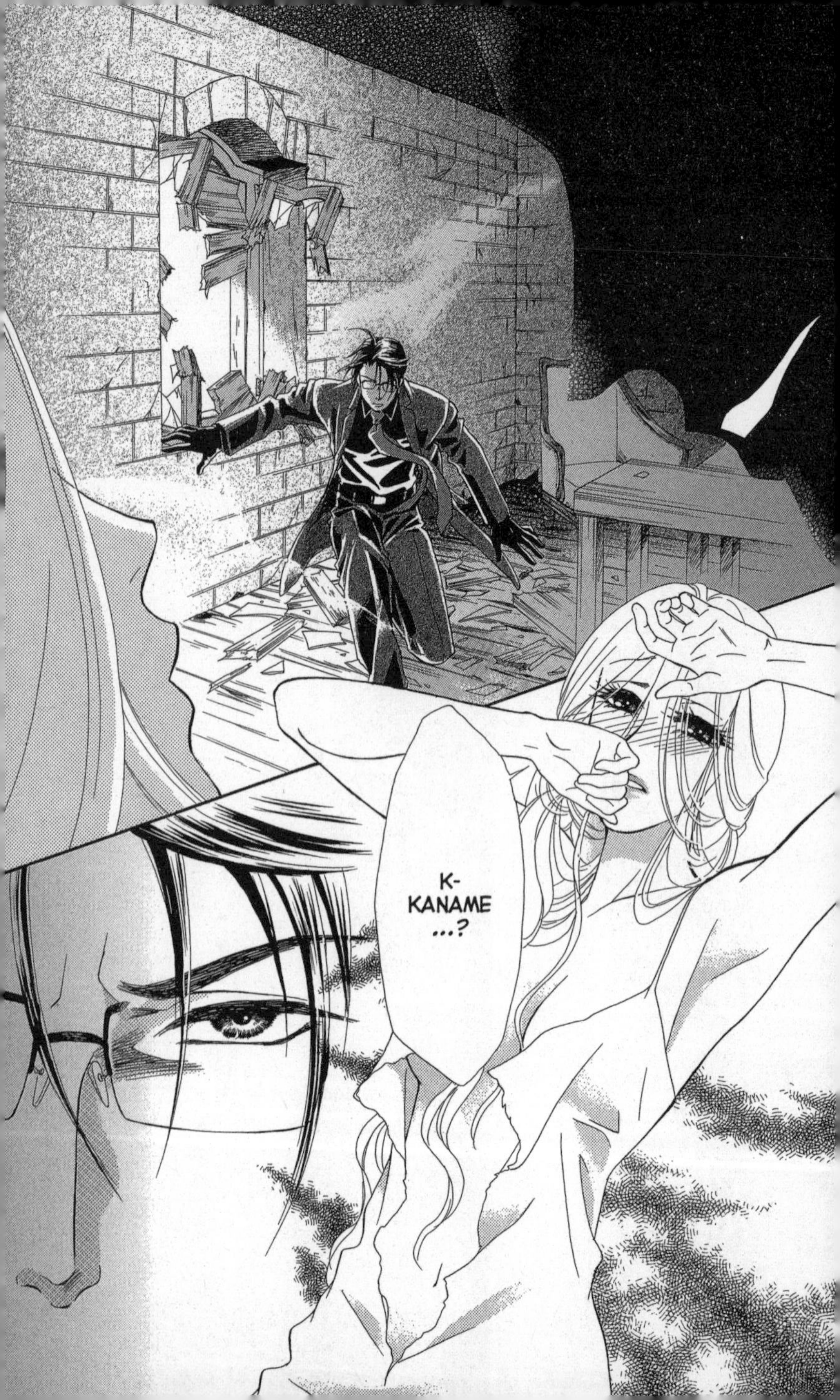
K-
KANAME
...?

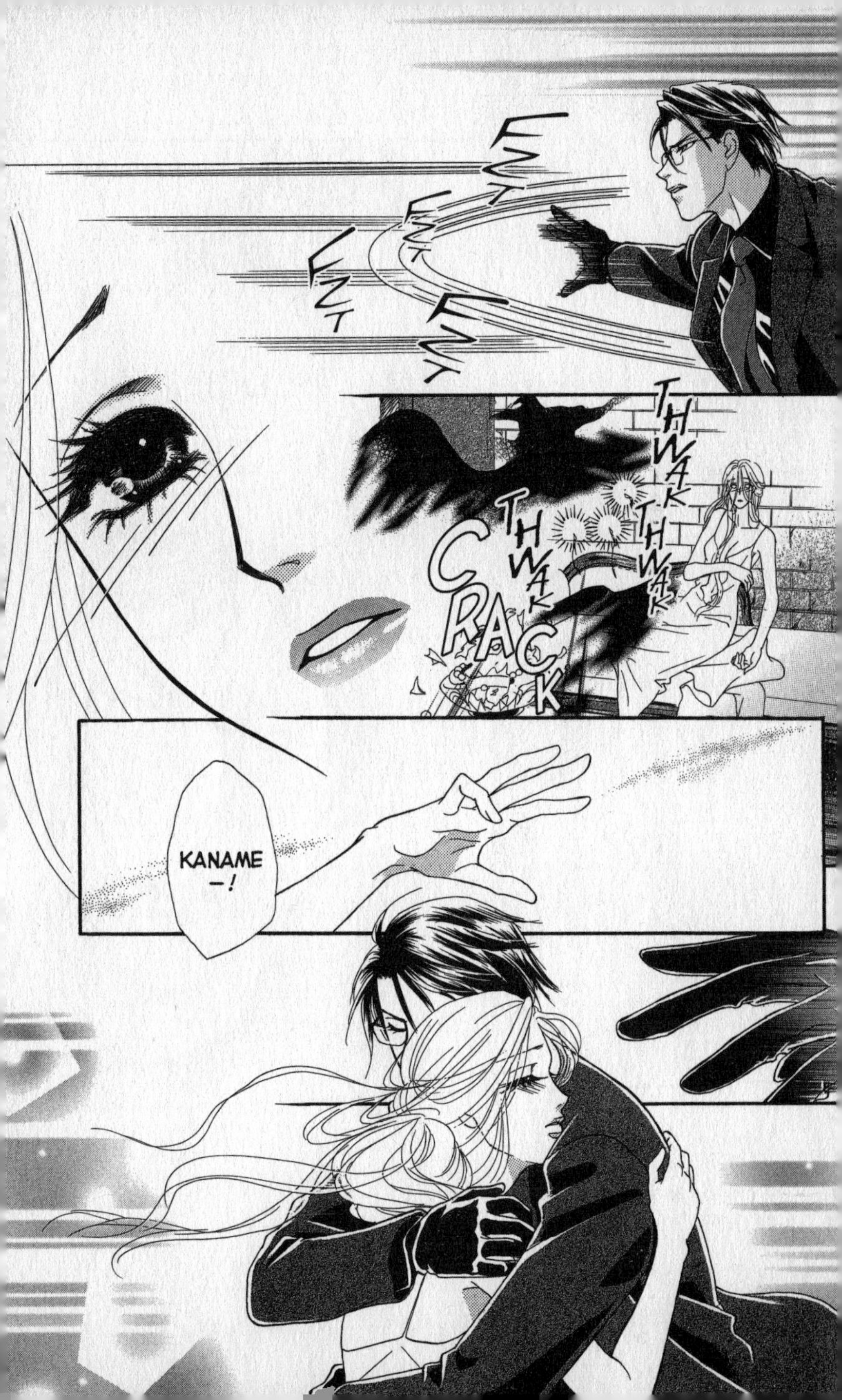
FWT
FWT
FWT
FWT
THWAK
THWAK
THWAK
CRACK
KANAME
—!

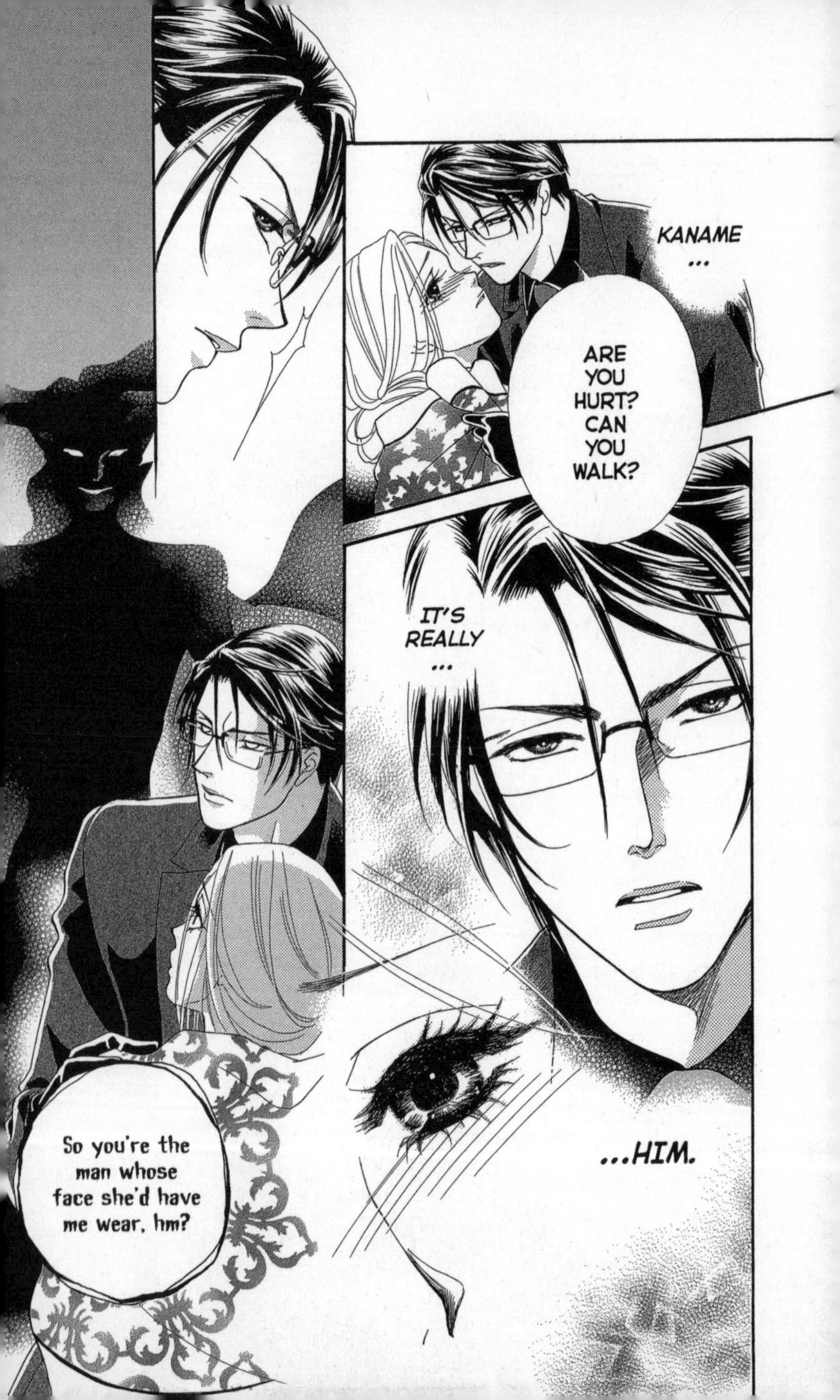
KANAME ...
ARE YOU HURT? CAN YOU WALK?
IT'S REALLY ...
...HIM.
So you're the man whose face she'd have me wear, hm?

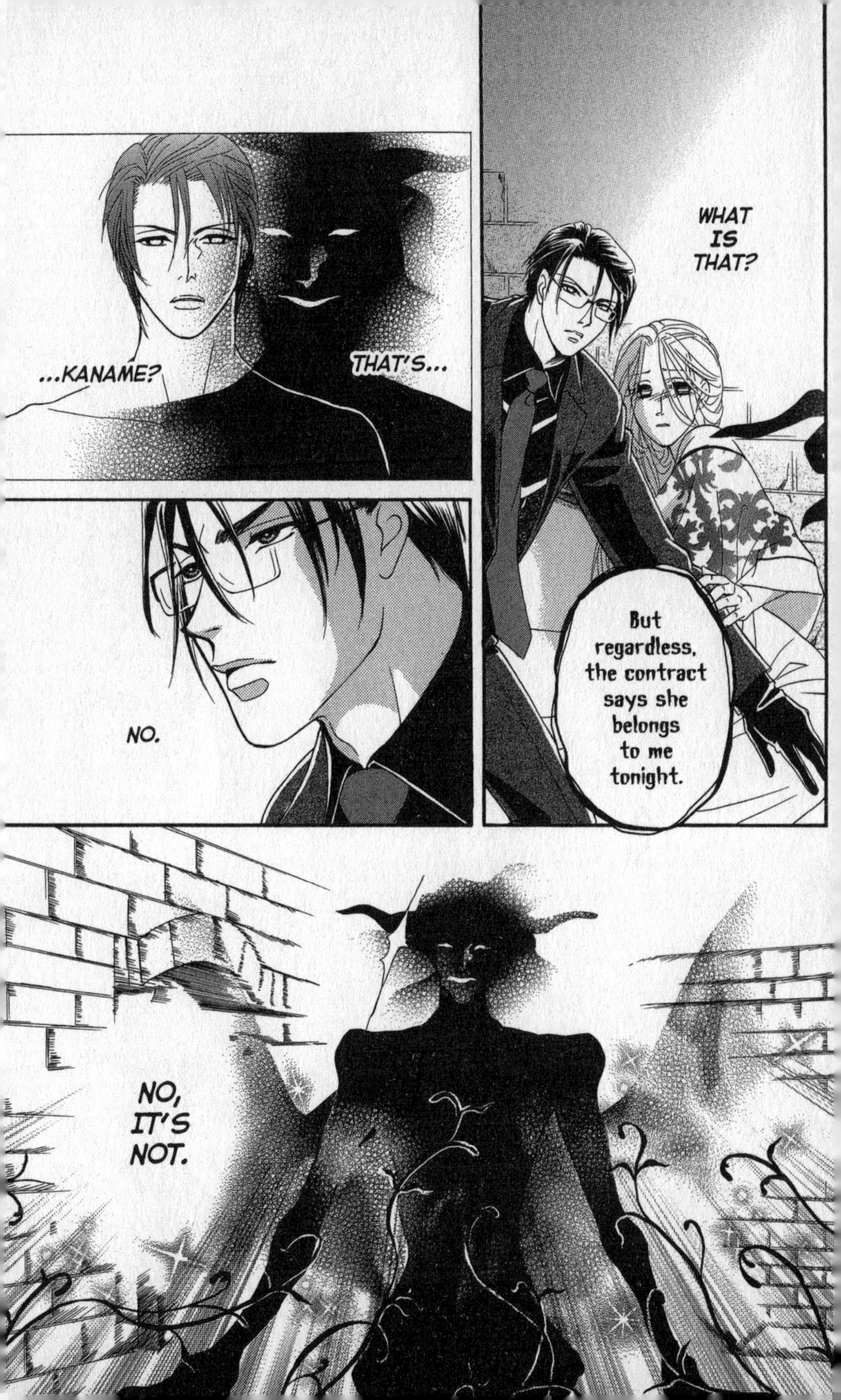
WHAT IS THAT?
But regardless, the contract says she belongs to me tonight.
THAT'S...
...KANAME?
NO.
NO, IT'S NOT.

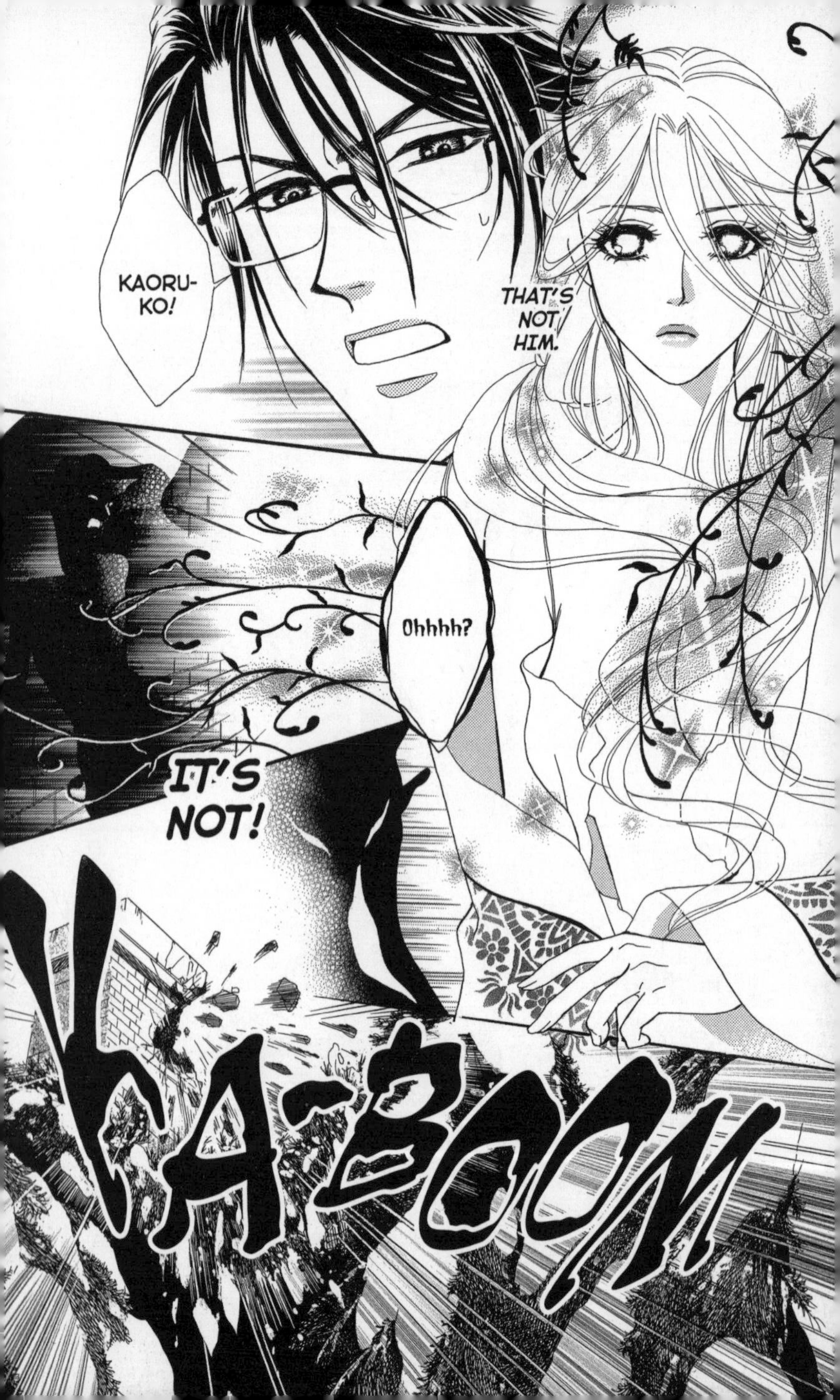
THAT'S NOT HIM.
KAORU-KO!
Ohhhh?
IT'S NOT!
KA-BOOM

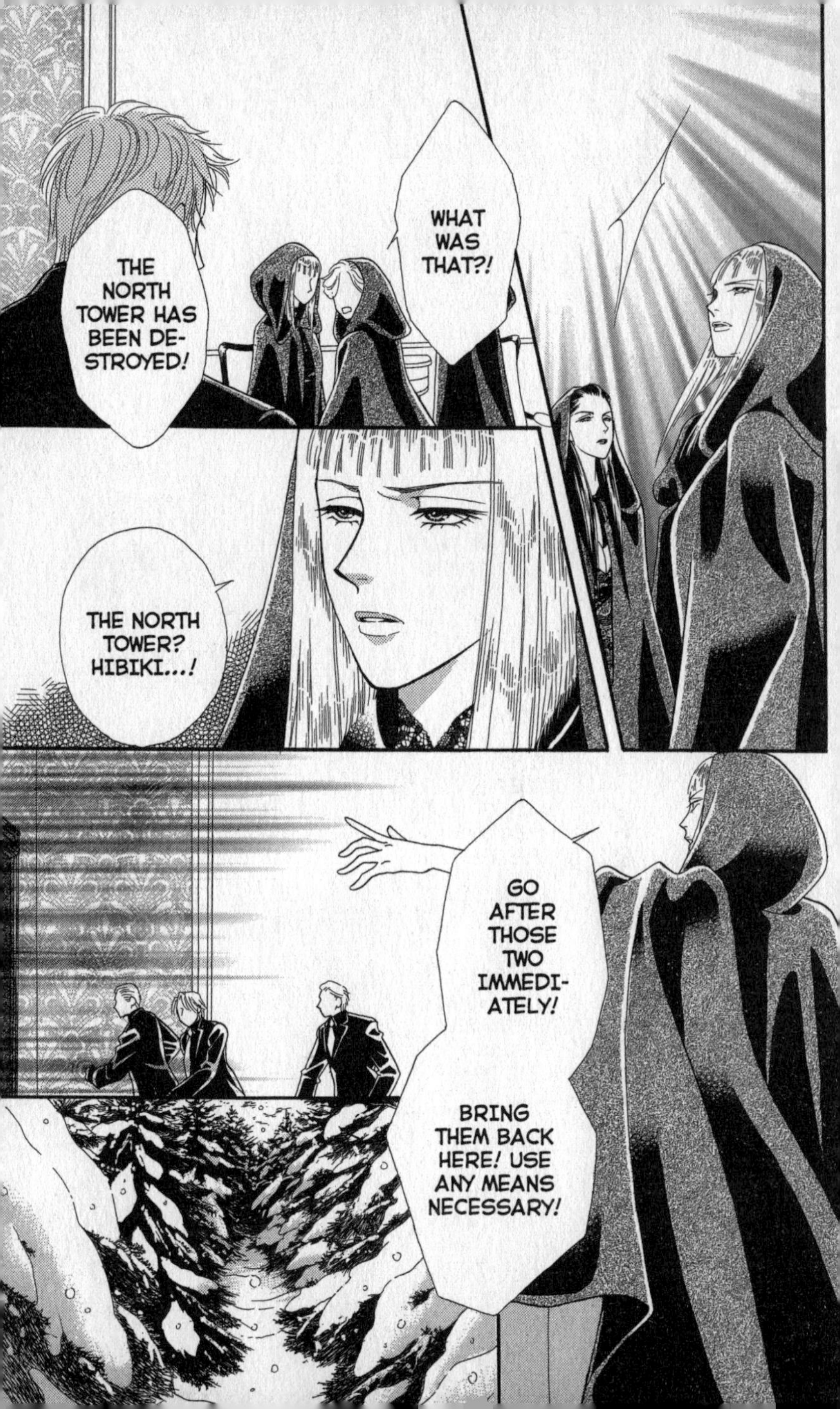

WHAT WAS THAT?!
THE NORTH TOWER HAS BEEN DE-STROYED!
THE NORTH TOWER? HIBIKI...!
GO AFTER THOSE TWO IMMEDI-ATELY!
BRING THEM BACK HERE! USE ANY MEANS NECESSARY!

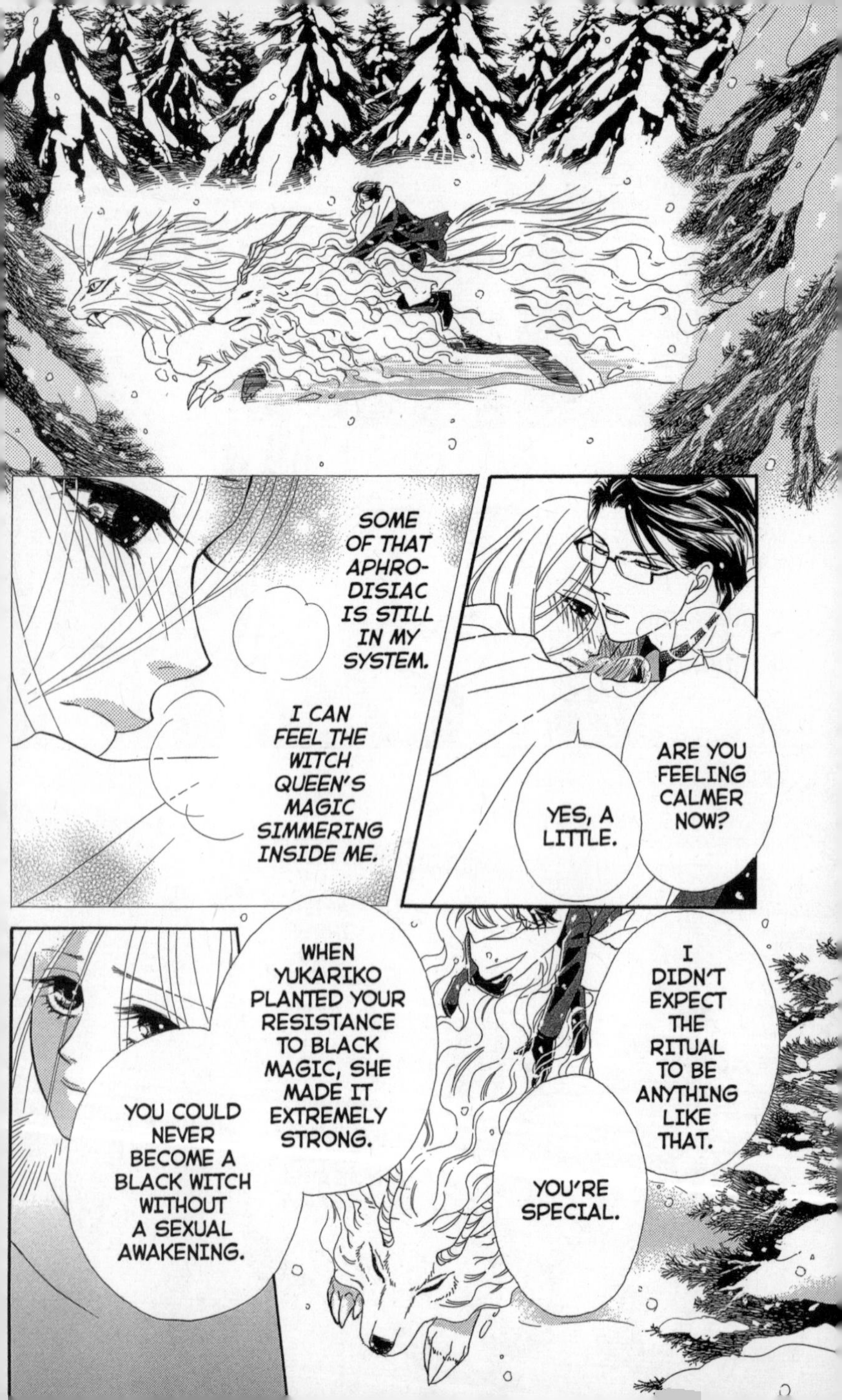
ARE YOU FEELING CALMER NOW?
YES, A LITTLE.
SOME OF THAT APHRODISIAC IS STILL IN MY SYSTEM.
I CAN FEEL THE WITCH QUEEN'S MAGIC SIMMERING INSIDE ME.
I DIDN'T EXPECT THE RITUAL TO BE ANYTHING LIKE THAT.
YOU'RE SPECIAL.
WHEN YUKARIKO PLANTED YOUR RESISTANCE TO BLACK MAGIC, SHE MADE IT EXTREMELY STRONG.
YOU COULD NEVER BECOME A BLACK WITCH WITHOUT A SEXUAL AWAKENING.

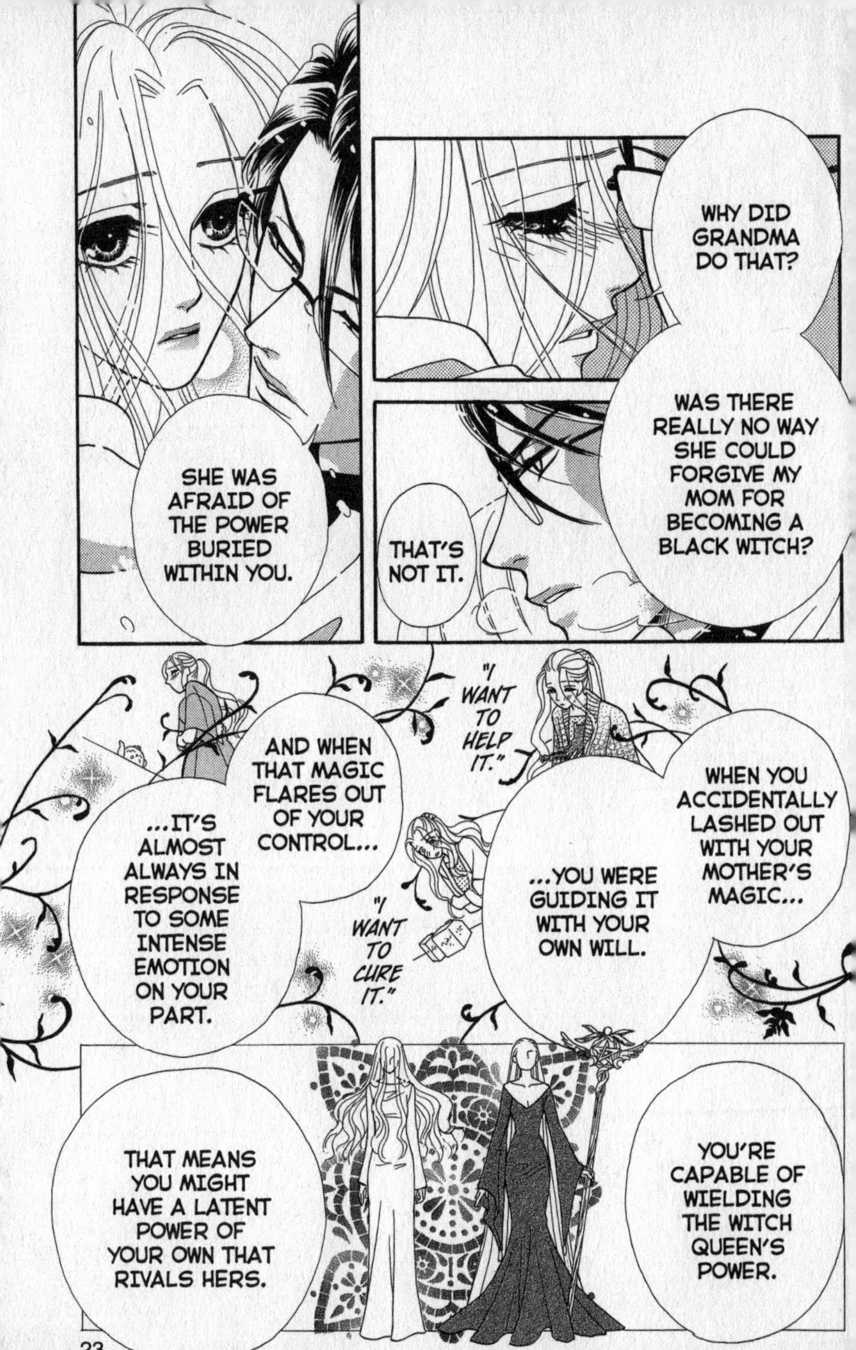
WHY DID GRANDMA DO THAT?
WAS THERE REALLY NO WAY SHE COULD FORGIVE MY MOM FOR BECOMING A BLACK WITCH?
THAT'S NOT IT.
SHE WAS AFRAID OF THE POWER BURIED WITHIN YOU.
WHEN YOU ACCIDENTALLY LASHED OUT WITH YOUR MOTHER'S MAGIC...
"I WANT TO HELP IT."
...YOU WERE GUIDING IT WITH YOUR OWN WILL.
"I WANT TO CURE IT."
AND WHEN THAT MAGIC FLARES OUT OF YOUR CONTROL...
...IT'S ALMOST ALWAYS IN RESPONSE TO SOME INTENSE EMOTION ON YOUR PART.
YOU'RE CAPABLE OF WIELDING THE WITCH QUEEN'S POWER.
THAT MEANS YOU MIGHT HAVE A LATENT POWER OF YOUR OWN THAT RIVALS HERS.

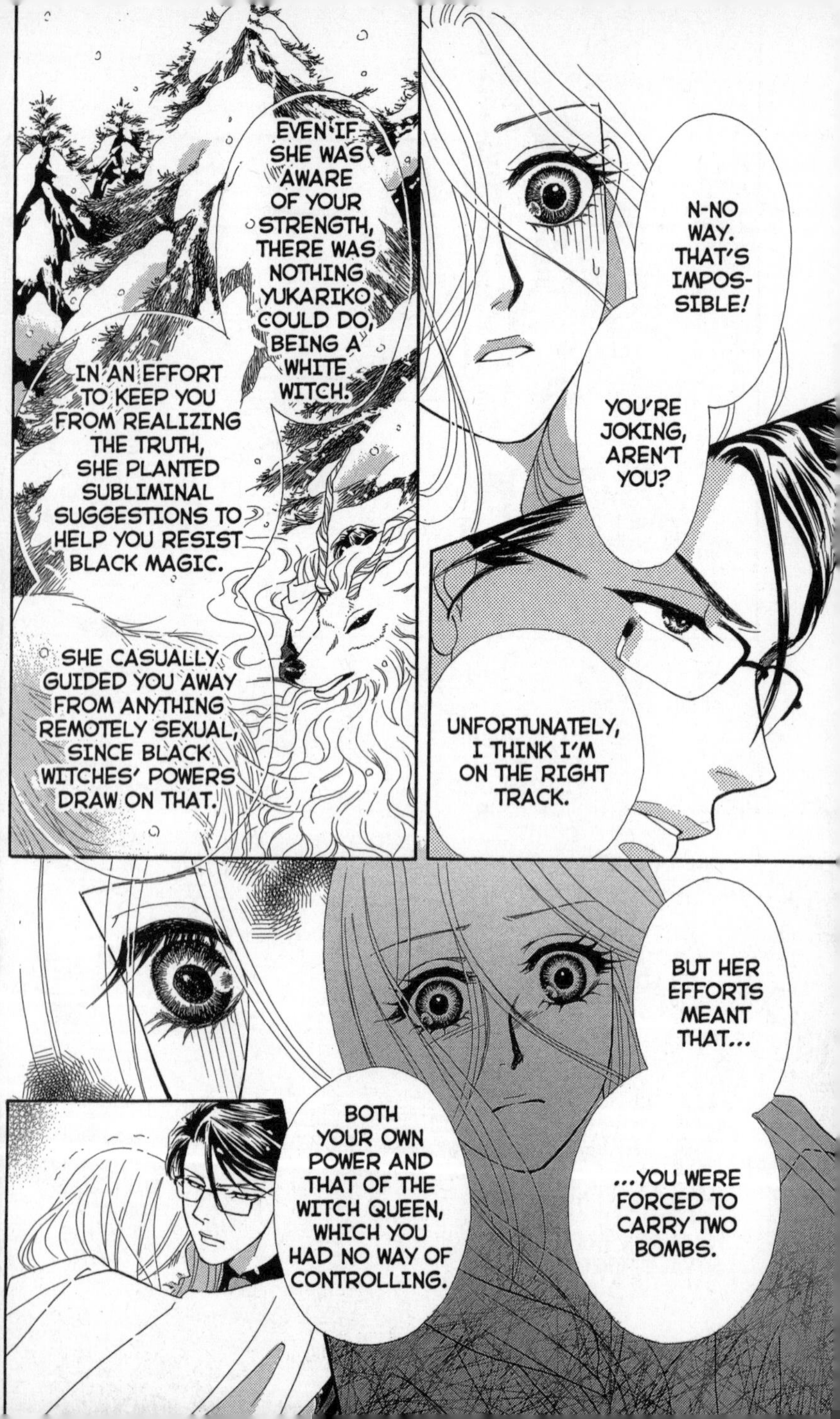
N-NO WAY. THAT'S IMPOS-SIBLE!
YOU'RE JOKING, AREN'T YOU?
UNFORTUNATELY, I THINK I'M ON THE RIGHT TRACK.
EVEN IF SHE WAS AWARE OF YOUR STRENGTH, THERE WAS NOTHING YUKARIKO COULD DO, BEING A WHITE WITCH.
IN AN EFFORT TO KEEP YOU FROM REALIZING THE TRUTH, SHE PLANTED SUBLIMINAL SUGGESTIONS TO HELP YOU RESIST BLACK MAGIC.
SHE CASUALLY GUIDED YOU AWAY FROM ANYTHING REMOTELY SEXUAL, SINCE BLACK WITCHES' POWERS DRAW ON THAT.
BUT HER EFFORTS MEANT THAT...
...YOU WERE FORCED TO CARRY TWO BOMBS.
BOTH YOUR OWN POWER AND THAT OF THE WITCH QUEEN, WHICH YOU HAD NO WAY OF CONTROLLING.

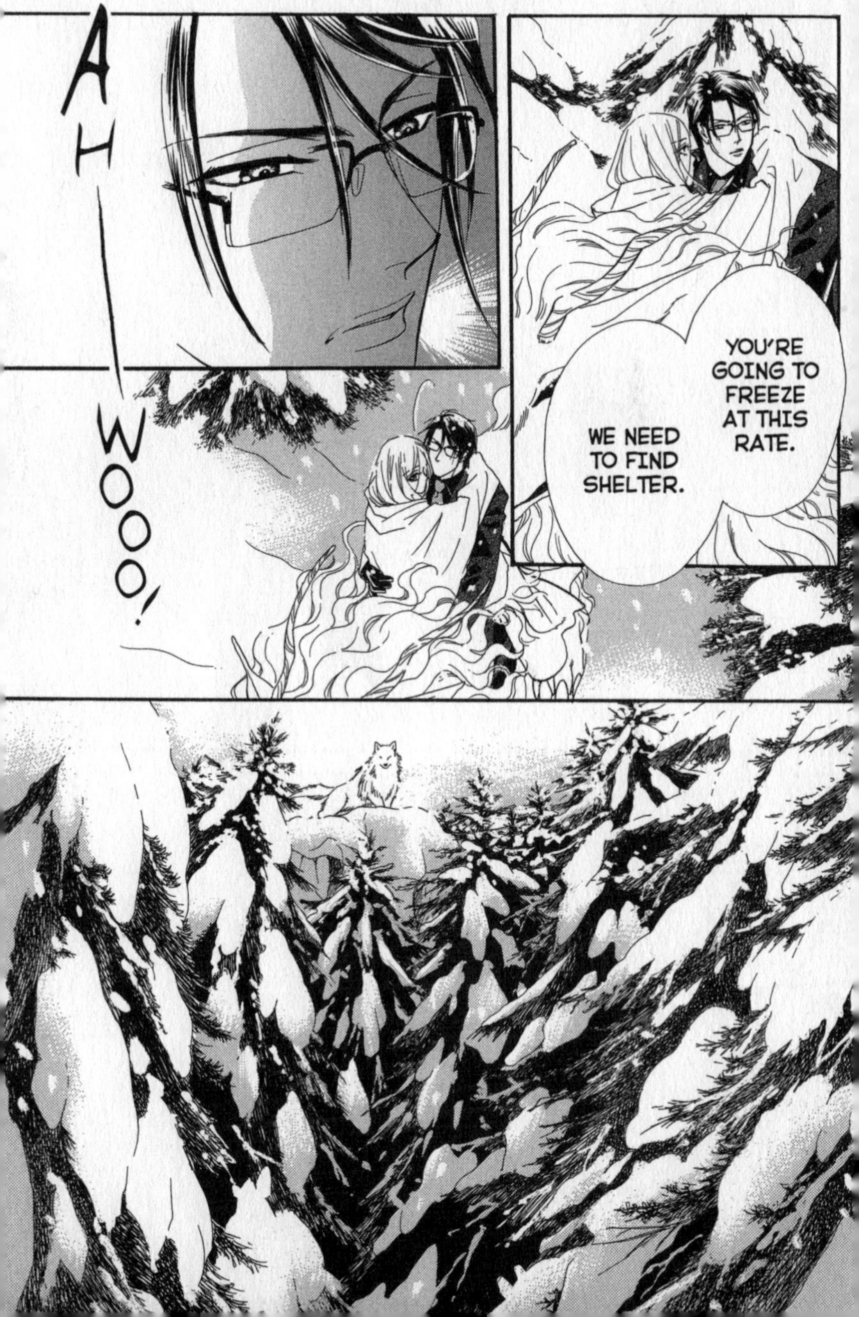
YOU'RE GOING TO FREEZE AT THIS RATE.
WE NEED TO FIND SHELTER.
AH—WOOO!

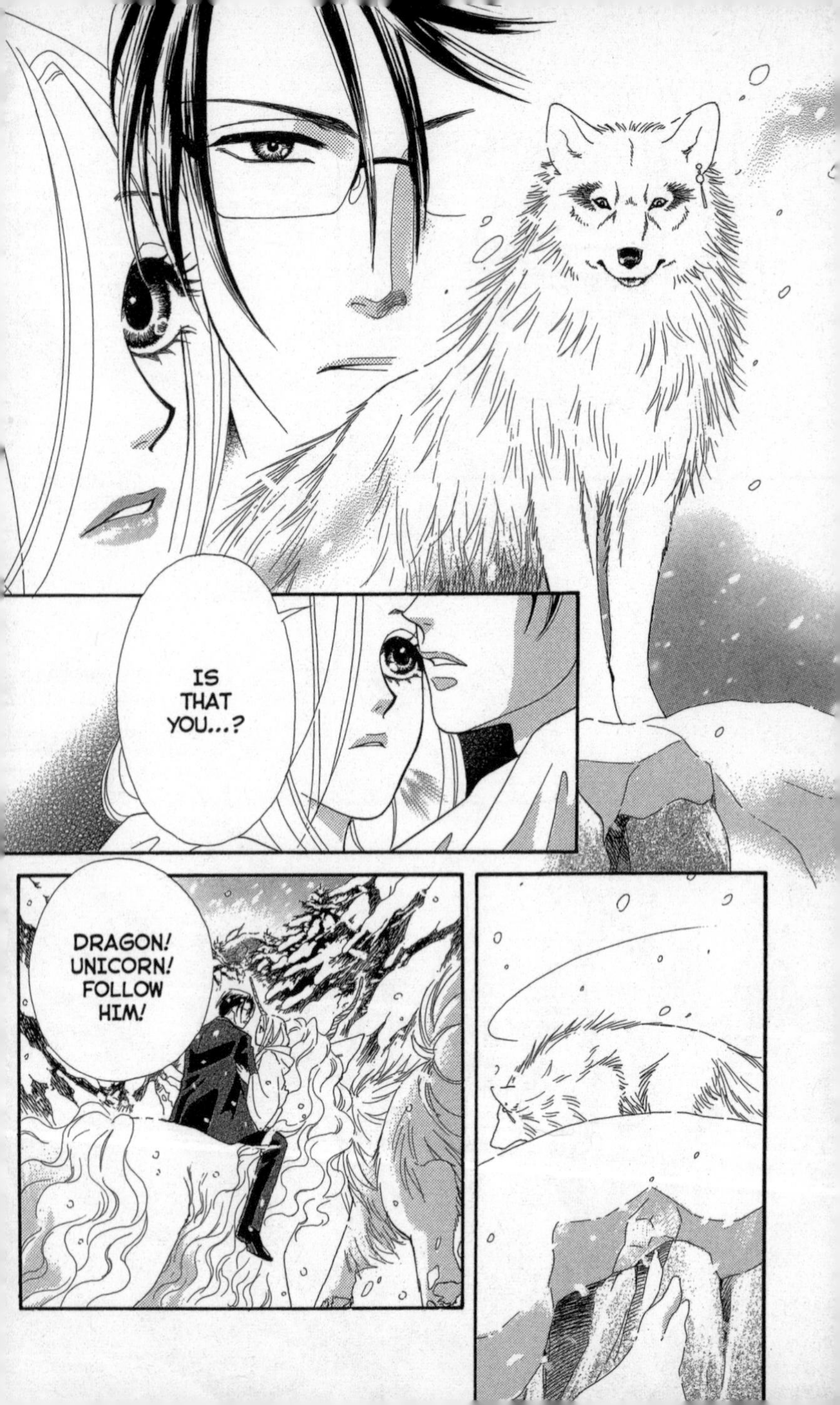
IS THAT YOU...?
DRAGON! UNICORN! FOLLOW HIM!

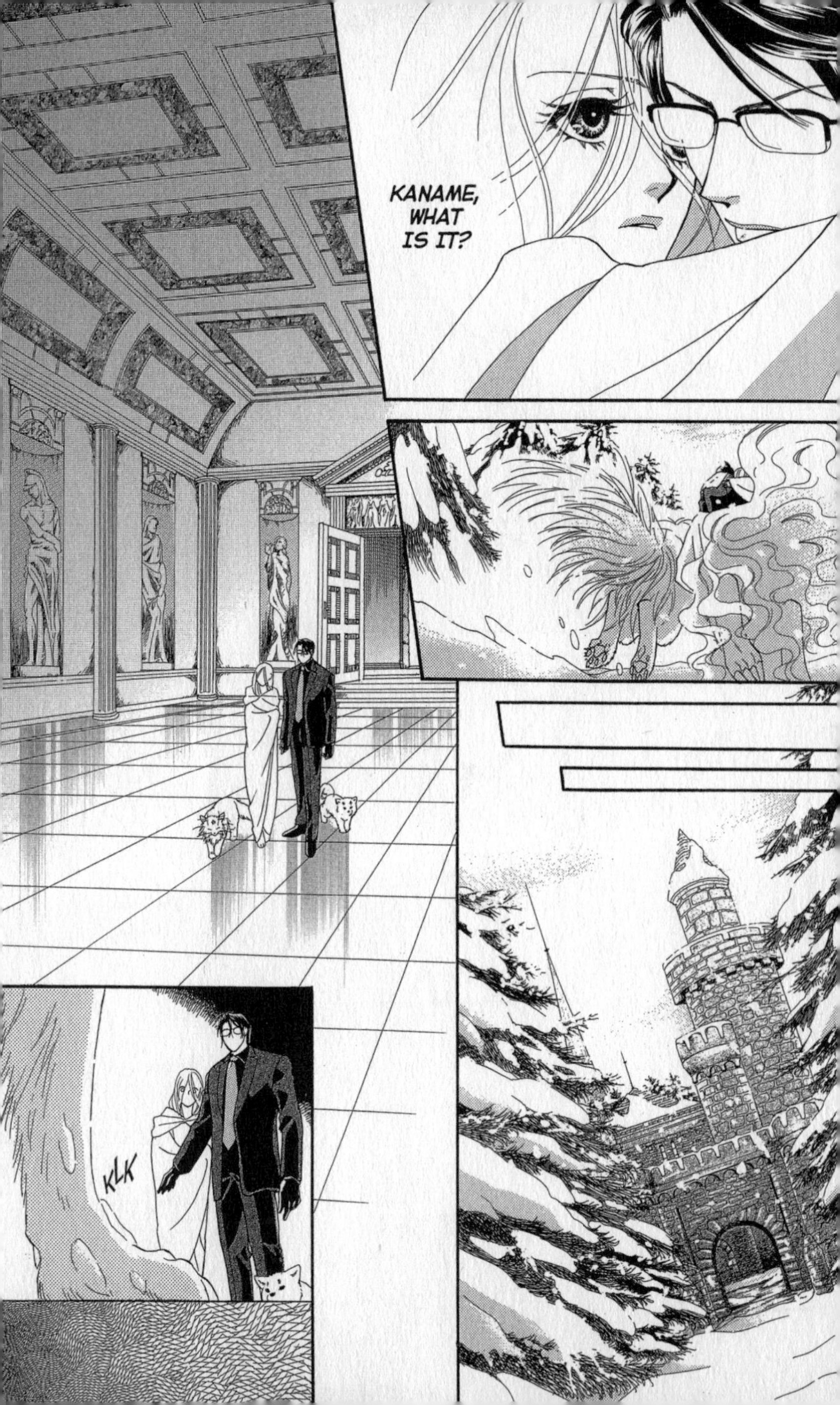
KANAME, WHAT IS IT?
KLK

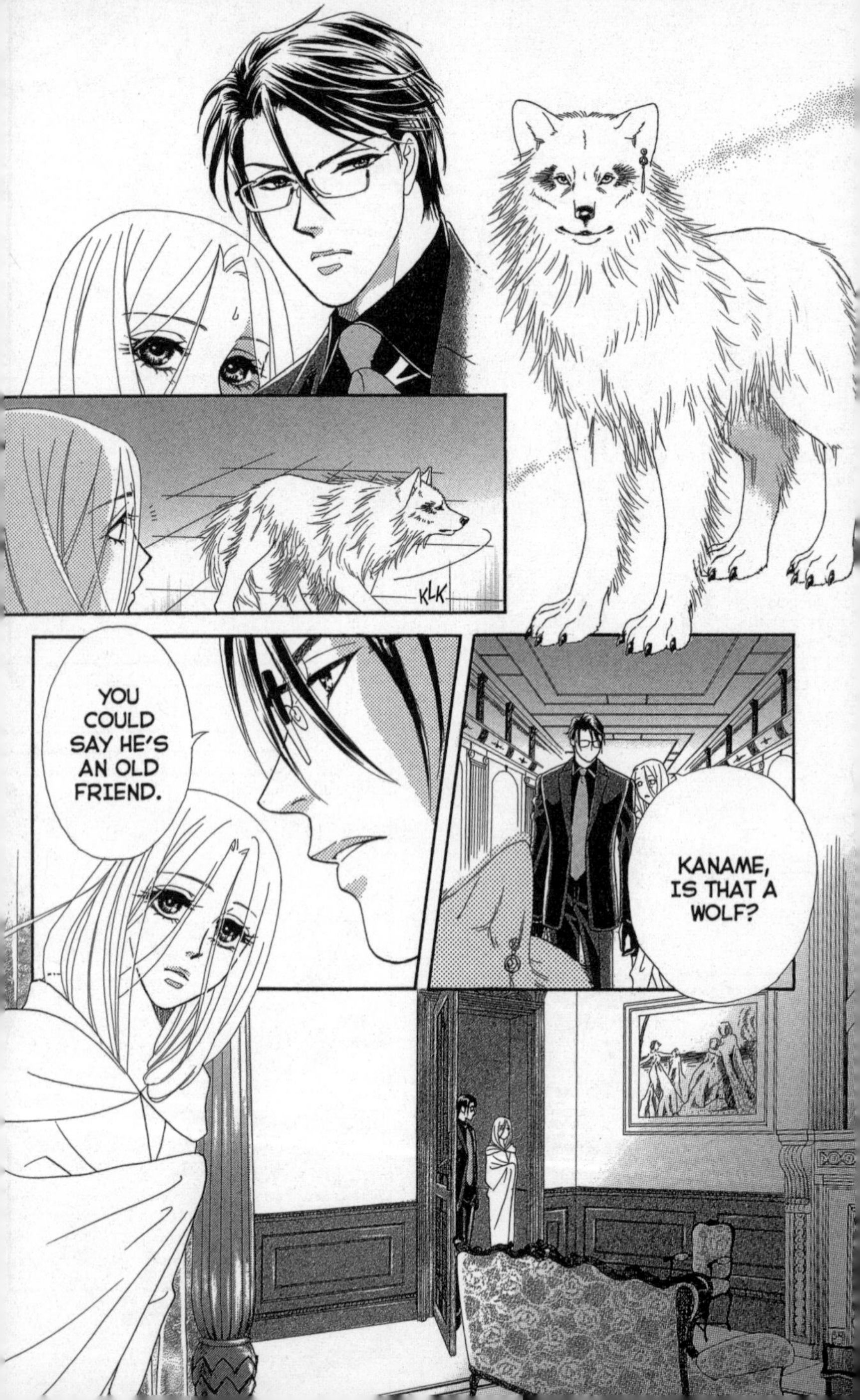
KLK
KANAME, IS THAT A WOLF?
YOU COULD SAY HE'S AN OLD FRIEND.

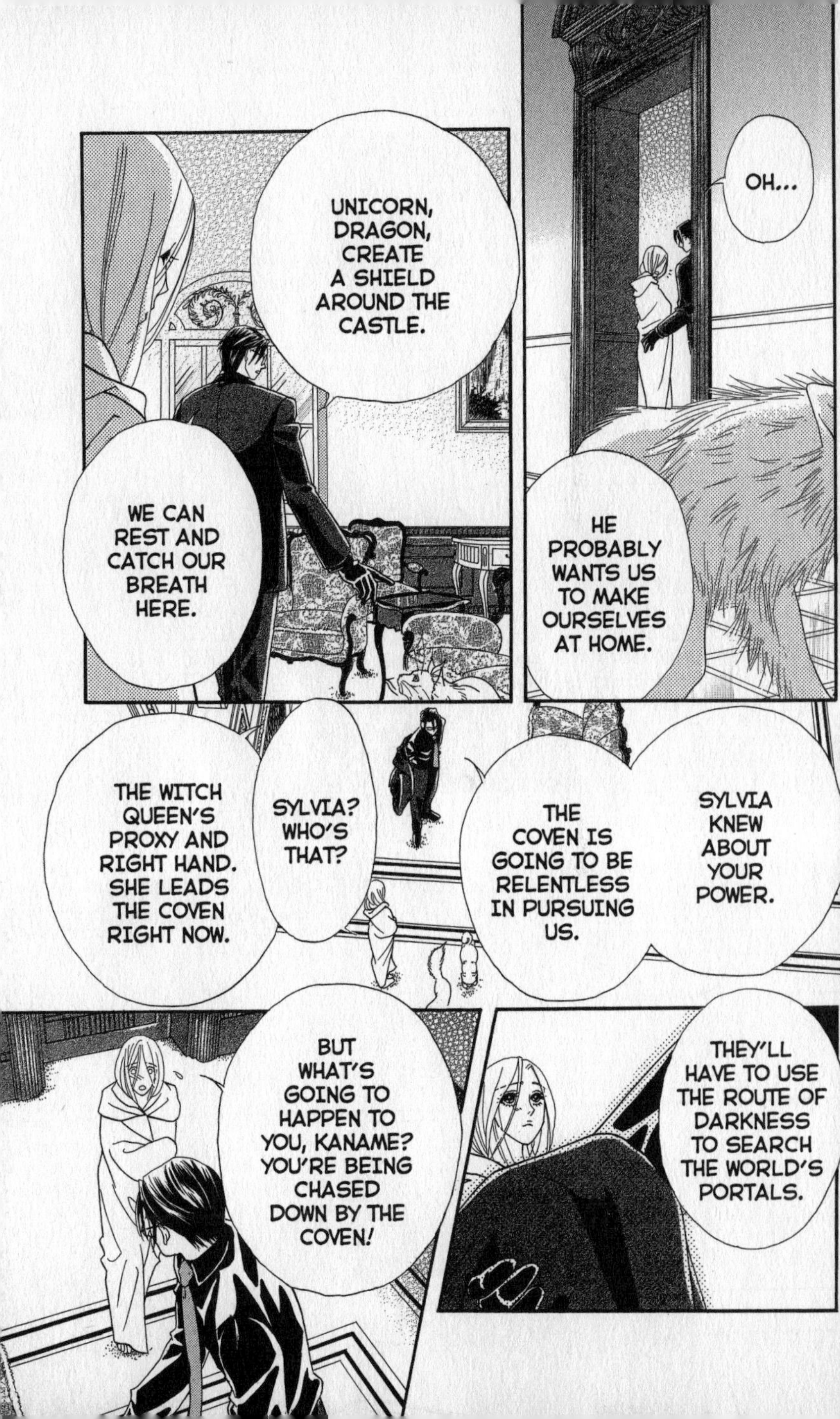
OH...
HE PROBABLY WANTS US TO MAKE OURSELVES AT HOME.
UNICORN, DRAGON, CREATE A SHIELD AROUND THE CASTLE.
WE CAN REST AND CATCH OUR BREATH HERE.
SYLVIA KNEW ABOUT YOUR POWER.
THE COVEN IS GOING TO BE RELENTLESS IN PURSUING US.
SYLVIA? WHO'S THAT?
THE WITCH QUEEN'S PROXY AND RIGHT HAND. SHE LEADS THE COVEN RIGHT NOW.
THEY'LL HAVE TO USE THE ROUTE OF DARKNESS TO SEARCH THE WORLD'S PORTALS.
BUT WHAT'S GOING TO HAPPEN TO YOU, KANAME? YOU'RE BEING CHASED DOWN BY THE COVEN!

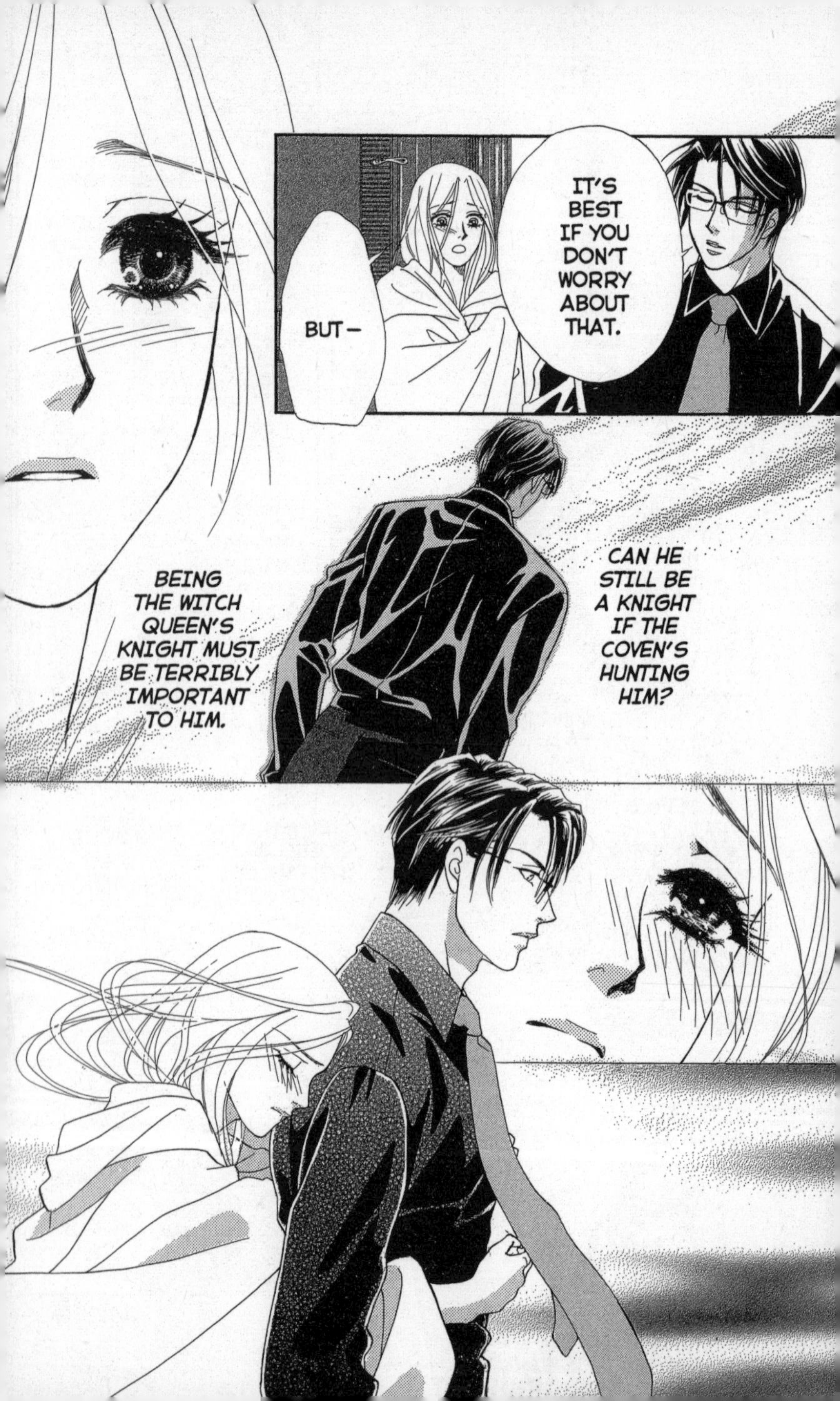
IT'S BEST IF YOU DON'T WORRY ABOUT THAT.
BUT—
CAN HE STILL BE A KNIGHT IF THE COVEN'S HUNTING HIM?
BEING THE WITCH QUEEN'S KNIGHT MUST BE TERRIBLY IMPORTANT TO HIM.

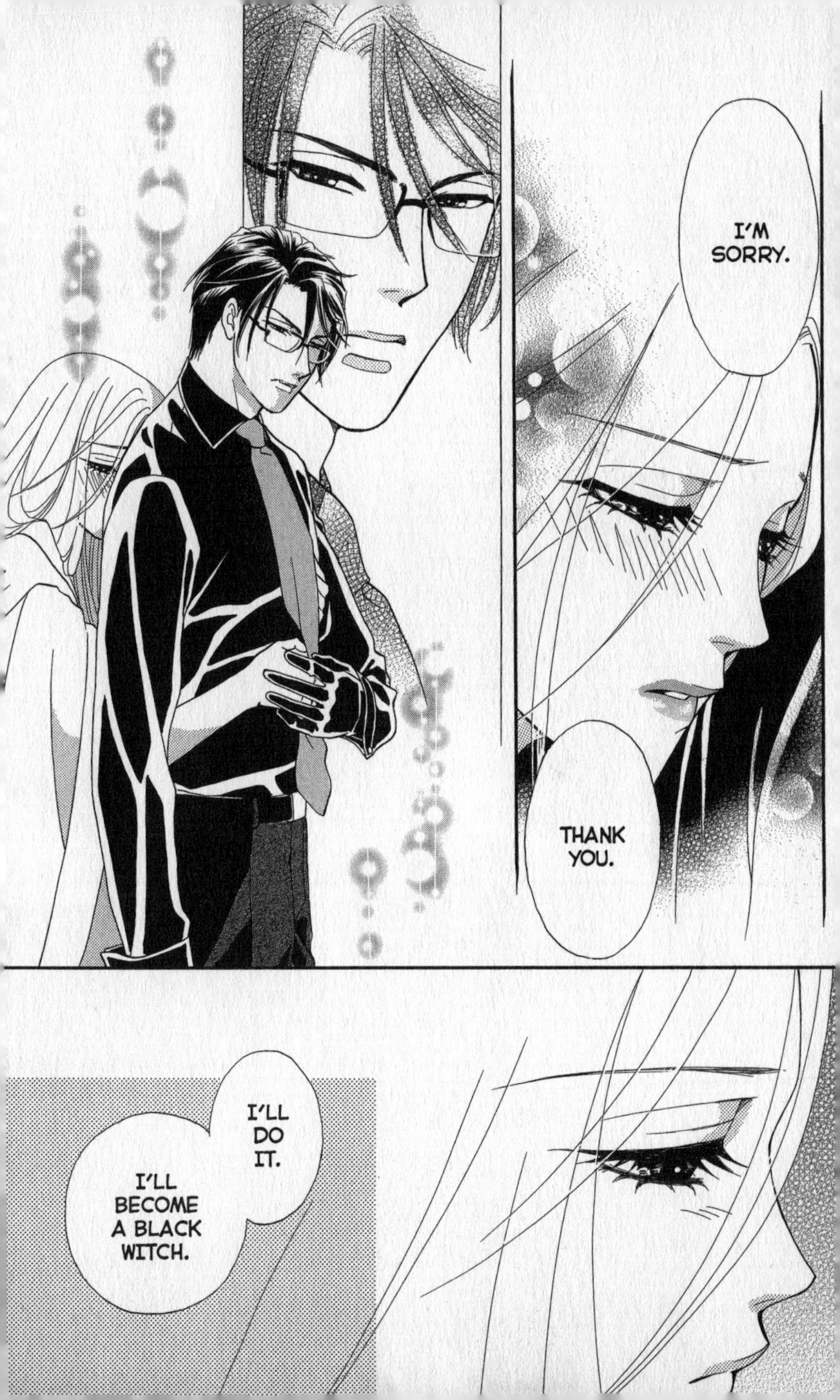
I'M SORRY.
THANK YOU.
I'LL DO IT.
I'LL BECOME A BLACK WITCH.

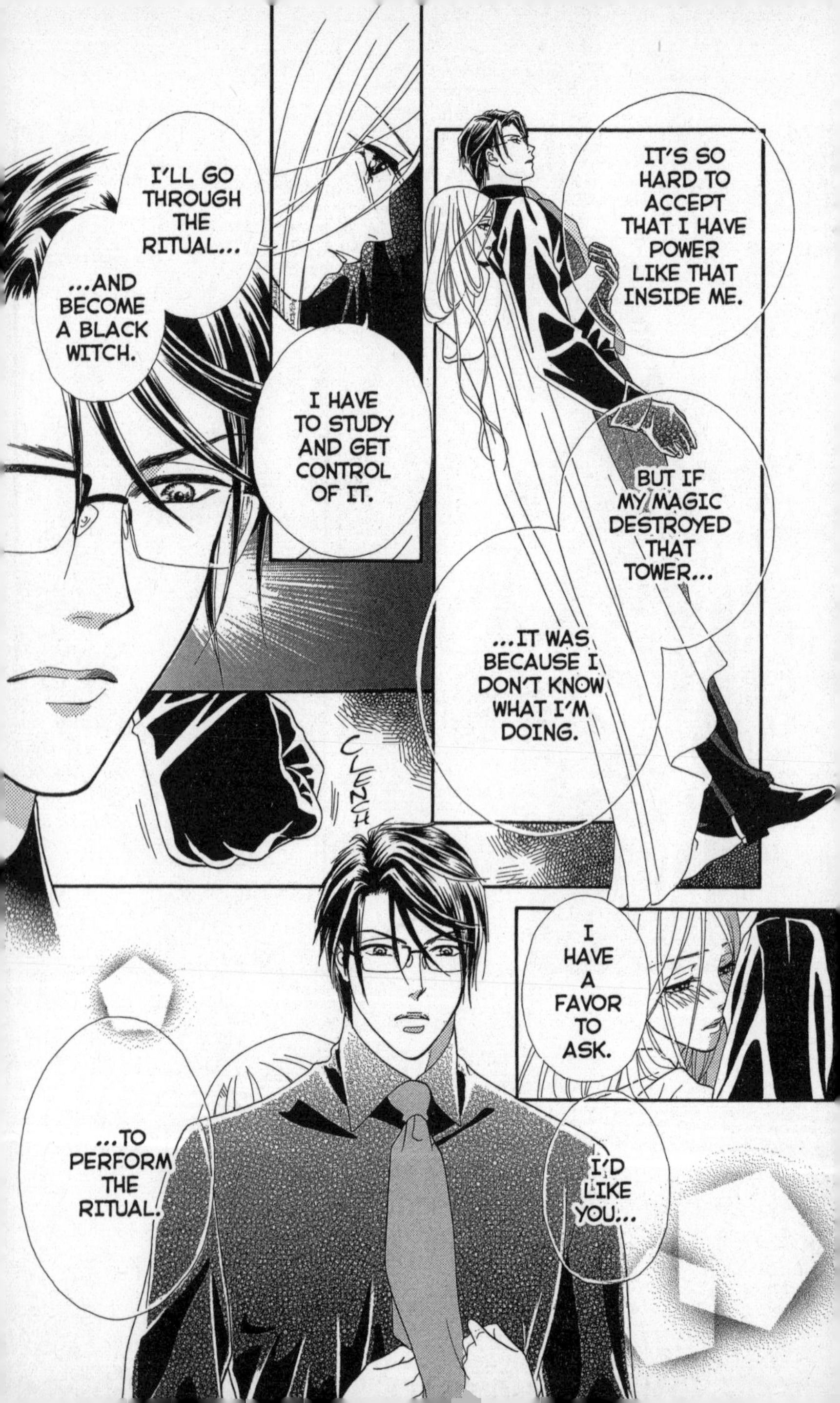
IT'S SO HARD TO ACCEPT THAT I HAVE POWER LIKE THAT INSIDE ME.
BUT IF MY MAGIC DESTROYED THAT TOWER...
...IT WAS BECAUSE I DON'T KNOW WHAT I'M DOING.
I HAVE TO STUDY AND GET CONTROL OF IT.
I'LL GO THROUGH THE RITUAL...
...AND BECOME A BLACK WITCH.
CLENCH
I HAVE A FAVOR TO ASK.
I'D LIKE YOU...
...TO PERFORM THE RITUAL.

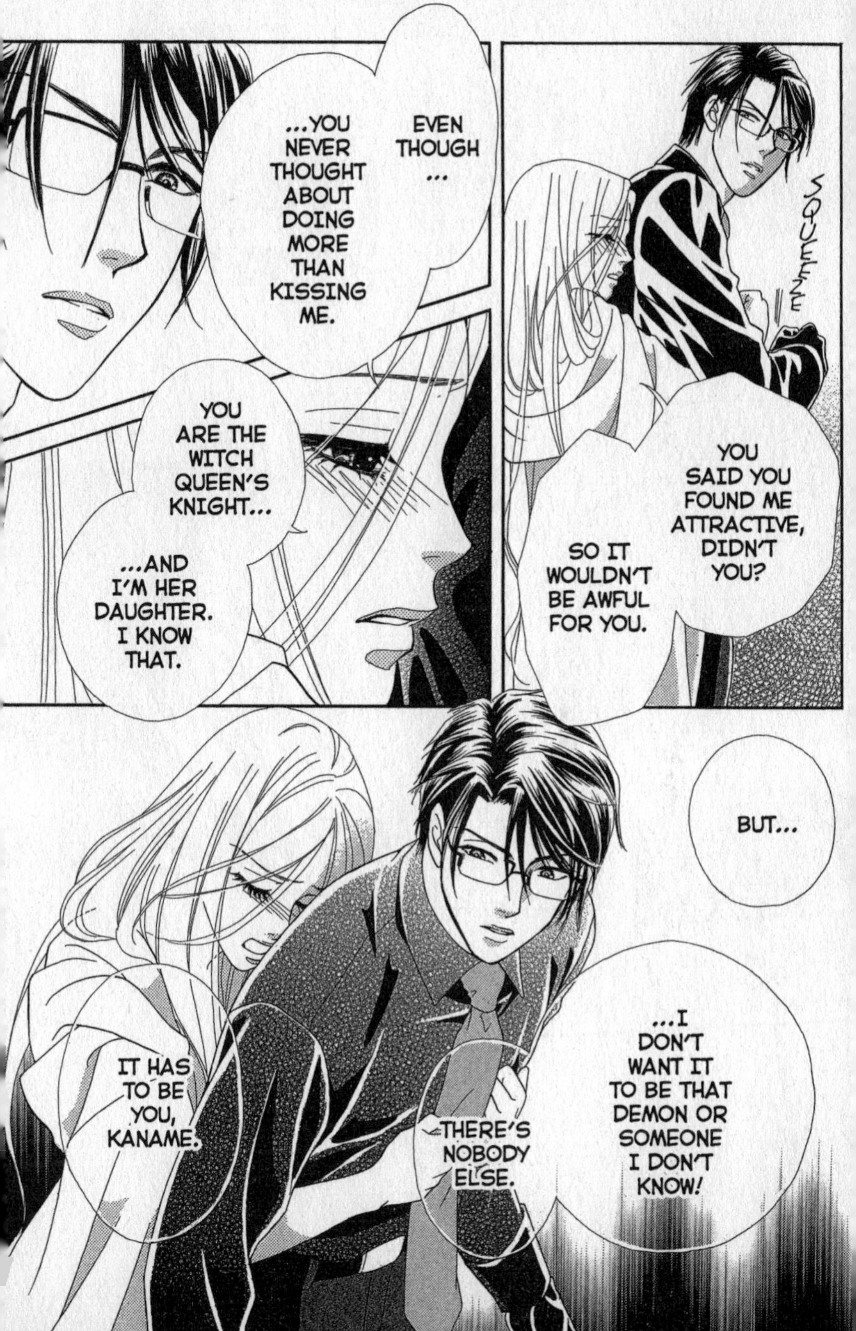
SQUEEEZE
YOU SAID YOU FOUND ME ATTRACTIVE, DIDN'T YOU?
SO IT WOULDN'T BE AWFUL FOR YOU.
EVEN THOUGH...
...YOU NEVER THOUGHT ABOUT DOING MORE THAN KISSING ME.
YOU ARE THE WITCH QUEEN'S KNIGHT...
...AND I'M HER DAUGHTER. I KNOW THAT.
BUT...
...I DON'T WANT IT TO BE THAT DEMON OR SOMEONE I DON'T KNOW!
THERE'S NOBODY ELSE.
IT HAS TO BE YOU, KANAME.

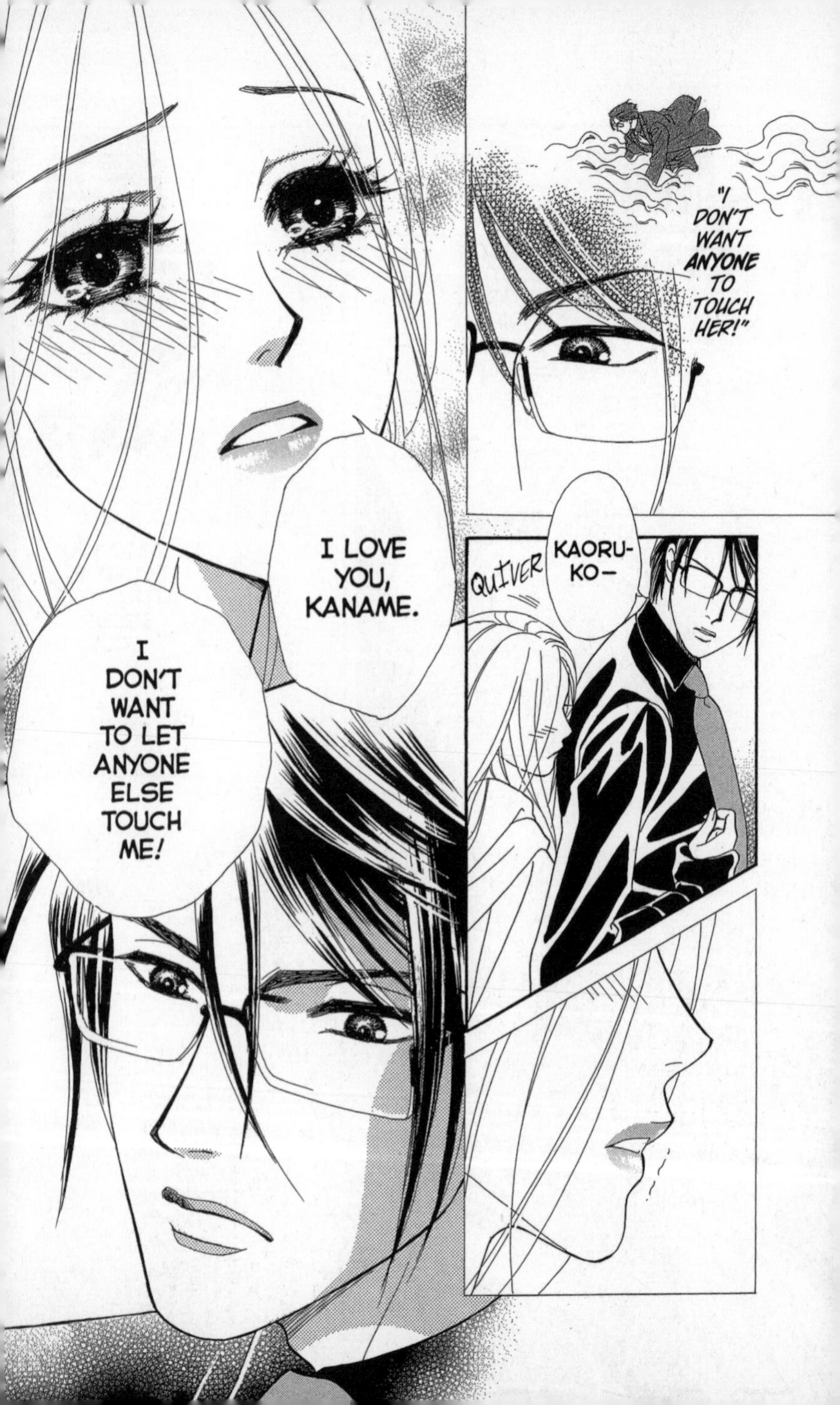
"I DON'T WANT ANYONE TO TOUCH HER!"
KAORU-KO–
QUIVER
I LOVE YOU, KANAME.
I DON'T WANT TO LET ANYONE ELSE TOUCH ME!

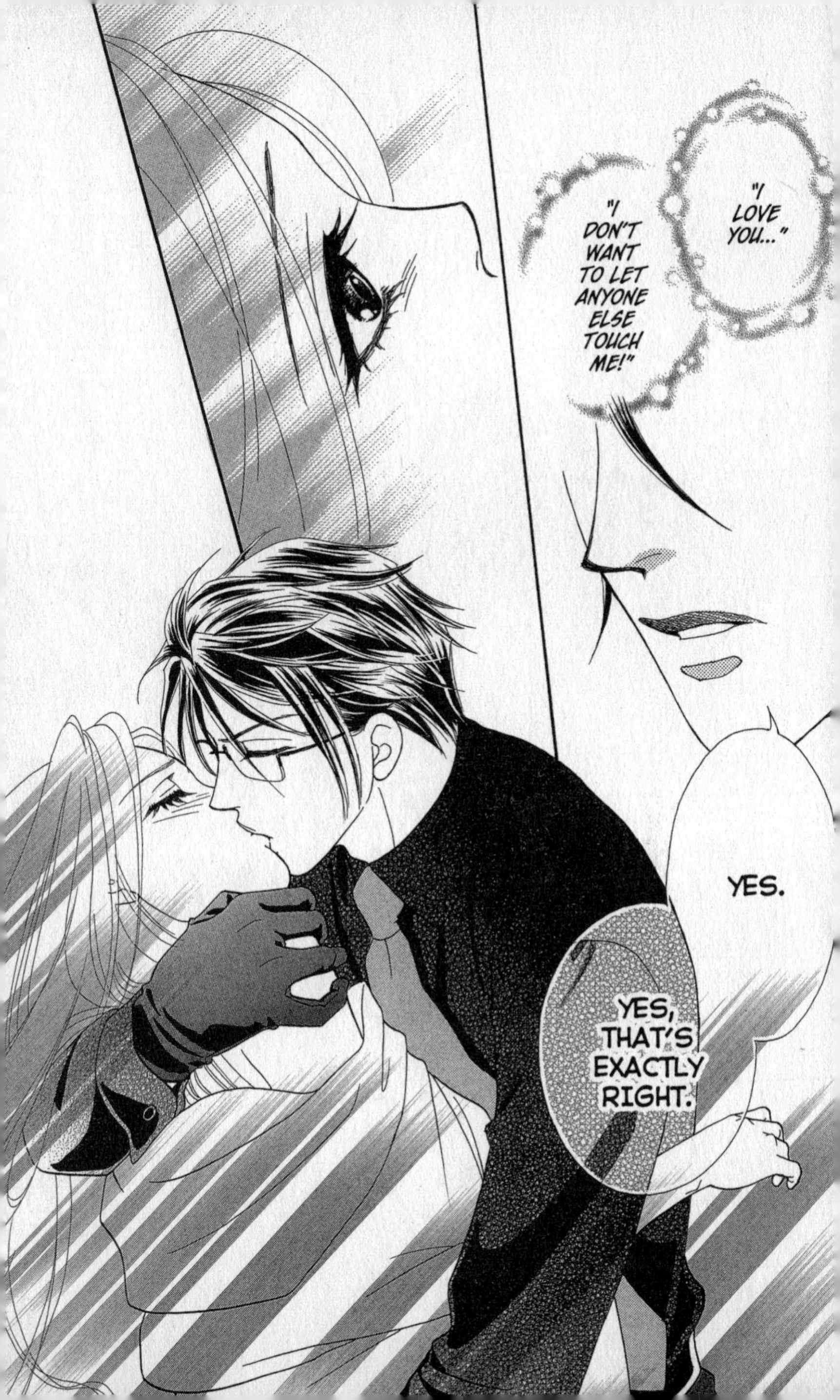
"I LOVE YOU..."
"I DON'T WANT TO LET ANYONE ELSE TOUCH ME!"
YES.
YES, THAT'S EXACTLY RIGHT.

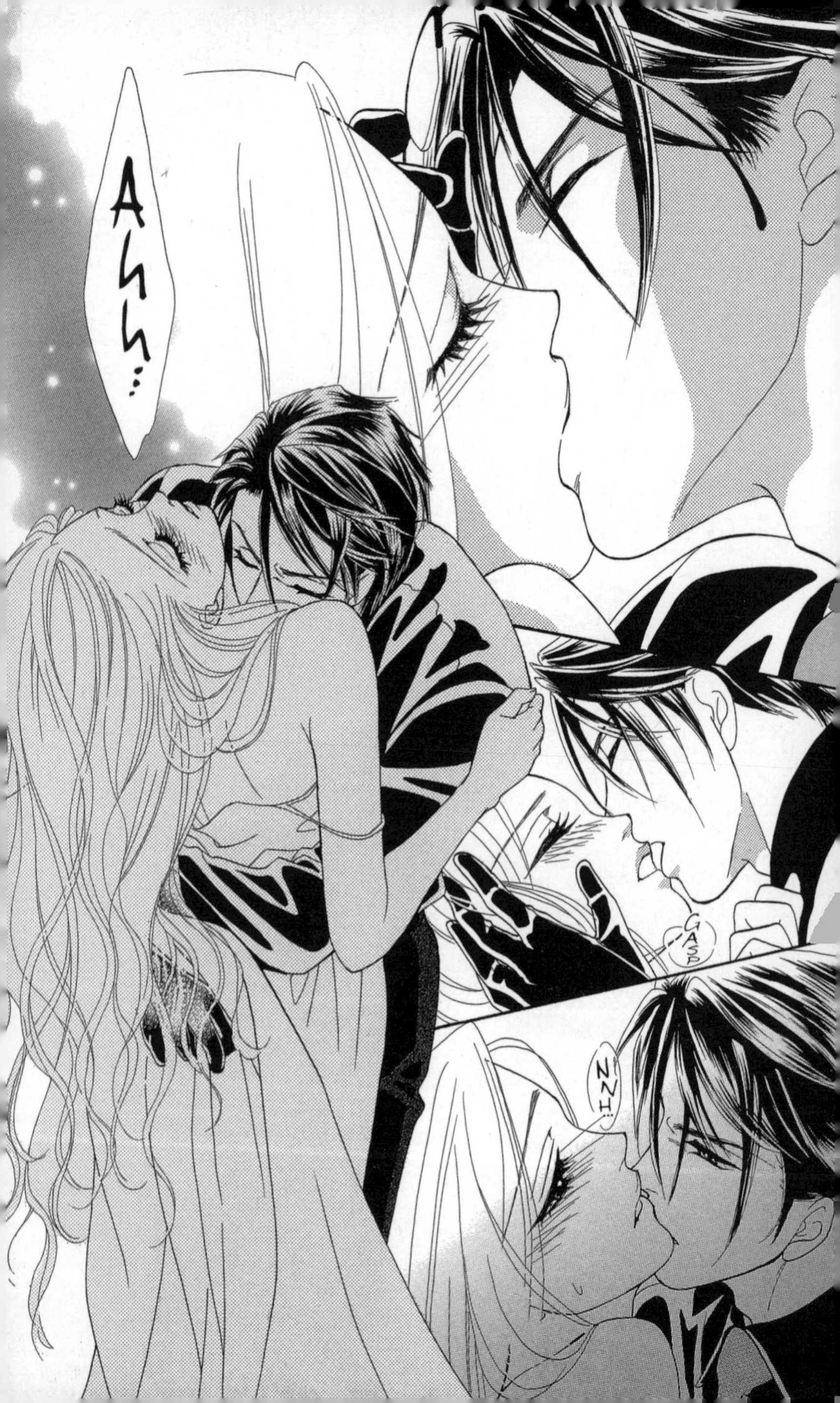

AHH...
GASP
NNH!!

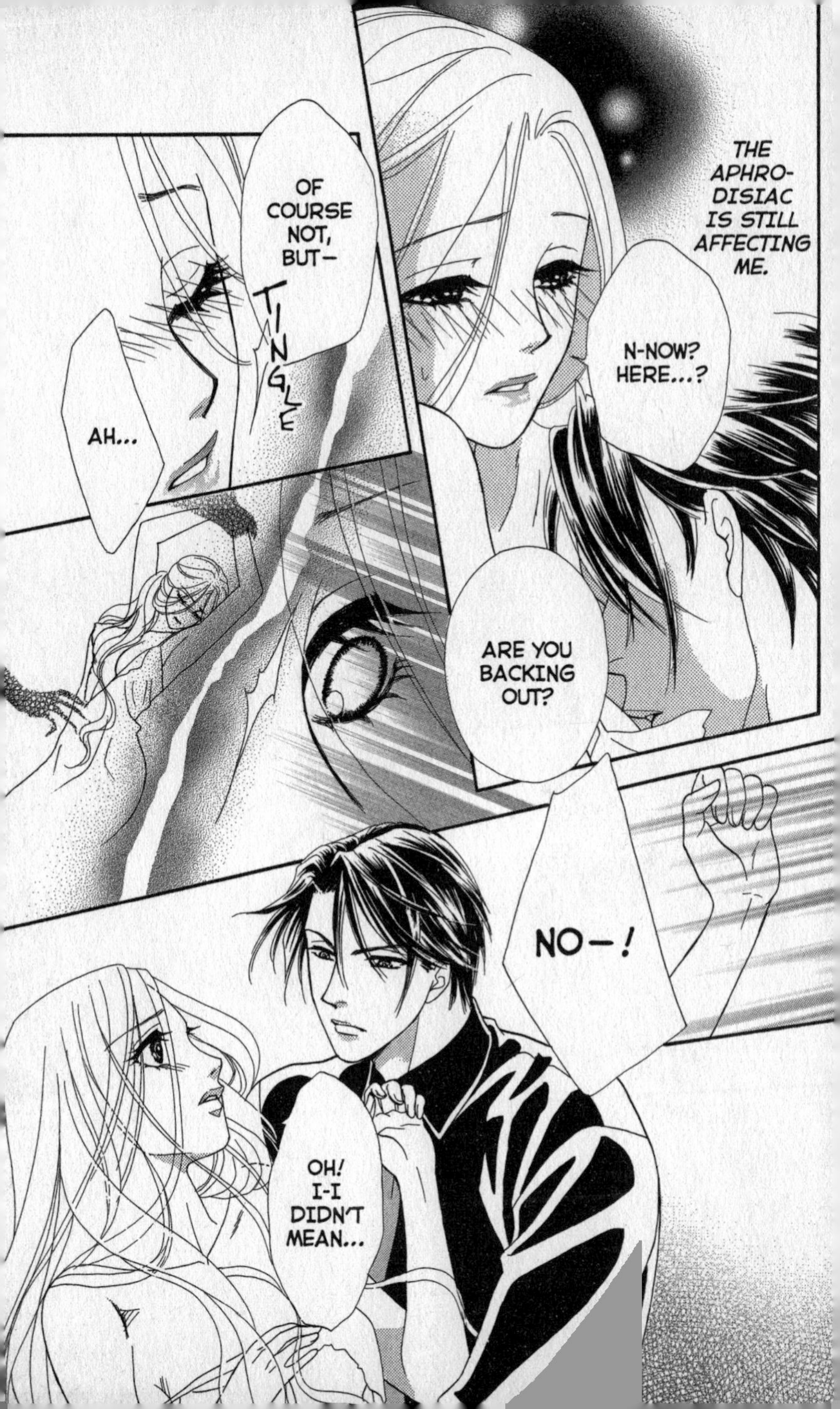
THE APHRO-DISIAC IS STILL AFFECTING ME.
N-NOW? HERE...?
ARE YOU BACKING OUT?
OF COURSE NOT, BUT—
TINGLE
AH...
NO—!
OH! I-I DIDN'T MEAN...

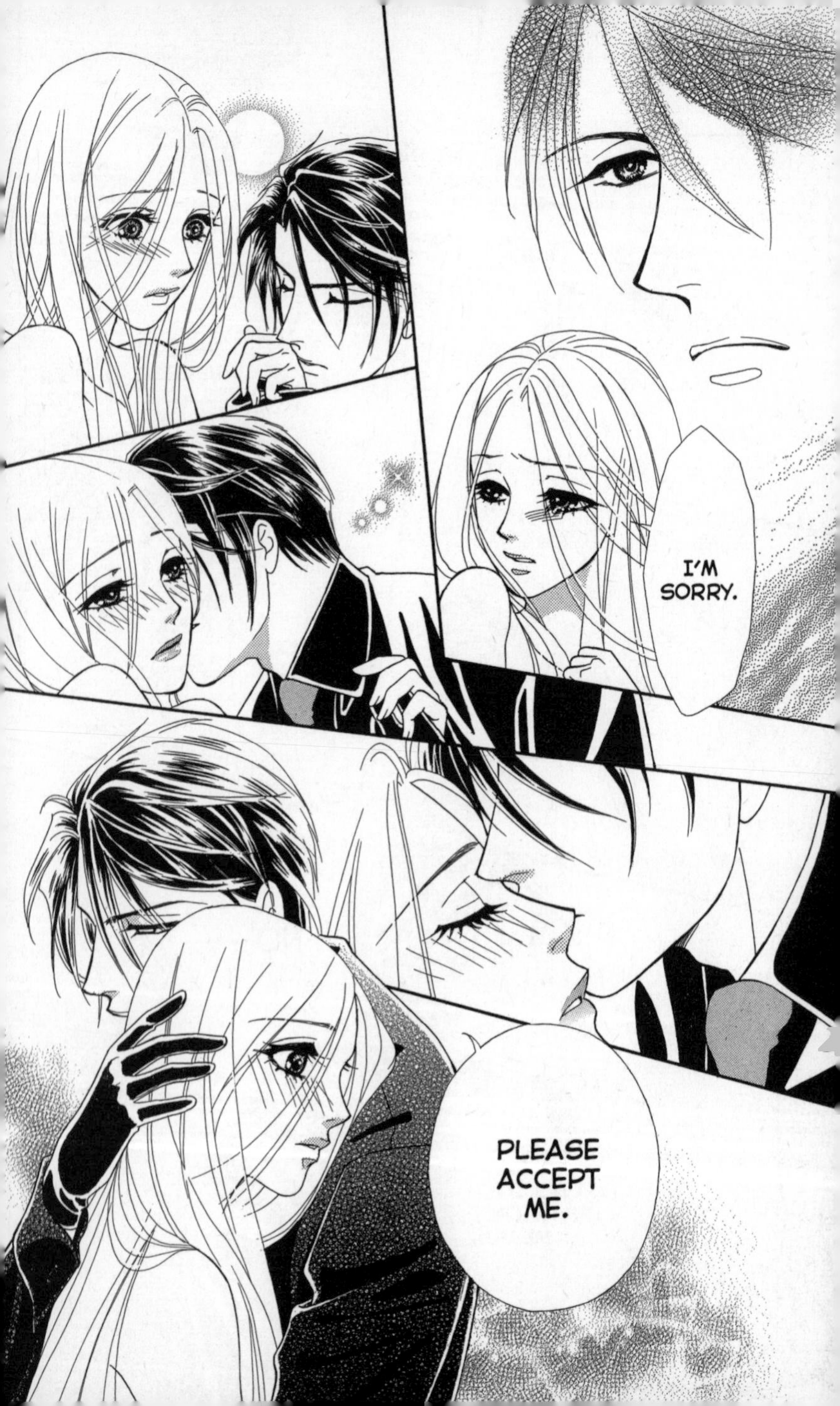
I'M SORRY.
PLEASE ACCEPT ME.

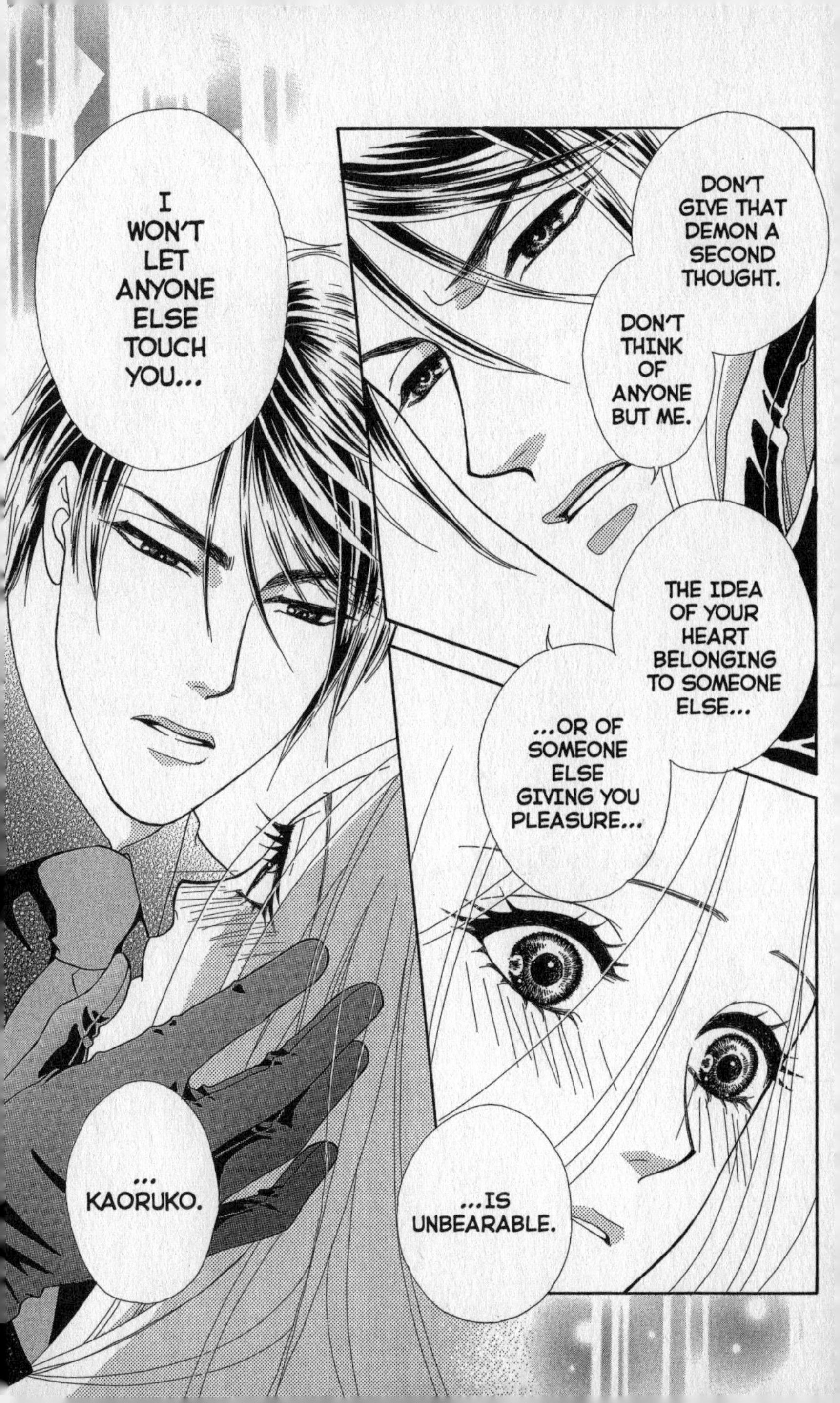
DON'T GIVE THAT DEMON A SECOND THOUGHT.
DON'T THINK OF ANYONE BUT ME.
THE IDEA OF YOUR HEART BELONGING TO SOMEONE ELSE...
...OR OF SOMEONE ELSE GIVING YOU PLEASURE...
...IS UNBEARABLE.
I WON'T LET ANYONE ELSE TOUCH YOU...
...KAORUKO.

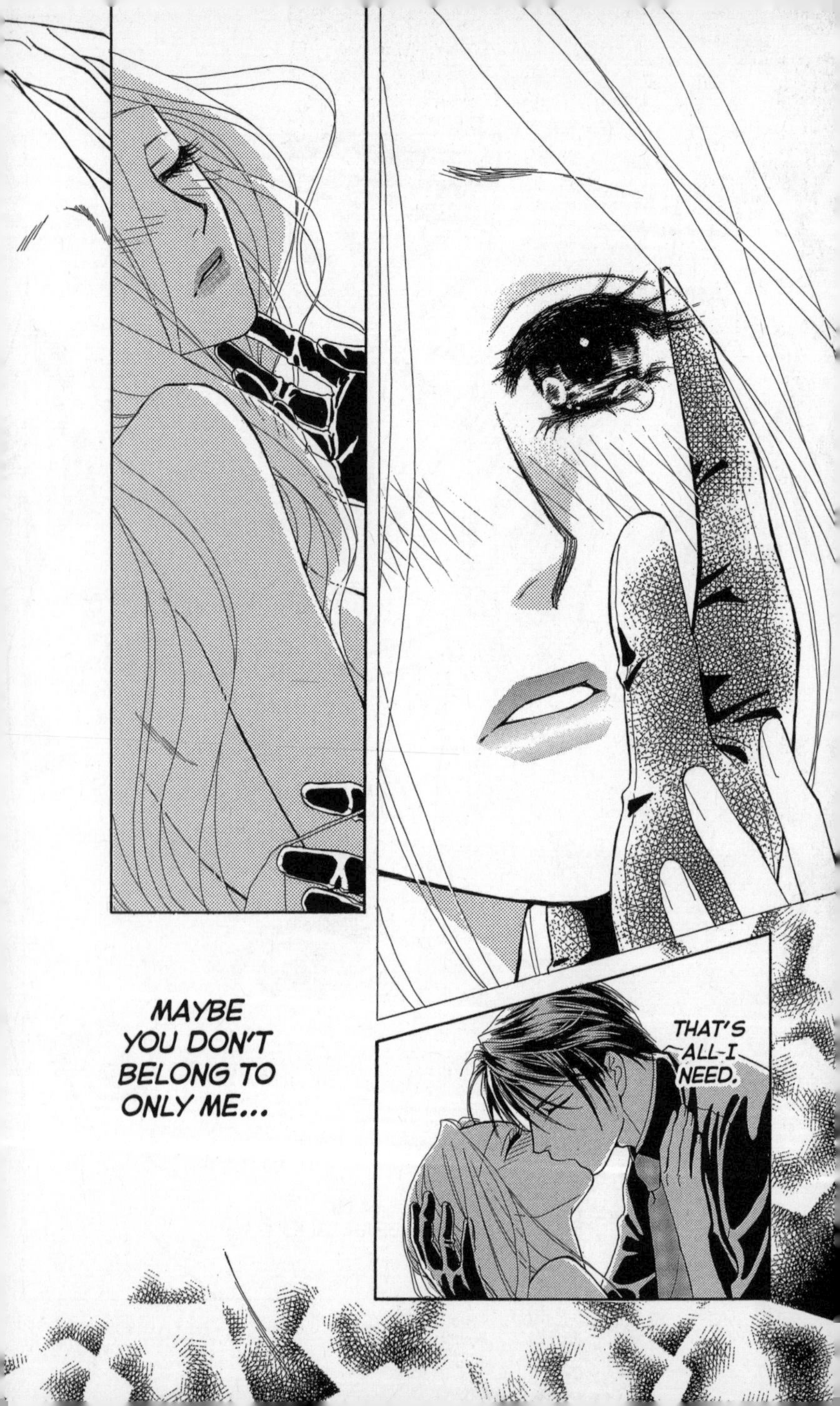
THAT'S ALL I NEED.
MAYBE YOU DON'T BELONG TO ONLY ME...

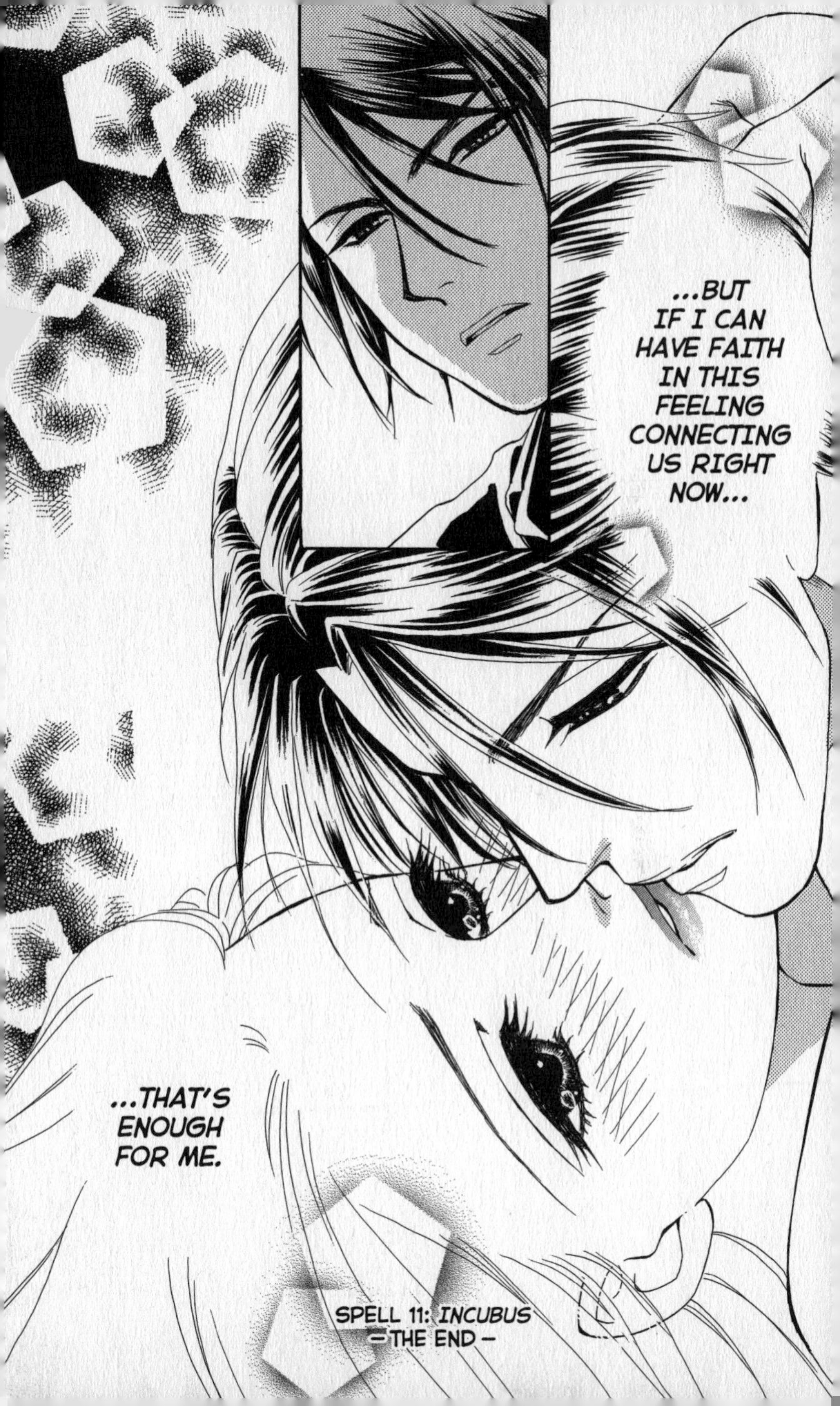
...BUT IF I CAN HAVE FAITH IN THIS FEELING CONNECTING US RIGHT NOW...
...THAT'S ENOUGH FOR ME.
SPELL 11: INCUBUS
–THE END–

- INCUBUS -

The cost of repairing the window
Kaname broke will probably
come out of his salary.

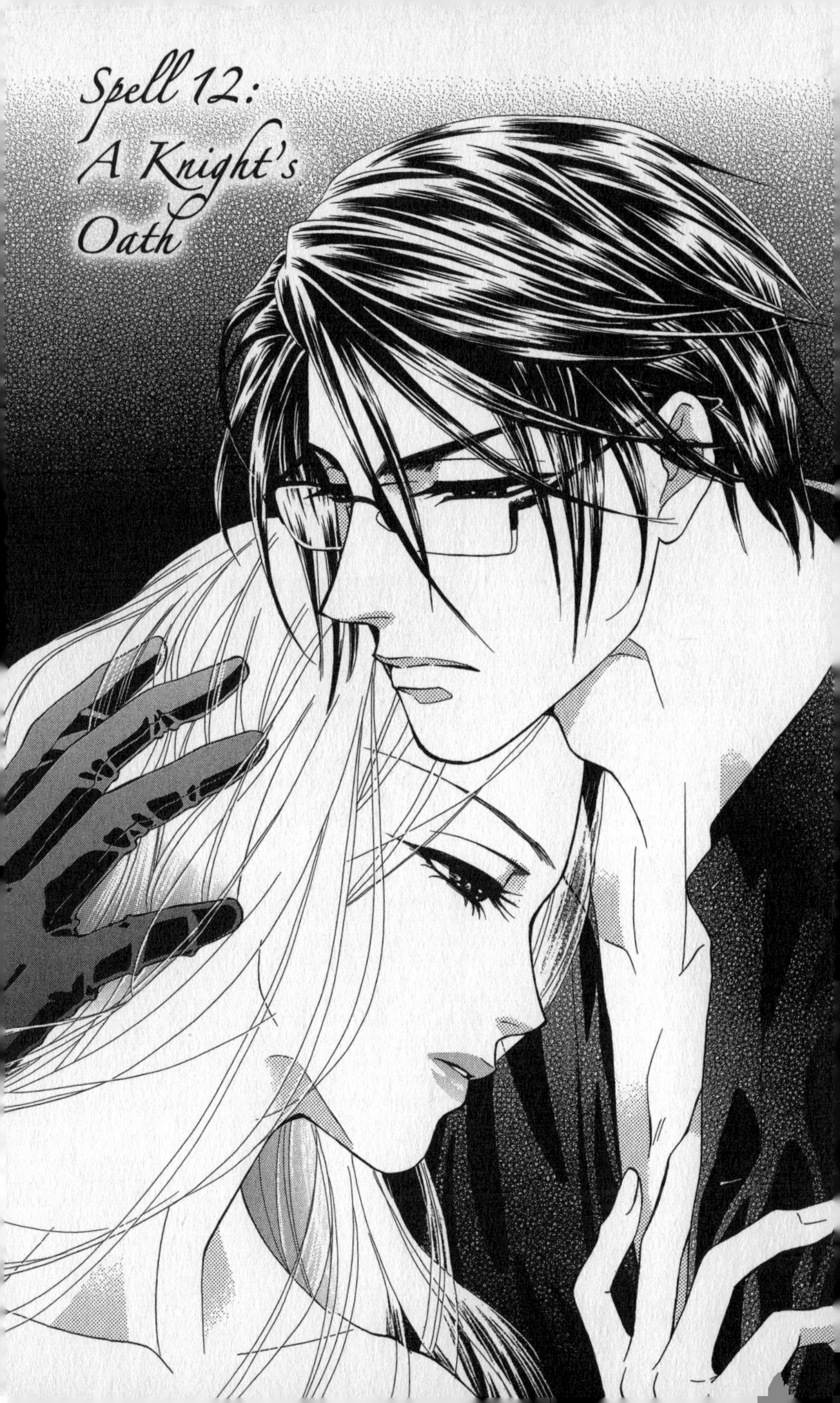
Spell 12:
A Knight's
Oath

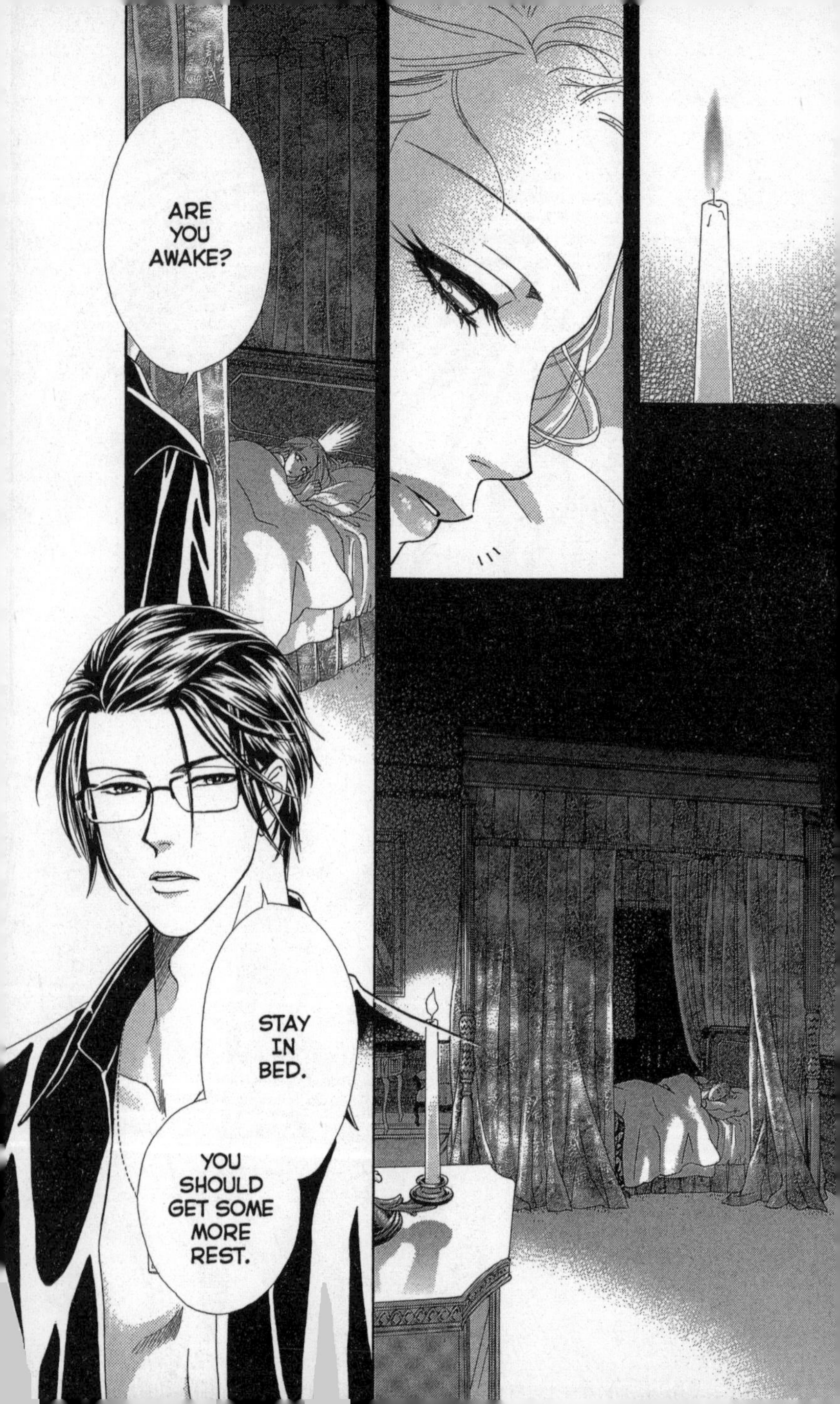
ARE YOU AWAKE?
STAY IN BED.
YOU SHOULD GET SOME MORE REST.

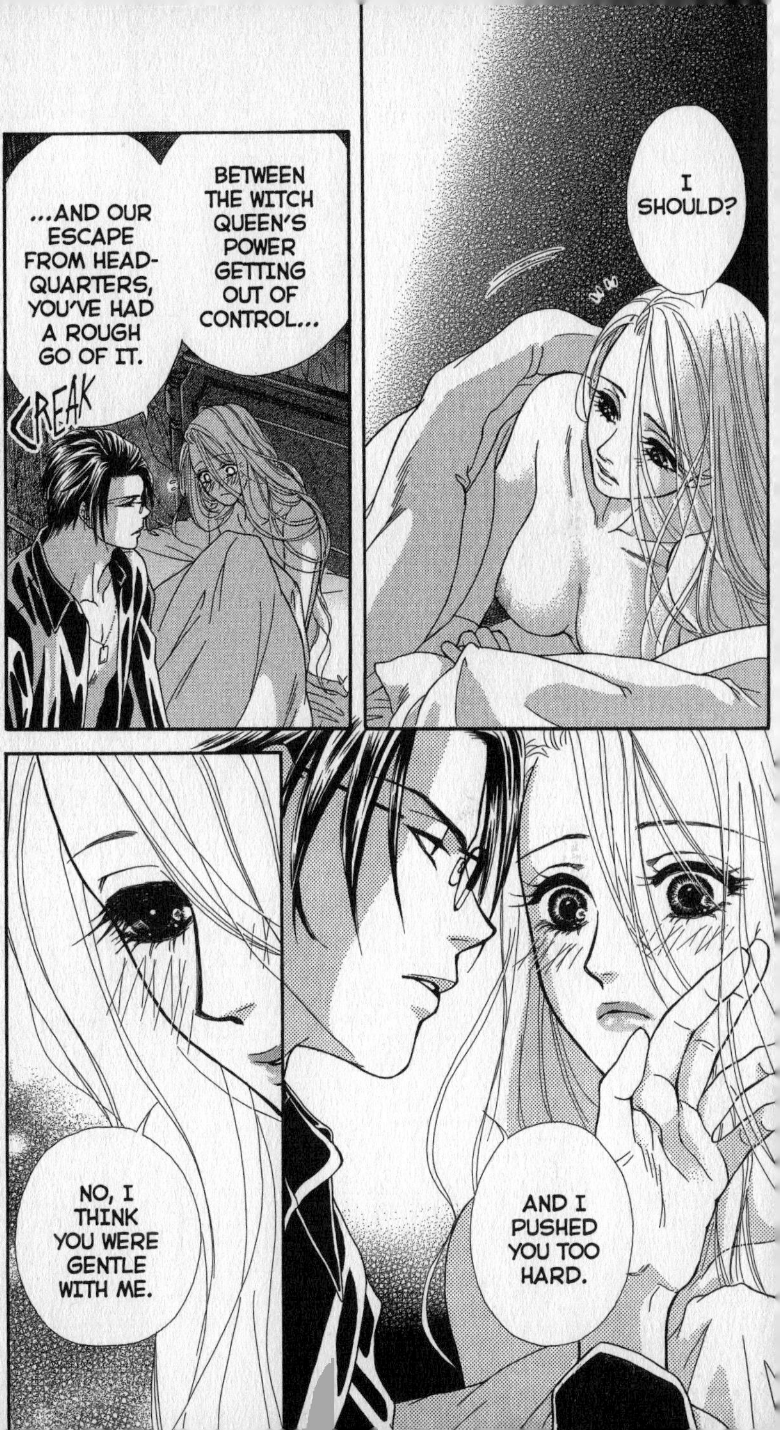
I SHOULD?
BETWEEN THE WITCH QUEEN'S POWER GETTING OUT OF CONTROL...
...AND OUR ESCAPE FROM HEAD-QUARTERS, YOU'VE HAD A ROUGH GO OF IT.
CREAK
AND I PUSHED YOU TOO HARD.
NO, I THINK YOU WERE GENTLE WITH ME.

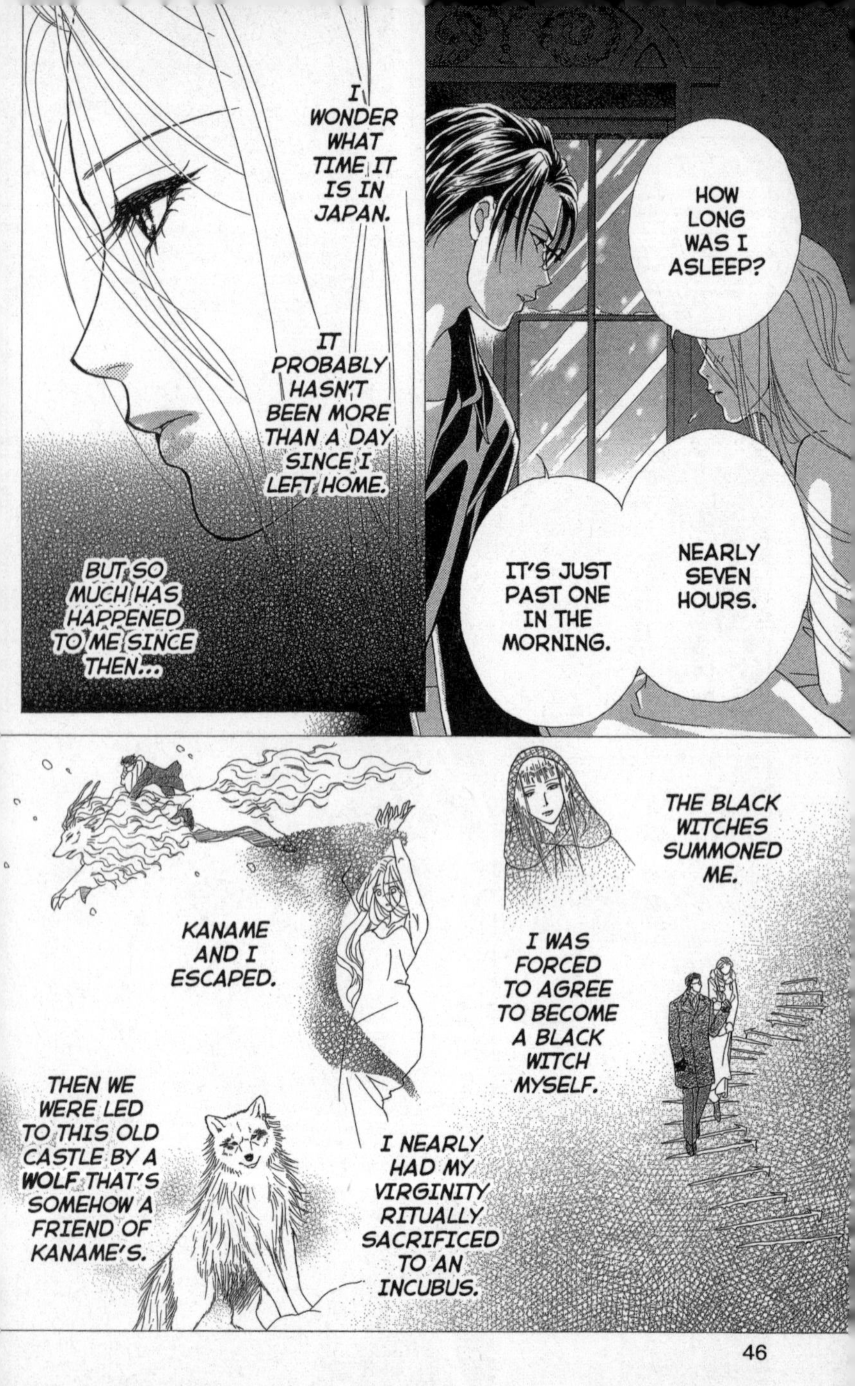
HOW LONG WAS I ASLEEP?
NEARLY SEVEN HOURS.
IT'S JUST PAST ONE IN THE MORNING.
I WONDER WHAT TIME IT IS IN JAPAN.
IT PROBABLY HASN'T BEEN MORE THAN A DAY SINCE I LEFT HOME.
BUT SO MUCH HAS HAPPENED TO ME SINCE THEN...
THE BLACK WITCHES SUMMONED ME.
I WAS FORCED TO AGREE TO BECOME A BLACK WITCH MYSELF.
I NEARLY HAD MY VIRGINITY RITUALLY SACRIFICED TO AN INCUBUS.
KANAME AND I ESCAPED.
THEN WE WERE LED TO THIS OLD CASTLE BY A WOLF THAT'S SOMEHOW A FRIEND OF KANAME'S.

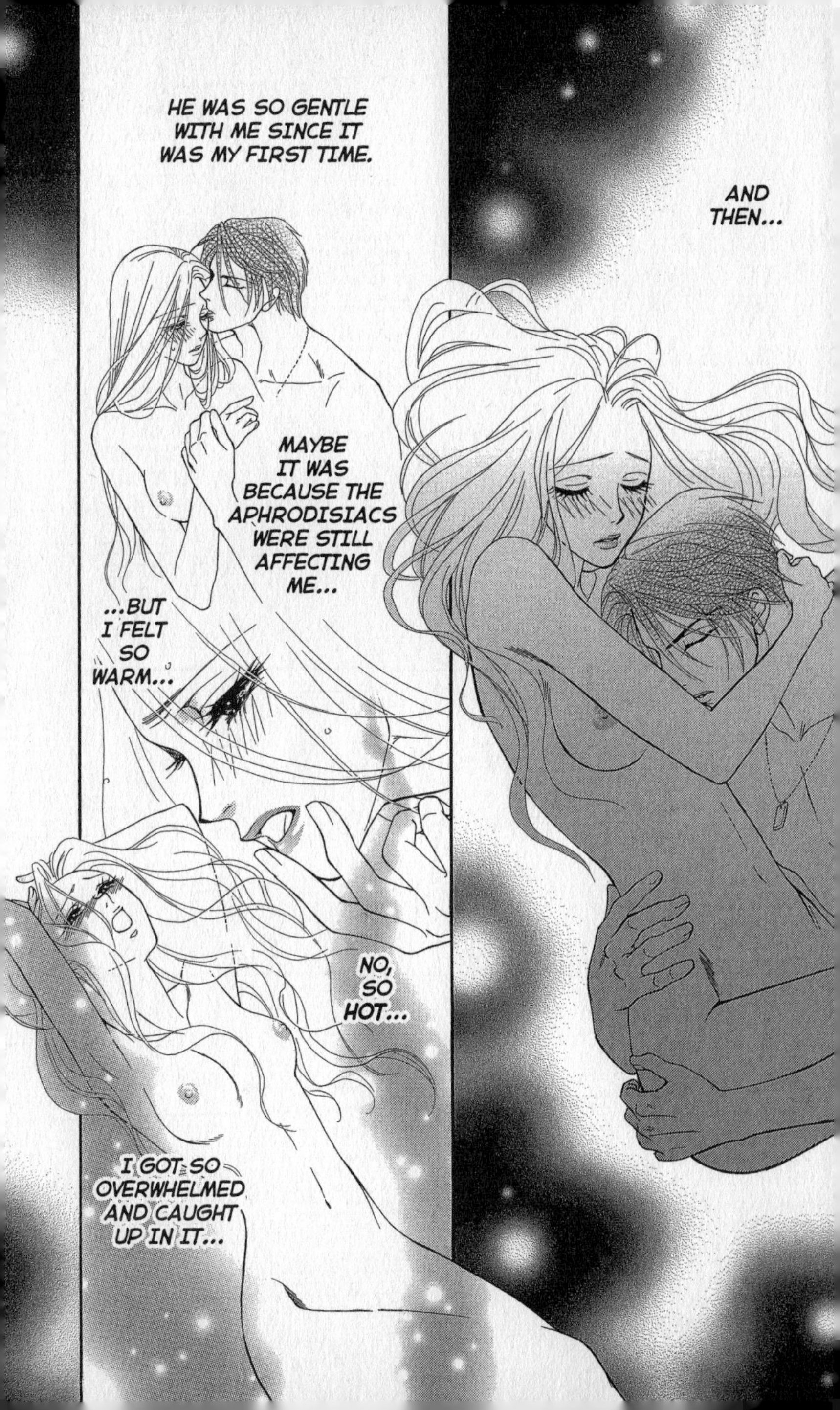
AND THEN...
HE WAS SO GENTLE WITH ME SINCE IT WAS MY FIRST TIME.
MAYBE IT WAS BECAUSE THE APHRODISIACS WERE STILL AFFECTING ME...
...BUT I FELT SO WARM...
NO, SO HOT...
I GOT SO OVERWHELMED AND CAUGHT UP IN IT...

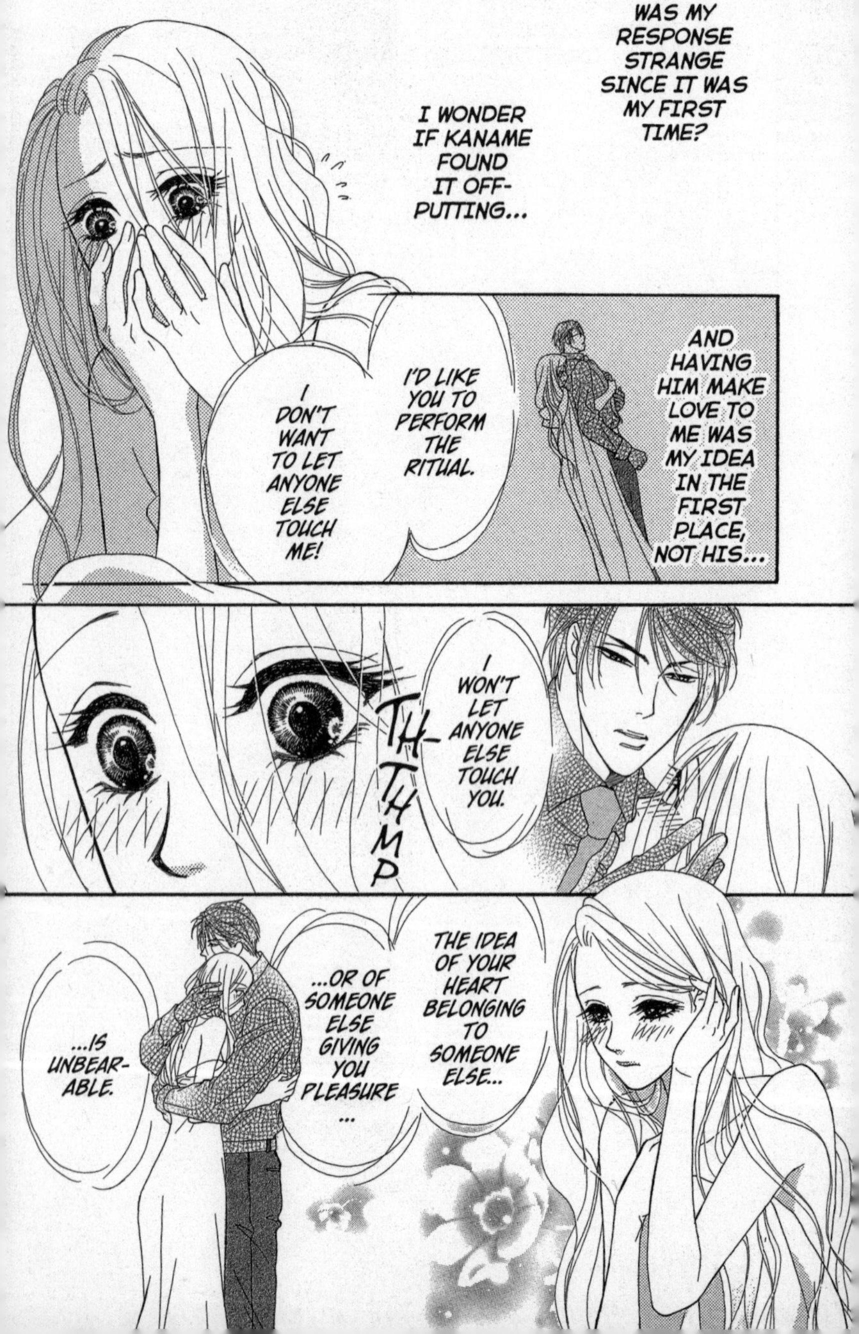
WAS MY RESPONSE STRANGE SINCE IT WAS MY FIRST TIME?
I WONDER IF KANAME FOUND IT OFF-PUTTING...
AND HAVING HIM MAKE LOVE TO ME WAS MY IDEA IN THE FIRST PLACE, NOT HIS...
I'D LIKE YOU TO PERFORM THE RITUAL.
I DON'T WANT TO LET ANYONE ELSE TOUCH ME!
I WON'T LET ANYONE ELSE TOUCH YOU.
TH-THMP
THE IDEA OF YOUR HEART BELONGING TO SOMEONE ELSE...
...OR OF SOMEONE ELSE GIVING YOU PLEASURE...
...IS UNBEAR-ABLE.

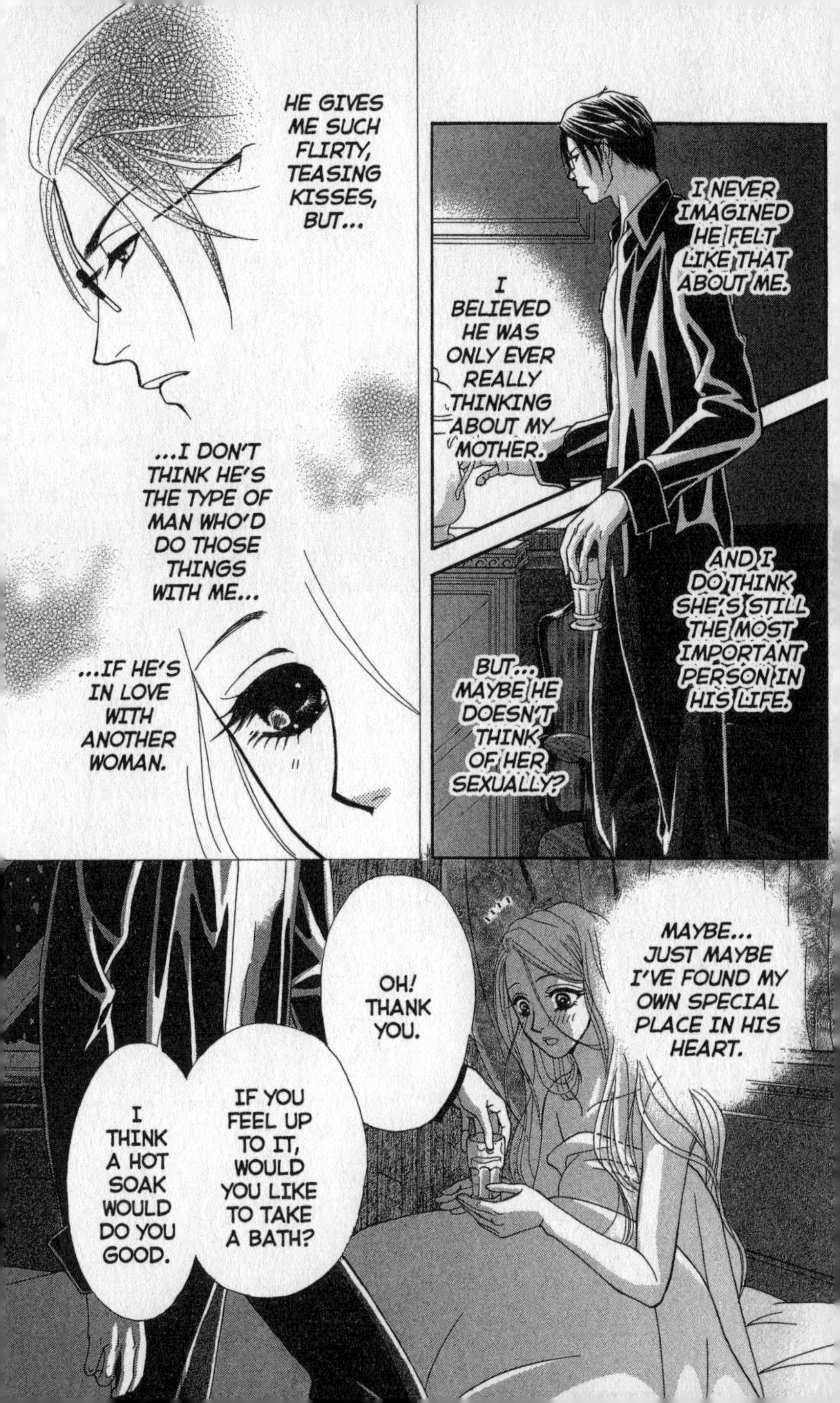
I NEVER IMAGINED HE FELT LIKE THAT ABOUT ME.
I BELIEVED HE WAS ONLY EVER REALLY THINKING ABOUT MY MOTHER.
AND I DO THINK SHE'S STILL THE MOST IMPORTANT PERSON IN HIS LIFE.
BUT... MAYBE HE DOESN'T THINK OF HER SEXUALLY?
HE GIVES ME SUCH FLIRTY, TEASING KISSES, BUT...
...I DON'T THINK HE'S THE TYPE OF MAN WHO'D DO THOSE THINGS WITH ME...
...IF HE'S IN LOVE WITH ANOTHER WOMAN.
MAYBE... JUST MAYBE I'VE FOUND MY OWN SPECIAL PLACE IN HIS HEART.
OH! THANK YOU.
IF YOU FEEL UP TO IT, WOULD YOU LIKE TO TAKE A BATH?
I THINK A HOT SOAK WOULD DO YOU GOOD.

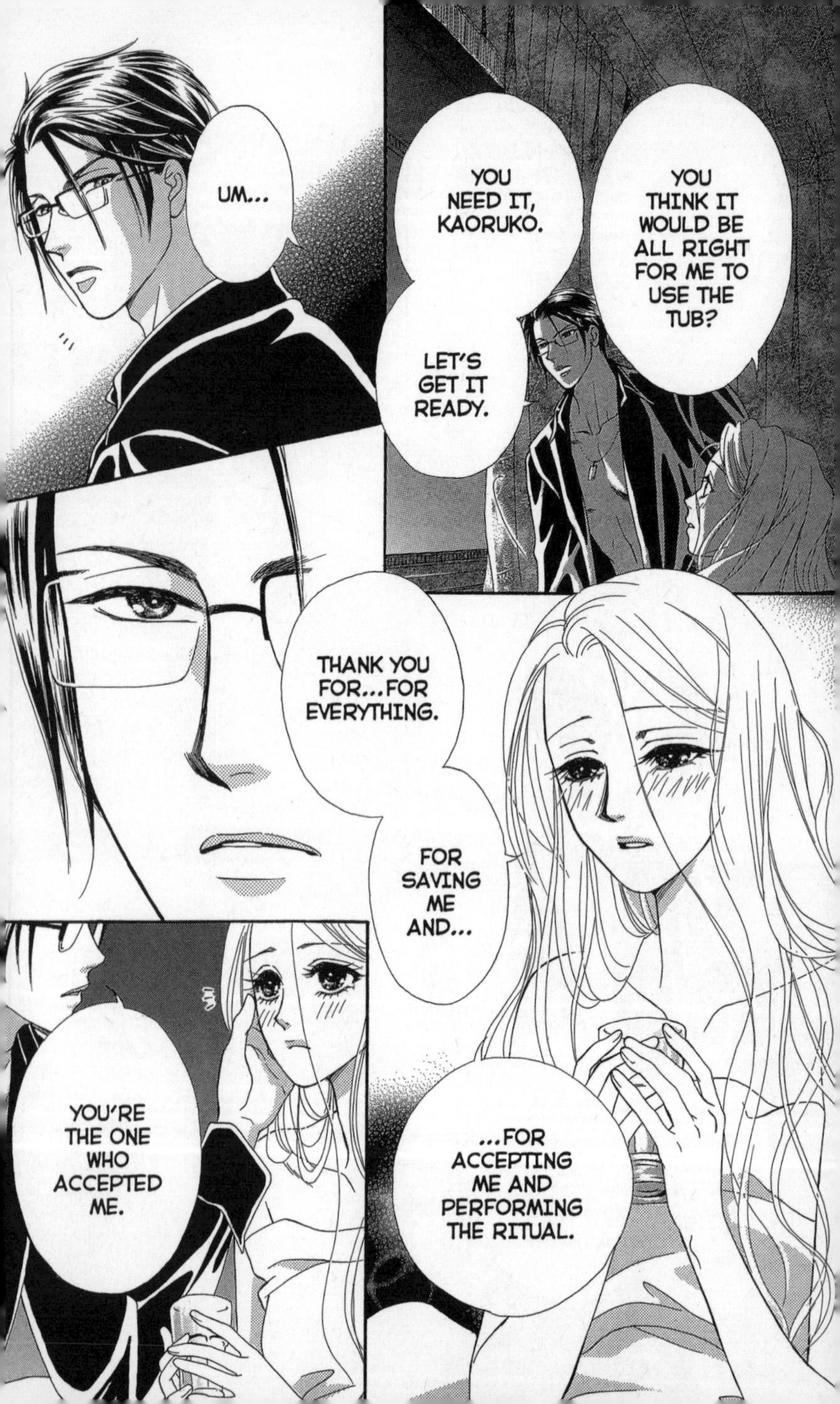
YOU THINK IT WOULD BE ALL RIGHT FOR ME TO USE THE TUB?
YOU NEED IT, KAORUKO.
LET'S GET IT READY.
UM...
THANK YOU FOR...FOR EVERYTHING.
FOR SAVING ME AND...
...FOR ACCEPTING ME AND PERFORMING THE RITUAL.
YOU'RE THE ONE WHO ACCEPTED ME.

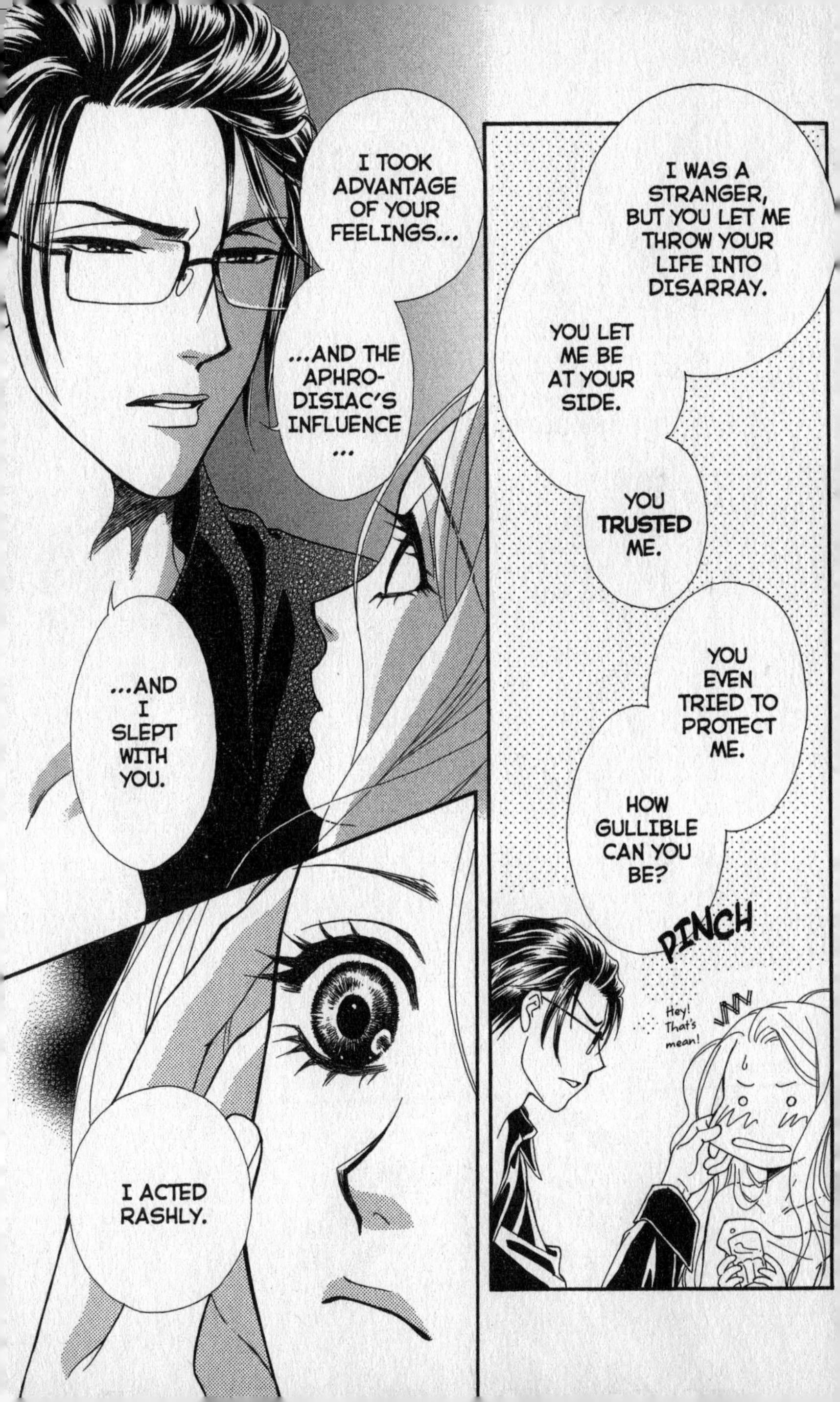

I WAS A STRANGER, BUT YOU LET ME THROW YOUR LIFE INTO DISARRAY.
YOU LET ME BE AT YOUR SIDE.
YOU TRUSTED ME.
YOU EVEN TRIED TO PROTECT ME.
HOW GULLIBLE CAN YOU BE?
PINCH
Hey! That's mean!
I TOOK ADVANTAGE OF YOUR FEELINGS...
...AND THE APHRO-DISIAC'S INFLUENCE ...
...AND I SLEPT WITH YOU.
I ACTED RASHLY.

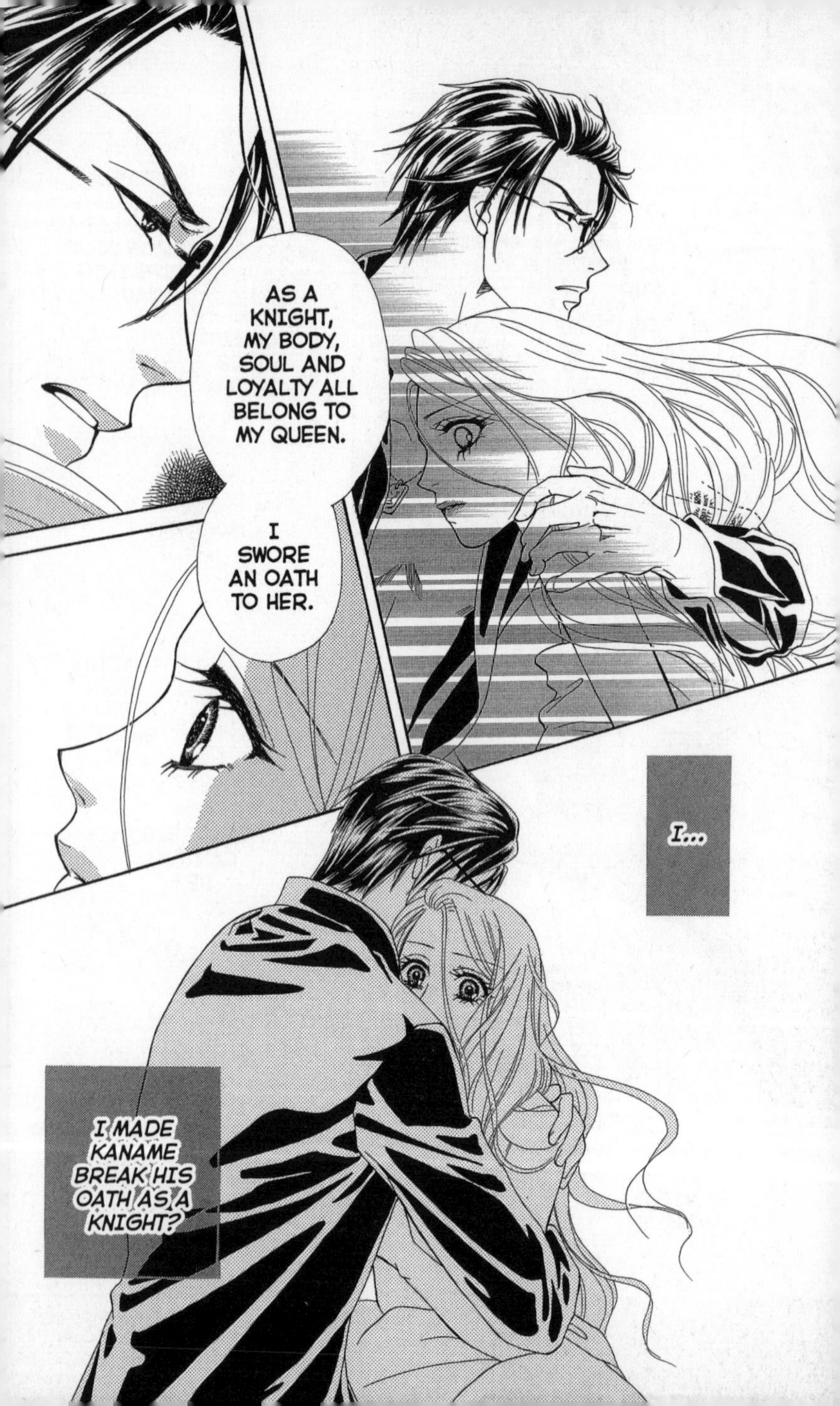
AS A KNIGHT, MY BODY, SOUL AND LOYALTY ALL BELONG TO MY QUEEN.
I SWORE AN OATH TO HER.
I...
I MADE KANAME BREAK HIS OATH AS A KNIGHT?

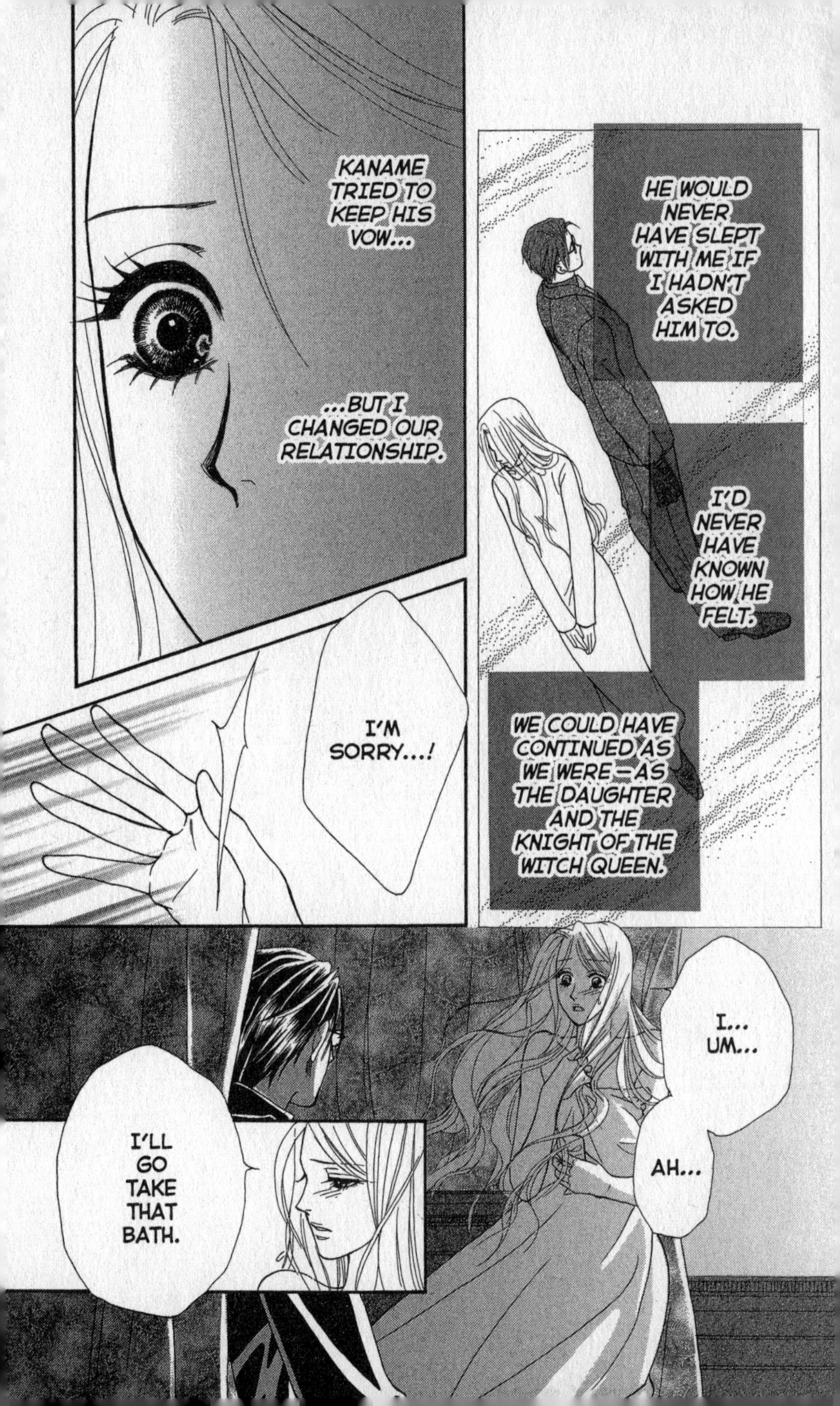
HE WOULD NEVER HAVE SLEPT WITH ME IF I HADN'T ASKED HIM TO.
I'D NEVER HAVE KNOWN HOW HE FELT.
WE COULD HAVE CONTINUED AS WE WERE—AS THE DAUGHTER AND THE KNIGHT OF THE WITCH QUEEN.
KANAME TRIED TO KEEP HIS VOW...
...BUT I CHANGED OUR RELATIONSHIP.
I'M SORRY...!
I... UM...
AH...
I'LL GO TAKE THAT BATH.

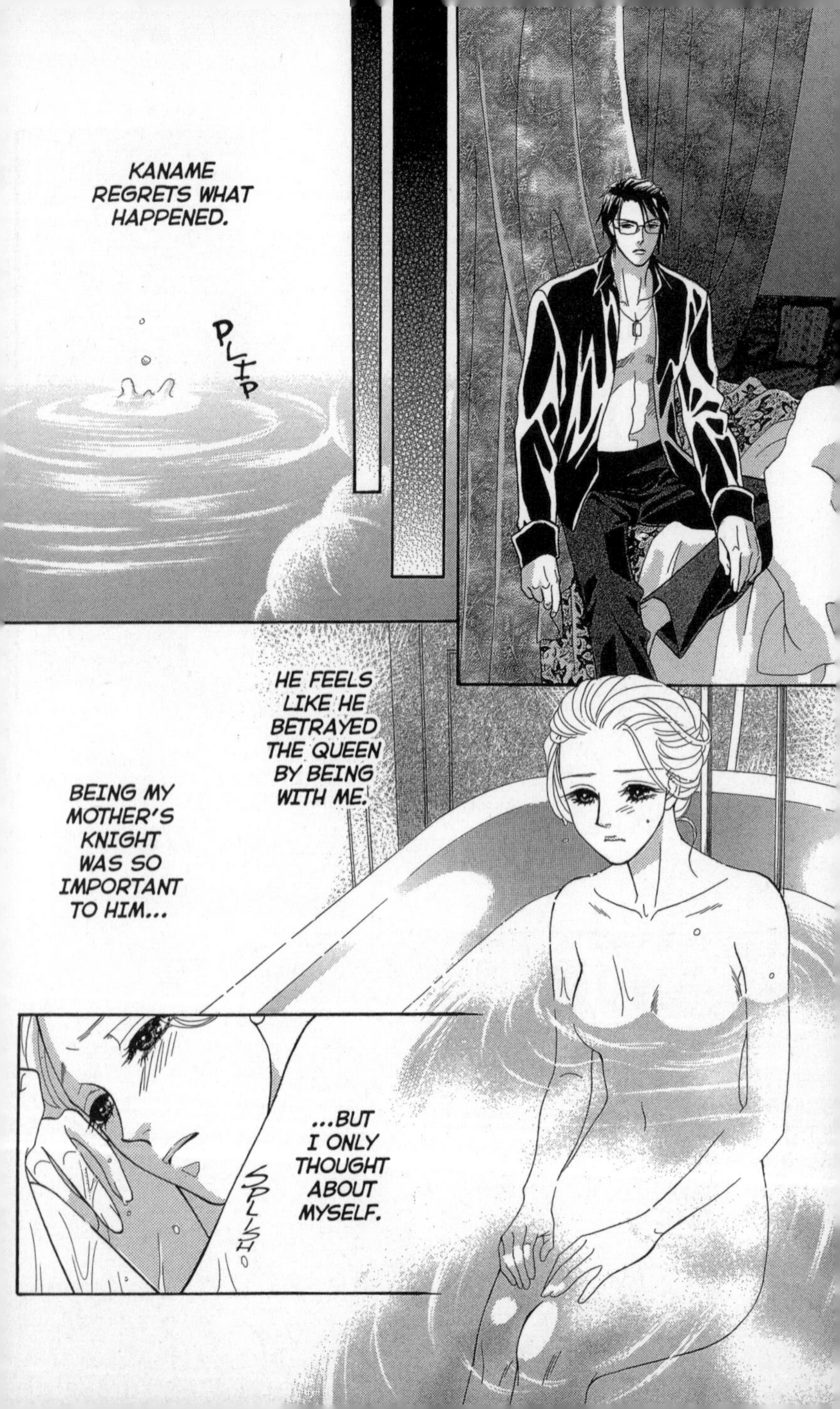
KANAME REGRETS WHAT HAPPENED.
PLIP
HE FEELS LIKE HE BETRAYED THE QUEEN BY BEING WITH ME.
BEING MY MOTHER'S KNIGHT WAS SO IMPORTANT TO HIM...
...BUT I ONLY THOUGHT ABOUT MYSELF.
SPLSH

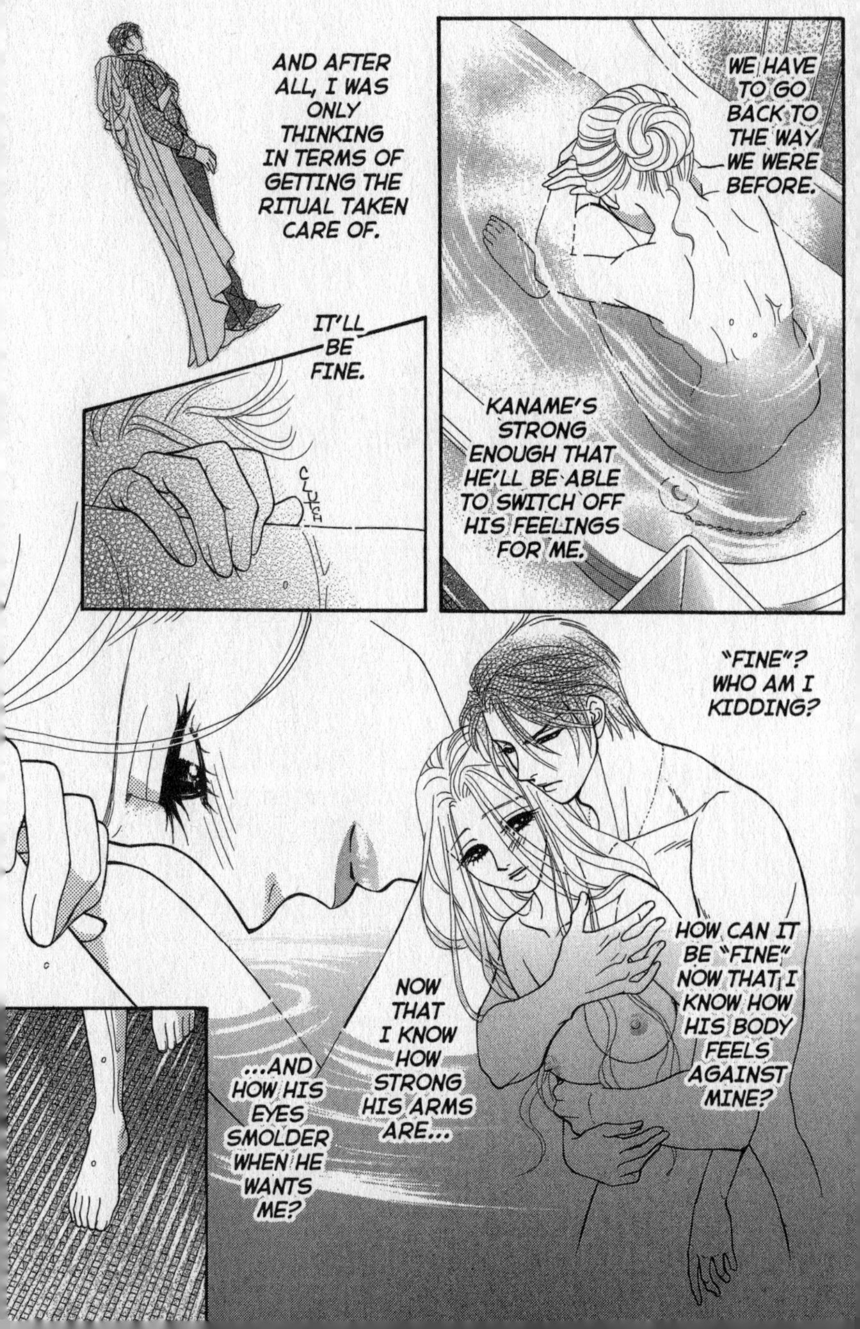
WE HAVE TO GO BACK TO THE WAY WE WERE BEFORE.
KANAME'S STRONG ENOUGH THAT HE'LL BE ABLE TO SWITCH OFF HIS FEELINGS FOR ME.
AND AFTER ALL, I WAS ONLY THINKING IN TERMS OF GETTING THE RITUAL TAKEN CARE OF.
IT'LL BE FINE.
CLUTCH
"FINE"? WHO AM I KIDDING?
HOW CAN IT BE "FINE" NOW THAT I KNOW HOW HIS BODY FEELS AGAINST MINE?
NOW THAT I KNOW HOW STRONG HIS ARMS ARE...
...AND HOW HIS EYES SMOLDER WHEN HE WANTS ME?

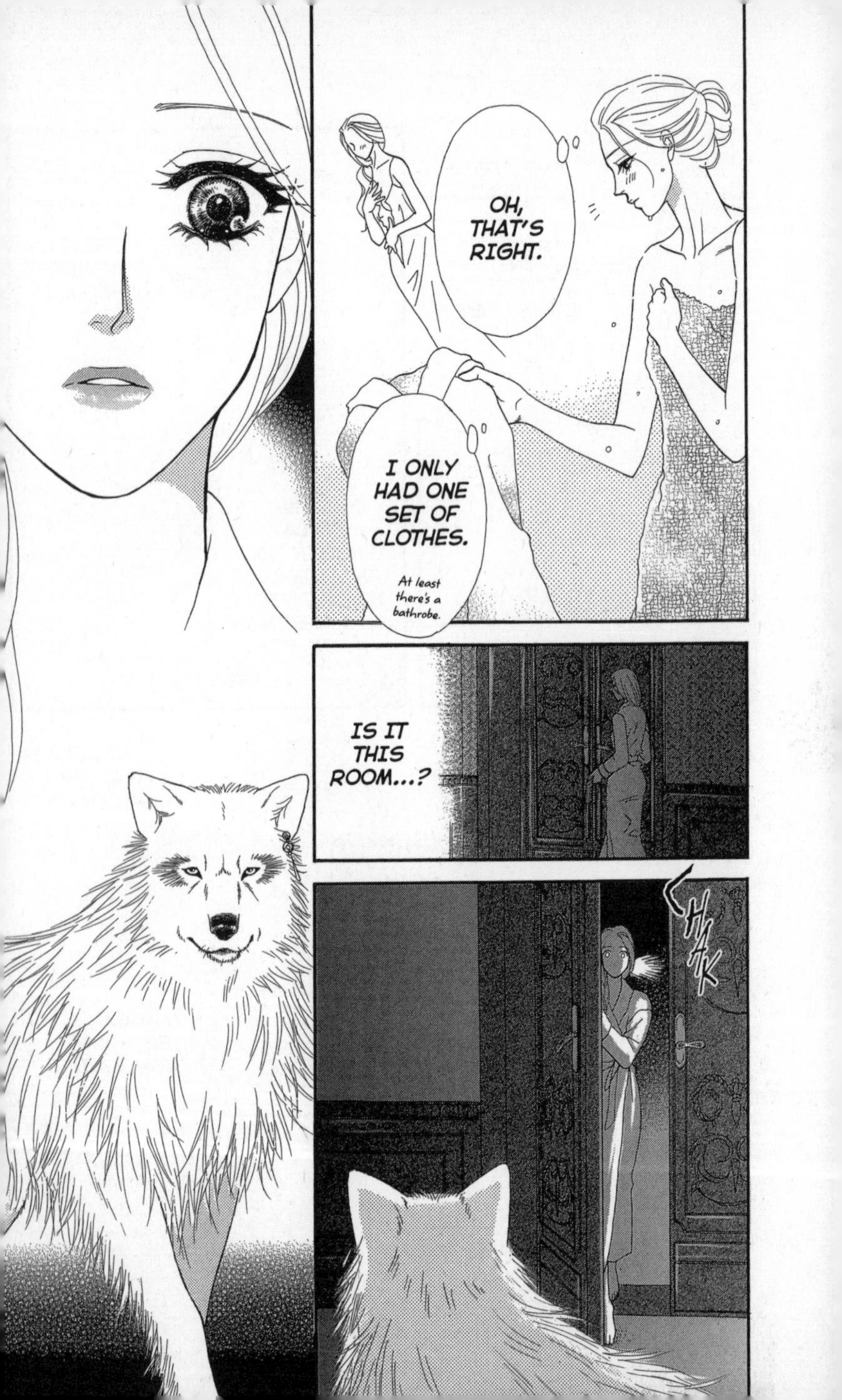
OH, THAT'S RIGHT.
I ONLY HAD ONE SET OF CLOTHES.
At least there's a bathrobe.
IS IT THIS ROOM...?
CHAK

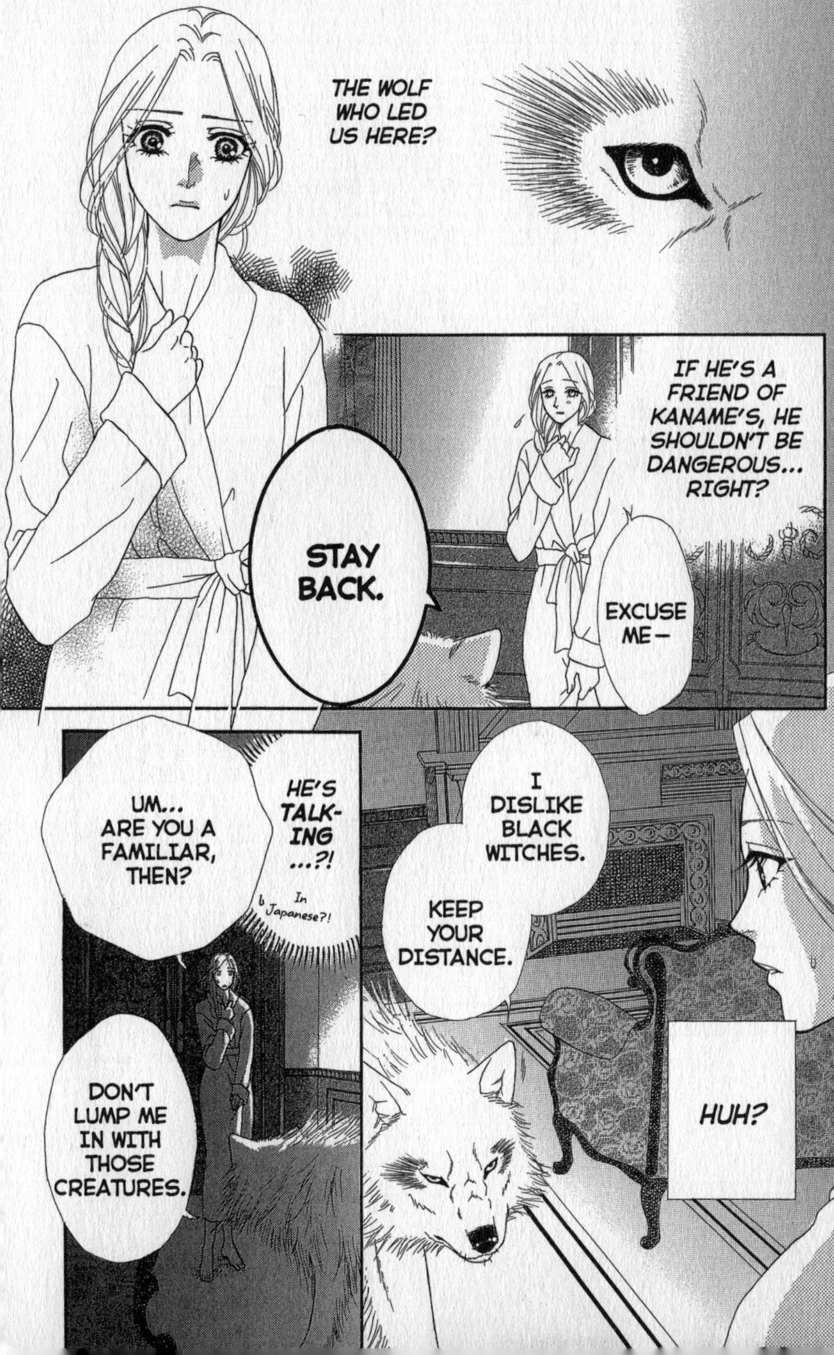
THE WOLF WHO LED US HERE?
IF HE'S A FRIEND OF KANAME'S, HE SHOULDN'T BE DANGEROUS... RIGHT?
EXCUSE ME—
STAY BACK.
I DISLIKE BLACK WITCHES.
KEEP YOUR DISTANCE.
HUH?
HE'S TALKING...?!
In Japanese?!
UM... ARE YOU A FAMILIAR, THEN?
DON'T LUMP ME IN WITH THOSE CREATURES.

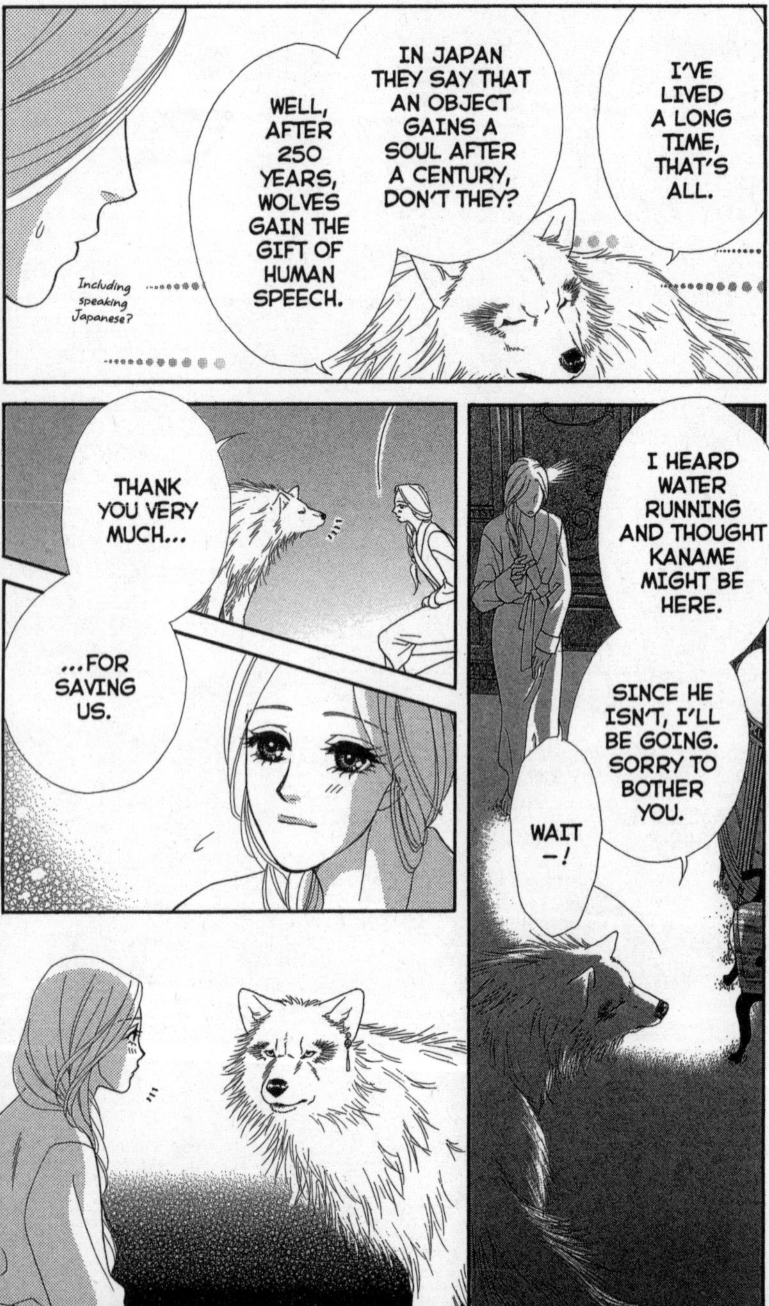
I'VE LIVED A LONG TIME, THAT'S ALL.
IN JAPAN THEY SAY THAT AN OBJECT GAINS A SOUL AFTER A CENTURY, DON'T THEY?
WELL, AFTER 250 YEARS, WOLVES GAIN THE GIFT OF HUMAN SPEECH.
Including speaking Japanese?
I HEARD WATER RUNNING AND THOUGHT KANAME MIGHT BE HERE.
SINCE HE ISN'T, I'LL BE GOING. SORRY TO BOTHER YOU.
WAIT —!
THANK YOU VERY MUCH...
...FOR SAVING US.

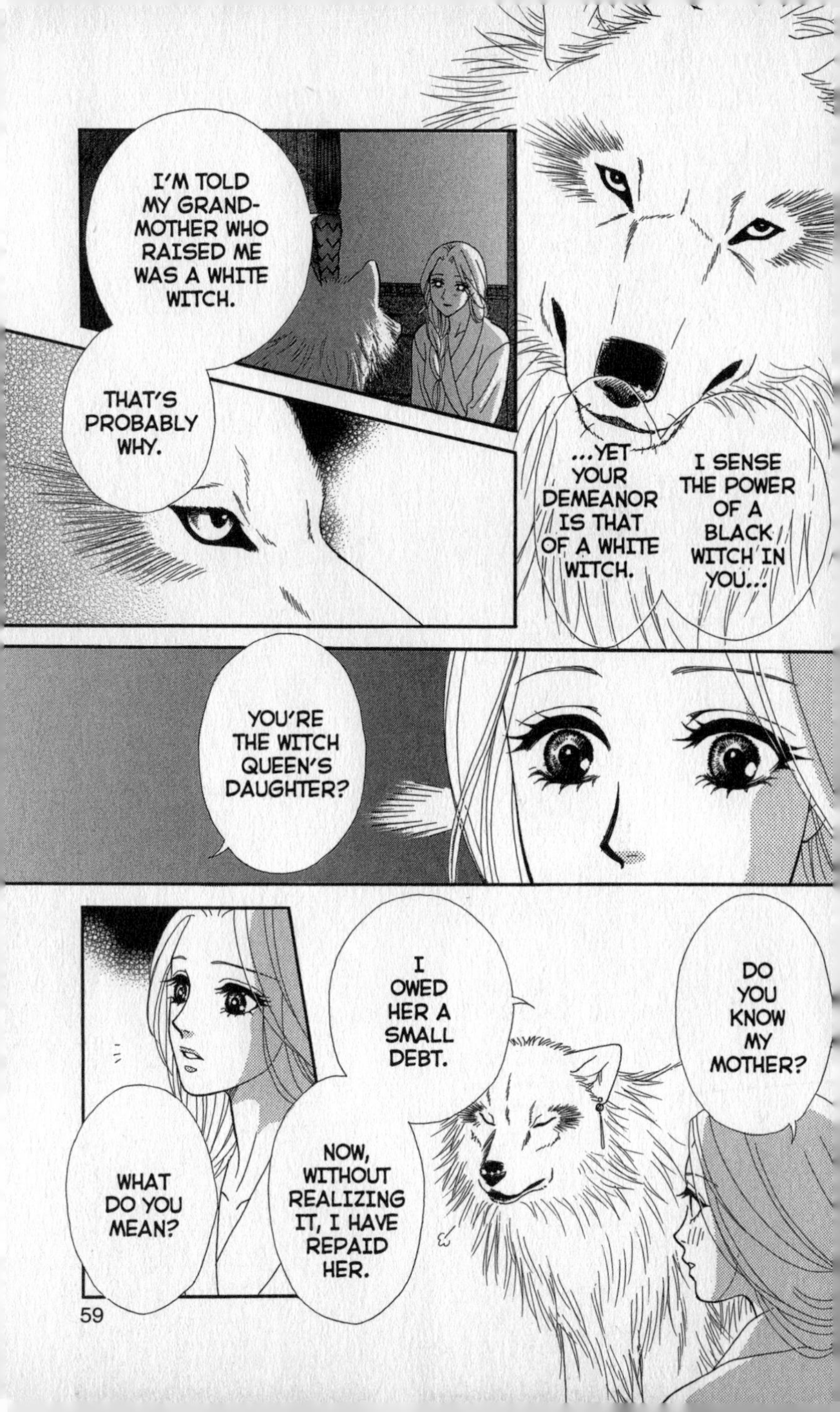
I SENSE THE POWER OF A BLACK WITCH IN YOU...
...YET YOUR DEMEANOR IS THAT OF A WHITE WITCH.
I'M TOLD MY GRAND-MOTHER WHO RAISED ME WAS A WHITE WITCH.
THAT'S PROBABLY WHY.
YOU'RE THE WITCH QUEEN'S DAUGHTER?
DO YOU KNOW MY MOTHER?
I OWED HER A SMALL DEBT.
NOW, WITHOUT REALIZING IT, I HAVE REPAID HER.
WHAT DO YOU MEAN?

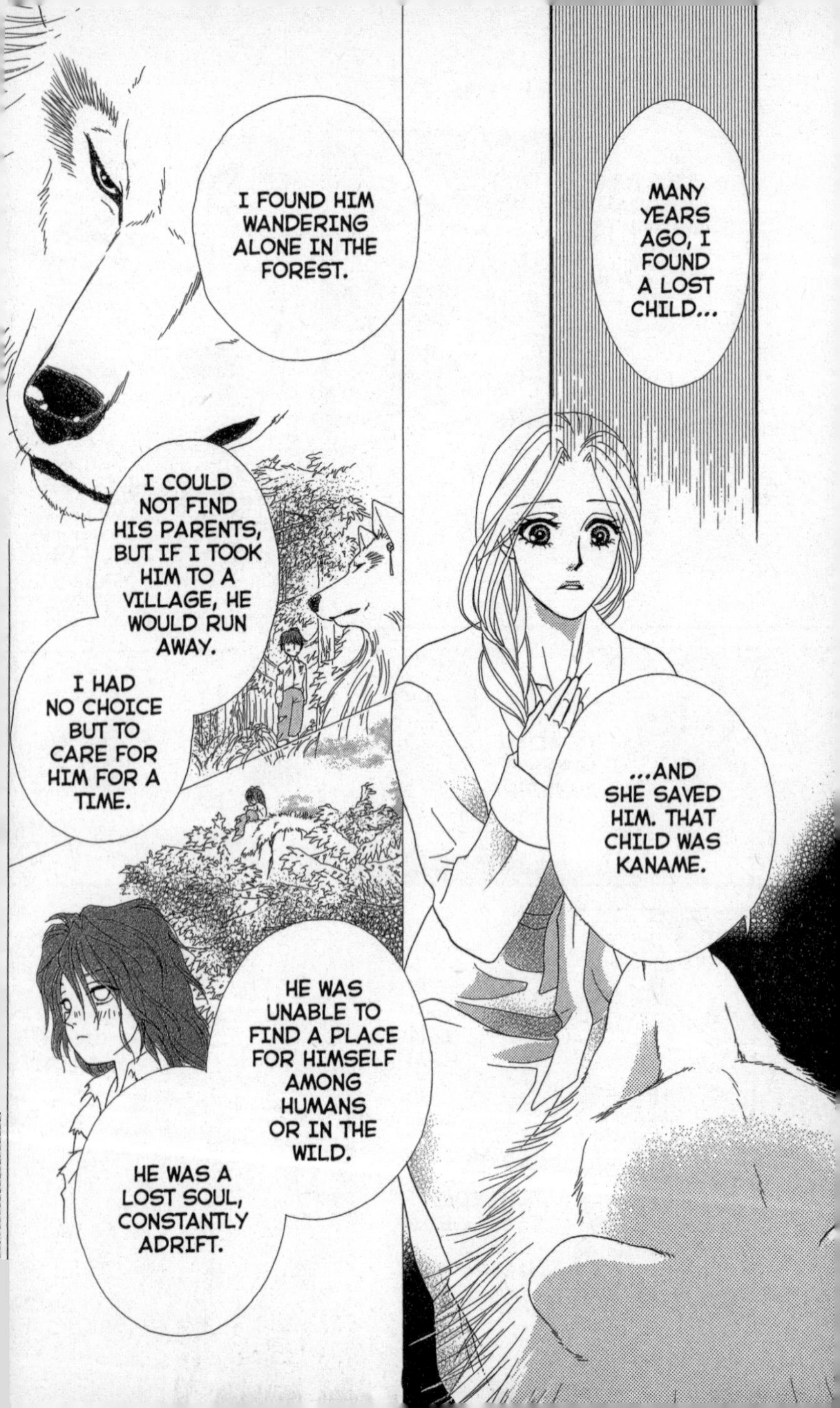
MANY YEARS AGO, I FOUND A LOST CHILD...
...AND SHE SAVED HIM. THAT CHILD WAS KANAME.
I FOUND HIM WANDERING ALONE IN THE FOREST.
I COULD NOT FIND HIS PARENTS, BUT IF I TOOK HIM TO A VILLAGE, HE WOULD RUN AWAY.
I HAD NO CHOICE BUT TO CARE FOR HIM FOR A TIME.
HE WAS UNABLE TO FIND A PLACE FOR HIMSELF AMONG HUMANS OR IN THE WILD.
HE WAS A LOST SOUL, CONSTANTLY ADRIFT.

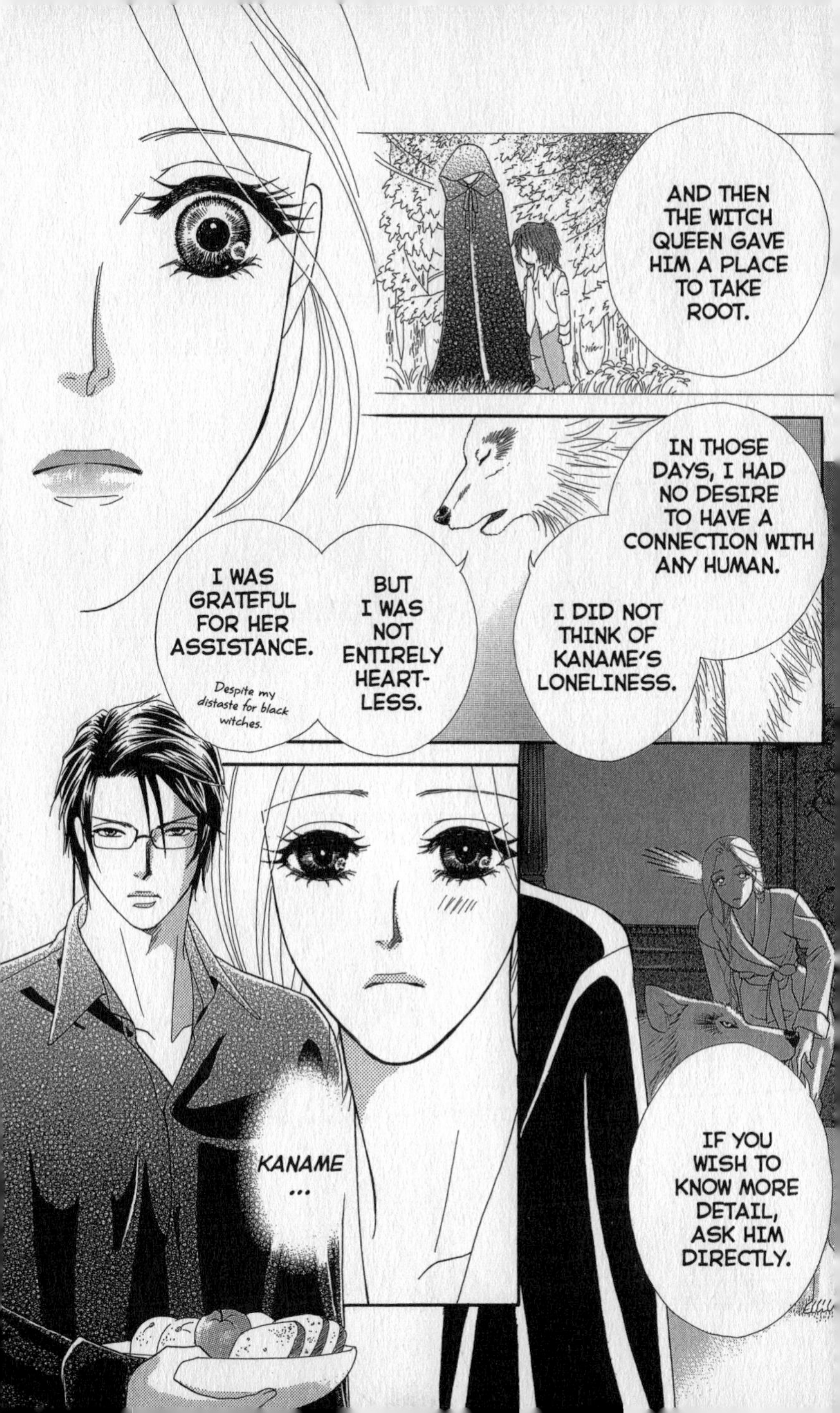
AND THEN THE WITCH QUEEN GAVE HIM A PLACE TO TAKE ROOT.
IN THOSE DAYS, I HAD NO DESIRE TO HAVE A CONNECTION WITH ANY HUMAN.
I DID NOT THINK OF KANAME'S LONELINESS.
BUT I WAS NOT ENTIRELY HEART-LESS.
I WAS GRATEFUL FOR HER ASSISTANCE.
Despite my distaste for black witches.
IF YOU WISH TO KNOW MORE DETAIL, ASK HIM DIRECTLY.
KANAME ...

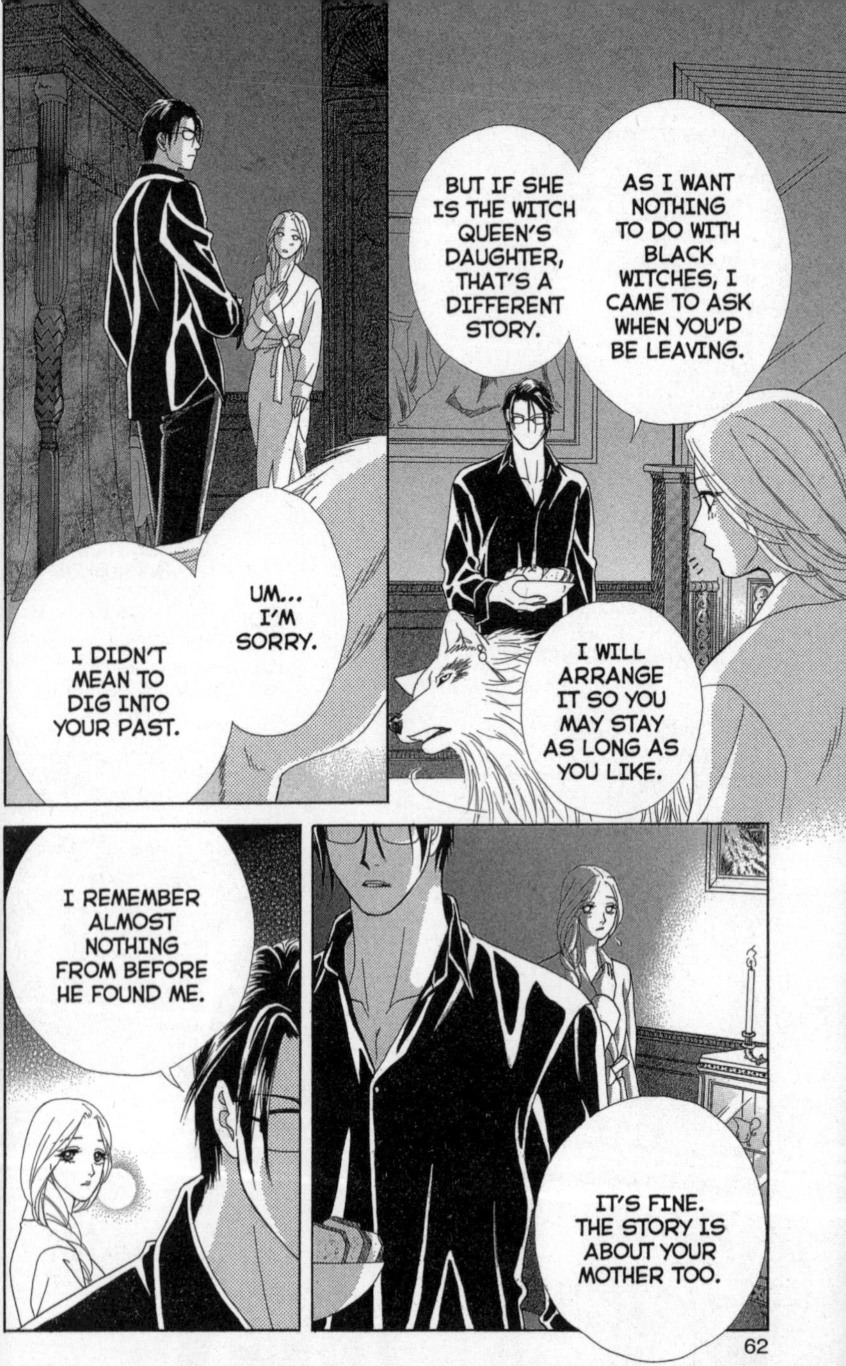
AS I WANT NOTHING TO DO WITH BLACK WITCHES, I CAME TO ASK WHEN YOU'D BE LEAVING.
BUT IF SHE IS THE WITCH QUEEN'S DAUGHTER, THAT'S A DIFFERENT STORY.
I WILL ARRANGE IT SO YOU MAY STAY AS LONG AS YOU LIKE.
UM... I'M SORRY.
I DIDN'T MEAN TO DIG INTO YOUR PAST.
IT'S FINE. THE STORY IS ABOUT YOUR MOTHER TOO.
I REMEMBER ALMOST NOTHING FROM BEFORE HE FOUND ME.

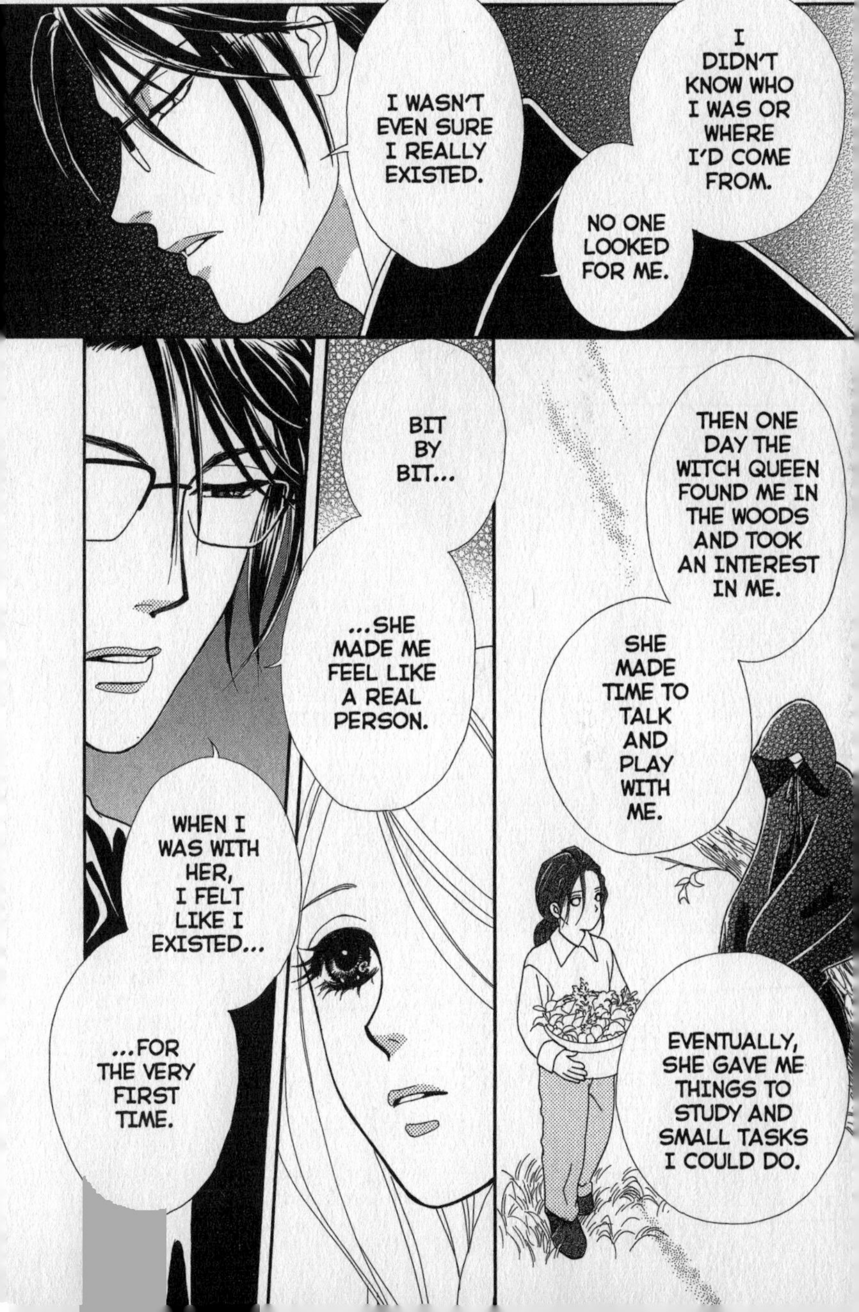
I DIDN'T KNOW WHO I WAS OR WHERE I'D COME FROM.
NO ONE LOOKED FOR ME.
I WASN'T EVEN SURE I REALLY EXISTED.
THEN ONE DAY THE WITCH QUEEN FOUND ME IN THE WOODS AND TOOK AN INTEREST IN ME.
SHE MADE TIME TO TALK AND PLAY WITH ME.
EVENTUALLY, SHE GAVE ME THINGS TO STUDY AND SMALL TASKS I COULD DO.
BIT BY BIT...
...SHE MADE ME FEEL LIKE A REAL PERSON.
WHEN I WAS WITH HER, I FELT LIKE I EXISTED...
...FOR THE VERY FIRST TIME.

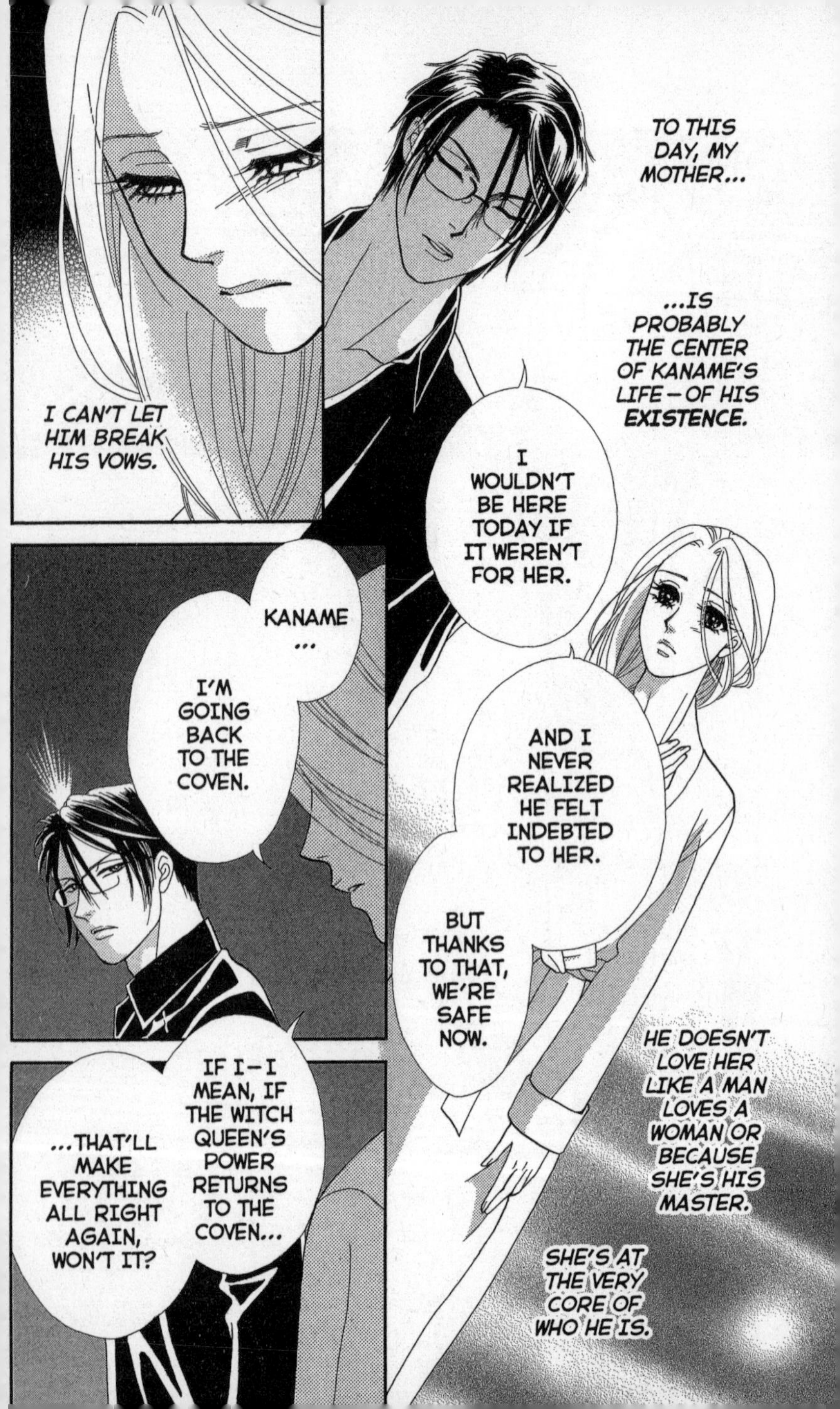
TO THIS DAY, MY MOTHER...
...IS PROBABLY THE CENTER OF KANAME'S LIFE—OF HIS **EXISTENCE.**
I WOULDN'T BE HERE TODAY IF IT WEREN'T FOR HER.
AND I NEVER REALIZED HE FELT INDEBTED TO HER.
BUT THANKS TO THAT, WE'RE SAFE NOW.
HE DOESN'T LOVE HER LIKE A MAN LOVES A WOMAN OR BECAUSE SHE'S HIS MASTER.
SHE'S AT THE VERY CORE OF WHO HE IS.
I CAN'T LET HIM BREAK HIS VOWS.
KANAME...
I'M GOING BACK TO THE COVEN.
IF I—I MEAN, IF THE WITCH QUEEN'S POWER RETURNS TO THE COVEN...
...THAT'LL MAKE EVERYTHING ALL RIGHT AGAIN, WON'T IT?

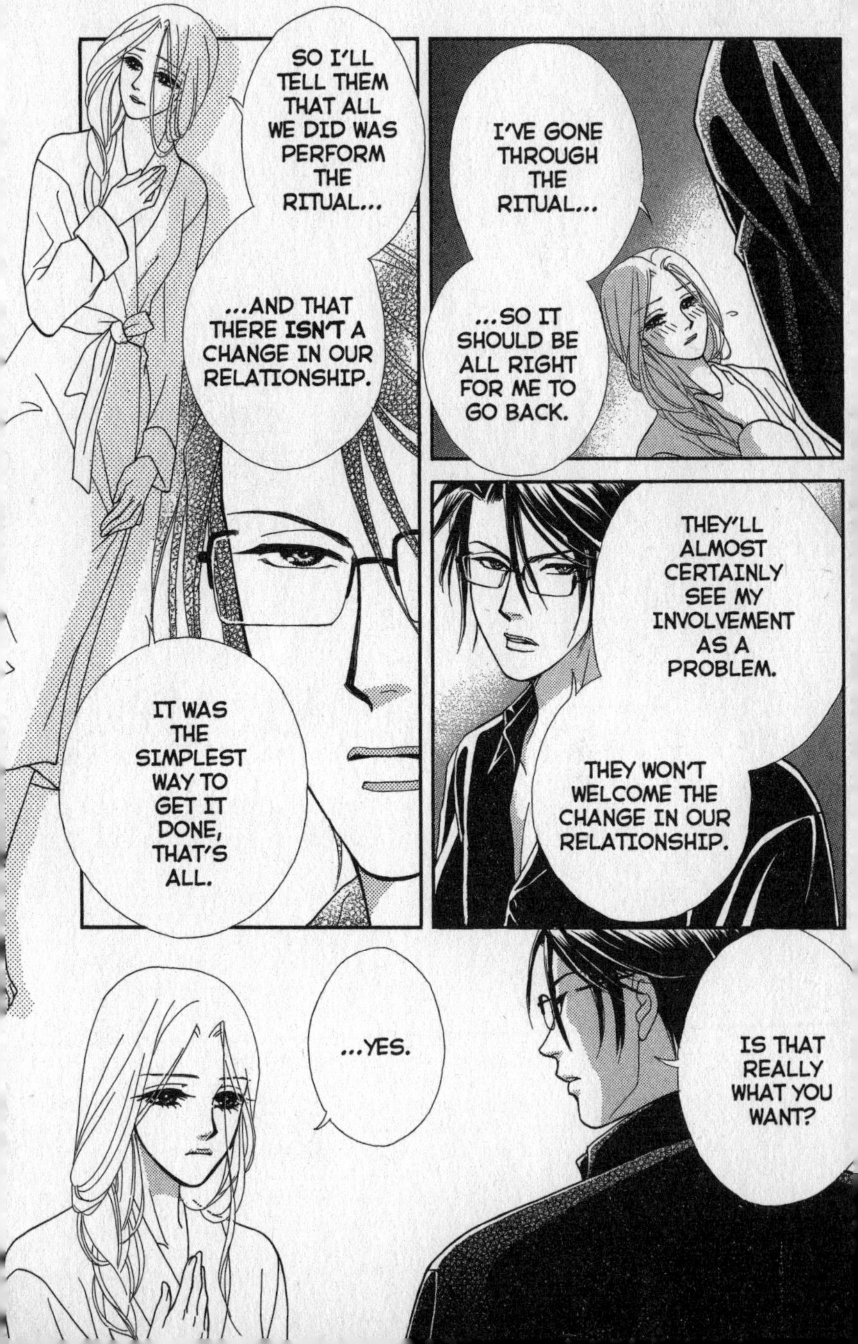
I'VE GONE THROUGH THE RITUAL...
...SO IT SHOULD BE ALL RIGHT FOR ME TO GO BACK.
THEY'LL ALMOST CERTAINLY SEE MY INVOLVEMENT AS A PROBLEM.
THEY WON'T WELCOME THE CHANGE IN OUR RELATIONSHIP.
SO I'LL TELL THEM THAT ALL WE DID WAS PERFORM THE RITUAL...
...AND THAT THERE **ISN'T** A CHANGE IN OUR RELATIONSHIP.
IT WAS THE SIMPLEST WAY TO GET IT DONE, THAT'S ALL.
IS THAT REALLY WHAT YOU WANT?
...YES.

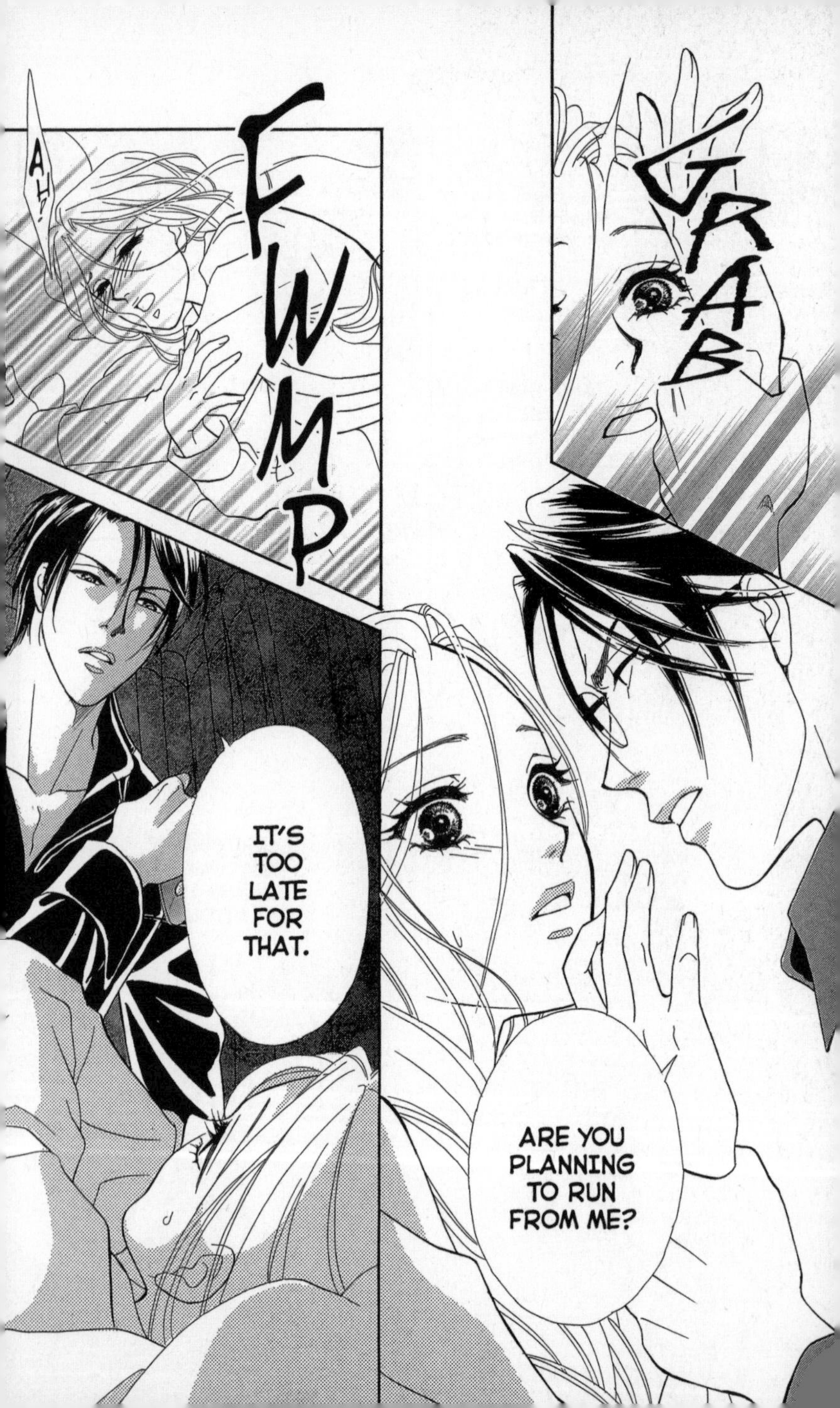
GRAB
ARE YOU PLANNING TO RUN FROM ME?
AH
FWMP
IT'S TOO LATE FOR THAT.

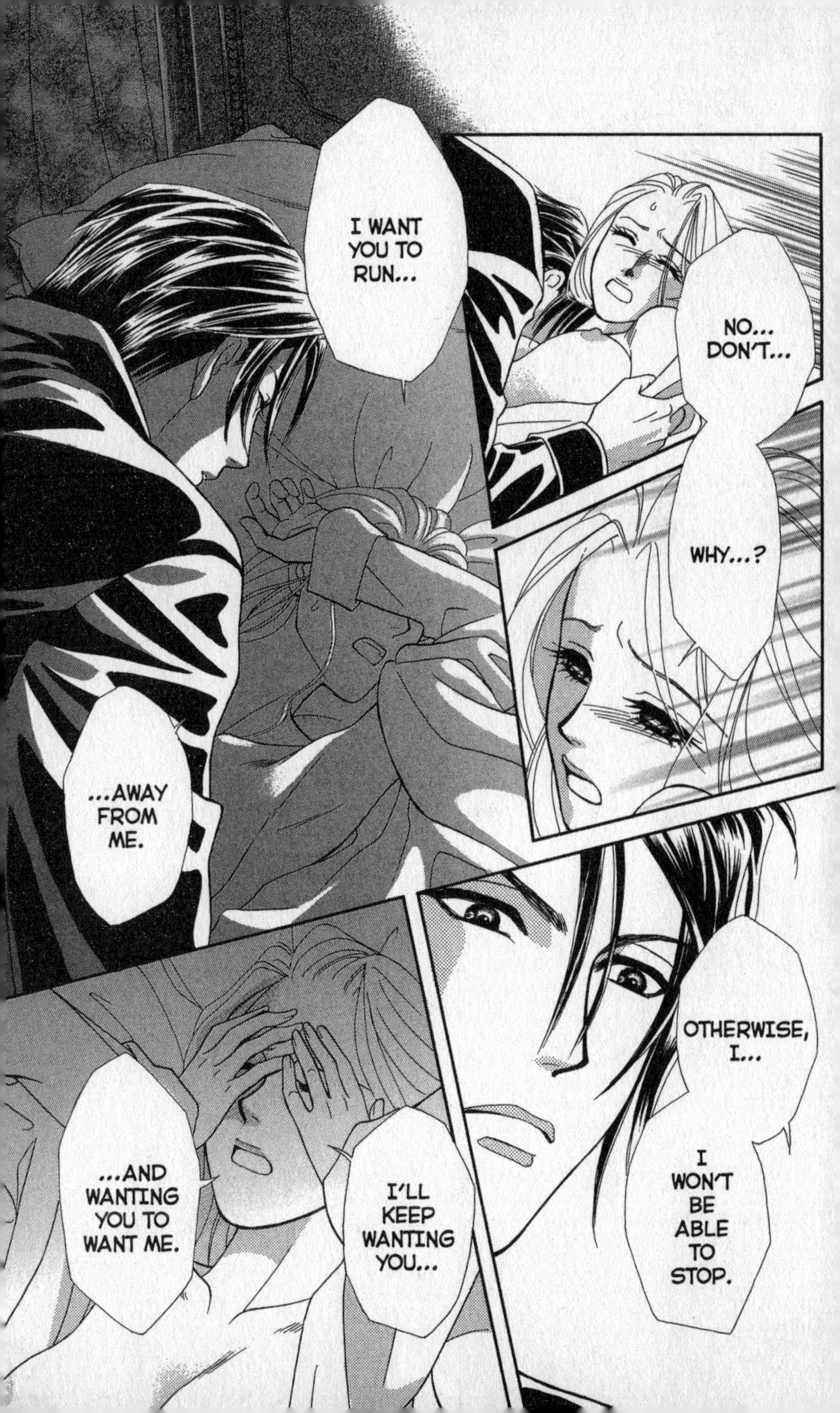
NO... DON'T...
WHY...?
I WANT YOU TO RUN...
...AWAY FROM ME.
OTHERWISE, I...
I WON'T BE ABLE TO STOP.
I'LL KEEP WANTING YOU...
...AND WANTING YOU TO WANT ME.

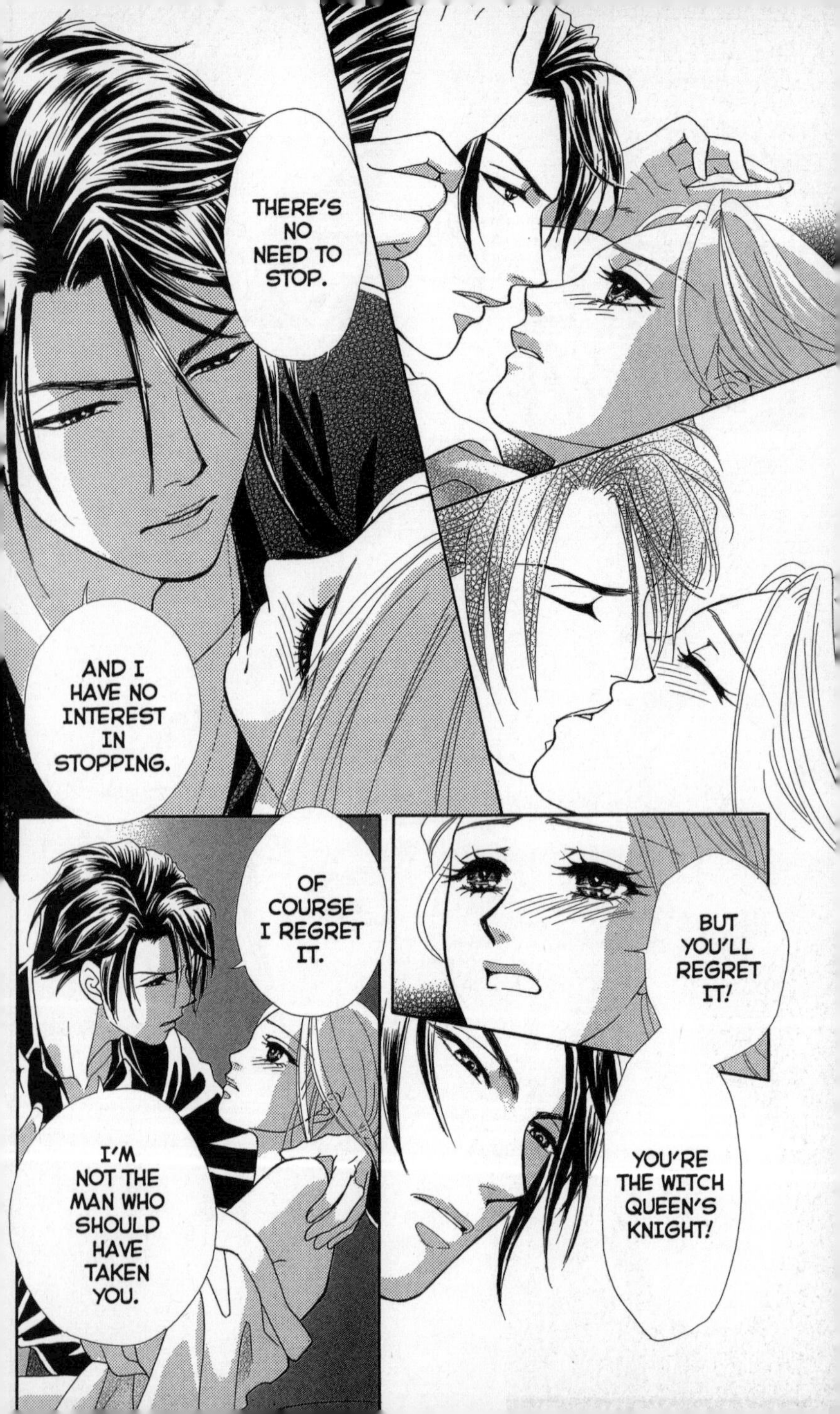
THERE'S NO NEED TO STOP.
AND I HAVE NO INTEREST IN STOPPING.
BUT YOU'LL REGRET IT!
YOU'RE THE WITCH QUEEN'S KNIGHT!
OF COURSE I REGRET IT.
I'M NOT THE MAN WHO SHOULD HAVE TAKEN YOU.

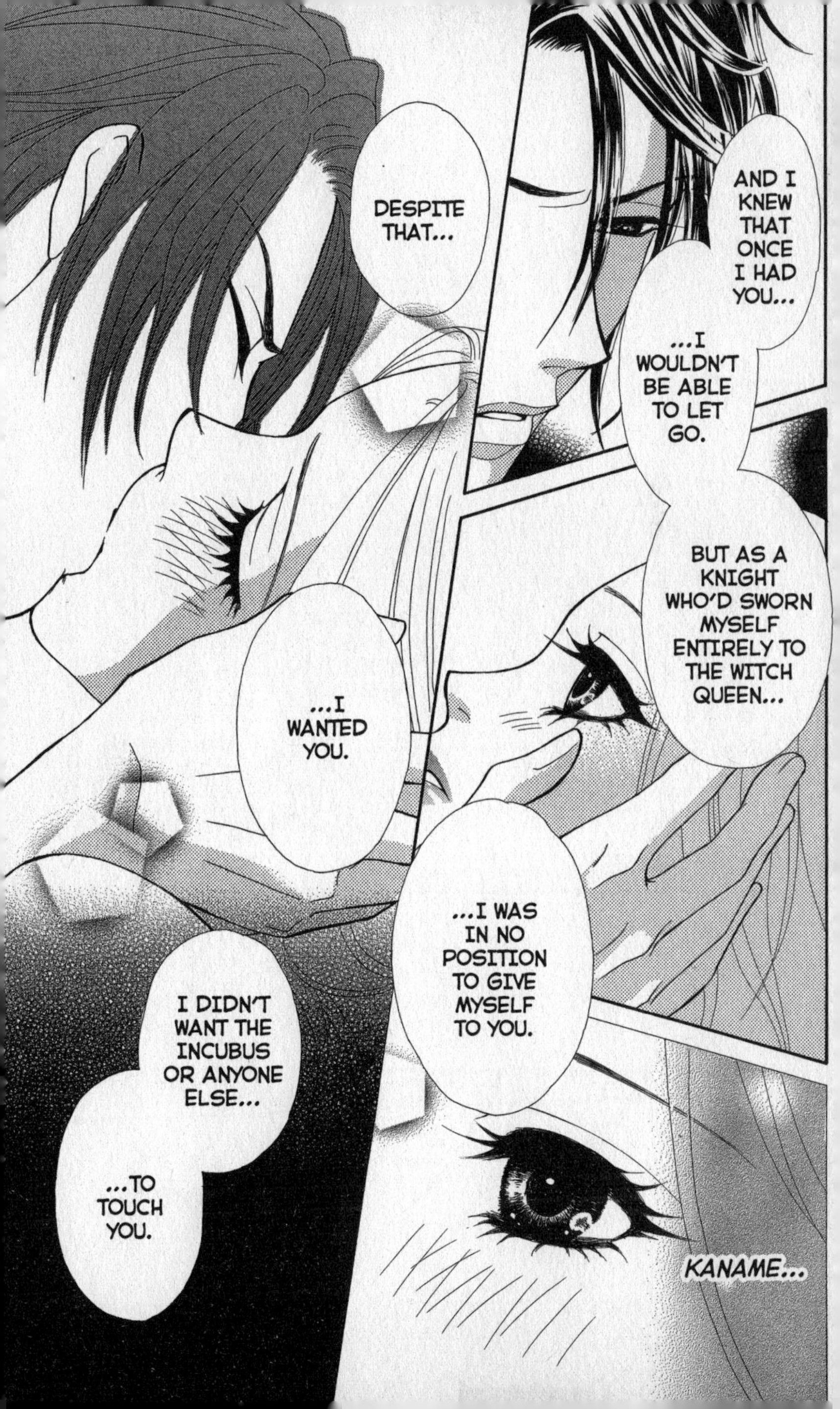
AND I KNEW THAT ONCE I HAD YOU...
...I WOULDN'T BE ABLE TO LET GO.
BUT AS A KNIGHT WHO'D SWORN MYSELF ENTIRELY TO THE WITCH QUEEN...
...I WAS IN NO POSITION TO GIVE MYSELF TO YOU.
KANAME...
DESPITE THAT...
...I WANTED YOU.
I DIDN'T WANT THE INCUBUS OR ANYONE ELSE...
...TO TOUCH YOU.

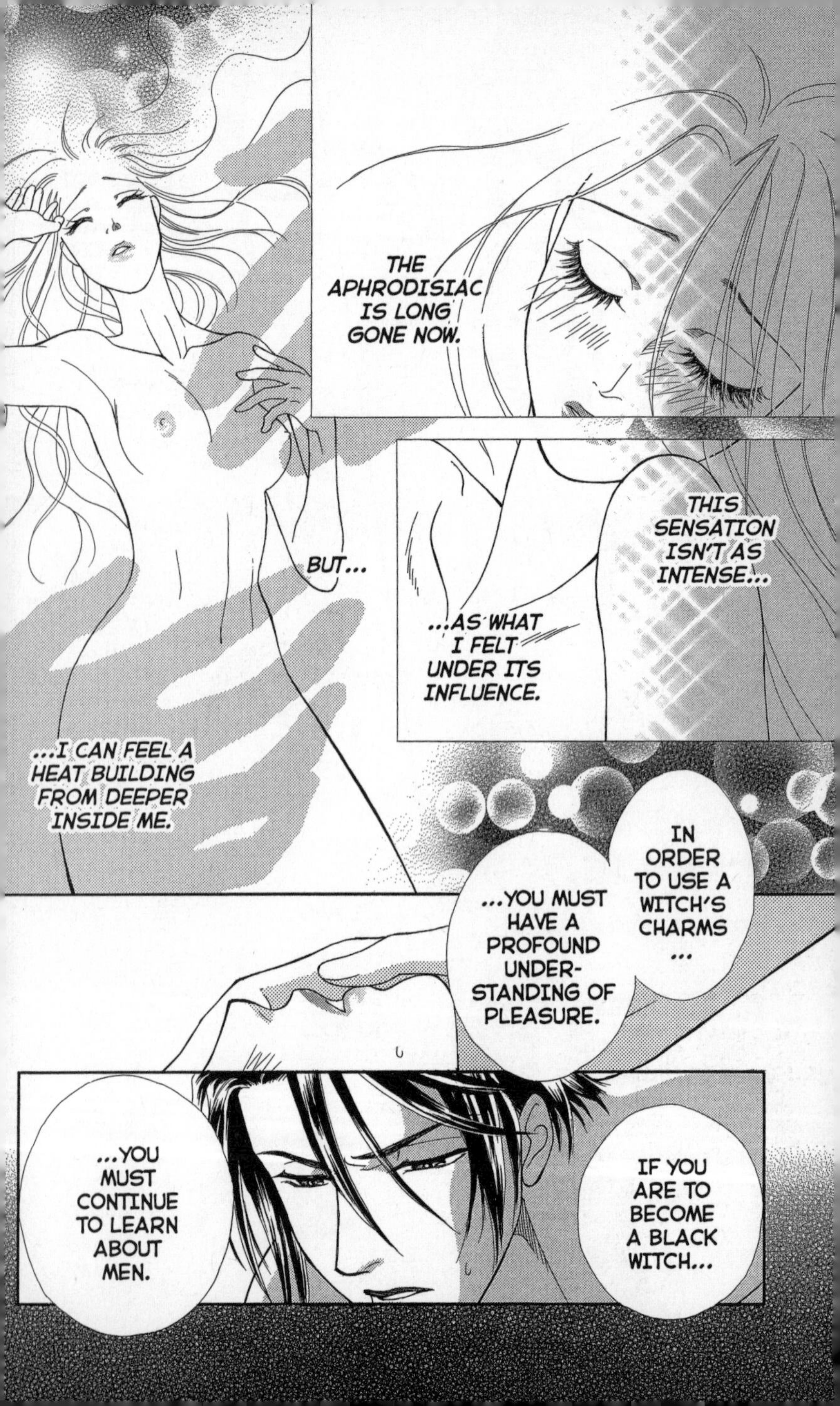
THE APHRODISIAC IS LONG GONE NOW.
THIS SENSATION ISN'T AS INTENSE...
...AS WHAT I FELT UNDER ITS INFLUENCE.
BUT...
...I CAN FEEL A HEAT BUILDING FROM DEEPER INSIDE ME.
IN ORDER TO USE A WITCH'S CHARMS...
...YOU MUST HAVE A PROFOUND UNDER-STANDING OF PLEASURE.
IF YOU ARE TO BECOME A BLACK WITCH...
...YOU MUST CONTINUE TO LEARN ABOUT MEN.

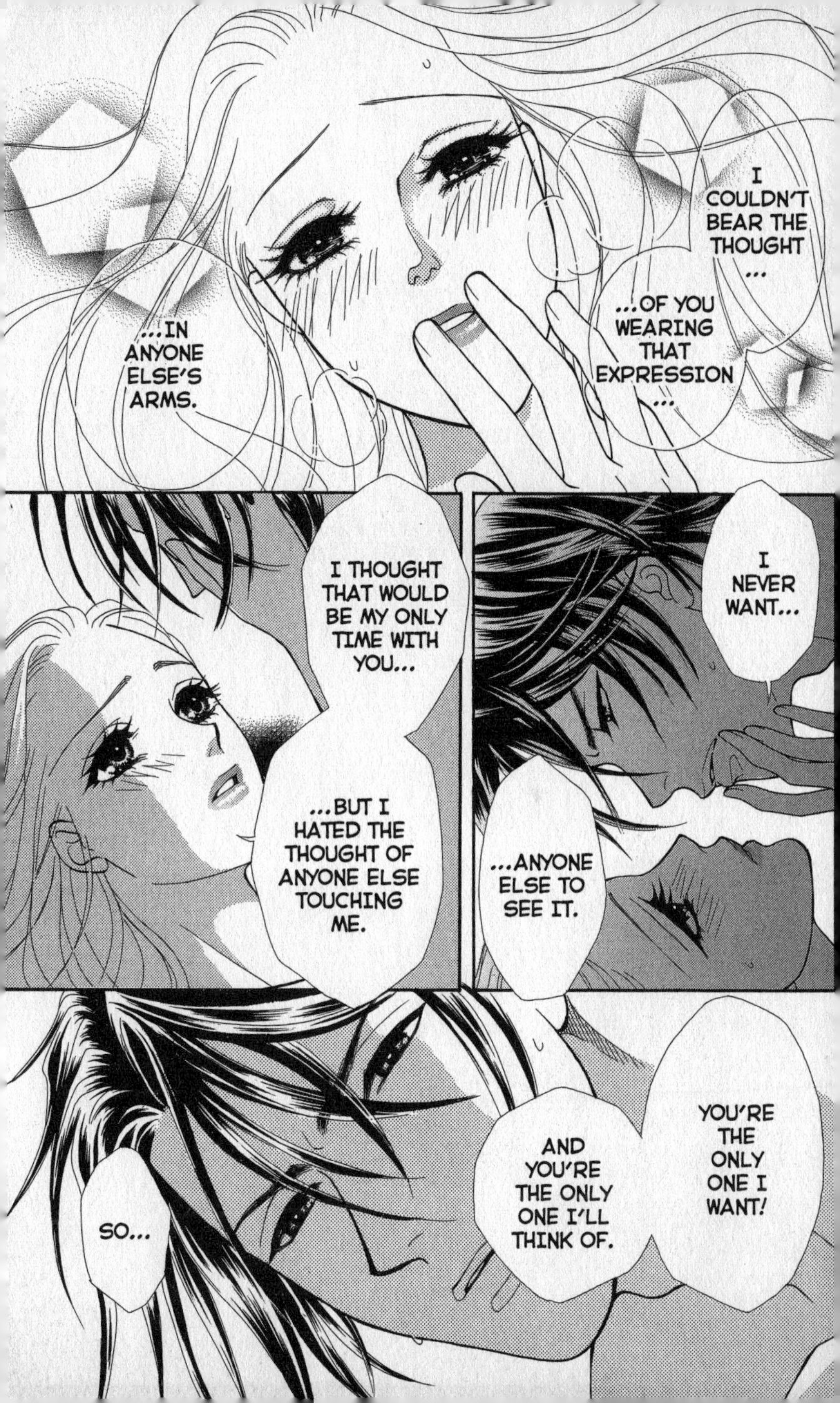
I COULDN'T BEAR THE THOUGHT...
...OF YOU WEARING THAT EXPRESSION...
...IN ANYONE ELSE'S ARMS.
I NEVER WANT...
...ANYONE ELSE TO SEE IT.
I THOUGHT THAT WOULD BE MY ONLY TIME WITH YOU...
...BUT I HATED THE THOUGHT OF ANYONE ELSE TOUCHING ME.
YOU'RE THE ONLY ONE I WANT!
AND YOU'RE THE ONLY ONE I'LL THINK OF.
SO...

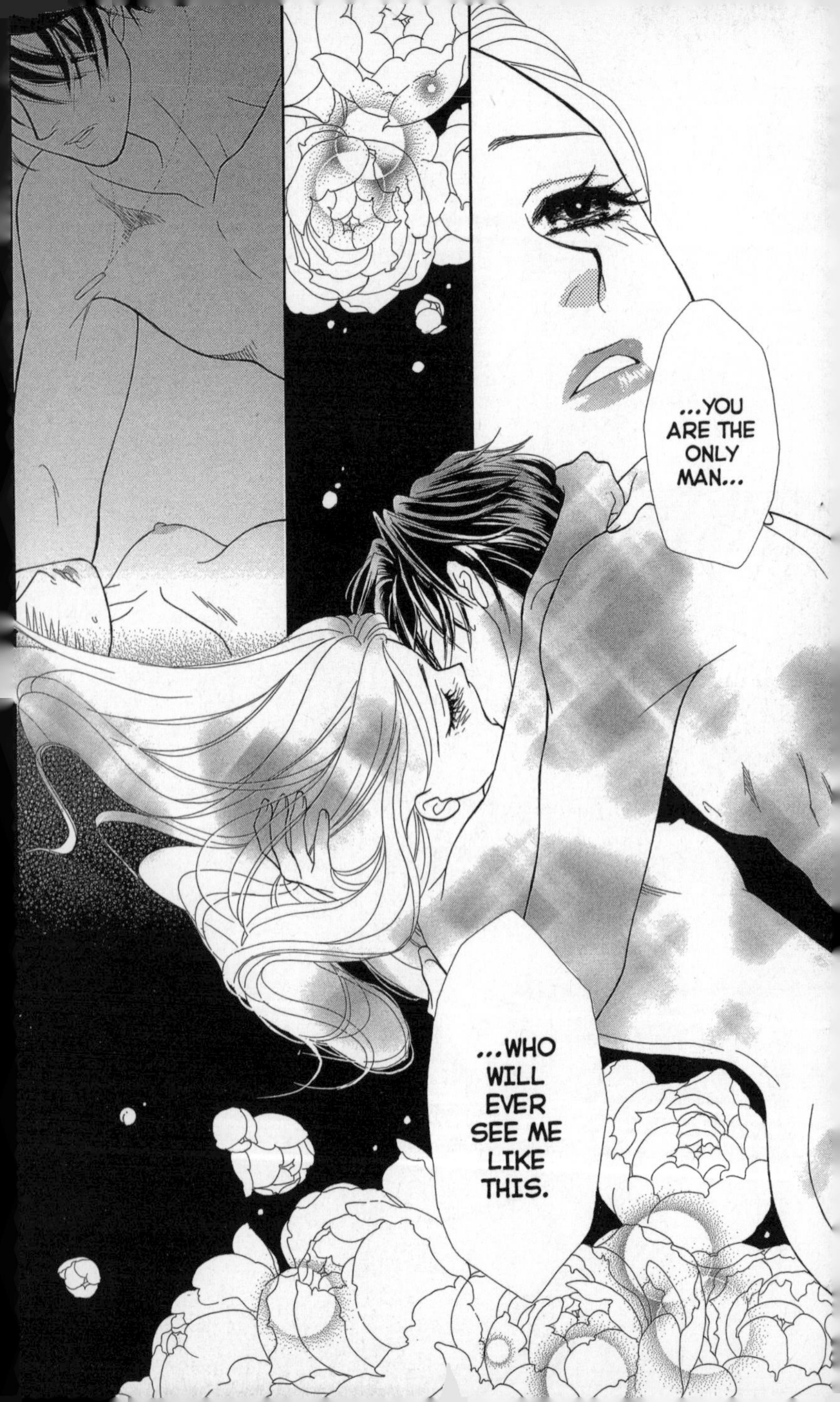
...YOU ARE THE ONLY MAN...
...WHO WILL EVER SEE ME LIKE THIS.

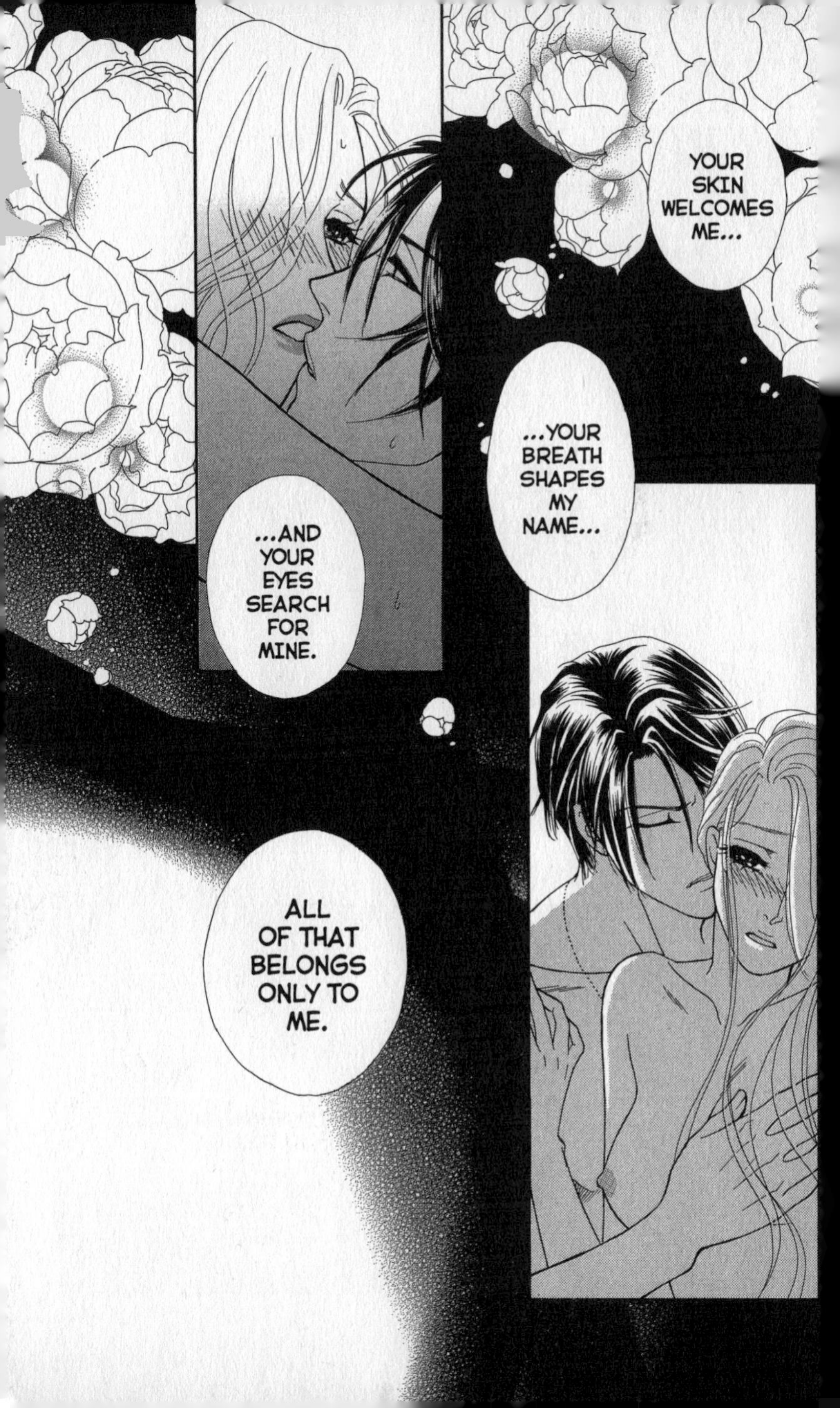
YOUR SKIN WELCOMES ME...
...YOUR BREATH SHAPES MY NAME...
...AND YOUR EYES SEARCH FOR MINE.
ALL OF THAT BELONGS ONLY TO ME.

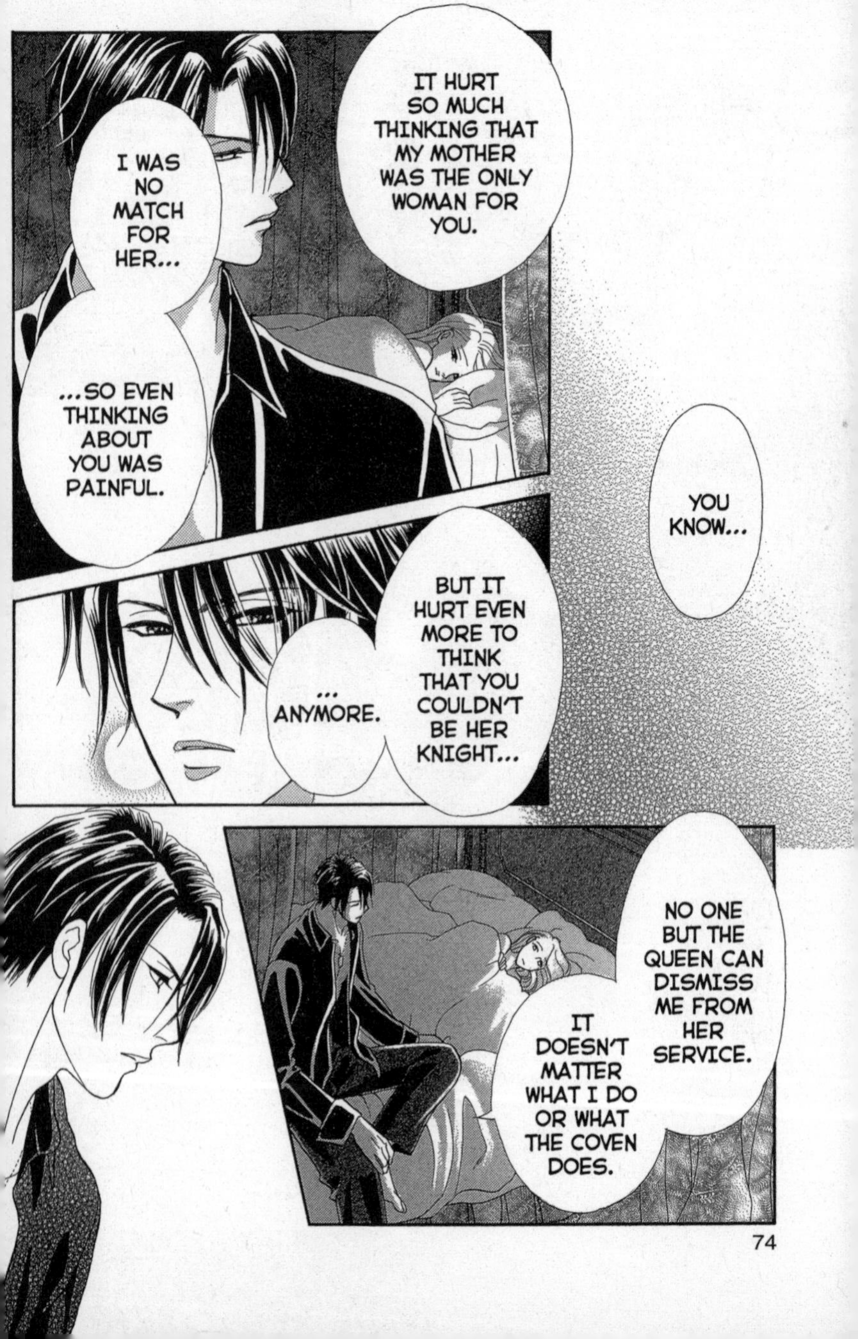
IT HURT SO MUCH THINKING THAT MY MOTHER WAS THE ONLY WOMAN FOR YOU.
I WAS NO MATCH FOR HER...
...SO EVEN THINKING ABOUT YOU WAS PAINFUL.
YOU KNOW...
BUT IT HURT EVEN MORE TO THINK THAT YOU COULDN'T BE HER KNIGHT...
... ANYMORE.
NO ONE BUT THE QUEEN CAN DISMISS ME FROM HER SERVICE.
IT DOESN'T MATTER WHAT I DO OR WHAT THE COVEN DOES.

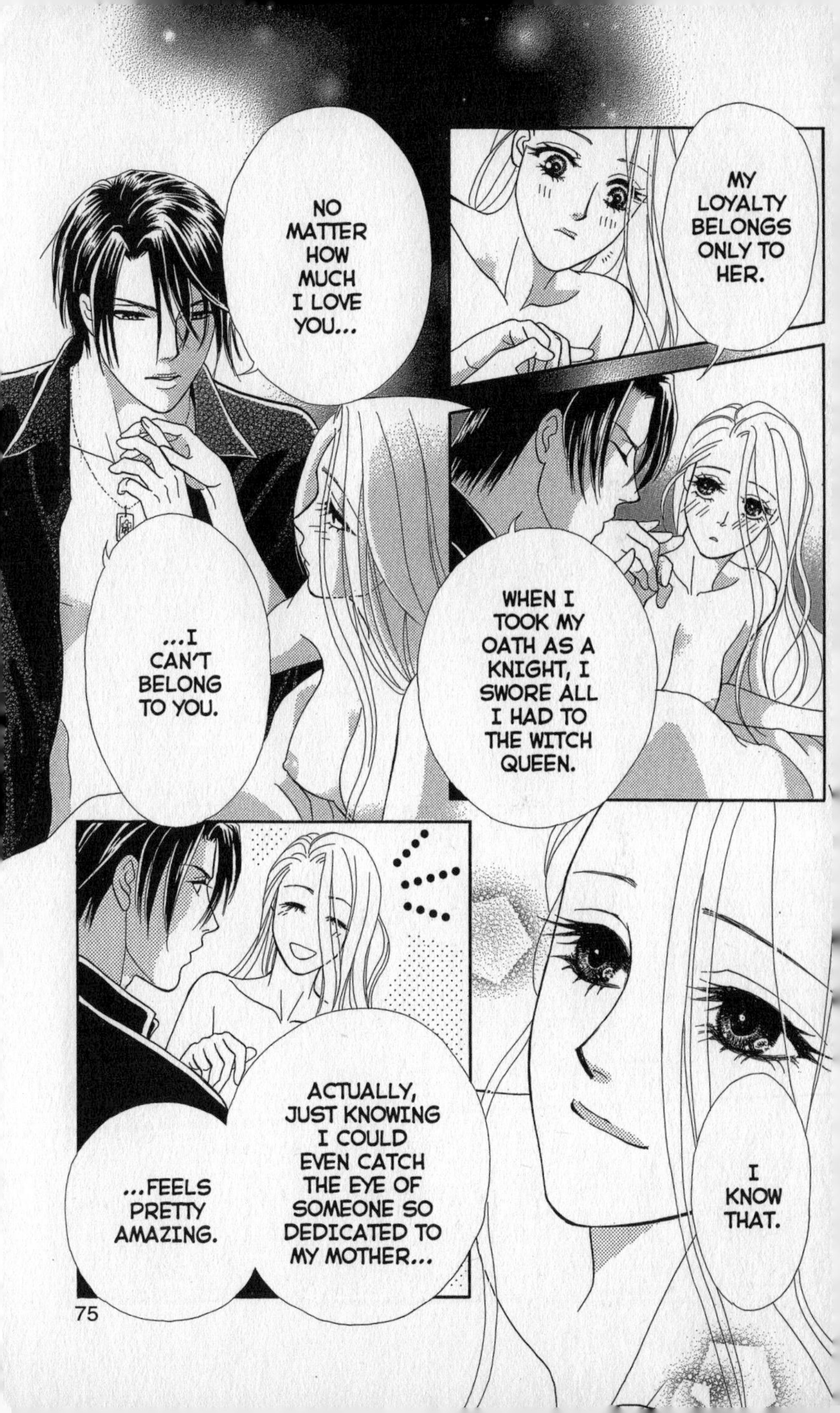
MY LOYALTY BELONGS ONLY TO HER.
WHEN I TOOK MY OATH AS A KNIGHT, I SWORE ALL I HAD TO THE WITCH QUEEN.
NO MATTER HOW MUCH I LOVE YOU...
...I CAN'T BELONG TO YOU.
I KNOW THAT.
ACTUALLY, JUST KNOWING I COULD EVEN CATCH THE EYE OF SOMEONE SO DEDICATED TO MY MOTHER...
...FEELS PRETTY AMAZING.

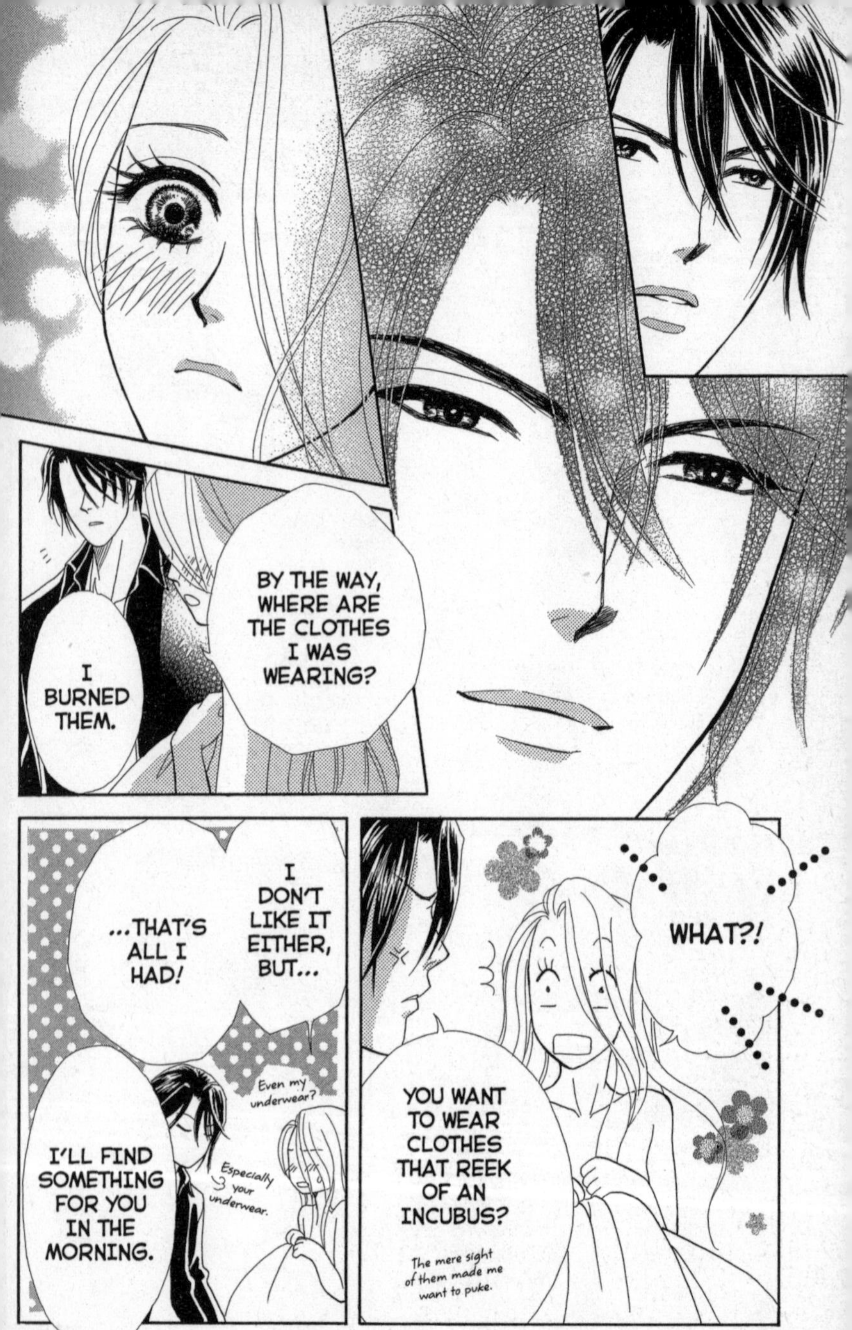
BY THE WAY, WHERE ARE THE CLOTHES I WAS WEARING?
I BURNED THEM.
WHAT?!
YOU WANT TO WEAR CLOTHES THAT REEK OF AN INCUBUS?
The mere sight of them made me want to puke.
I DON'T LIKE IT EITHER, BUT...
...THAT'S ALL I HAD!
Even my underwear?
Especially your underwear.
I'LL FIND SOMETHING FOR YOU IN THE MORNING.

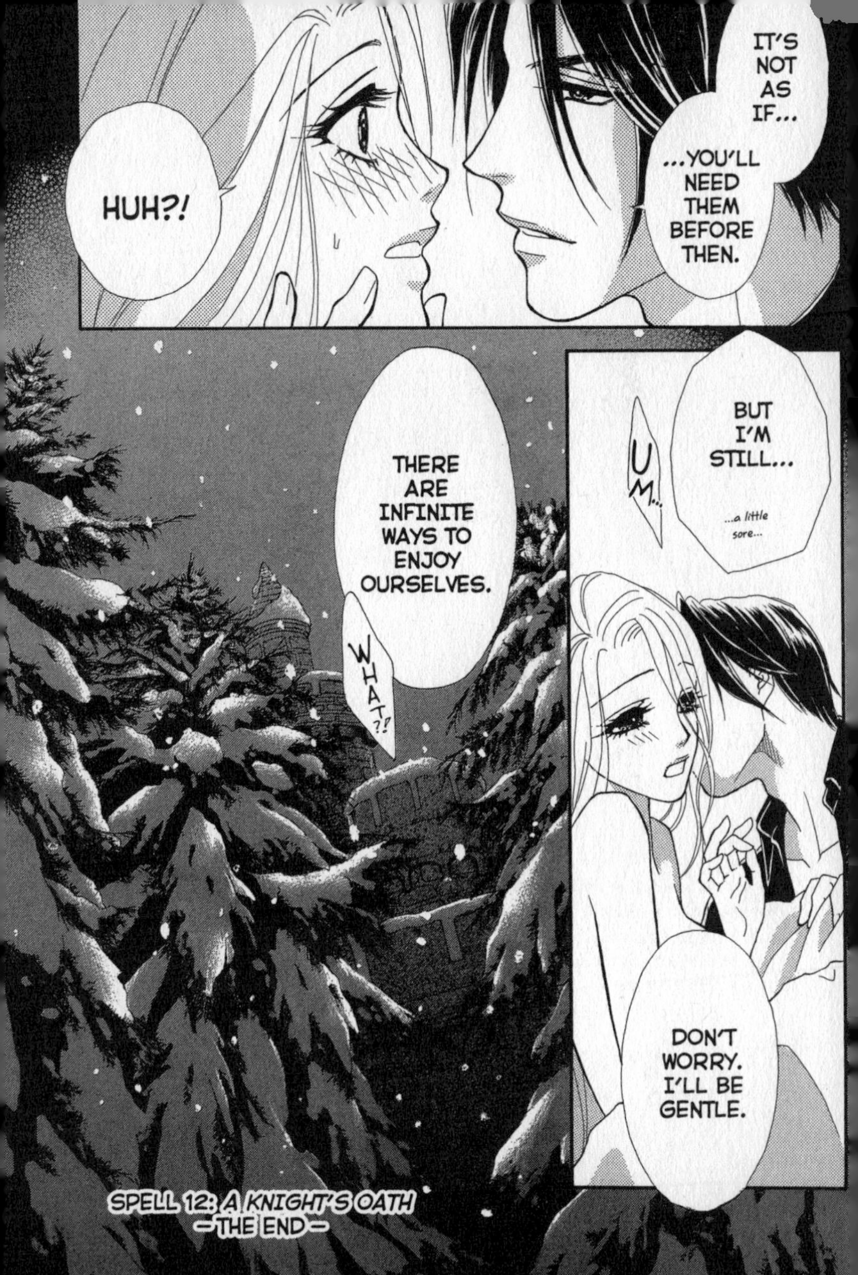
IT'S NOT AS IF...
...YOU'LL NEED THEM BEFORE THEN.
HUH?!
UM...
BUT I'M STILL...
...a little sore...
DON'T WORRY. I'LL BE GENTLE.
THERE ARE INFINITE WAYS TO ENJOY OURSELVES.
WHAT?!
SPELL 12: A KNIGHT'S OATH
—THE END—

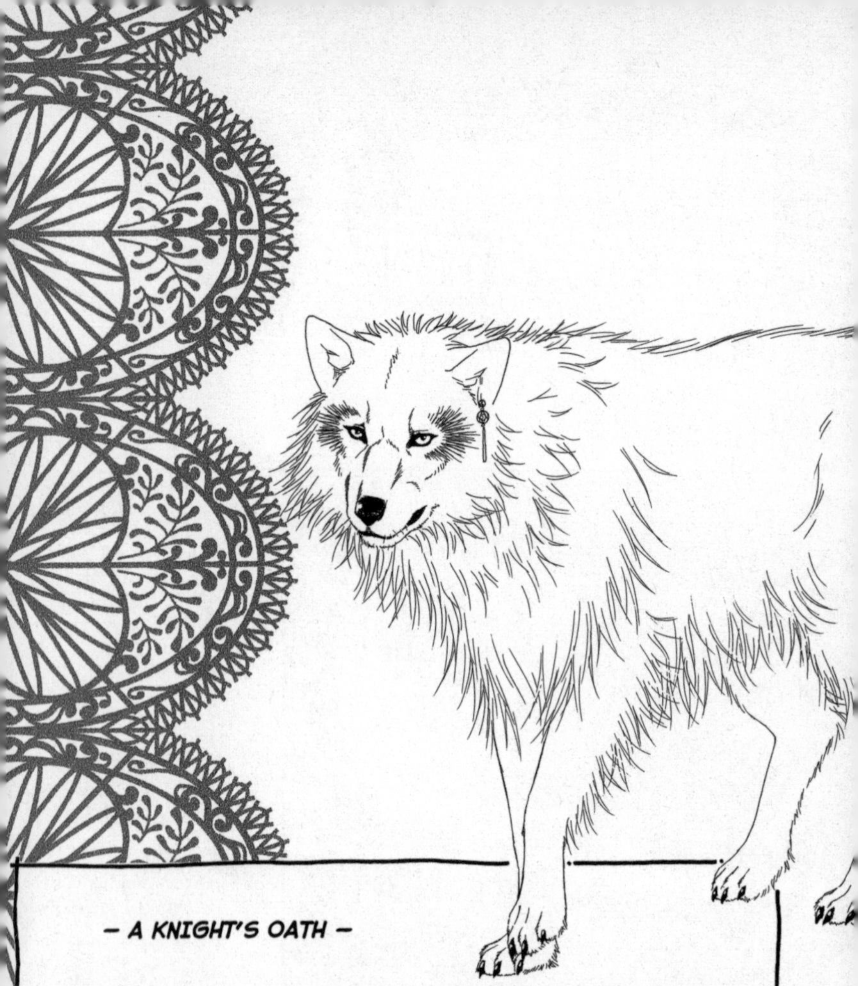

– A KNIGHT'S OATH –

The ancient castle and 250-year-old wolf that first appeared in the "Incubus" chapter may be familiar to some of you! They both made an appearance in one of my earlier works, **Kindan no Koi de Ikou**. I was thrilled to be able to draw that wolf again! And I'm so glad that he didn't turn out to be a black wolf like his father! If he had, the scenes where he appeared with Kaname would have been entirely black... (Wry smile)

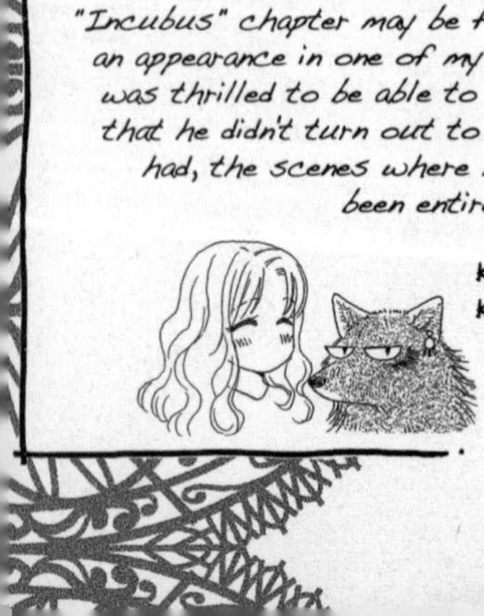

Kindan no Koi de Ikou, along with **Kindan no Koi o Shiyoh** and **Kindan no Koi o Shiyoh 2**, is a series of 12 volumes. At this point you can probably only get the e-book version, but please check it out if you get the chance!

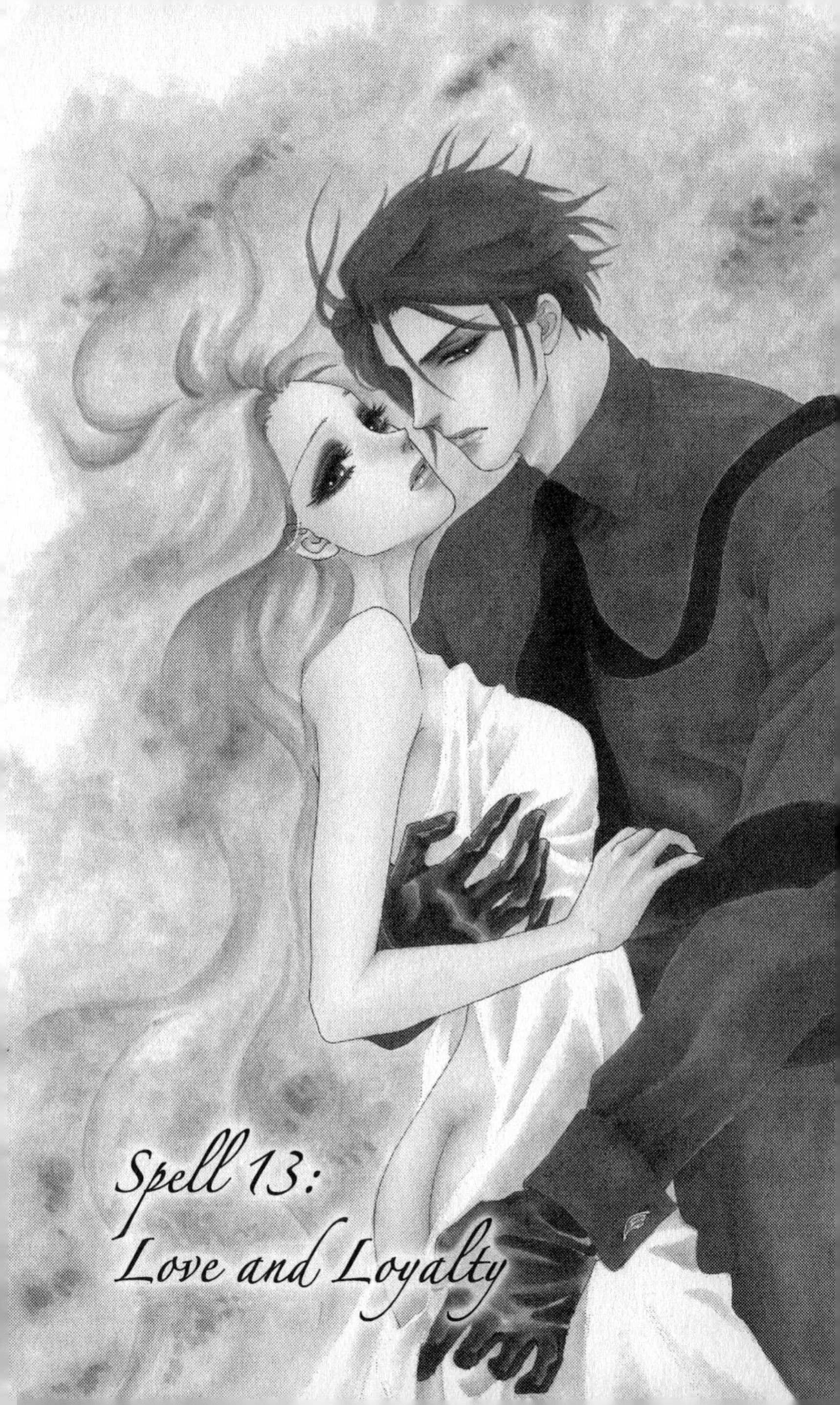
Spell 13:
Love and Loyalty

In this volume, Koko finally becomes a black witch. There's a lot of talk about "white" and "black" witches and magic, but I made most of it up myself.

I did do some research, but I've rearranged the information I found to fit my needs. It bears no resemblance to actual magic or modern Wiccan practices.

Thank you for your understanding!

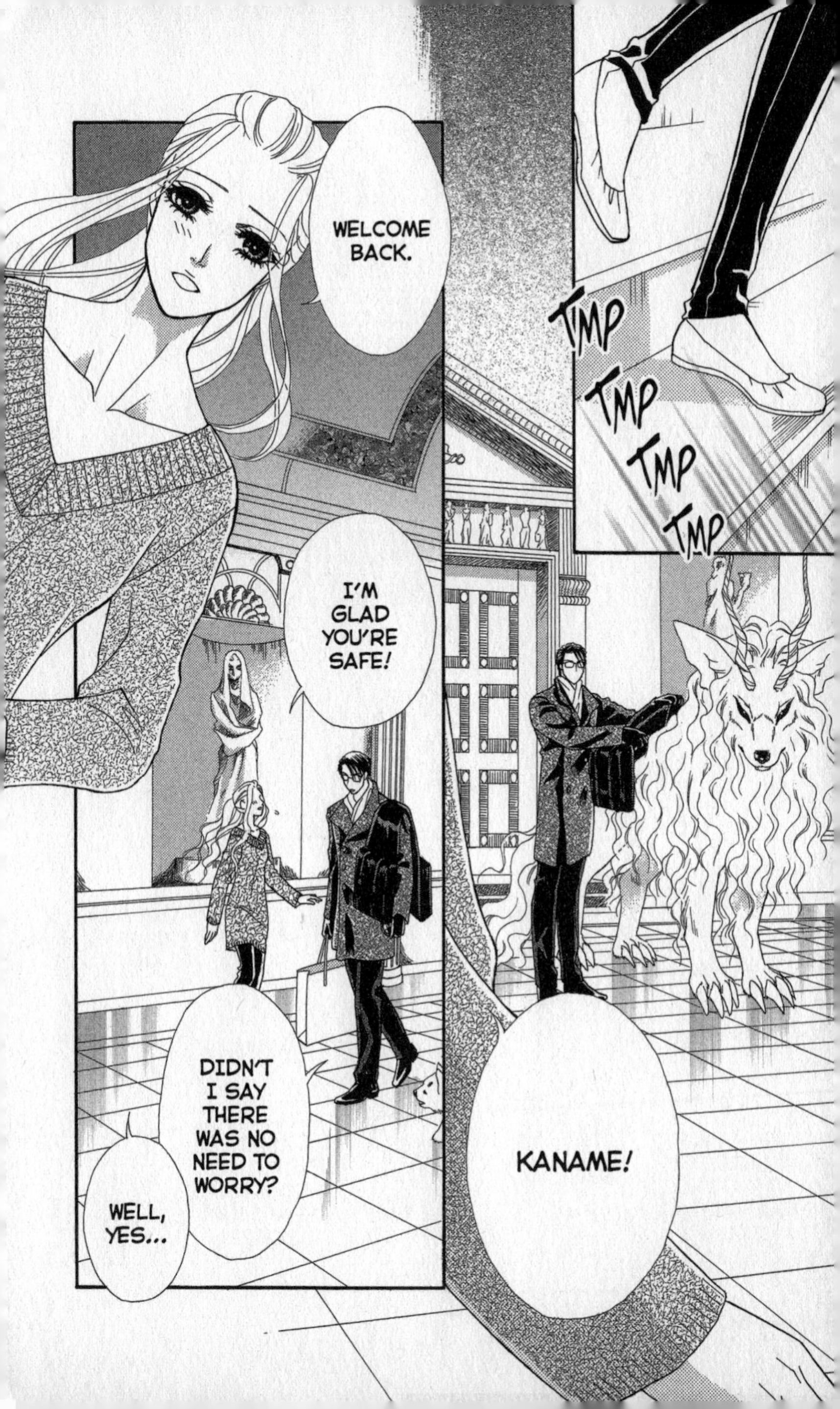
TMP
TMP
TMP
TMP
KANAME!
WELCOME BACK.
I'M GLAD YOU'RE SAFE!
DIDN'T I SAY THERE WAS NO NEED TO WORRY?
WELL, YES...

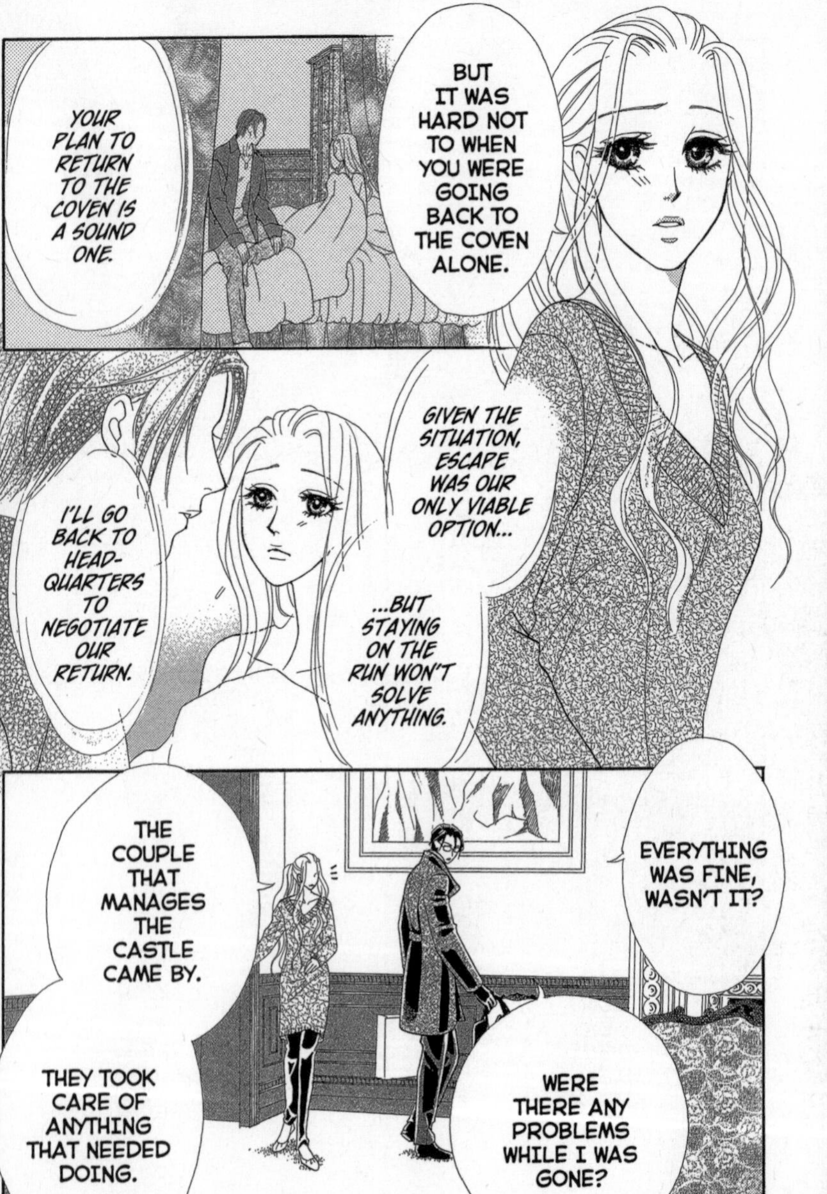
BUT IT WAS HARD NOT TO WHEN YOU WERE GOING BACK TO THE COVEN ALONE.
YOUR PLAN TO RETURN TO THE COVEN IS A SOUND ONE.
GIVEN THE SITUATION, ESCAPE WAS OUR ONLY VIABLE OPTION...
...BUT STAYING ON THE RUN WON'T SOLVE ANYTHING.
I'LL GO BACK TO HEAD-QUARTERS TO NEGOTIATE OUR RETURN.
EVERYTHING WAS FINE, WASN'T IT?
THE COUPLE THAT MANAGES THE CASTLE CAME BY.
WERE THERE ANY PROBLEMS WHILE I WAS GONE?
THEY TOOK CARE OF ANYTHING THAT NEEDED DOING.

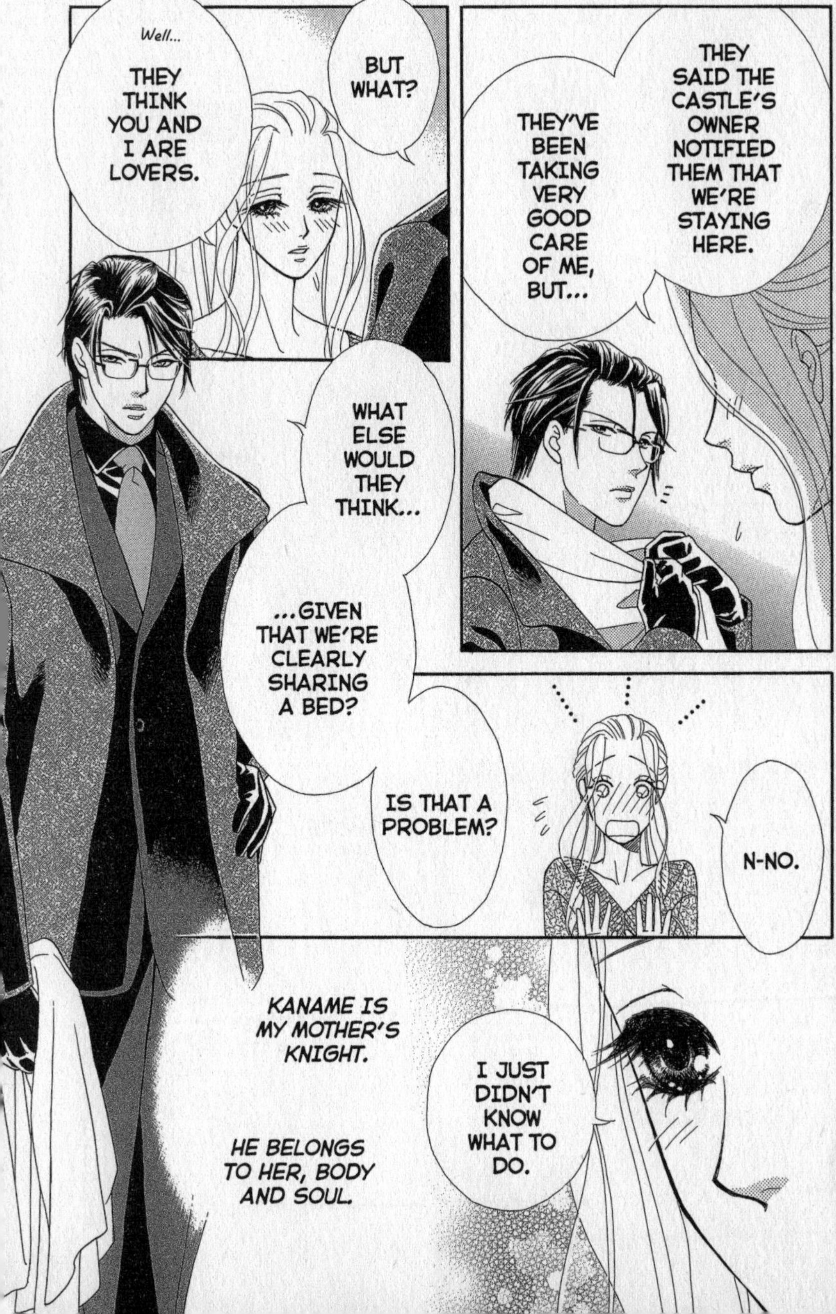
THEY SAID THE CASTLE'S OWNER NOTIFIED THEM THAT WE'RE STAYING HERE.
THEY'VE BEEN TAKING VERY GOOD CARE OF ME, BUT...
BUT WHAT?
Well... THEY THINK YOU AND I ARE LOVERS.
WHAT ELSE WOULD THEY THINK...
...GIVEN THAT WE'RE CLEARLY SHARING A BED?
IS THAT A PROBLEM?
N-NO.
I JUST DIDN'T KNOW WHAT TO DO.
KANAME IS MY MOTHER'S KNIGHT.
HE BELONGS TO HER, BODY AND SOUL.

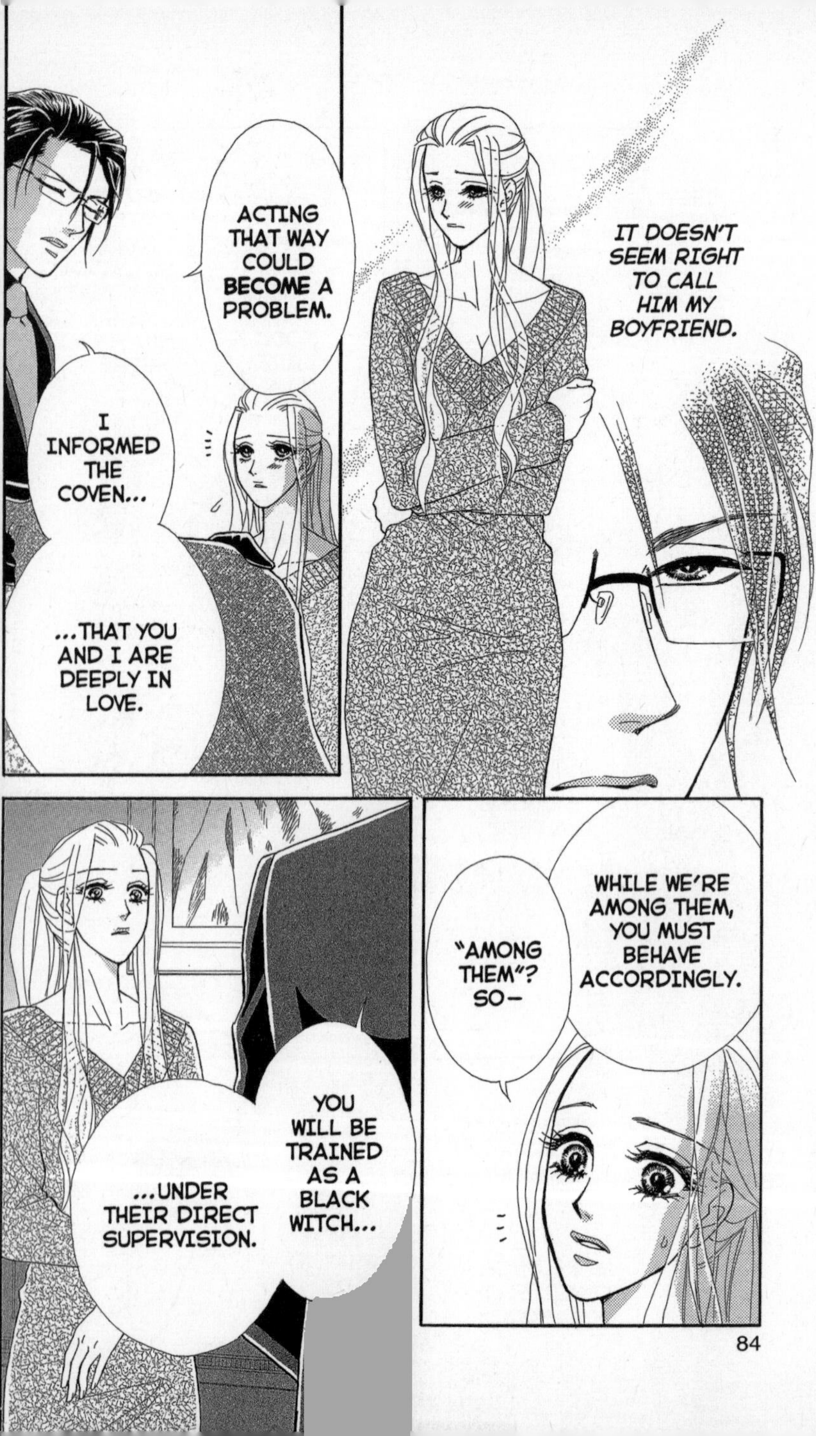
IT DOESN'T SEEM RIGHT TO CALL HIM MY BOYFRIEND.
ACTING THAT WAY COULD BECOME A PROBLEM.
I INFORMED THE COVEN...
...THAT YOU AND I ARE DEEPLY IN LOVE.
WHILE WE'RE AMONG THEM, YOU MUST BEHAVE ACCORDINGLY.
"AMONG THEM"? SO—
YOU WILL BE TRAINED AS A BLACK WITCH...
...UNDER THEIR DIRECT SUPERVISION.

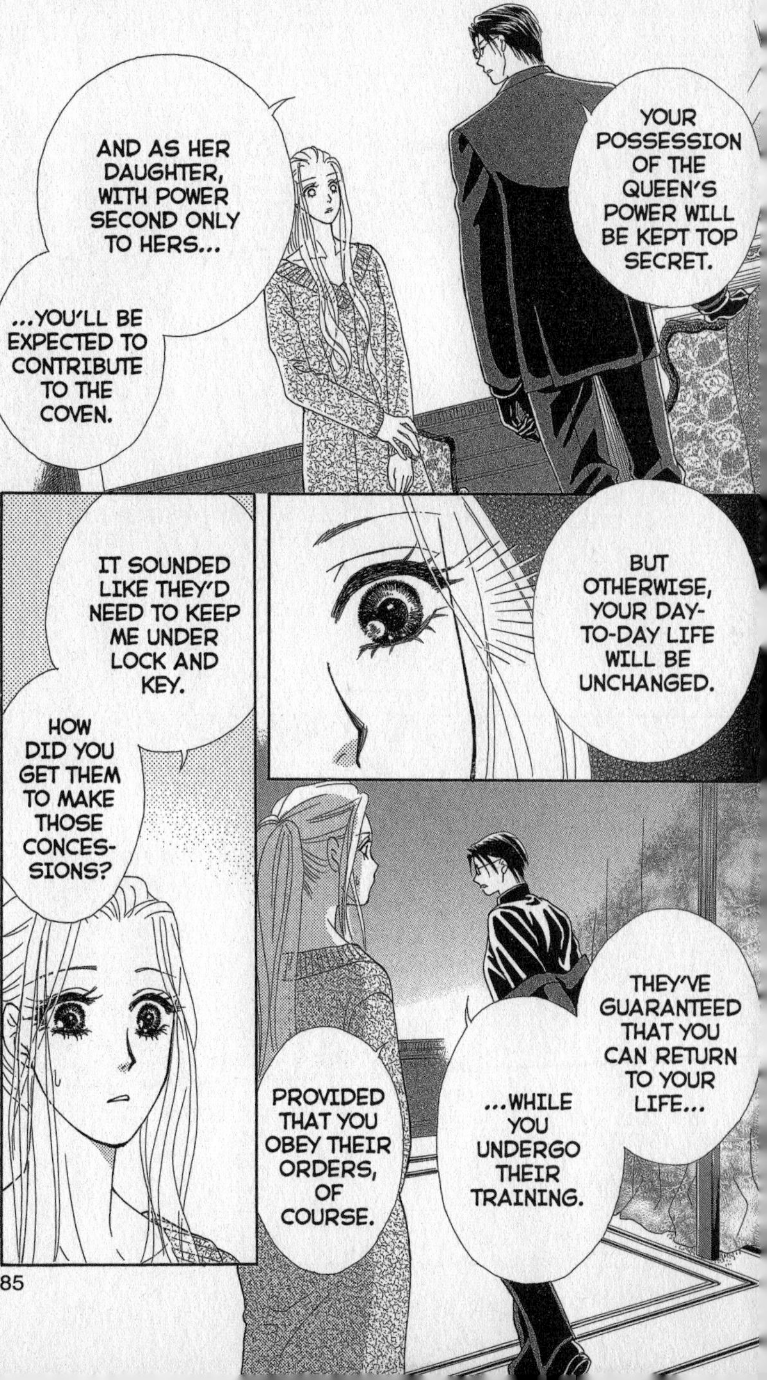
YOUR POSSESSION OF THE QUEEN'S POWER WILL BE KEPT TOP SECRET.
AND AS HER DAUGHTER, WITH POWER SECOND ONLY TO HERS...
...YOU'LL BE EXPECTED TO CONTRIBUTE TO THE COVEN.
BUT OTHERWISE, YOUR DAY-TO-DAY LIFE WILL BE UNCHANGED.
THEY'VE GUARANTEED THAT YOU CAN RETURN TO YOUR LIFE...
...WHILE YOU UNDERGO THEIR TRAINING.
PROVIDED THAT YOU OBEY THEIR ORDERS, OF COURSE.
IT SOUNDED LIKE THEY'D NEED TO KEEP ME UNDER LOCK AND KEY.
HOW DID YOU GET THEM TO MAKE THOSE CONCESSIONS?

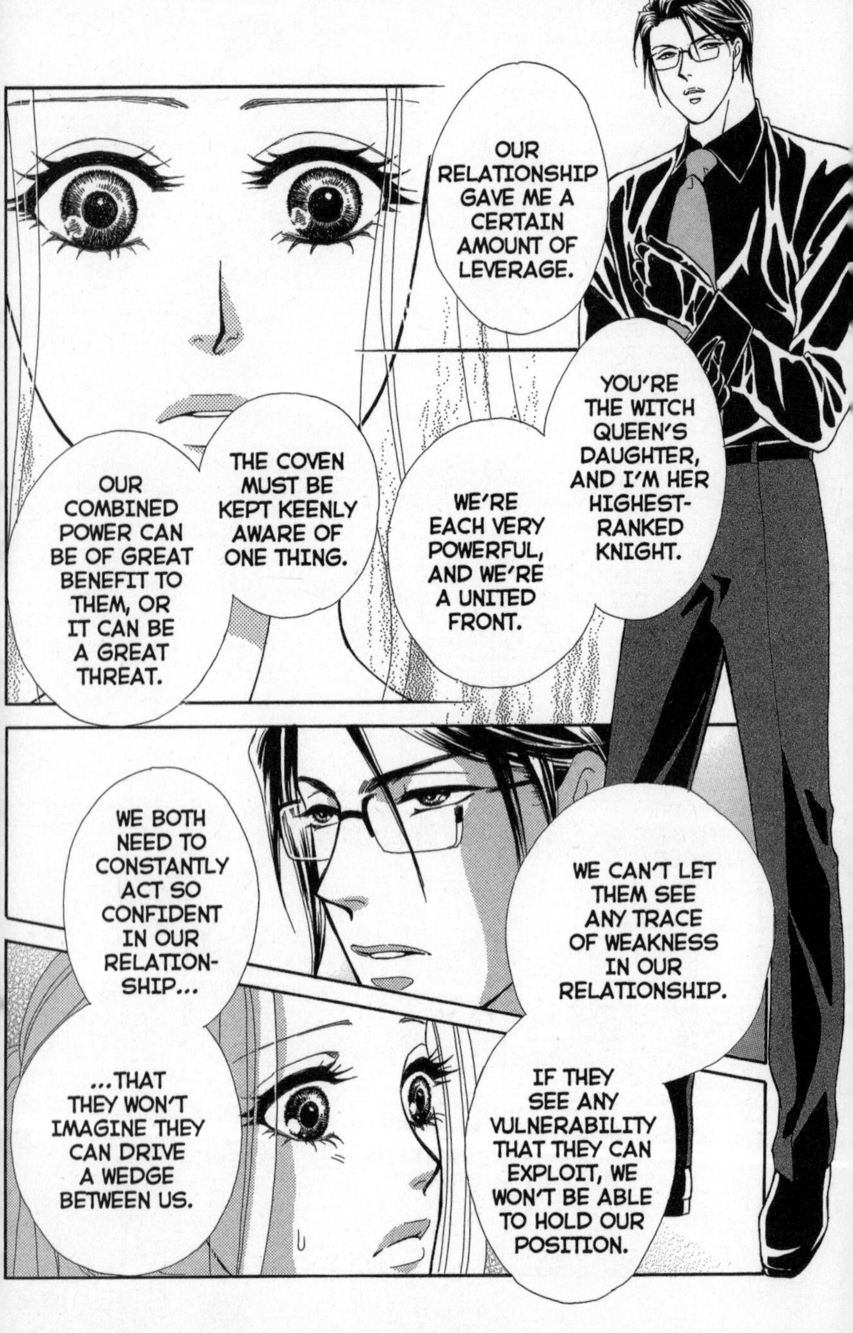
OUR RELATIONSHIP GAVE ME A CERTAIN AMOUNT OF LEVERAGE.
YOU'RE THE WITCH QUEEN'S DAUGHTER, AND I'M HER HIGHEST-RANKED KNIGHT.
WE'RE EACH VERY POWERFUL, AND WE'RE A UNITED FRONT.
THE COVEN MUST BE KEPT KEENLY AWARE OF ONE THING.
OUR COMBINED POWER CAN BE OF GREAT BENEFIT TO THEM, OR IT CAN BE A GREAT THREAT.
WE CAN'T LET THEM SEE ANY TRACE OF WEAKNESS IN OUR RELATIONSHIP.
IF THEY SEE ANY VULNERABILITY THAT THEY CAN EXPLOIT, WE WON'T BE ABLE TO HOLD OUR POSITION.
WE BOTH NEED TO CONSTANTLY ACT SO CONFIDENT IN OUR RELATION-SHIP...
...THAT THEY WON'T IMAGINE THEY CAN DRIVE A WEDGE BETWEEN US.

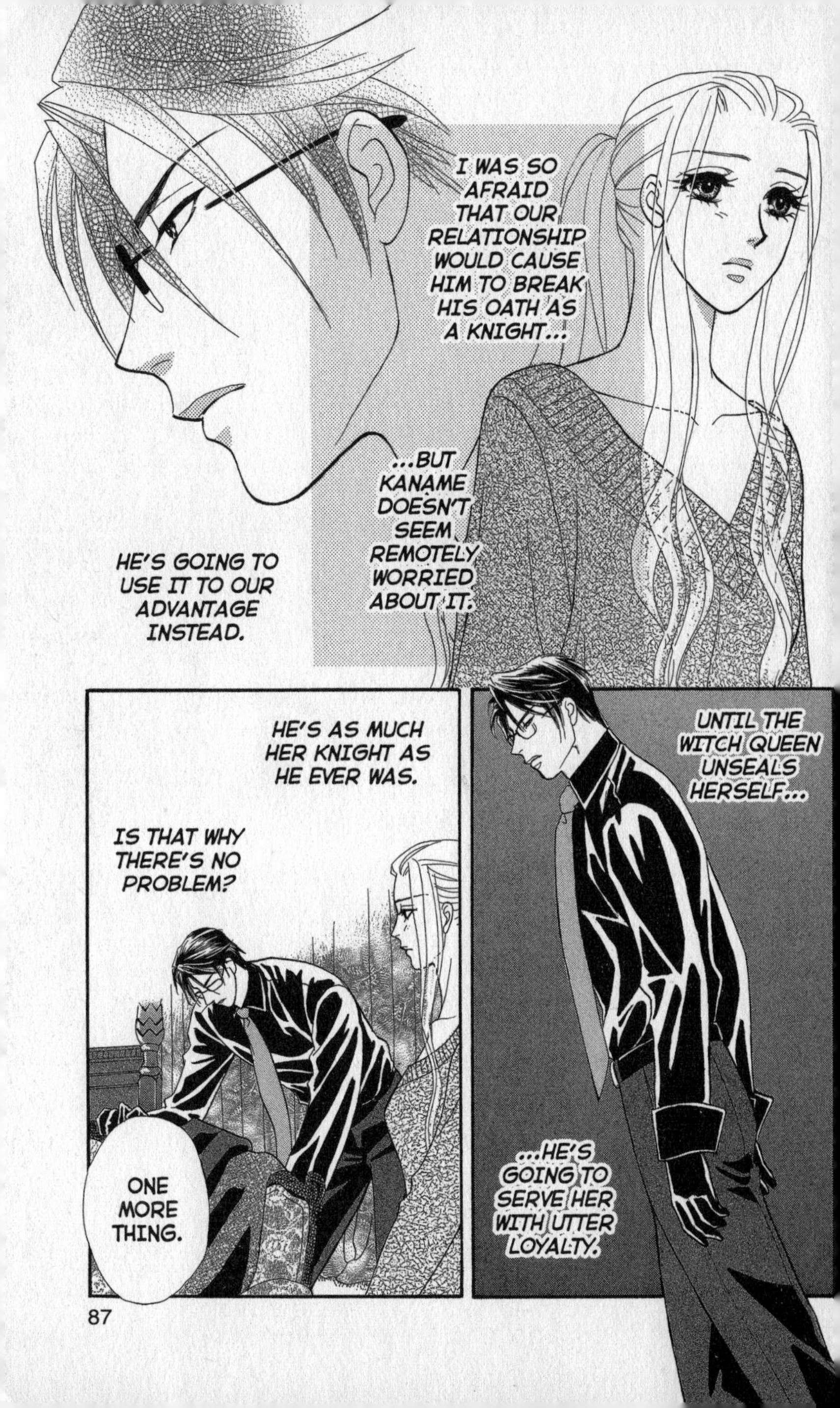
I WAS SO AFRAID THAT OUR RELATIONSHIP WOULD CAUSE HIM TO BREAK HIS OATH AS A KNIGHT...
...BUT KANAME DOESN'T SEEM REMOTELY WORRIED ABOUT IT.
HE'S GOING TO USE IT TO OUR ADVANTAGE INSTEAD.
UNTIL THE WITCH QUEEN UNSEALS HERSELF...
...HE'S GOING TO SERVE HER WITH UTTER LOYALTY.
HE'S AS MUCH HER KNIGHT AS HE EVER WAS.
IS THAT WHY THERE'S NO PROBLEM?
ONE MORE THING.

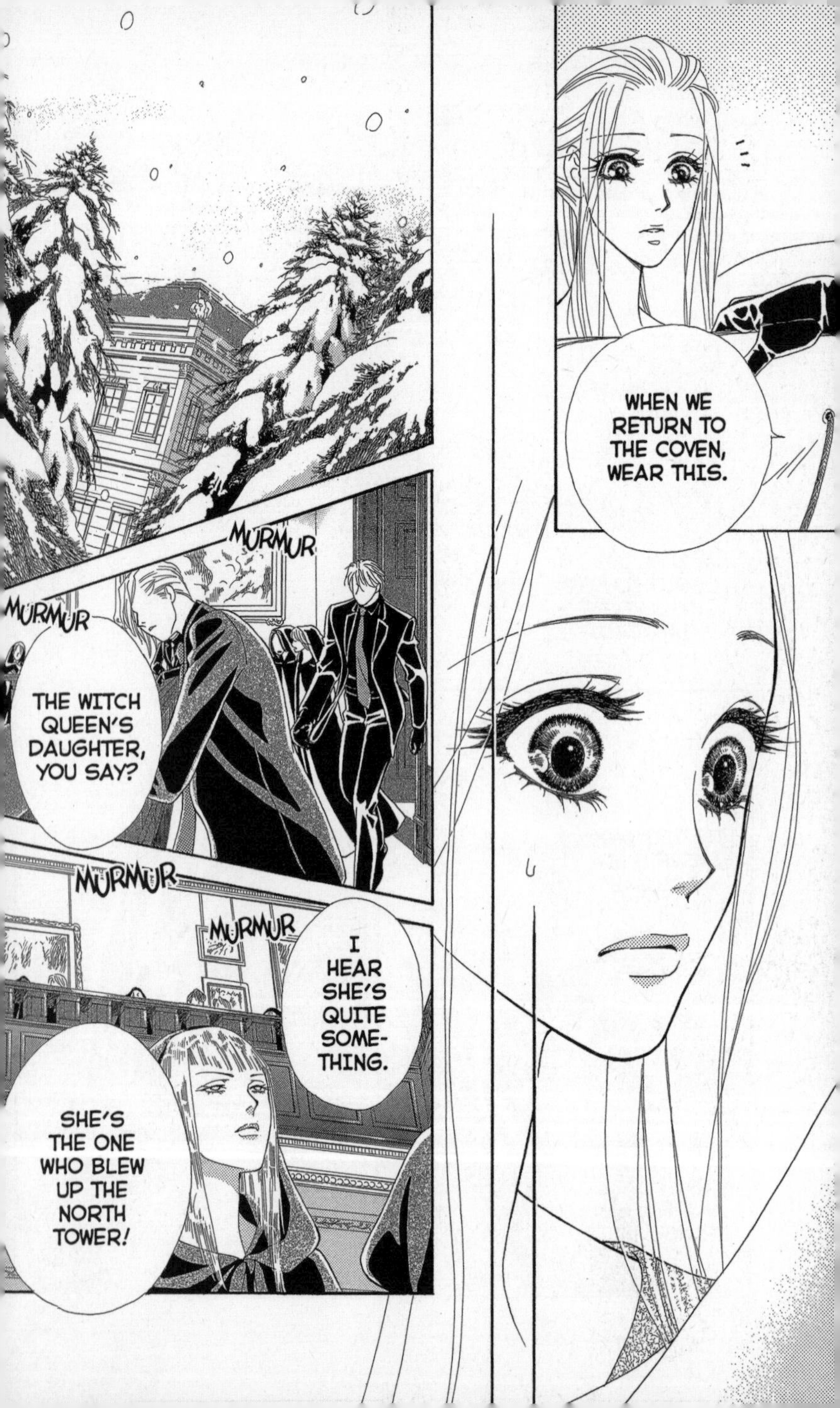
WHEN WE RETURN TO THE COVEN, WEAR THIS.
MURMUR
MURMUR
THE WITCH QUEEN'S DAUGHTER, YOU SAY?
MURMUR
MURMUR
I HEAR SHE'S QUITE SOME-THING.
SHE'S THE ONE WHO BLEW UP THE NORTH TOWER!

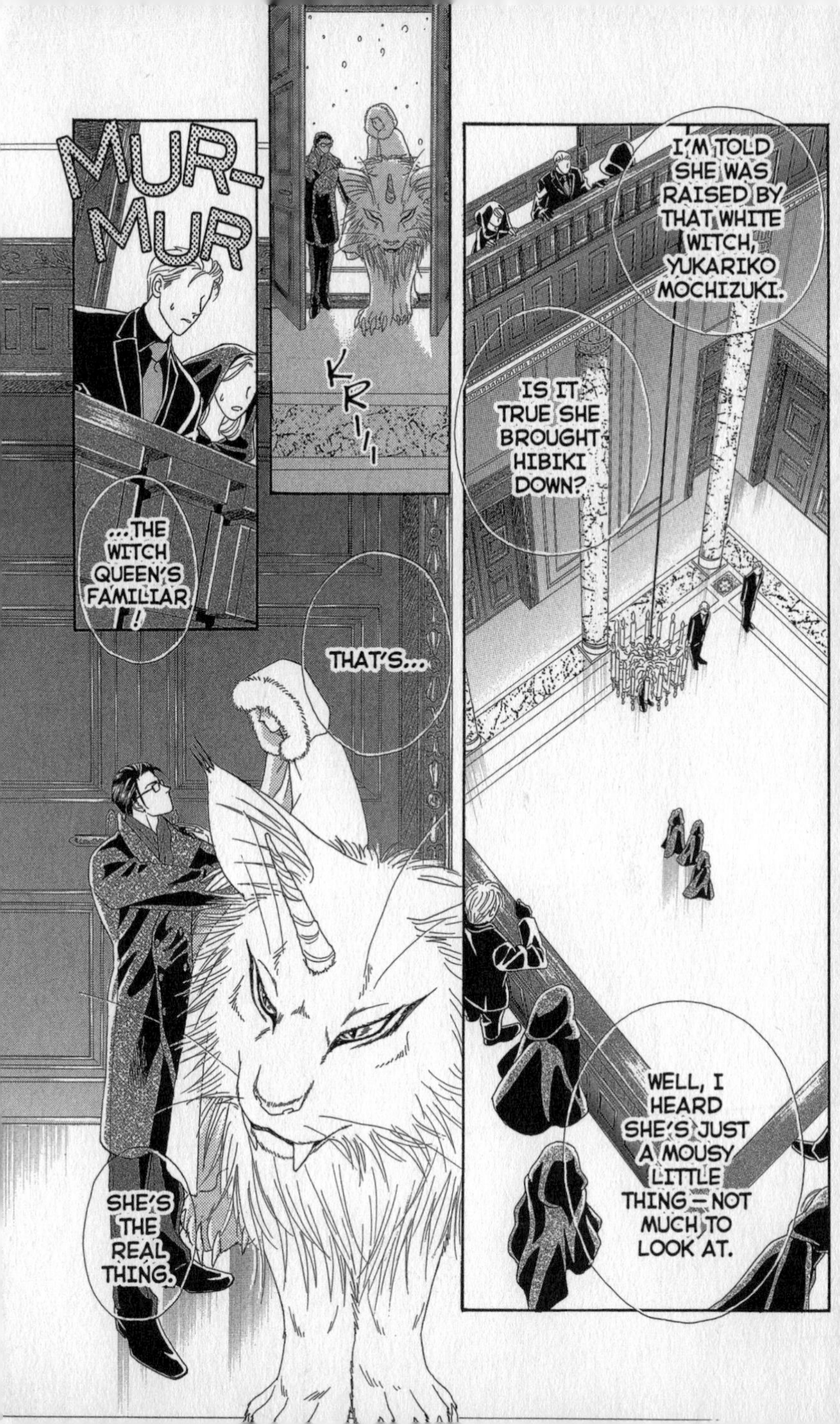
I'M TOLD SHE WAS RAISED BY THAT WHITE WITCH, YUKARIKO MOCHIZUKI.
IS IT TRUE SHE BROUGHT HIBIKI DOWN?
WELL, I HEARD SHE'S JUST A MOUSY LITTLE THING—NOT MUCH TO LOOK AT.
KRIII
MUR-MUR
...THE WITCH QUEEN'S FAMILIAR!
THAT'S...
SHE'S THE REAL THING.

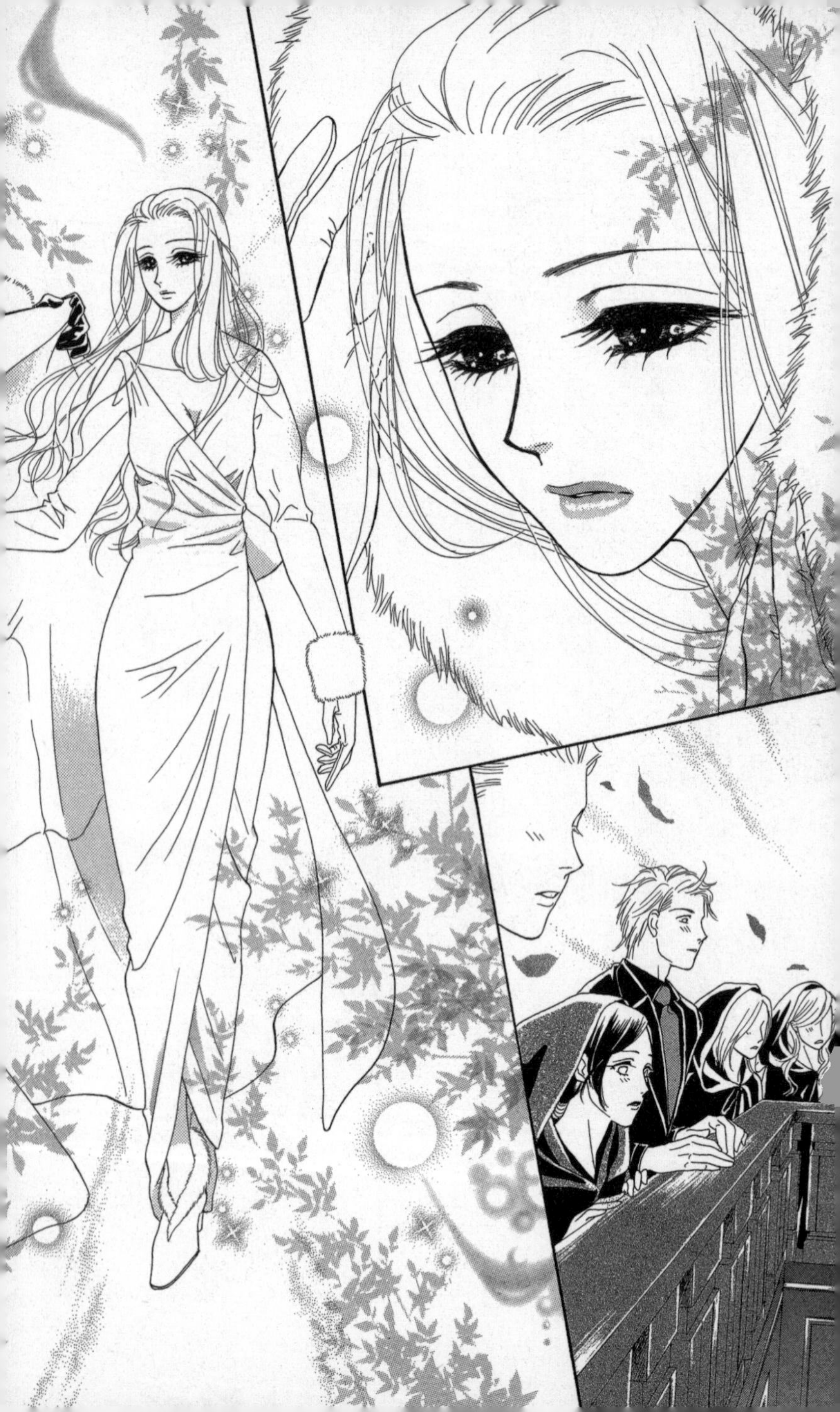

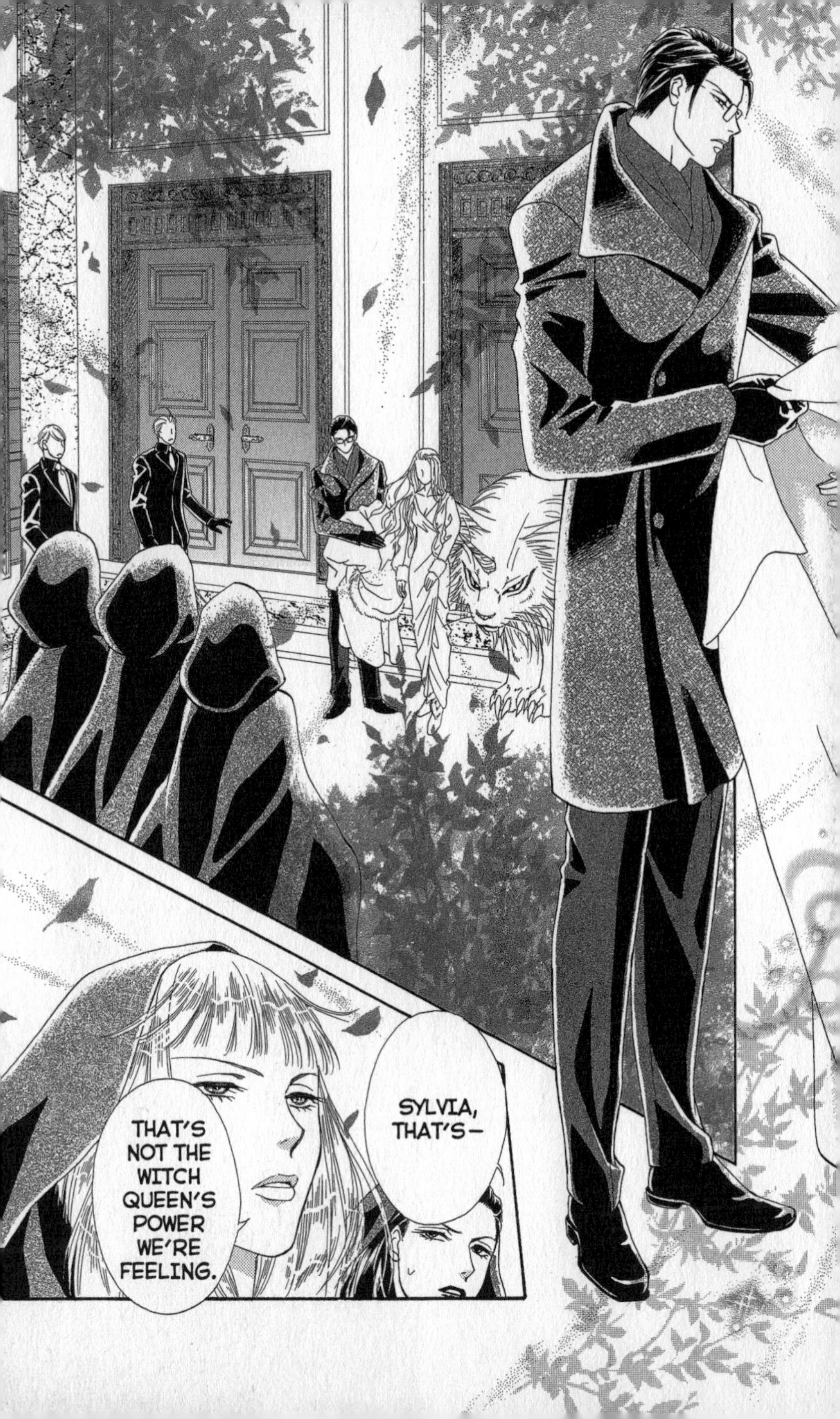
SYLVIA, THAT'S—
THAT'S NOT THE WITCH QUEEN'S POWER WE'RE FEELING.

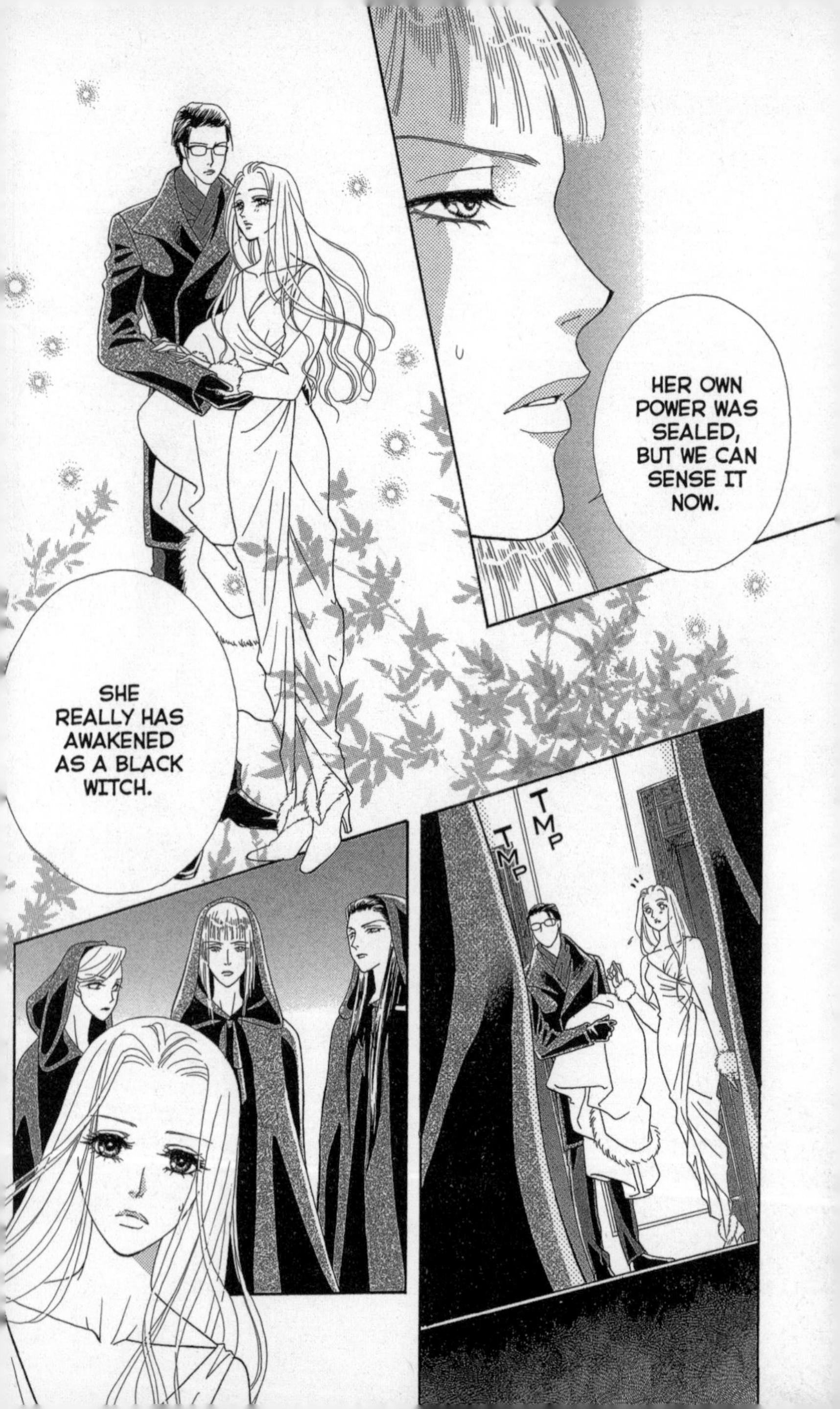
HER OWN POWER WAS SEALED, BUT WE CAN SENSE IT NOW.
SHE REALLY HAS AWAKENED AS A BLACK WITCH.
TMP
TMP

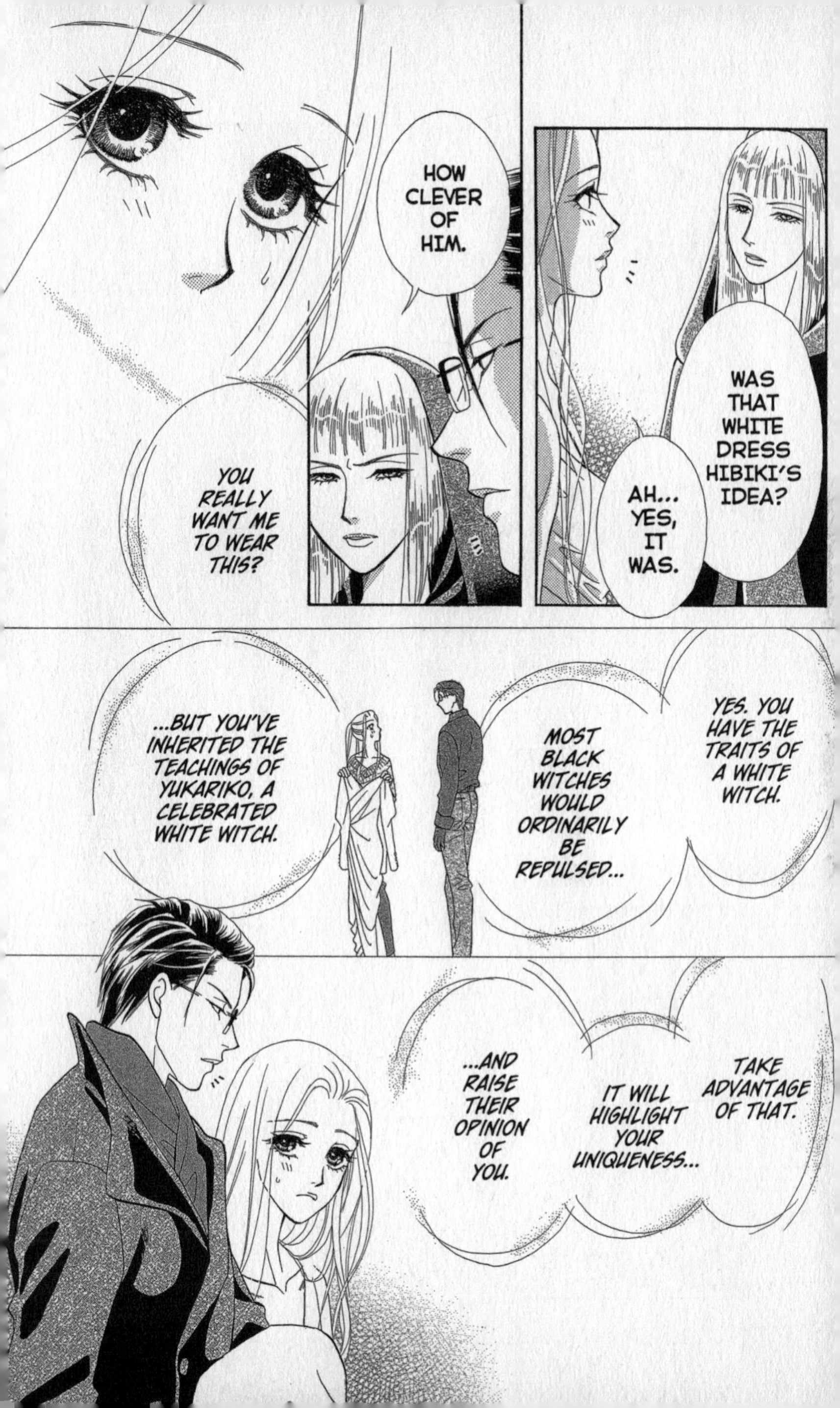
WAS THAT WHITE DRESS HIBIKI'S IDEA?
AH... YES, IT WAS.
HOW CLEVER OF HIM.
YOU REALLY WANT ME TO WEAR THIS?
YES. YOU HAVE THE TRAITS OF A WHITE WITCH.
MOST BLACK WITCHES WOULD ORDINARILY BE REPULSED...
...BUT YOU'VE INHERITED THE TEACHINGS OF YUKARIKO, A CELEBRATED WHITE WITCH.
TAKE ADVANTAGE OF THAT.
IT WILL HIGHLIGHT YOUR UNIQUENESS...
...AND RAISE THEIR OPINION OF YOU.

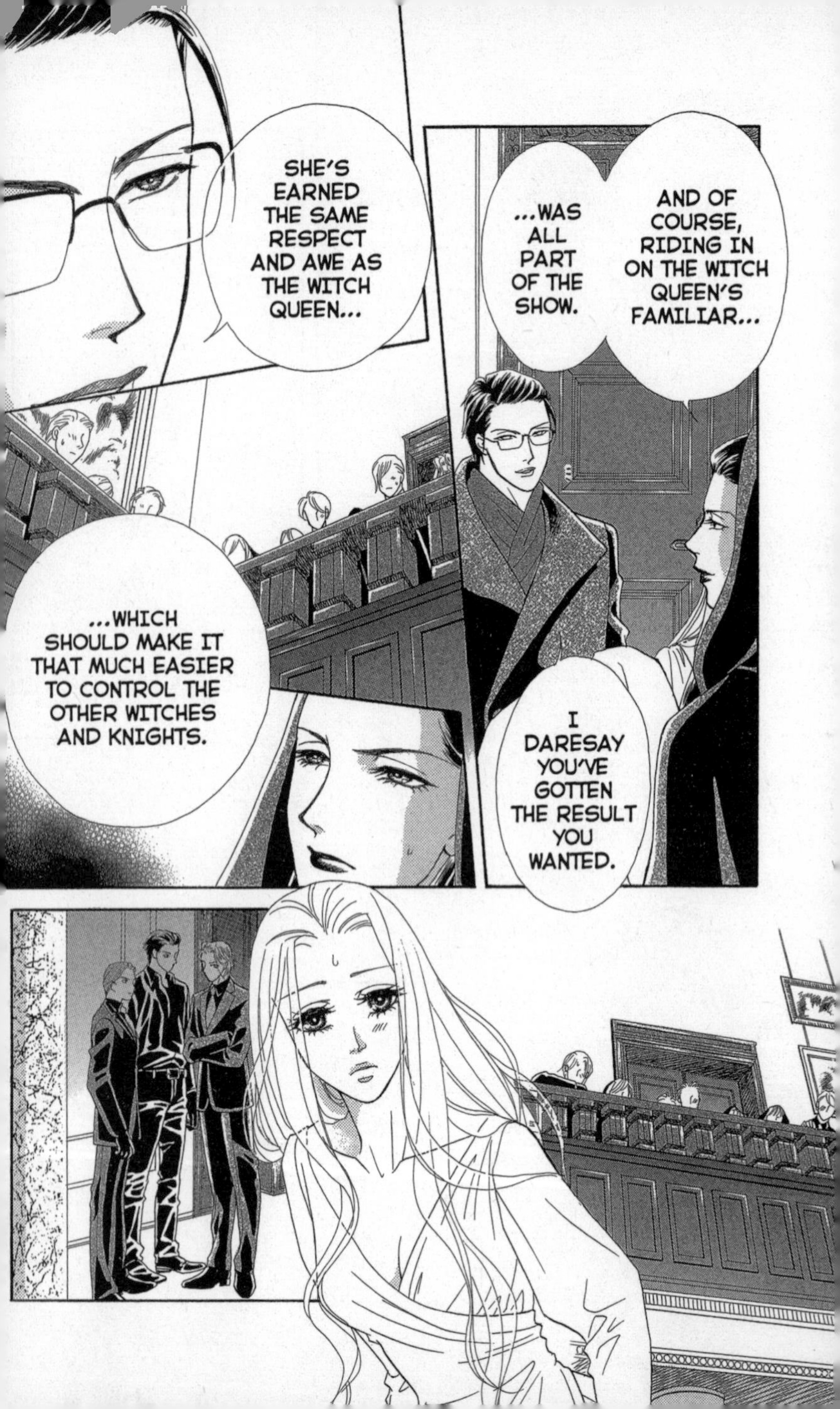
AND OF COURSE, RIDING IN ON THE WITCH QUEEN'S FAMILIAR...
...WAS ALL PART OF THE SHOW.
SHE'S EARNED THE SAME RESPECT AND AWE AS THE WITCH QUEEN...
...WHICH SHOULD MAKE IT THAT MUCH EASIER TO CONTROL THE OTHER WITCHES AND KNIGHTS.
I DARESAY YOU'VE GOTTEN THE RESULT YOU WANTED.

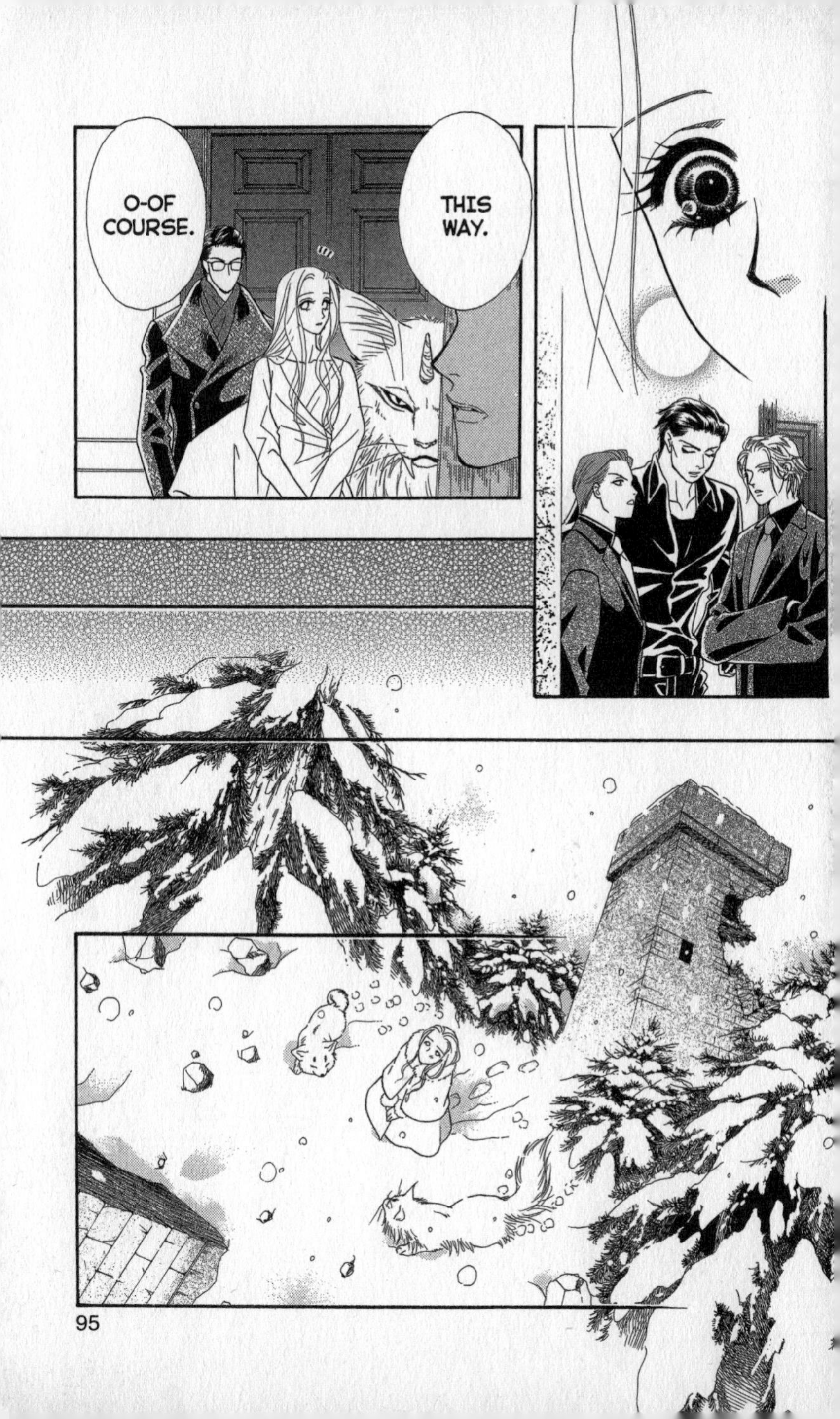
THIS WAY.
O-OF COURSE.

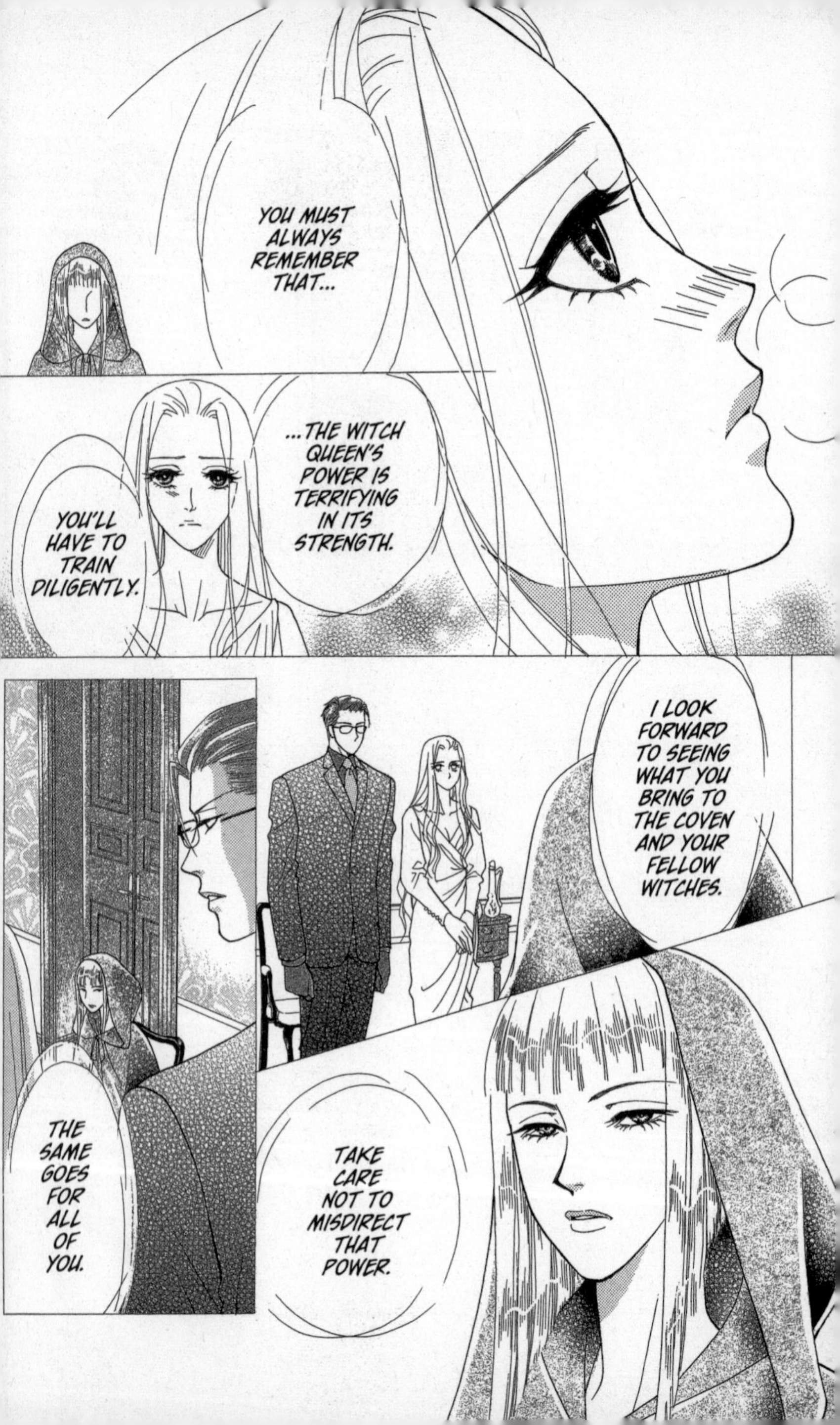
YOU MUST ALWAYS REMEMBER THAT...
...THE WITCH QUEEN'S POWER IS TERRIFYING IN ITS STRENGTH.
YOU'LL HAVE TO TRAIN DILIGENTLY.
I LOOK FORWARD TO SEEING WHAT YOU BRING TO THE COVEN AND YOUR FELLOW WITCHES.
TAKE CARE NOT TO MISDIRECT THAT POWER.
THE SAME GOES FOR ALL OF YOU.

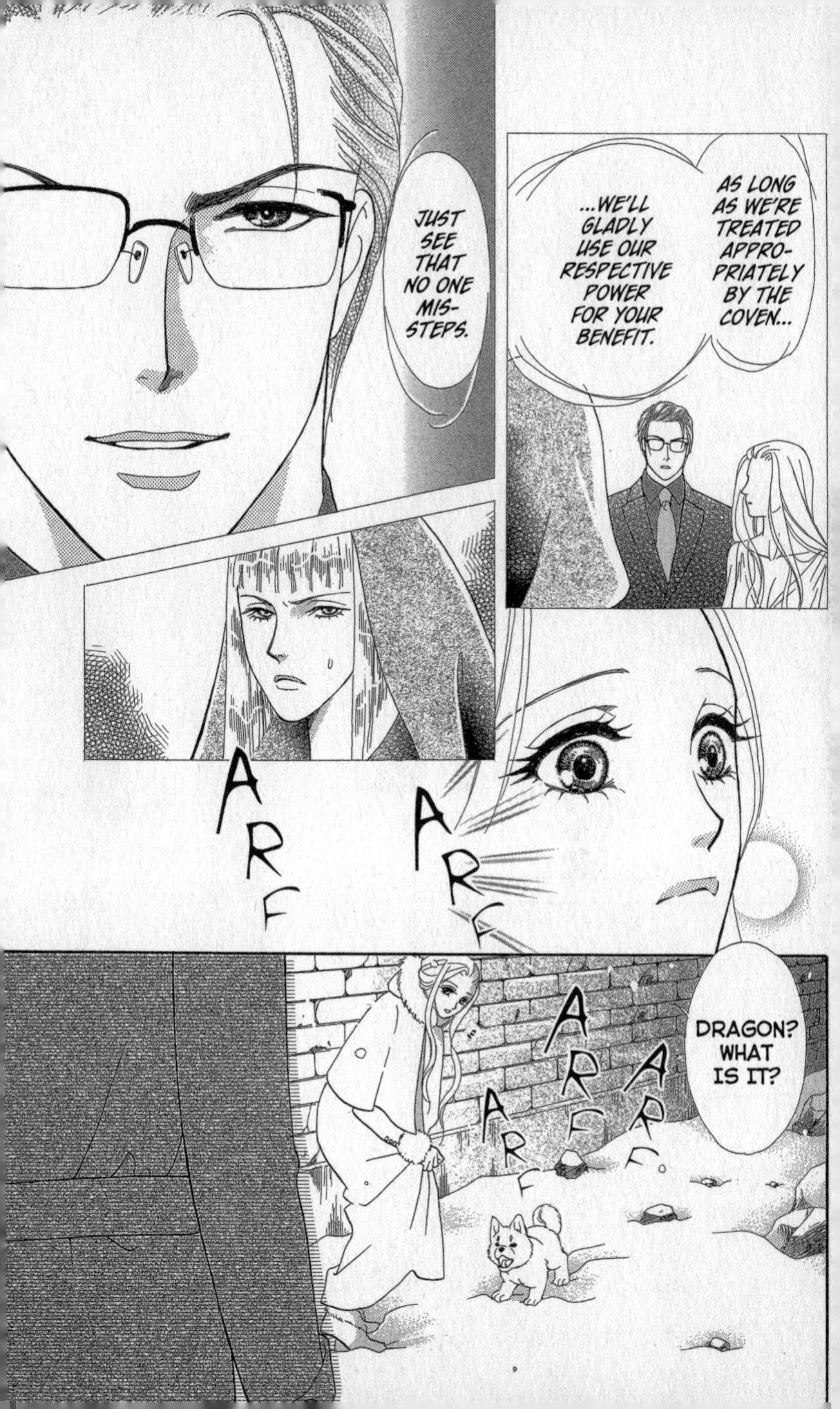
AS LONG AS WE'RE TREATED APPRO-PRIATELY BY THE COVEN...
...WE'LL GLADLY USE OUR RESPECTIVE POWER FOR YOUR BENEFIT.
JUST SEE THAT NO ONE MIS-STEPS.
ARF
ARF
DRAGON? WHAT IS IT?
ARF
ARF
ARF

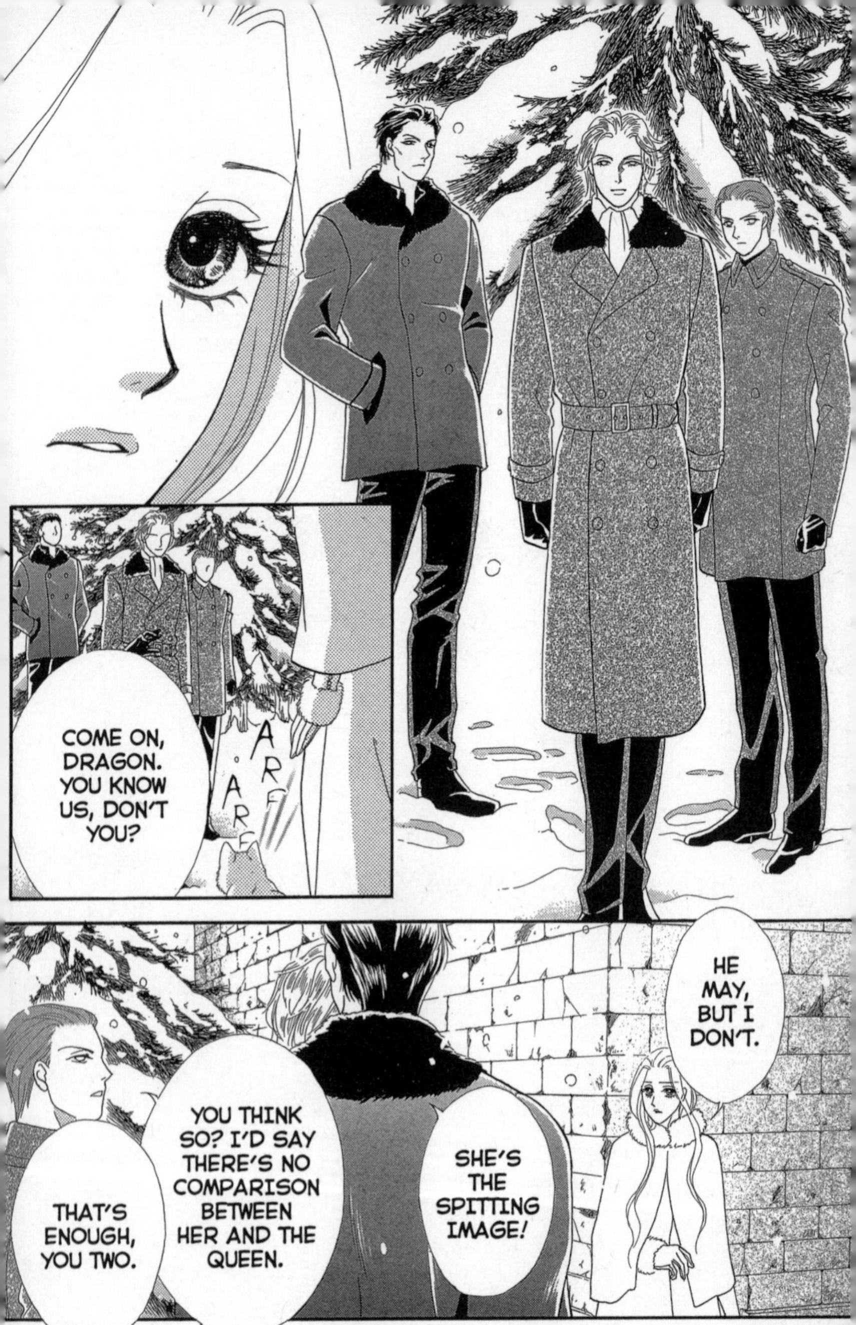
ARF
ARF
COME ON, DRAGON. YOU KNOW US, DON'T YOU?
HE MAY, BUT I DON'T.
SHE'S THE SPITTING IMAGE!
YOU THINK SO? I'D SAY THERE'S NO COMPARISON BETWEEN HER AND THE QUEEN.
THAT'S ENOUGH, YOU TWO.

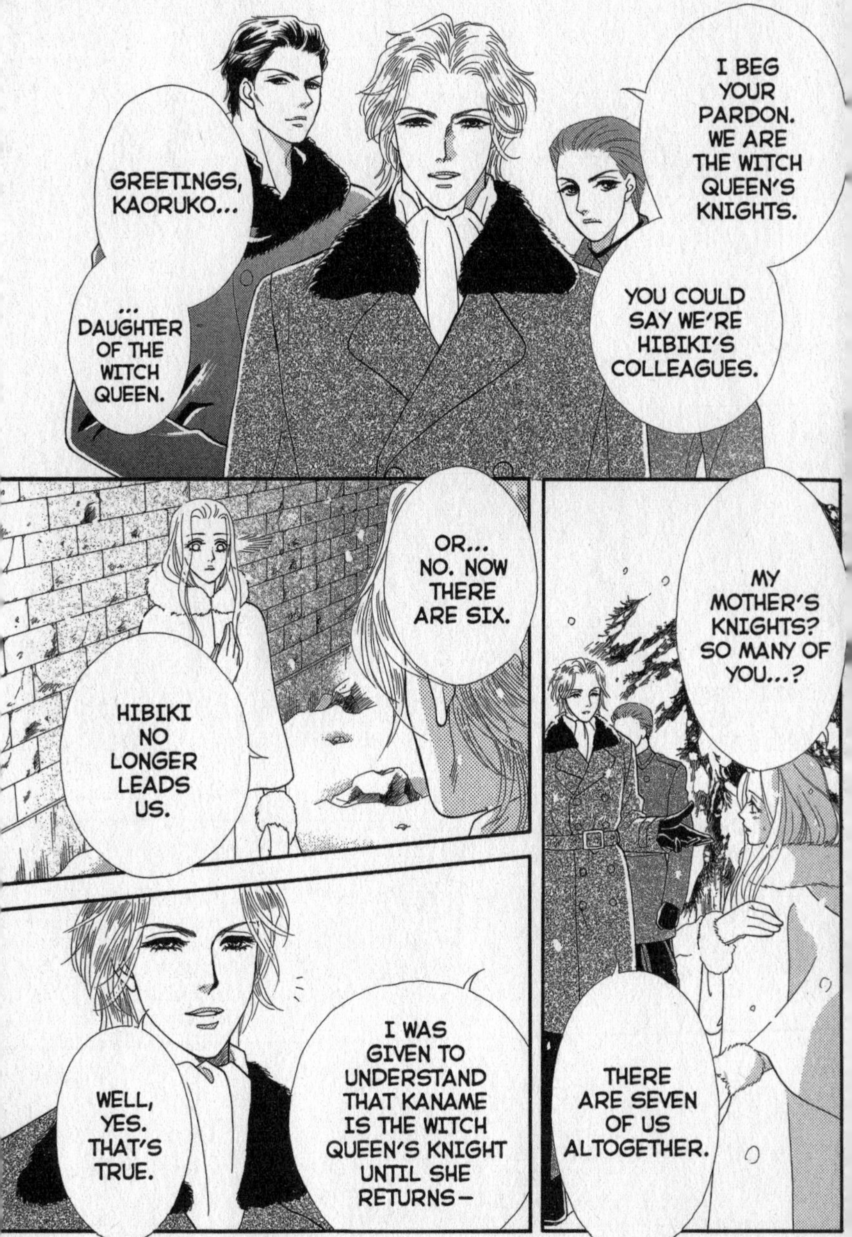
I BEG YOUR PARDON. WE ARE THE WITCH QUEEN'S KNIGHTS.
YOU COULD SAY WE'RE HIBIKI'S COLLEAGUES.
GREETINGS, KAORUKO...
...DAUGHTER OF THE WITCH QUEEN.
MY MOTHER'S KNIGHTS? SO MANY OF YOU...?
THERE ARE SEVEN OF US ALTOGETHER.
OR... NO. NOW THERE ARE SIX.
HIBIKI NO LONGER LEADS US.
I WAS GIVEN TO UNDERSTAND THAT KANAME IS THE WITCH QUEEN'S KNIGHT UNTIL SHE RETURNS—
WELL, YES. THAT'S TRUE.

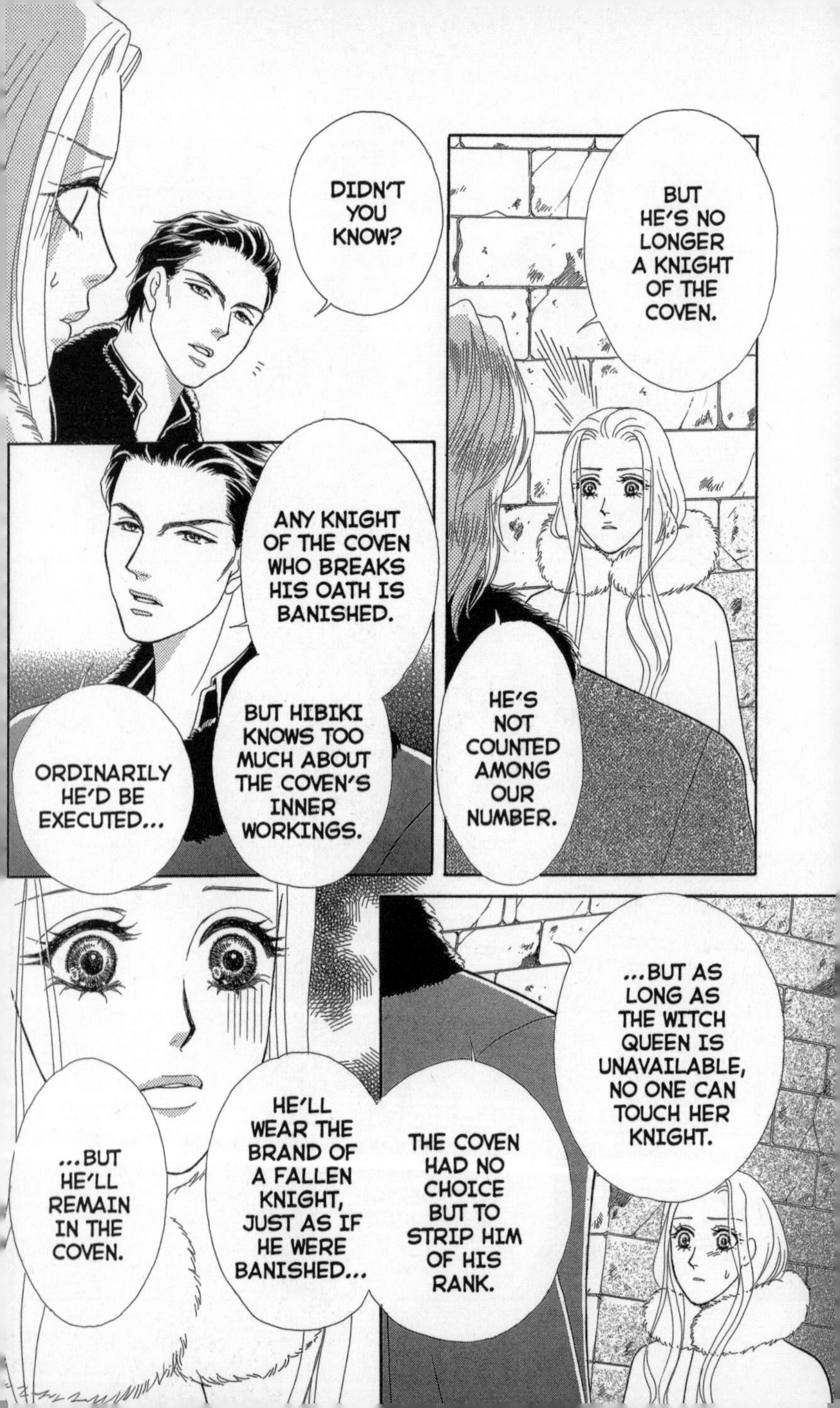
DIDN'T YOU KNOW?
BUT HE'S NO LONGER A KNIGHT OF THE COVEN.
HE'S NOT COUNTED AMONG OUR NUMBER.
ANY KNIGHT OF THE COVEN WHO BREAKS HIS OATH IS BANISHED.
BUT HIBIKI KNOWS TOO MUCH ABOUT THE COVEN'S INNER WORKINGS.
ORDINARILY HE'D BE EXECUTED...
...BUT AS LONG AS THE WITCH QUEEN IS UNAVAILABLE, NO ONE CAN TOUCH HER KNIGHT.
THE COVEN HAD NO CHOICE BUT TO STRIP HIM OF HIS RANK.
HE'LL WEAR THE BRAND OF A FALLEN KNIGHT, JUST AS IF HE WERE BANISHED...
...BUT HE'LL REMAIN IN THE COVEN.

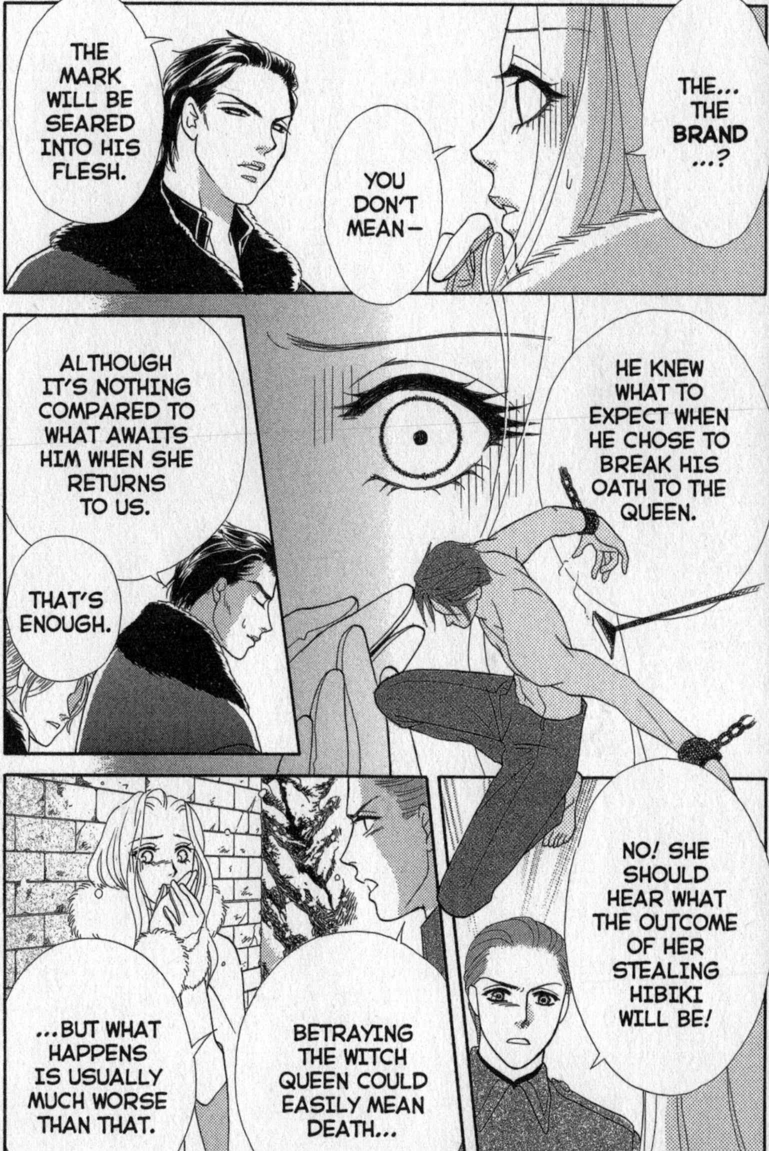
THE... THE BRAND ...?
YOU DON'T MEAN—
THE MARK WILL BE SEARED INTO HIS FLESH.
HE KNEW WHAT TO EXPECT WHEN HE CHOSE TO BREAK HIS OATH TO THE QUEEN.
ALTHOUGH IT'S NOTHING COMPARED TO WHAT AWAITS HIM WHEN SHE RETURNS TO US.
THAT'S ENOUGH.
NO! SHE SHOULD HEAR WHAT THE OUTCOME OF HER STEALING HIBIKI WILL BE!
BETRAYING THE WITCH QUEEN COULD EASILY MEAN DEATH...
...BUT WHAT HAPPENS IS USUALLY MUCH WORSE THAN THAT.

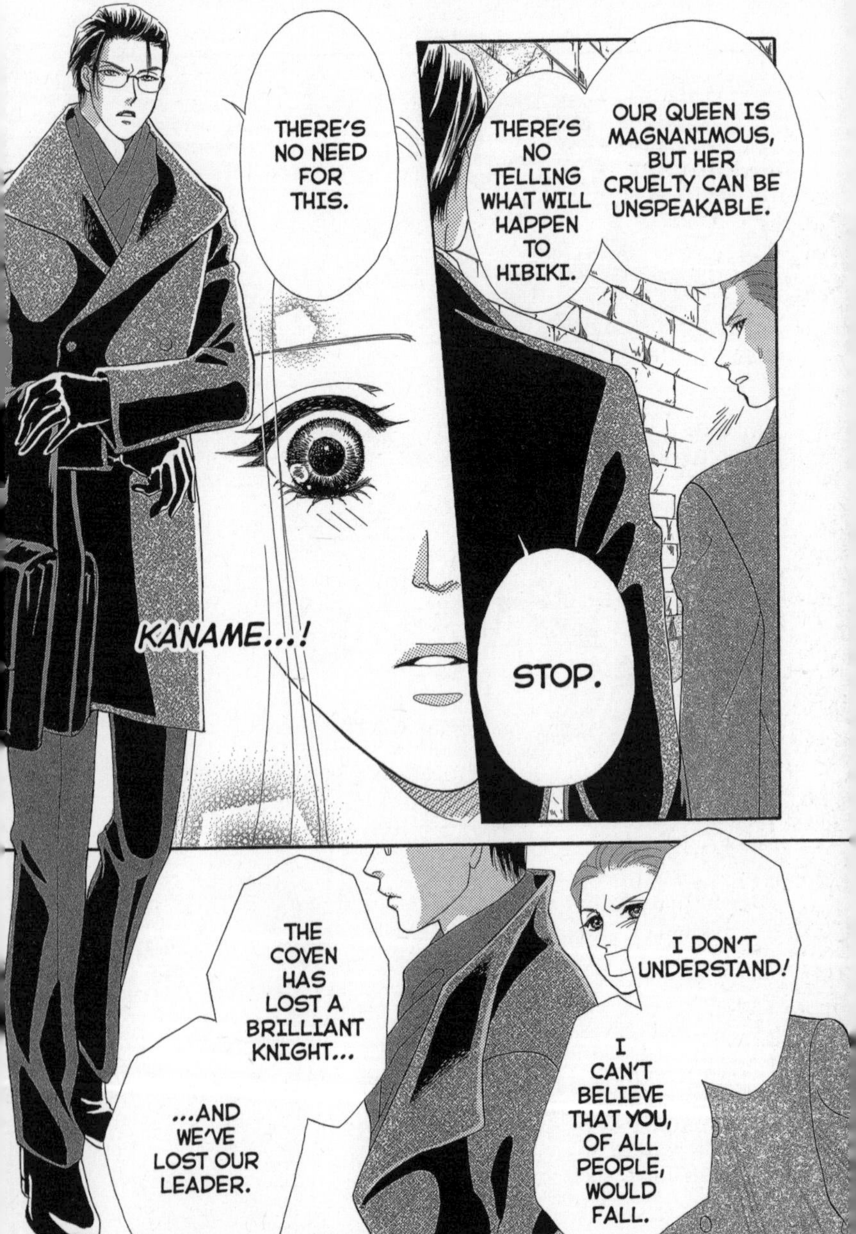
OUR QUEEN IS MAGNANIMOUS, BUT HER CRUELTY CAN BE UNSPEAKABLE.
THERE'S NO TELLING WHAT WILL HAPPEN TO HIBIKI.
STOP.
THERE'S NO NEED FOR THIS.
KANAME...!
I DON'T UNDERSTAND!
I CAN'T BELIEVE THAT YOU, OF ALL PEOPLE, WOULD FALL.
THE COVEN HAS LOST A BRILLIANT KNIGHT...
...AND WE'VE LOST OUR LEADER.

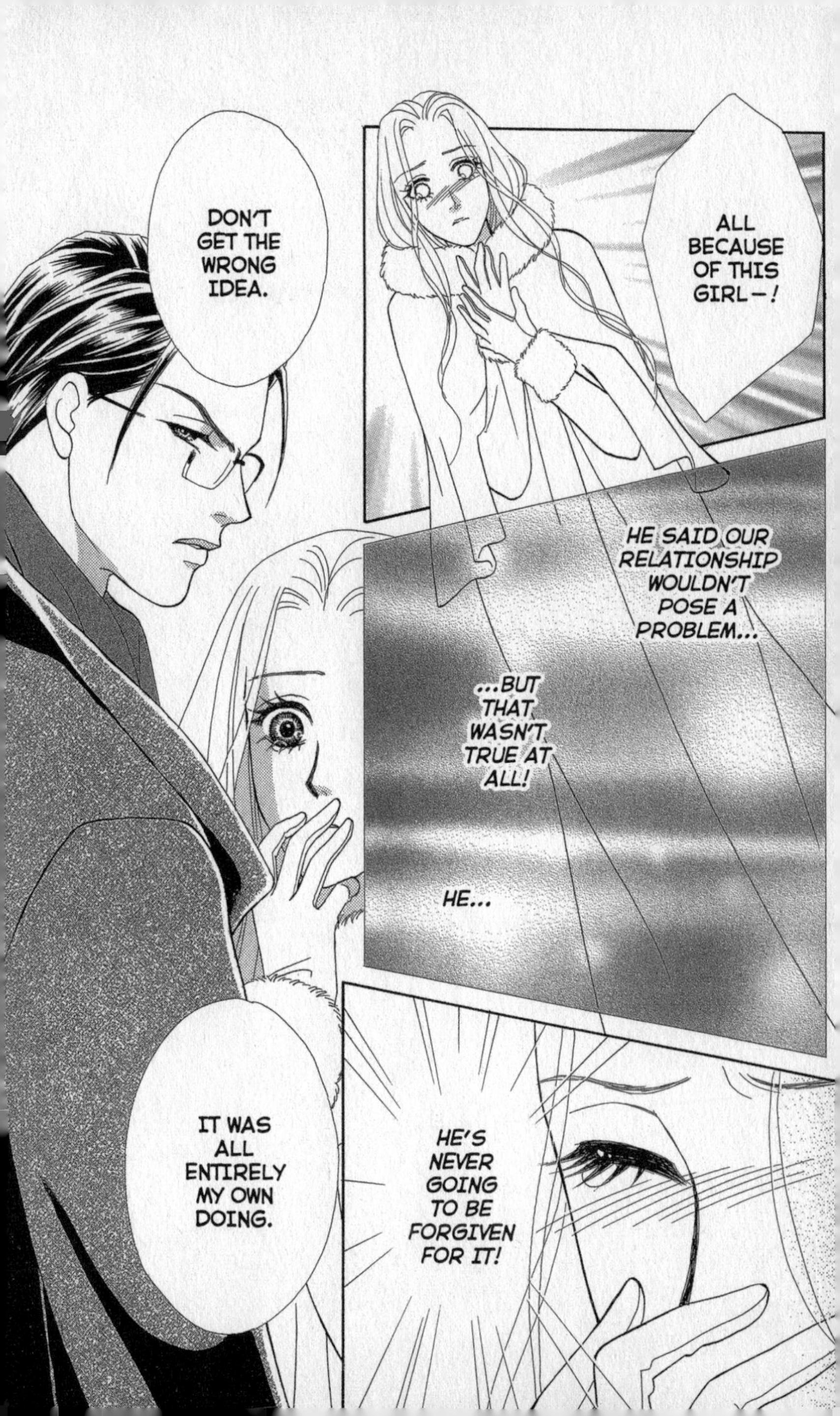
ALL BECAUSE OF THIS GIRL—!
DON'T GET THE WRONG IDEA.
HE SAID OUR RELATIONSHIP WOULDN'T POSE A PROBLEM...
...BUT THAT WASN'T TRUE AT ALL!
HE...
HE'S NEVER GOING TO BE FORGIVEN FOR IT!
IT WAS ALL ENTIRELY MY OWN DOING.

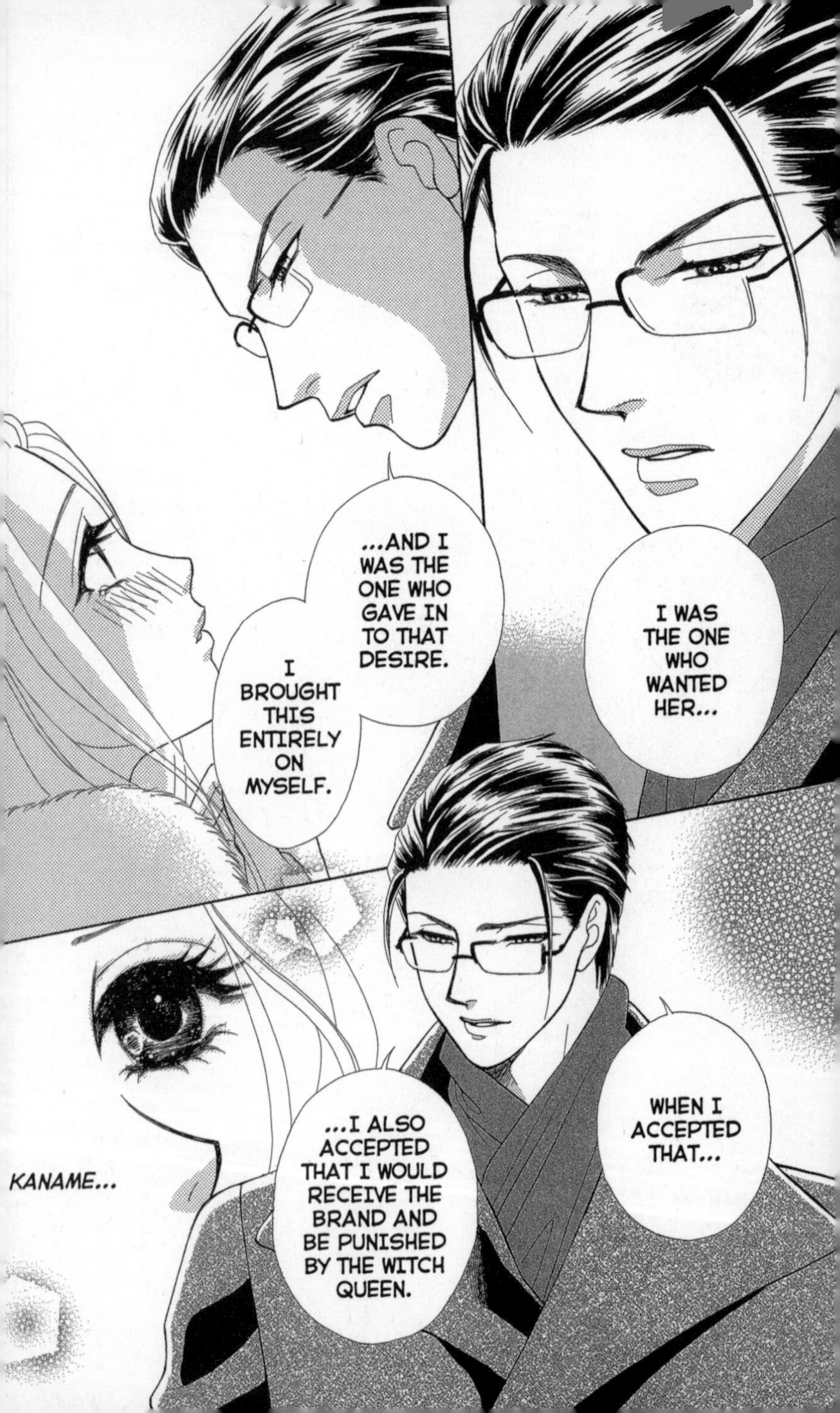
I WAS THE ONE WHO WANTED HER...
...AND I WAS THE ONE WHO GAVE IN TO THAT DESIRE.
I BROUGHT THIS ENTIRELY ON MYSELF.
WHEN I ACCEPTED THAT...
...I ALSO ACCEPTED THAT I WOULD RECEIVE THE BRAND AND BE PUNISHED BY THE WITCH QUEEN.
KANAME...

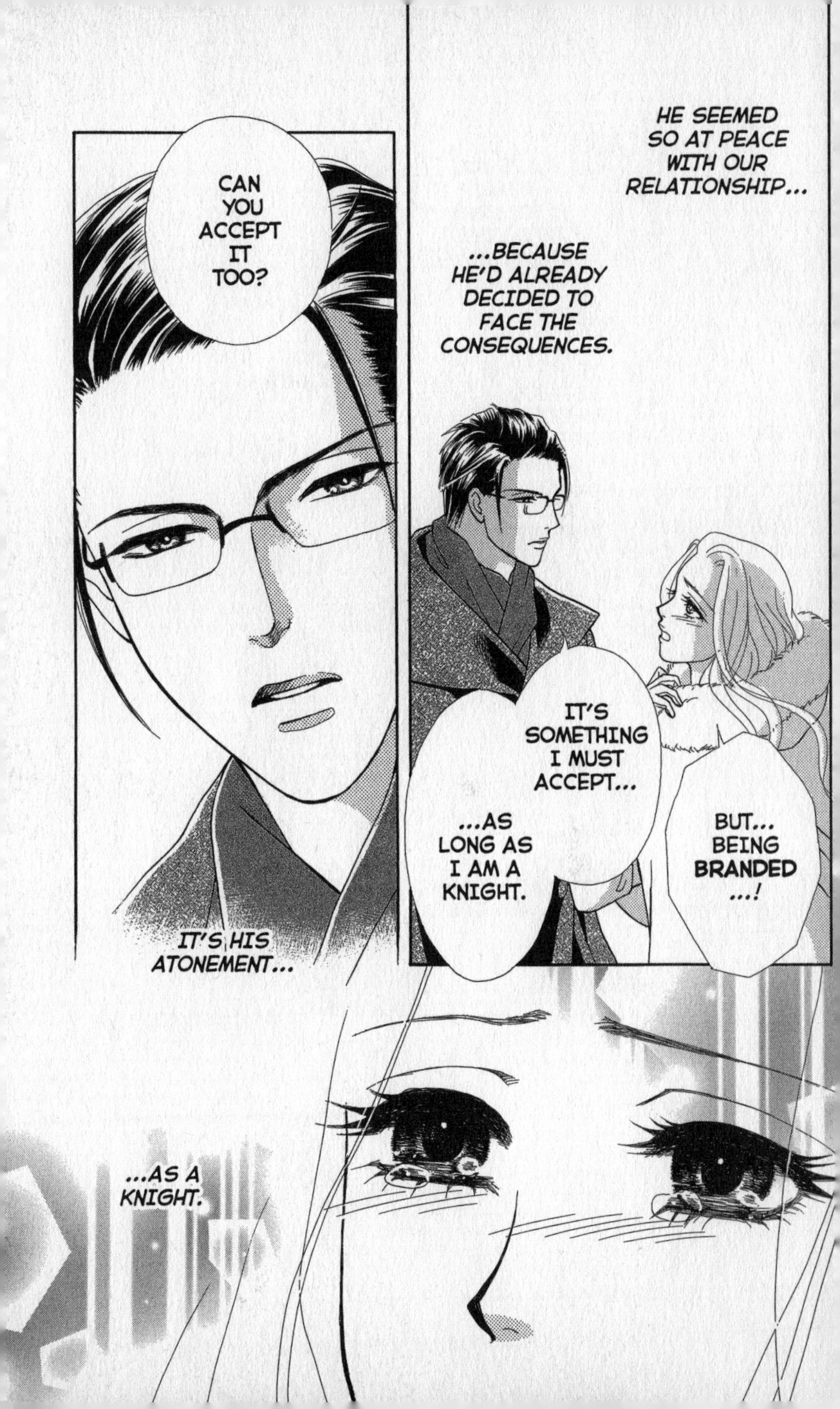
HE SEEMED SO AT PEACE WITH OUR RELATIONSHIP...
...BECAUSE HE'D ALREADY DECIDED TO FACE THE CONSEQUENCES.
BUT... BEING BRANDED ...!
IT'S SOMETHING I MUST ACCEPT...
...AS LONG AS I AM A KNIGHT.
CAN YOU ACCEPT IT TOO?
IT'S HIS ATONEMENT...
...AS A KNIGHT.

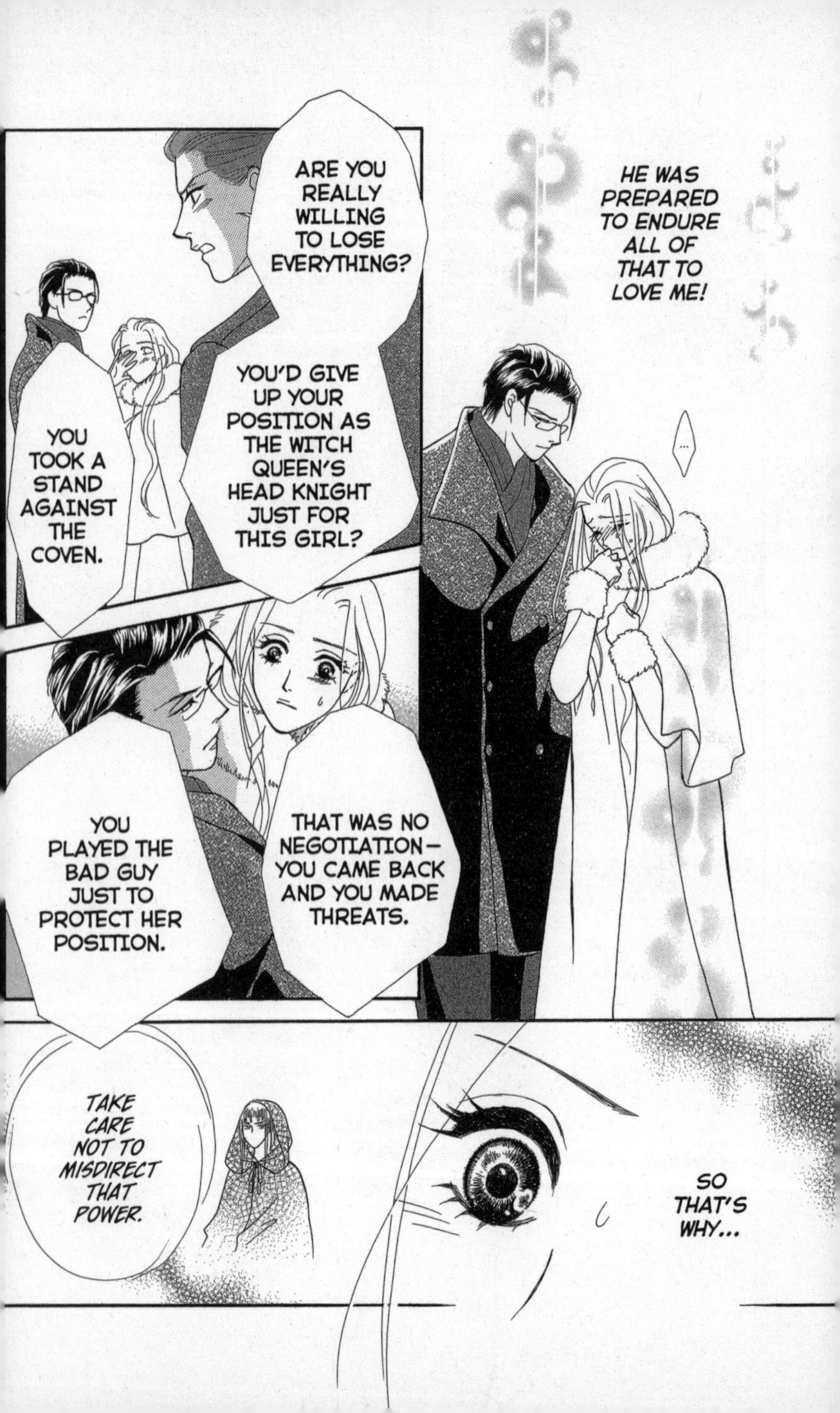
HE WAS PREPARED TO ENDURE ALL OF THAT TO LOVE ME!
...
ARE YOU REALLY WILLING TO LOSE EVERYTHING?
YOU'D GIVE UP YOUR POSITION AS THE WITCH QUEEN'S HEAD KNIGHT JUST FOR THIS GIRL?
YOU TOOK A STAND AGAINST THE COVEN.
THAT WAS NO NEGOTIATION—YOU CAME BACK AND YOU MADE THREATS.
YOU PLAYED THE BAD GUY JUST TO PROTECT HER POSITION.
SO THAT'S WHY...
TAKE CARE NOT TO MISDIRECT THAT POWER.

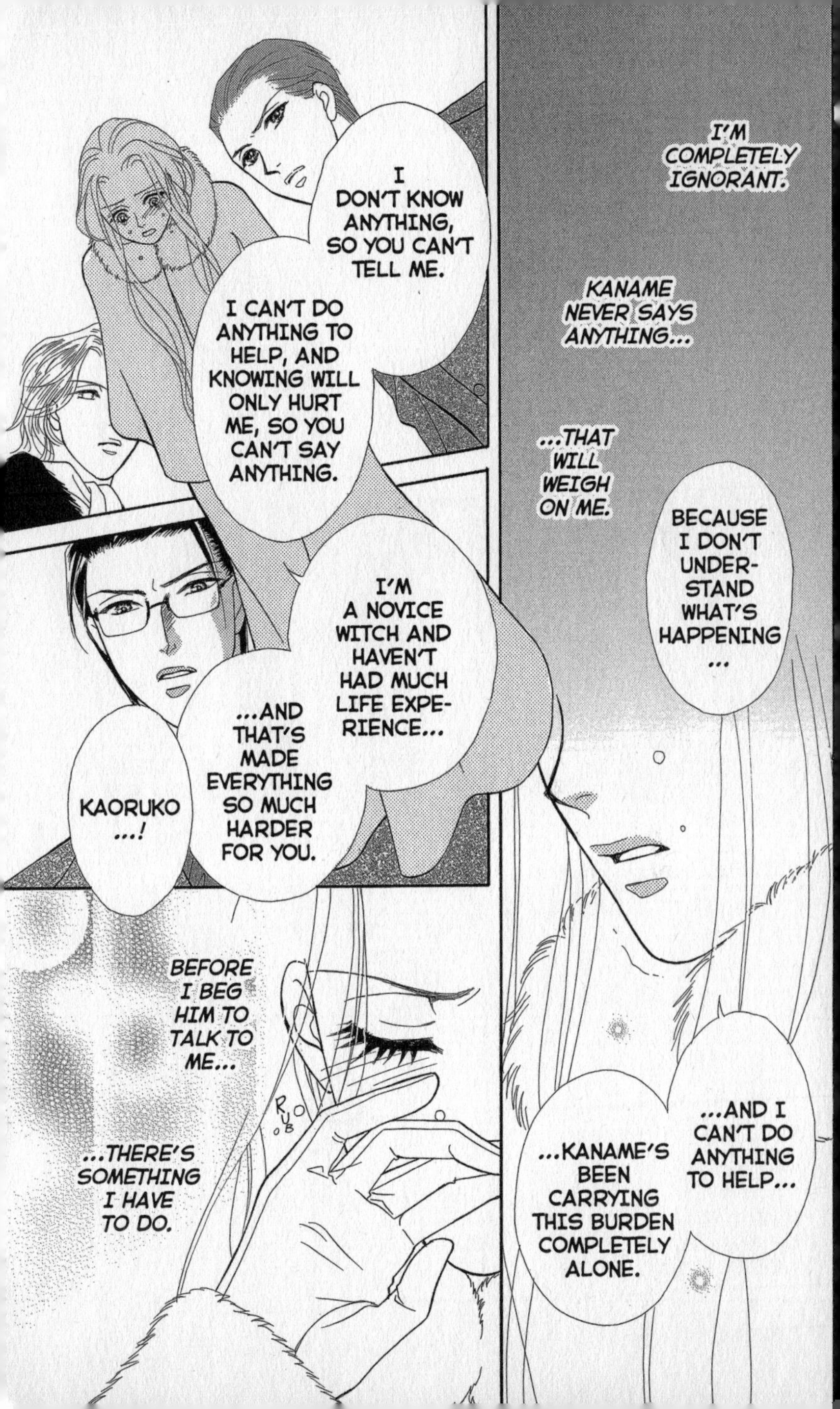
I'M COMPLETELY IGNORANT.
KANAME NEVER SAYS ANYTHING...
...THAT WILL WEIGH ON ME.
BECAUSE I DON'T UNDERSTAND WHAT'S HAPPENING...
...AND I CAN'T DO ANYTHING TO HELP...
...KANAME'S BEEN CARRYING THIS BURDEN COMPLETELY ALONE.
I DON'T KNOW ANYTHING, SO YOU CAN'T TELL ME.
I CAN'T DO ANYTHING TO HELP, AND KNOWING WILL ONLY HURT ME, SO YOU CAN'T SAY ANYTHING.
I'M A NOVICE WITCH AND HAVEN'T HAD MUCH LIFE EXPERIENCE...
...AND THAT'S MADE EVERYTHING SO MUCH HARDER FOR YOU.
KAORUKO...!
BEFORE I BEG HIM TO TALK TO ME...
...THERE'S SOMETHING I HAVE TO DO.
RUB

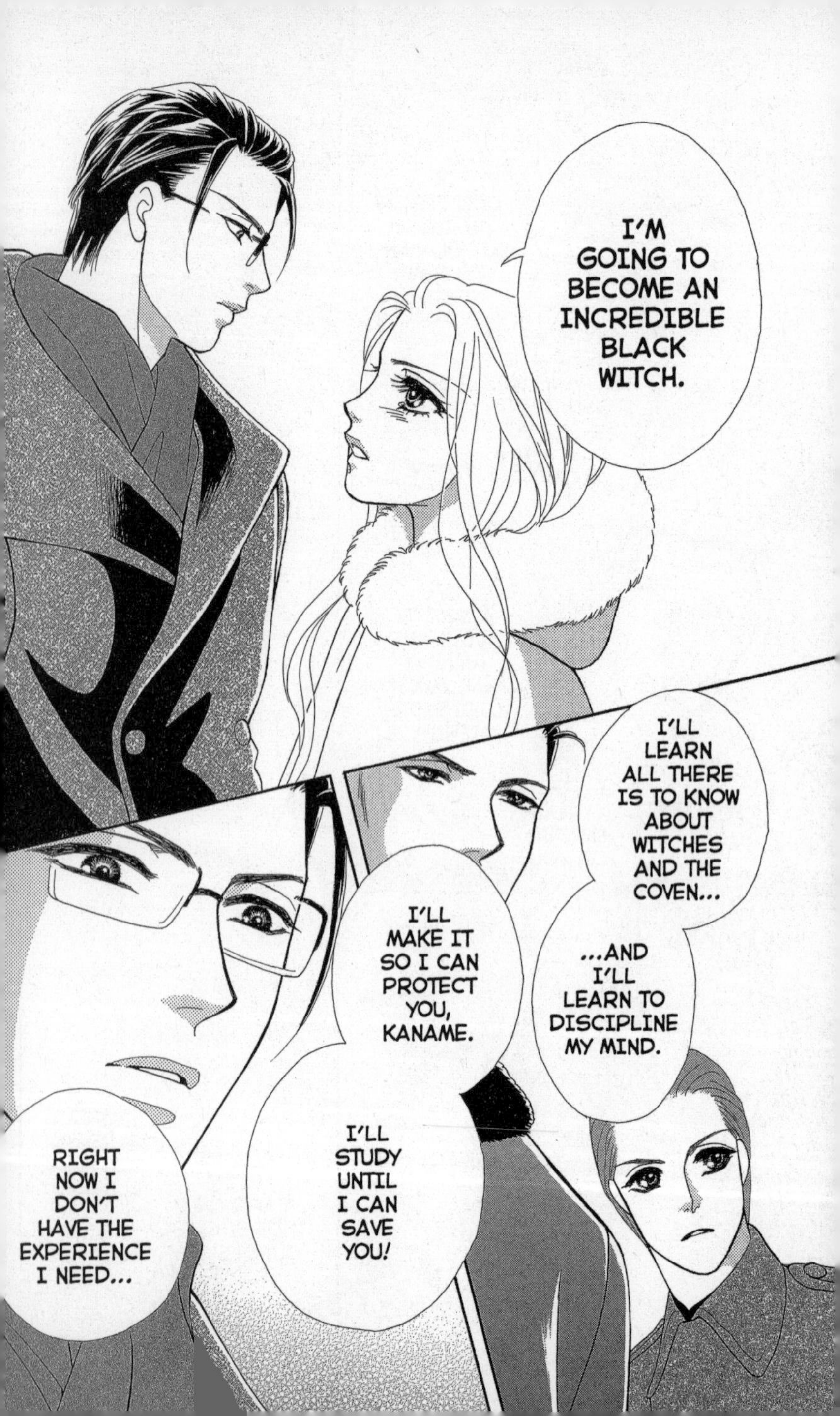
I'M GOING TO BECOME AN INCREDIBLE BLACK WITCH.
I'LL LEARN ALL THERE IS TO KNOW ABOUT WITCHES AND THE COVEN...
...AND I'LL LEARN TO DISCIPLINE MY MIND.
I'LL MAKE IT SO I CAN PROTECT YOU, KANAME.
I'LL STUDY UNTIL I CAN SAVE YOU!
RIGHT NOW I DON'T HAVE THE EXPERIENCE I NEED...

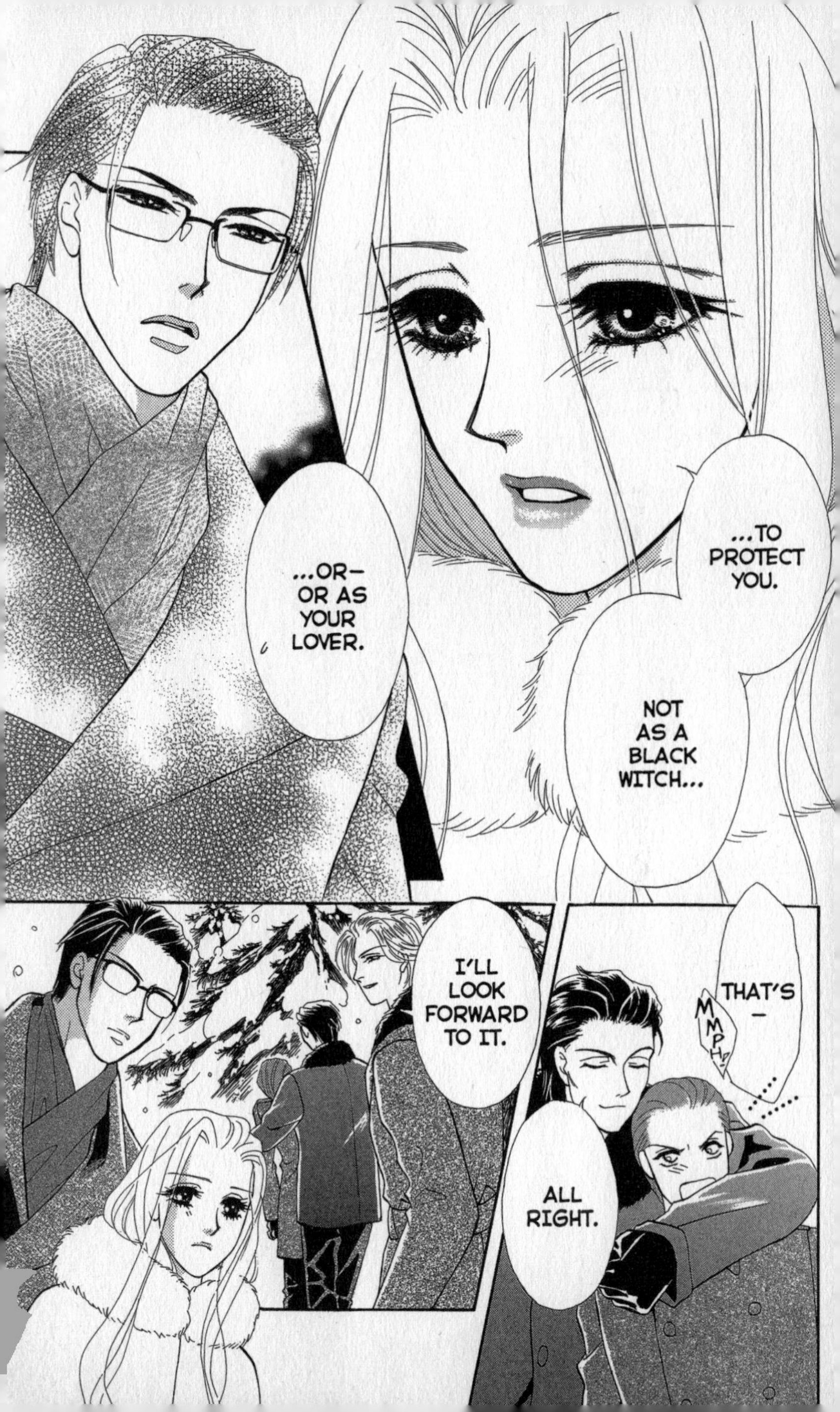
...TO PROTECT YOU.
NOT AS A BLACK WITCH...
...OR— OR AS YOUR LOVER.
THAT'S—
MMPH!
ALL RIGHT.
I'LL LOOK FORWARD TO IT.

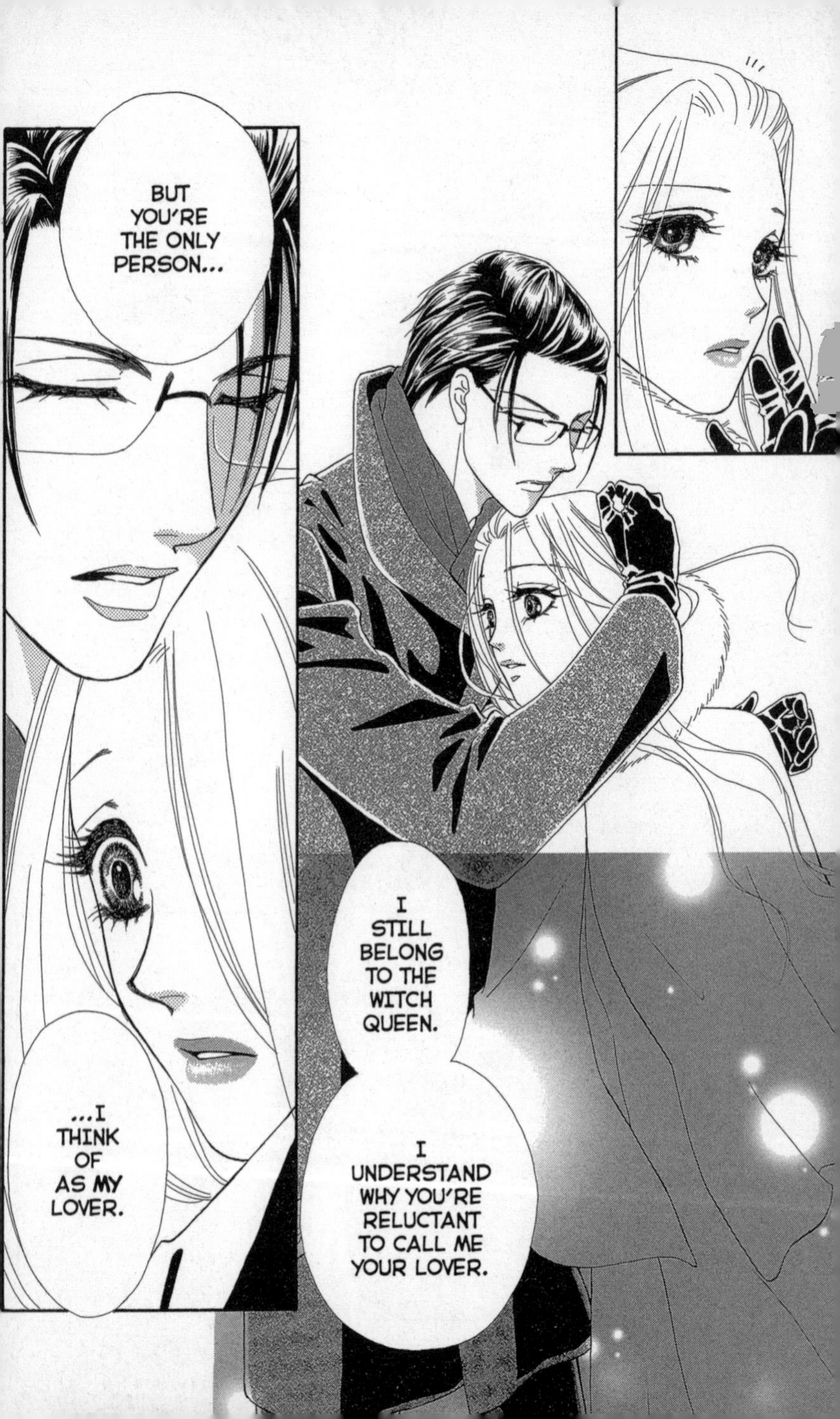
I STILL BELONG TO THE WITCH QUEEN.
I UNDERSTAND WHY YOU'RE RELUCTANT TO CALL ME YOUR LOVER.
BUT YOU'RE THE ONLY PERSON...
...I THINK OF AS MY LOVER.

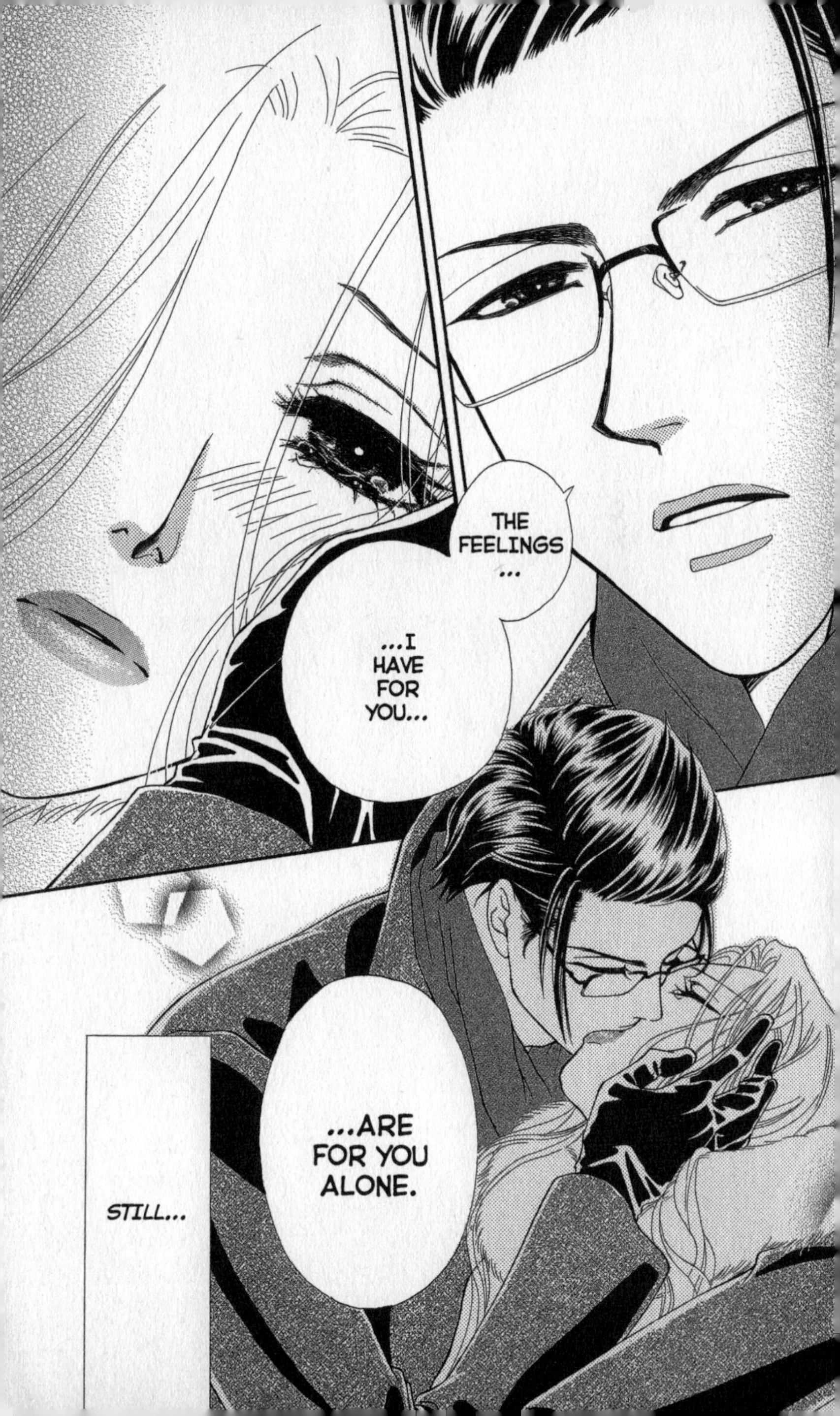
THE FEELINGS...
...I HAVE FOR YOU...
...ARE FOR YOU ALONE.
STILL...

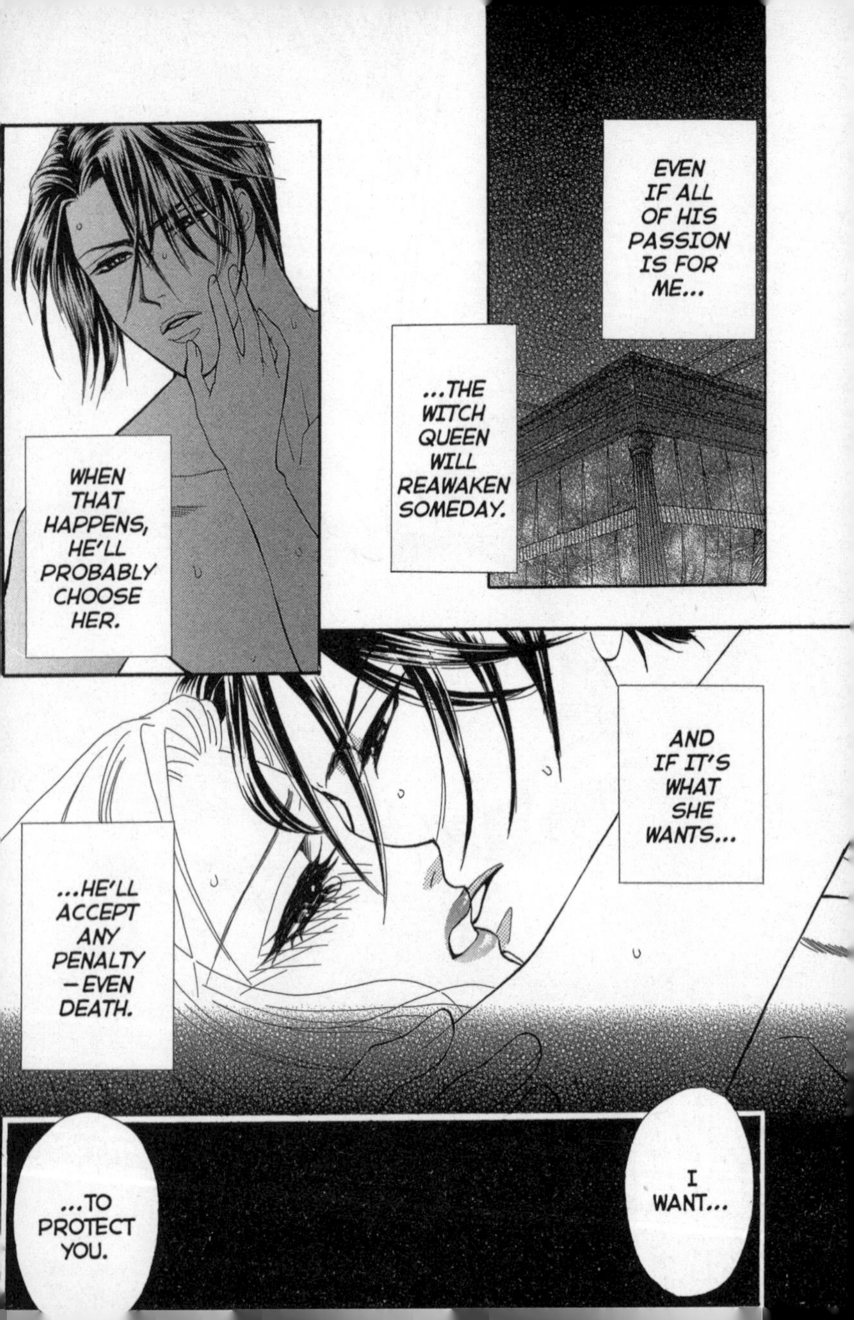
EVEN IF ALL OF HIS PASSION IS FOR ME...
...THE WITCH QUEEN WILL REAWAKEN SOMEDAY.
WHEN THAT HAPPENS, HE'LL PROBABLY CHOOSE HER.
AND IF IT'S WHAT SHE WANTS...
...HE'LL ACCEPT ANY PENALTY—EVEN DEATH.
I WANT...
...TO PROTECT YOU.

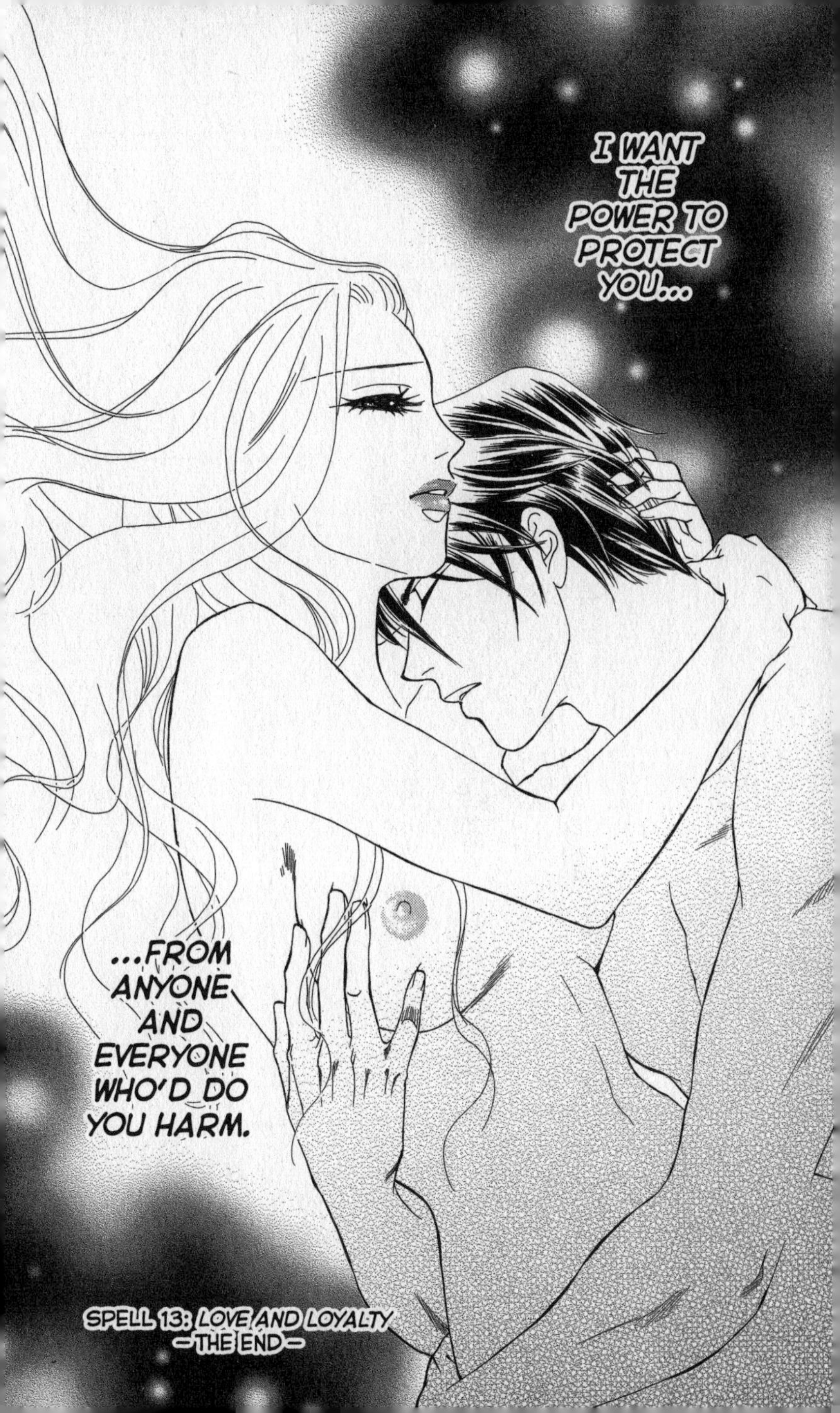
I WANT THE POWER TO PROTECT YOU...
...FROM ANYONE AND EVERYONE WHO'D DO YOU HARM.
SPELL 13: LOVE AND LOYALTY
-THE END-

– LOVE AND LOYALTY –

Enter the Witch Queen's knights!
They say there are seven of them,
including Kaname.

I wonder if I'll be able to draw them all...

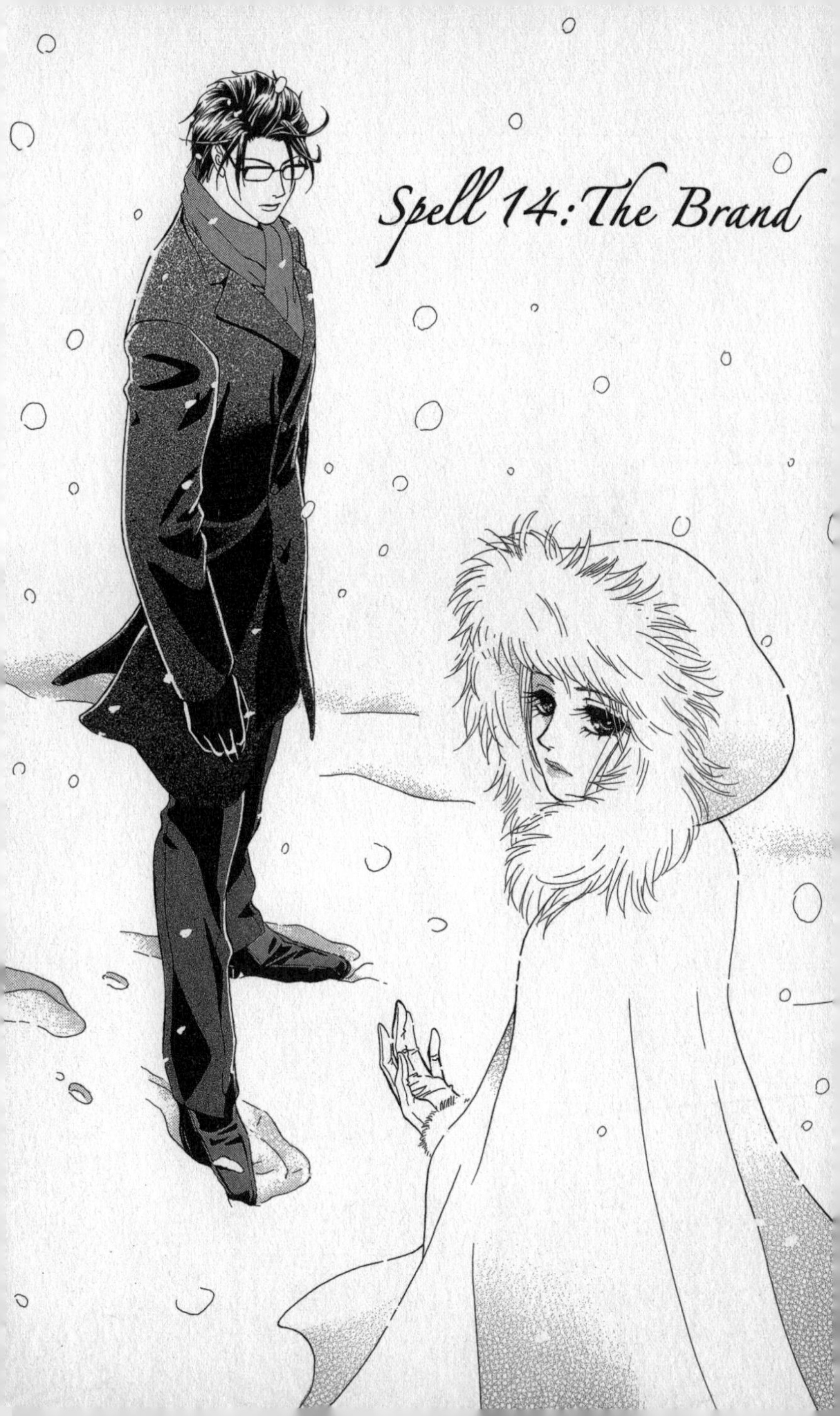
Spell 14: The Brand

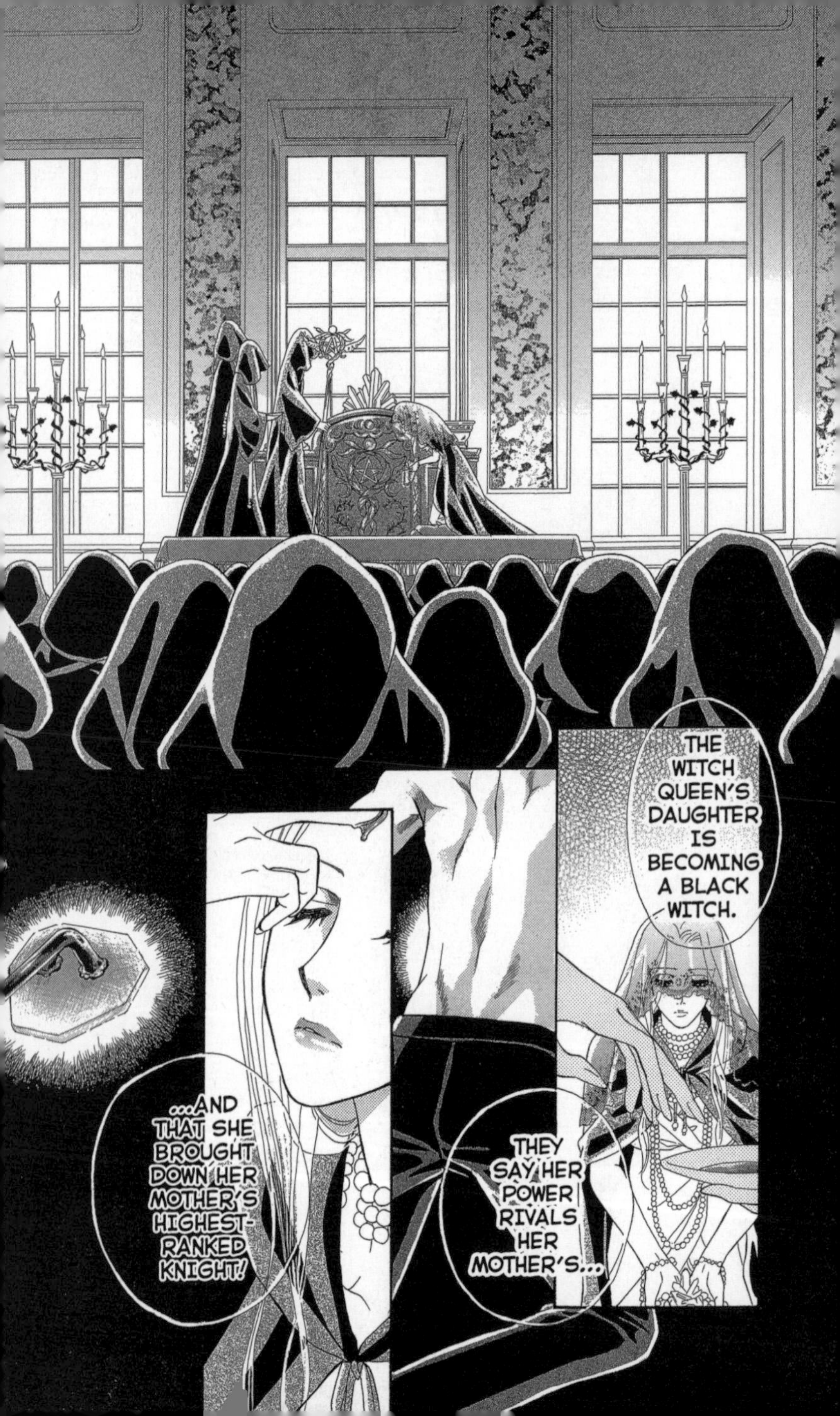
THE WITCH QUEEN'S DAUGHTER IS BECOMING A BLACK WITCH.
THEY SAY HER POWER RIVALS HER MOTHER'S...
...AND THAT SHE BROUGHT DOWN HER MOTHER'S HIGHEST-RANKED KNIGHT!

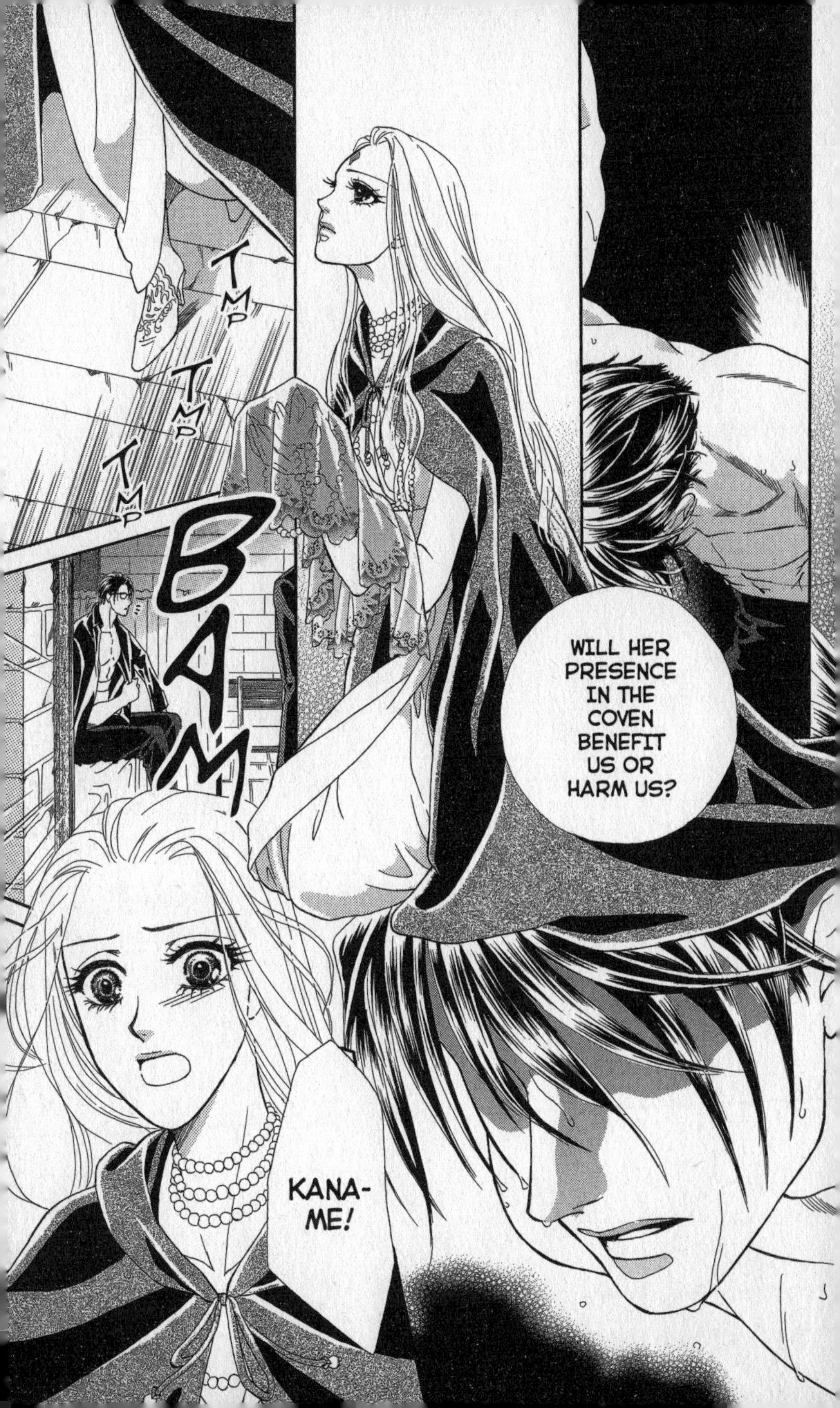

WILL HER PRESENCE IN THE COVEN BENEFIT US OR HARM US?
TMP
TMP
TMP
BAM
KANA-ME!

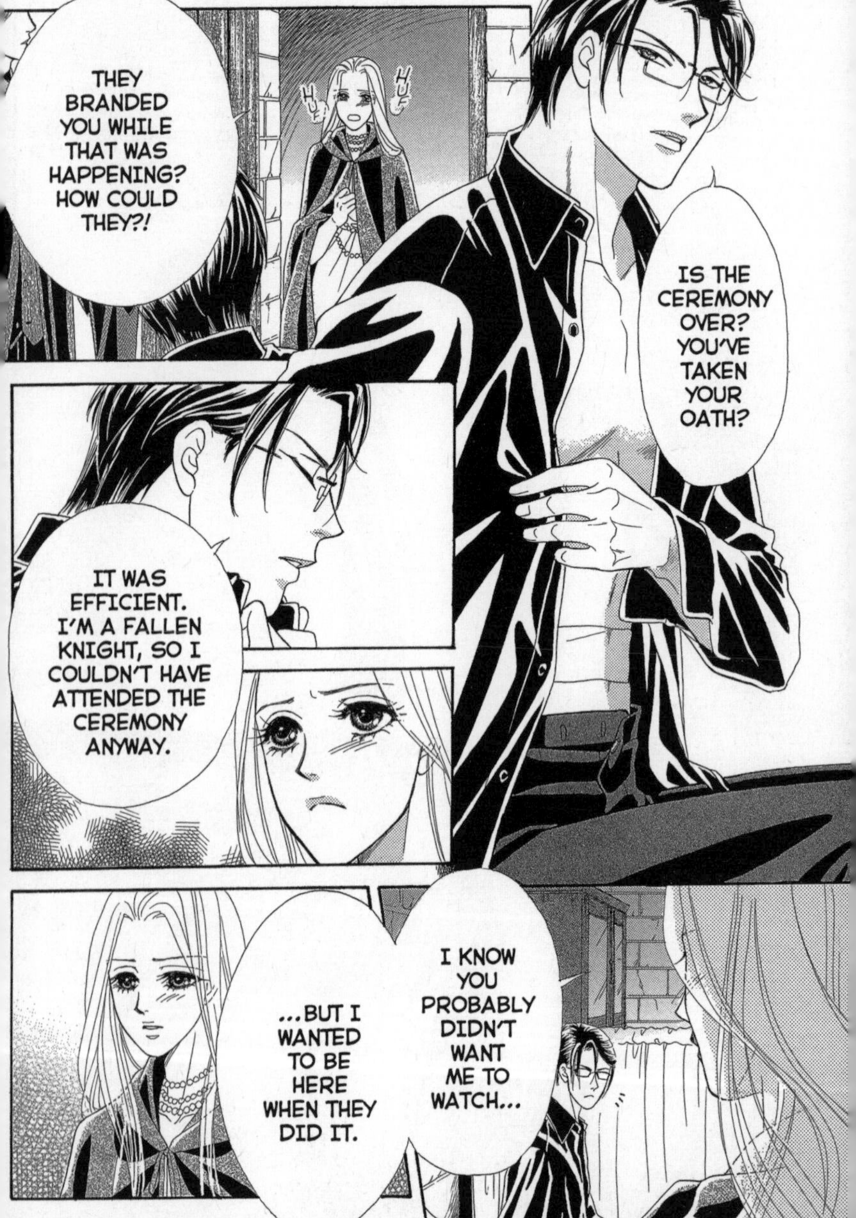
IS THE CEREMONY OVER? YOU'VE TAKEN YOUR OATH?
THEY BRANDED YOU WHILE THAT WAS HAPPENING? HOW COULD THEY?!
HUF HUF
IT WAS EFFICIENT. I'M A FALLEN KNIGHT, SO I COULDN'T HAVE ATTENDED THE CEREMONY ANYWAY.
I KNOW YOU PROBABLY DIDN'T WANT ME TO WATCH...
...BUT I WANTED TO BE HERE WHEN THEY DID IT.

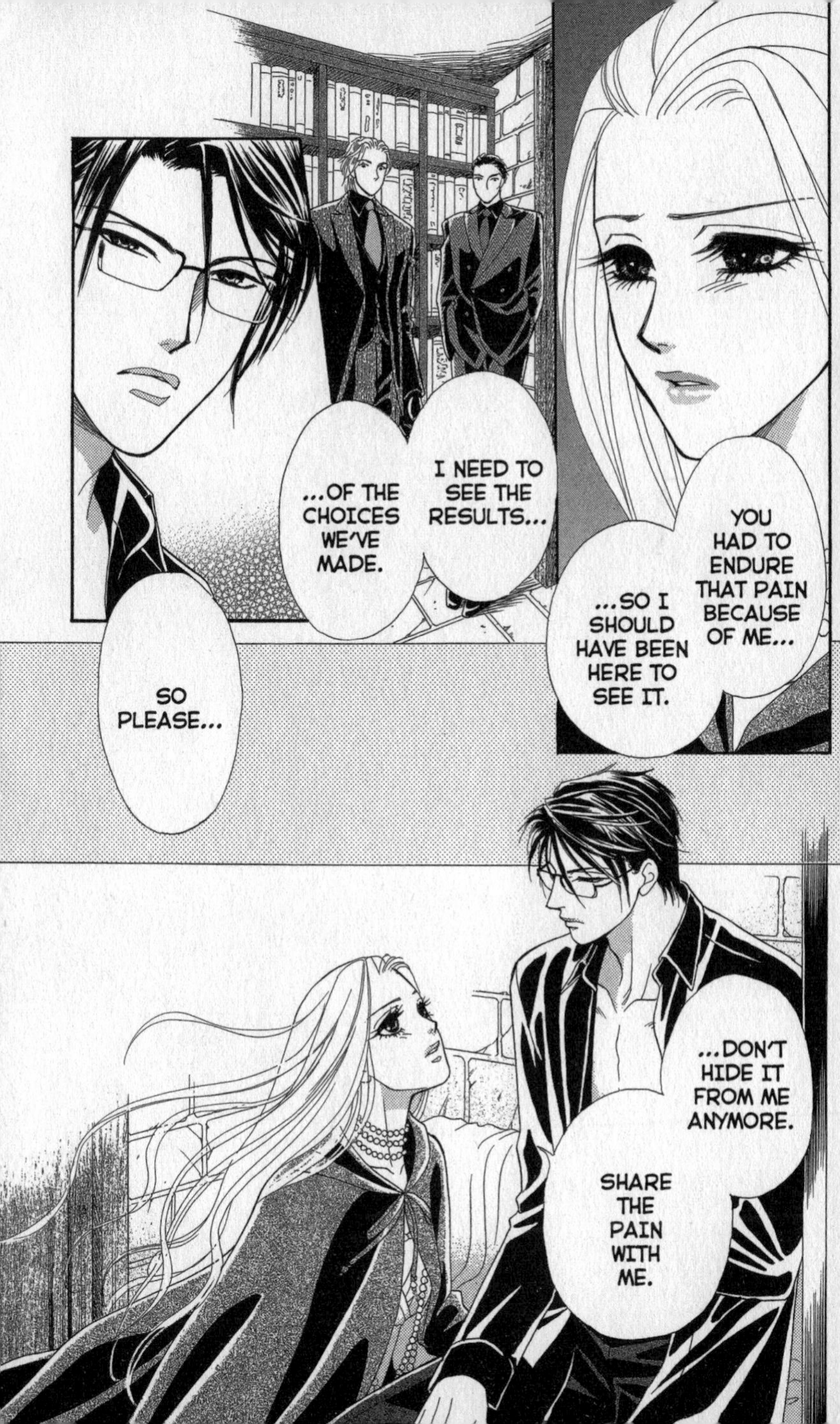
YOU HAD TO ENDURE THAT PAIN BECAUSE OF ME...
...SO I SHOULD HAVE BEEN HERE TO SEE IT.
I NEED TO SEE THE RESULTS...
...OF THE CHOICES WE'VE MADE.
SO PLEASE...
...DON'T HIDE IT FROM ME ANYMORE.
SHARE THE PAIN WITH ME.

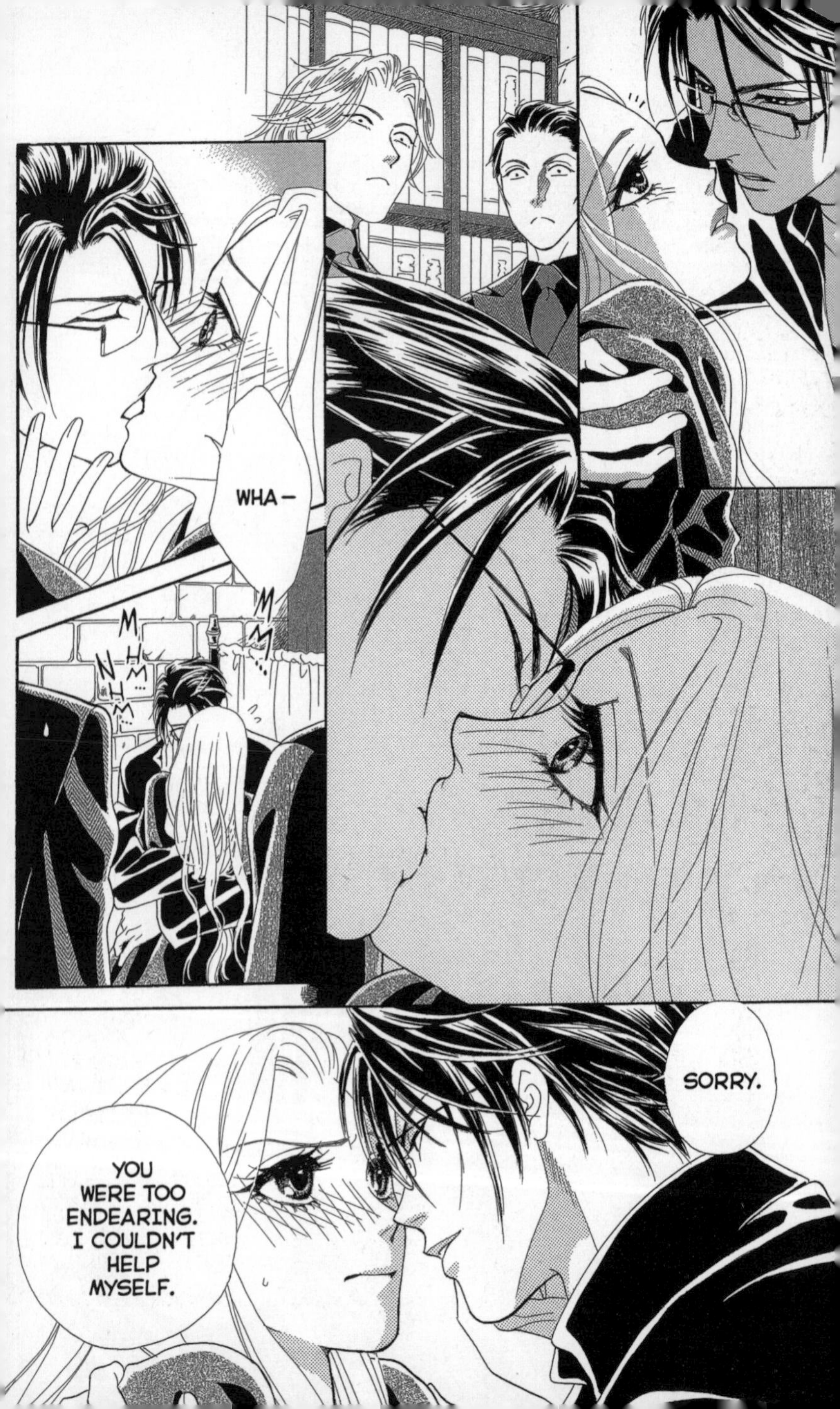

WHA—
MM...
MHM...
NHM...
SORRY.
YOU WERE TOO ENDEARING. I COULDN'T HELP MYSELF.

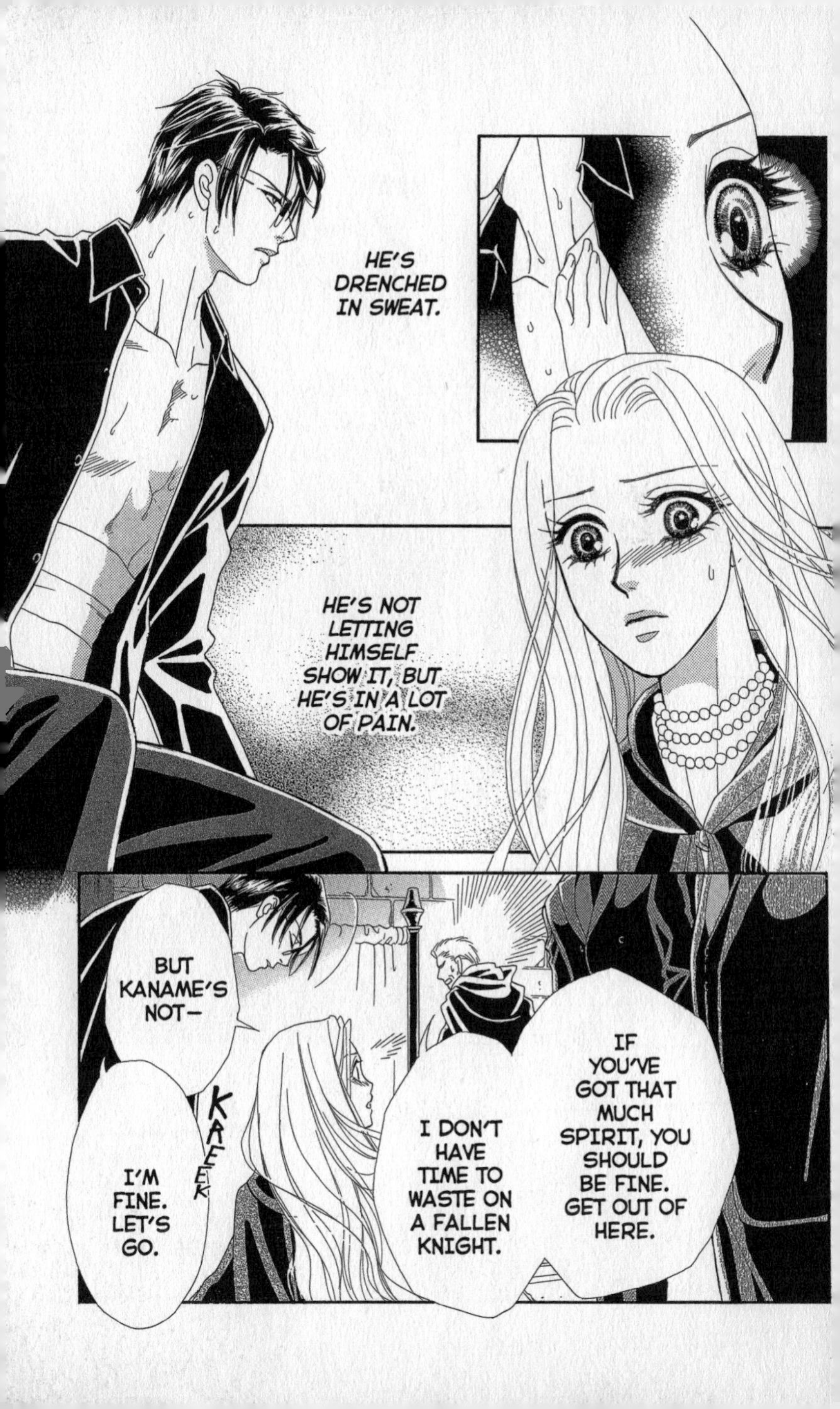
HE'S DRENCHED IN SWEAT.
HE'S NOT LETTING HIMSELF SHOW IT, BUT HE'S IN A LOT OF PAIN.
IF YOU'VE GOT THAT MUCH SPIRIT, YOU SHOULD BE FINE. GET OUT OF HERE.
I DON'T HAVE TIME TO WASTE ON A FALLEN KNIGHT.
BUT KANAME'S NOT—
KREEK
I'M FINE. LET'S GO.

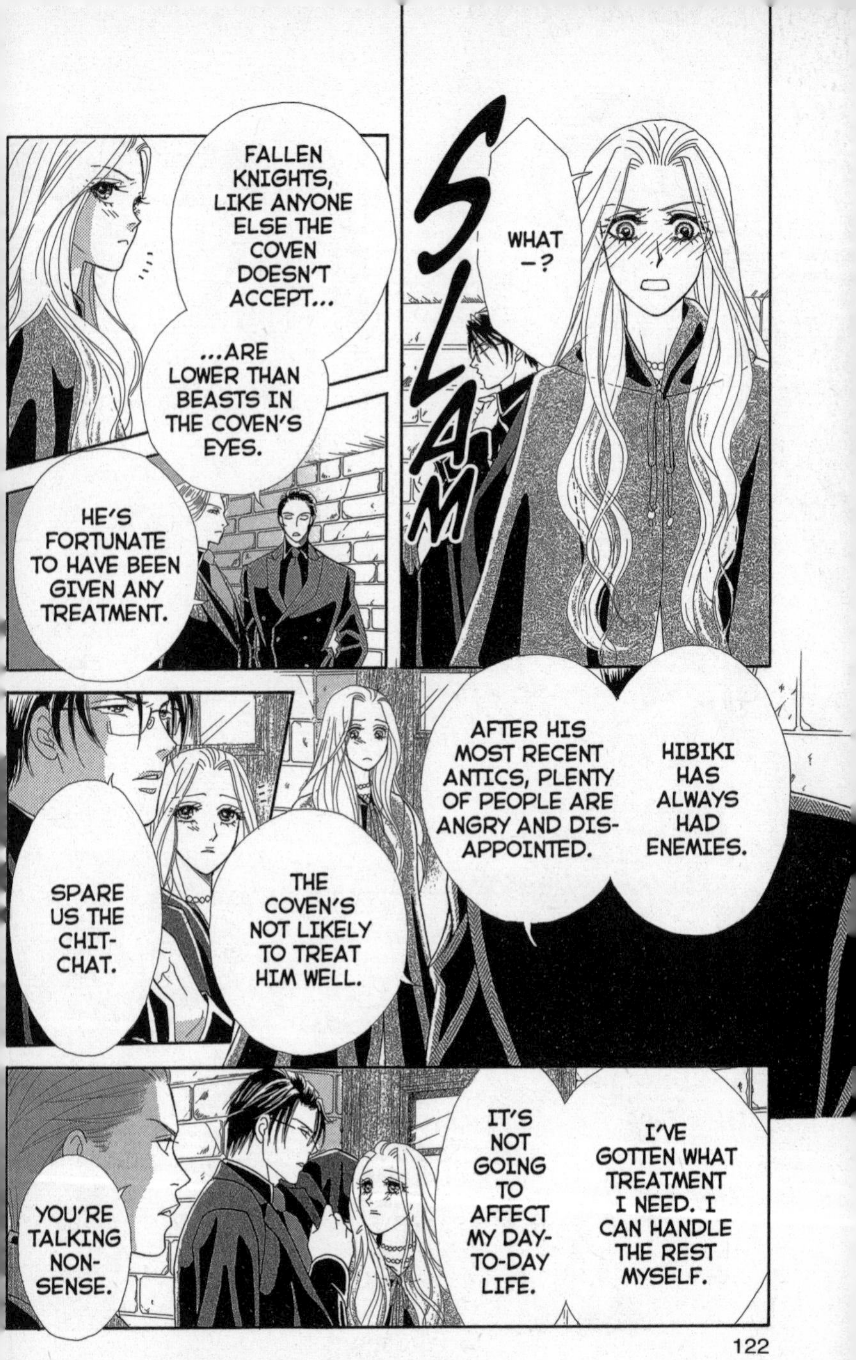
SLAM
WHAT—?
FALLEN KNIGHTS, LIKE ANYONE ELSE THE COVEN DOESN'T ACCEPT...
...ARE LOWER THAN BEASTS IN THE COVEN'S EYES.
HE'S FORTUNATE TO HAVE BEEN GIVEN ANY TREATMENT.
HIBIKI HAS ALWAYS HAD ENEMIES.
AFTER HIS MOST RECENT ANTICS, PLENTY OF PEOPLE ARE ANGRY AND DIS-APPOINTED.
THE COVEN'S NOT LIKELY TO TREAT HIM WELL.
SPARE US THE CHIT-CHAT.
I'VE GOTTEN WHAT TREATMENT I NEED. I CAN HANDLE THE REST MYSELF.
IT'S NOT GOING TO AFFECT MY DAY-TO-DAY LIFE.
YOU'RE TALKING NON-SENSE.

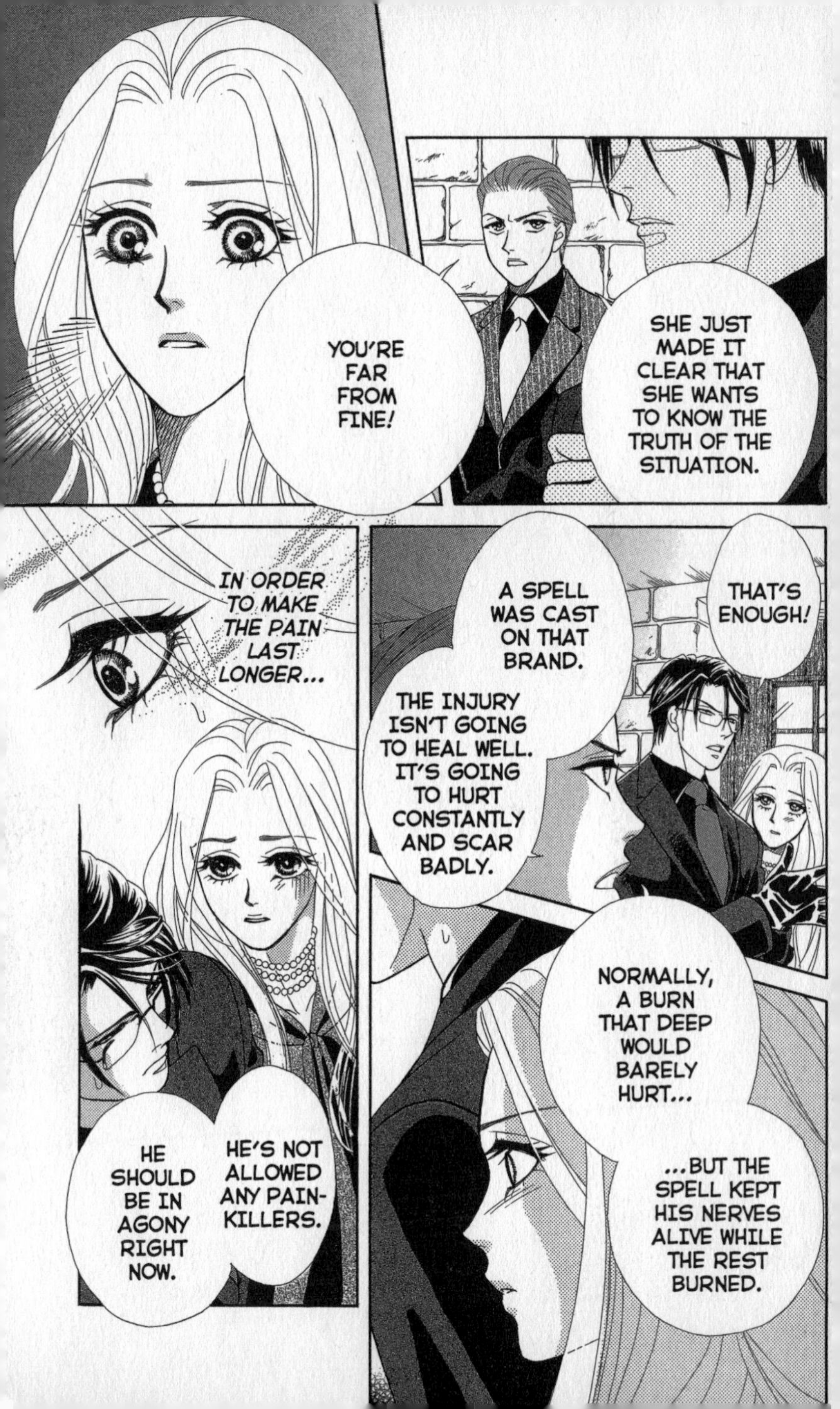
SHE JUST MADE IT CLEAR THAT SHE WANTS TO KNOW THE TRUTH OF THE SITUATION.
YOU'RE FAR FROM FINE!
THAT'S ENOUGH!
A SPELL WAS CAST ON THAT BRAND.
THE INJURY ISN'T GOING TO HEAL WELL. IT'S GOING TO HURT CONSTANTLY AND SCAR BADLY.
NORMALLY, A BURN THAT DEEP WOULD BARELY HURT...
...BUT THE SPELL KEPT HIS NERVES ALIVE WHILE THE REST BURNED.
IN ORDER TO MAKE THE PAIN LAST LONGER...
HE'S NOT ALLOWED ANY PAIN-KILLERS.
HE SHOULD BE IN AGONY RIGHT NOW.

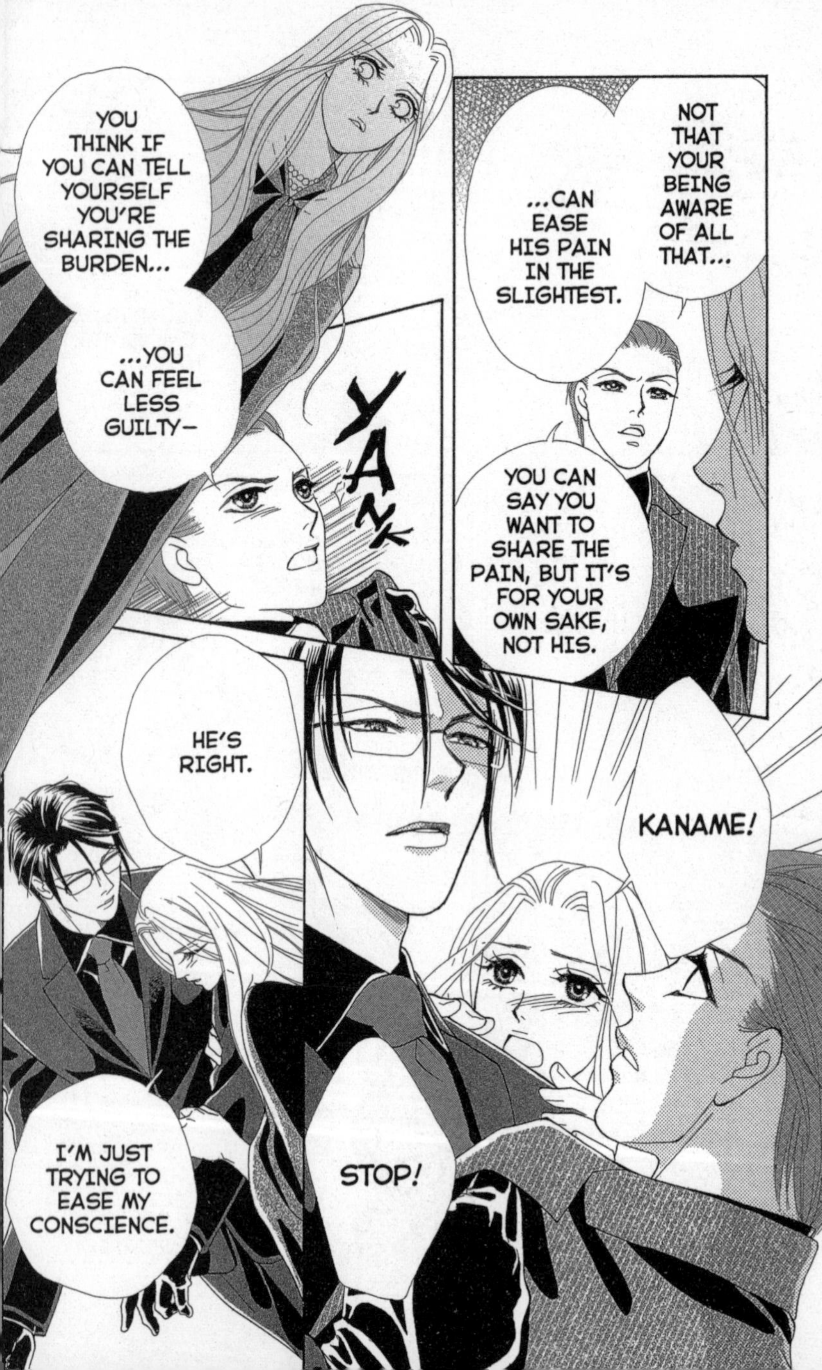
NOT THAT YOUR BEING AWARE OF ALL THAT...
...CAN EASE HIS PAIN IN THE SLIGHTEST.
YOU CAN SAY YOU WANT TO SHARE THE PAIN, BUT IT'S FOR YOUR OWN SAKE, NOT HIS.
YOU THINK IF YOU CAN TELL YOURSELF YOU'RE SHARING THE BURDEN...
...YOU CAN FEEL LESS GUILTY—
YANK
KANAME!
STOP!
HE'S RIGHT.
I'M JUST TRYING TO EASE MY CONSCIENCE.

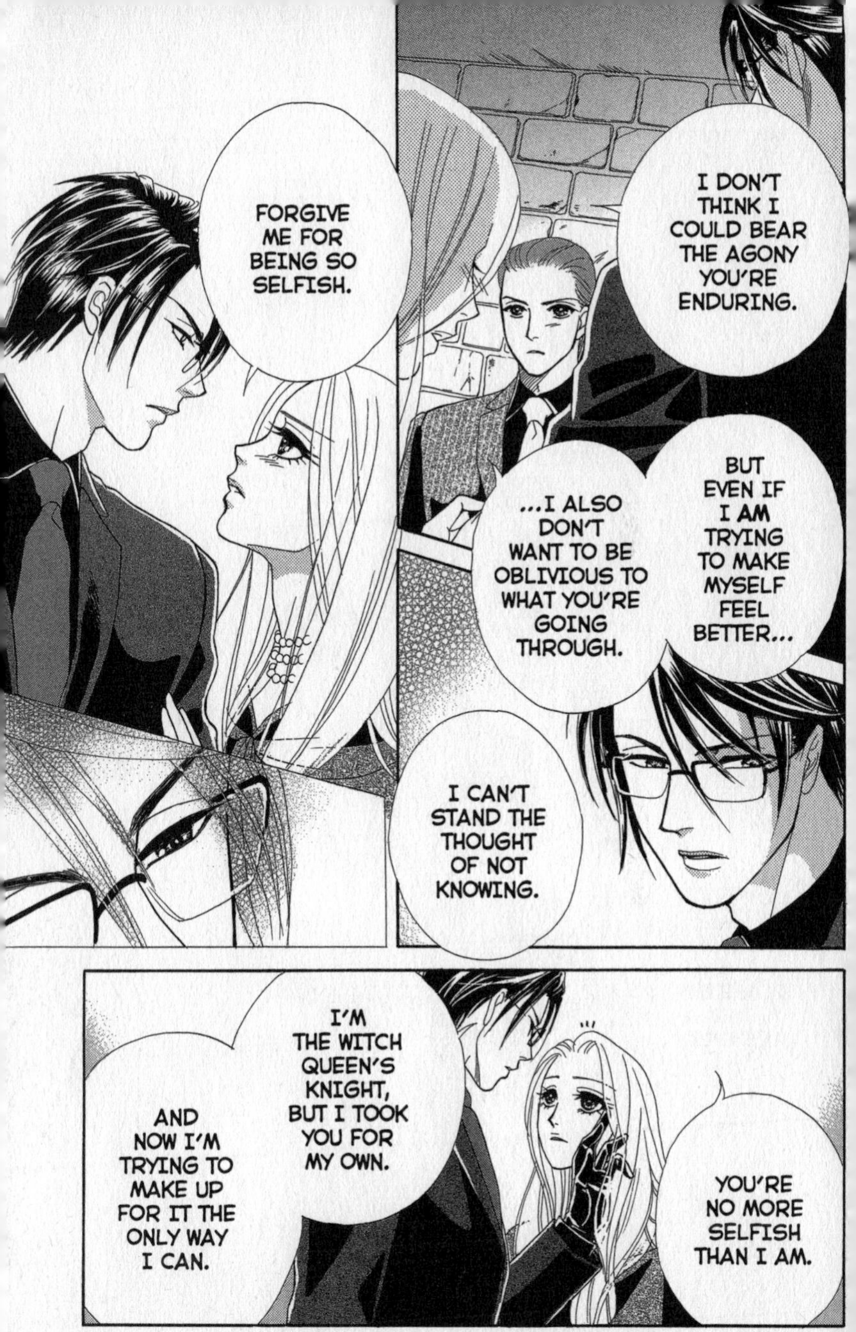
I DON'T THINK I COULD BEAR THE AGONY YOU'RE ENDURING.
BUT EVEN IF I AM TRYING TO MAKE MYSELF FEEL BETTER...
...I ALSO DON'T WANT TO BE OBLIVIOUS TO WHAT YOU'RE GOING THROUGH.
I CAN'T STAND THE THOUGHT OF NOT KNOWING.
FORGIVE ME FOR BEING SO SELFISH.
YOU'RE NO MORE SELFISH THAN I AM.
I'M THE WITCH QUEEN'S KNIGHT, BUT I TOOK YOU FOR MY OWN.
AND NOW I'M TRYING TO MAKE UP FOR IT THE ONLY WAY I CAN.

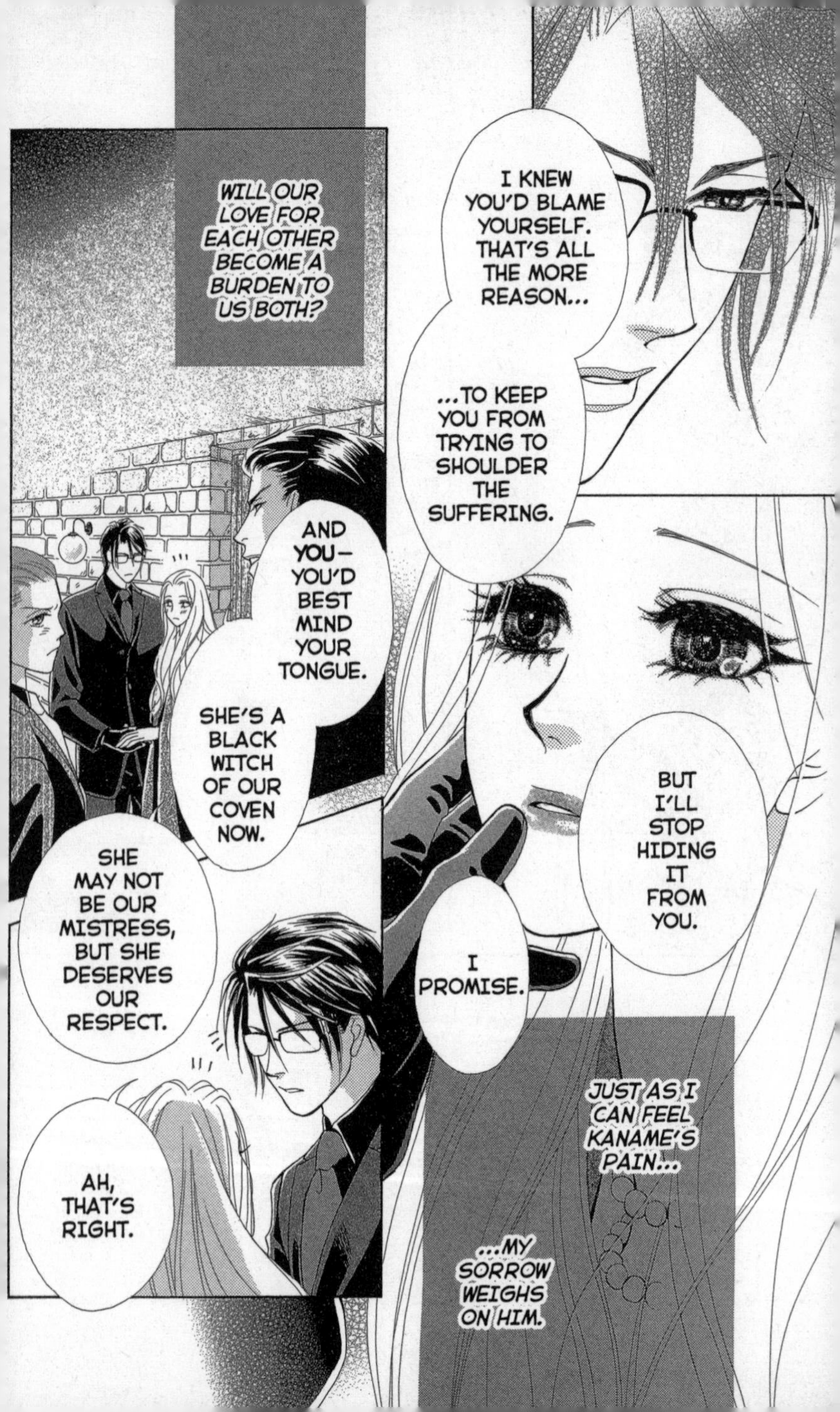
I KNEW YOU'D BLAME YOURSELF. THAT'S ALL THE MORE REASON...
...TO KEEP YOU FROM TRYING TO SHOULDER THE SUFFERING.
BUT I'LL STOP HIDING IT FROM YOU.
I PROMISE.
JUST AS I CAN FEEL KANAME'S PAIN...
...MY SORROW WEIGHS ON HIM.
WILL OUR LOVE FOR EACH OTHER BECOME A BURDEN TO US BOTH?
AND YOU—YOU'D BEST MIND YOUR TONGUE.
SHE'S A BLACK WITCH OF OUR COVEN NOW.
SHE MAY NOT BE OUR MISTRESS, BUT SHE DESERVES OUR RESPECT.
AH, THAT'S RIGHT.

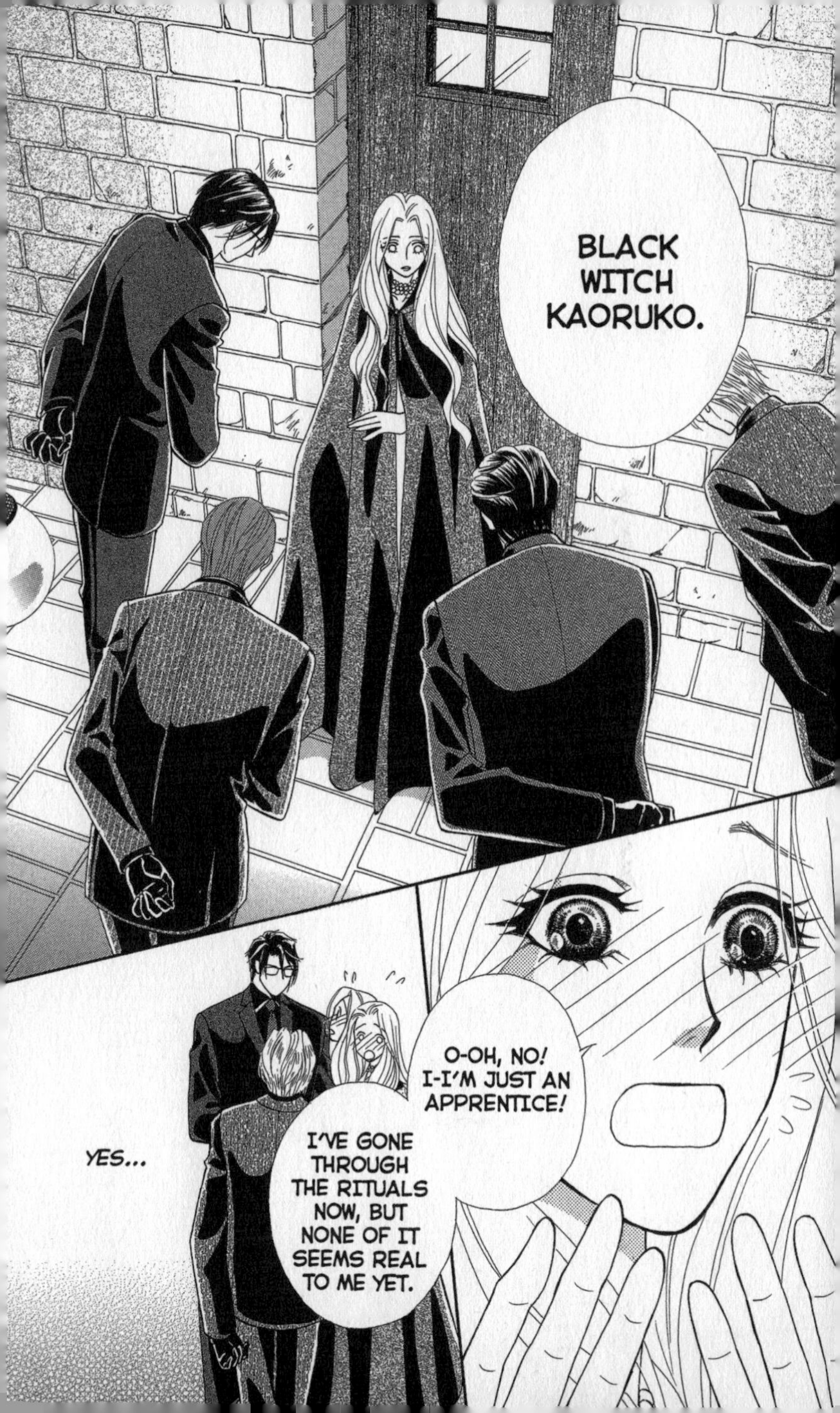
BLACK WITCH KAORUKO.
O-OH, NO! I-I'M JUST AN APPRENTICE!
I'VE GONE THROUGH THE RITUALS NOW, BUT NONE OF IT SEEMS REAL TO ME YET.
YES...

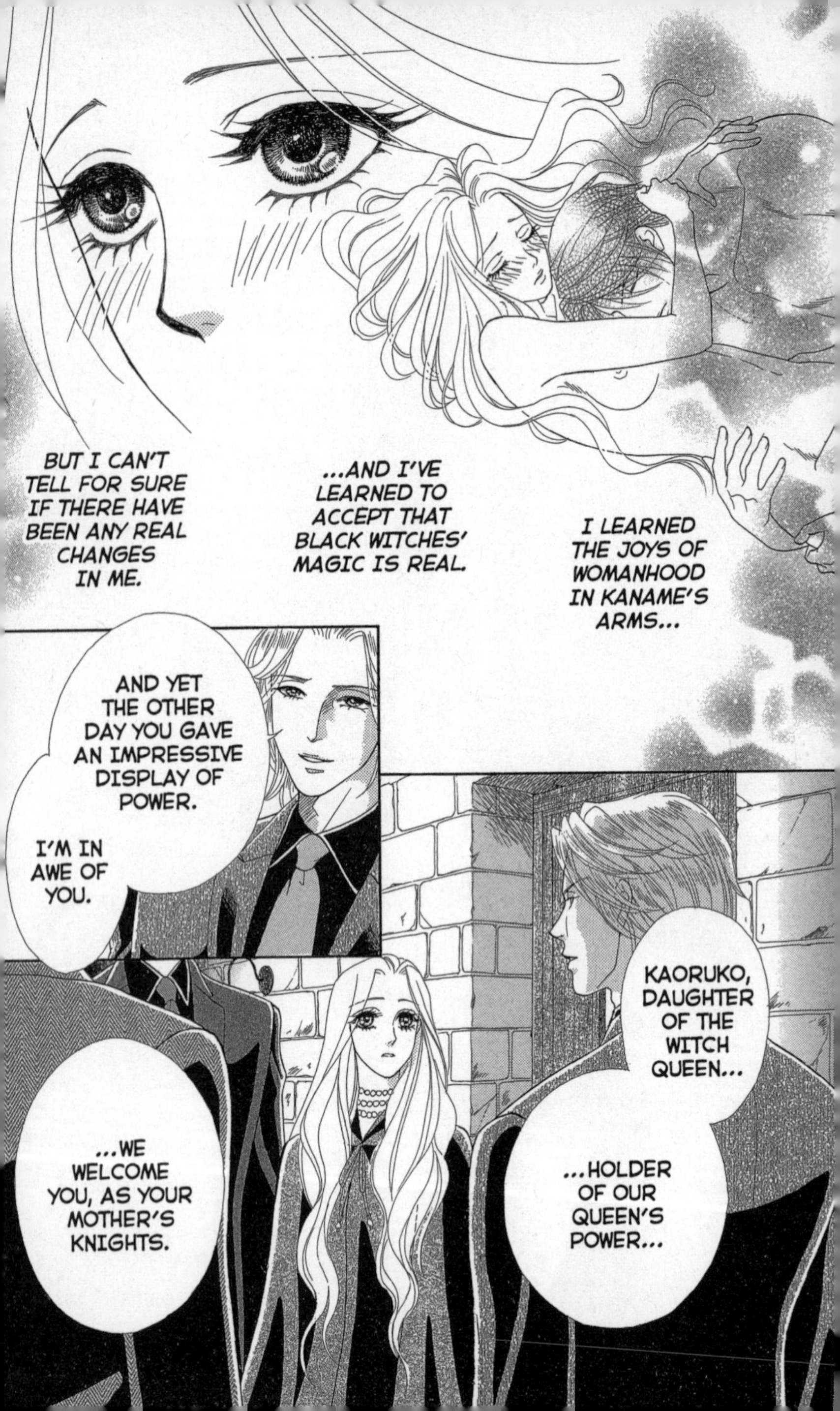
I LEARNED THE JOYS OF WOMANHOOD IN KANAME'S ARMS...
...AND I'VE LEARNED TO ACCEPT THAT BLACK WITCHES' MAGIC IS REAL.
BUT I CAN'T TELL FOR SURE IF THERE HAVE BEEN ANY REAL CHANGES IN ME.
AND YET THE OTHER DAY YOU GAVE AN IMPRESSIVE DISPLAY OF POWER.
I'M IN AWE OF YOU.
KAORUKO, DAUGHTER OF THE WITCH QUEEN...
...HOLDER OF OUR QUEEN'S POWER...
...WE WELCOME YOU, AS YOUR MOTHER'S KNIGHTS.

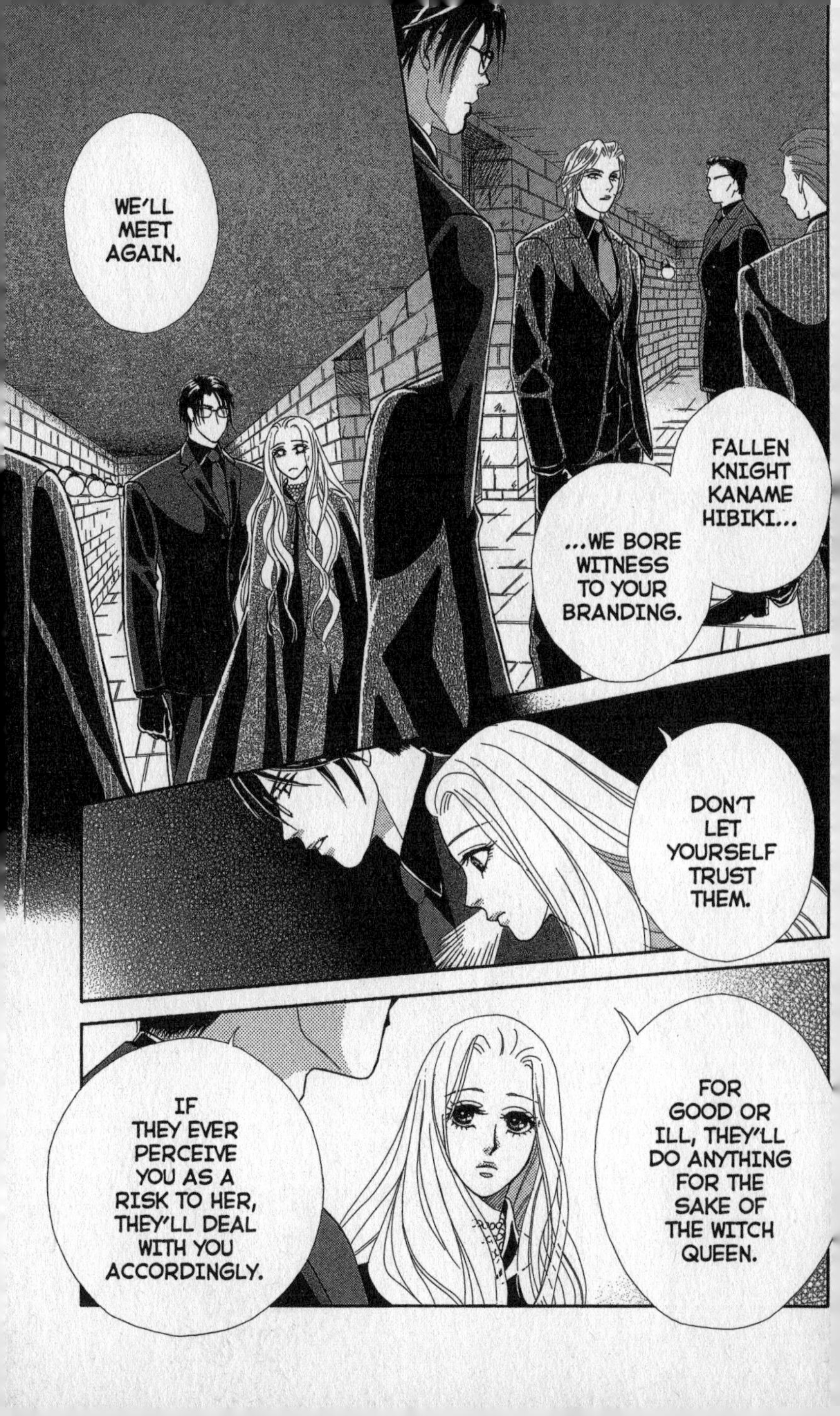
FALLEN KNIGHT KANAME HIBIKI...
...WE BORE WITNESS TO YOUR BRANDING.
WE'LL MEET AGAIN.
DON'T LET YOURSELF TRUST THEM.
FOR GOOD OR ILL, THEY'LL DO ANYTHING FOR THE SAKE OF THE WITCH QUEEN.
IF THEY EVER PERCEIVE YOU AS A RISK TO HER, THEY'LL DEAL WITH YOU ACCORDINGLY.

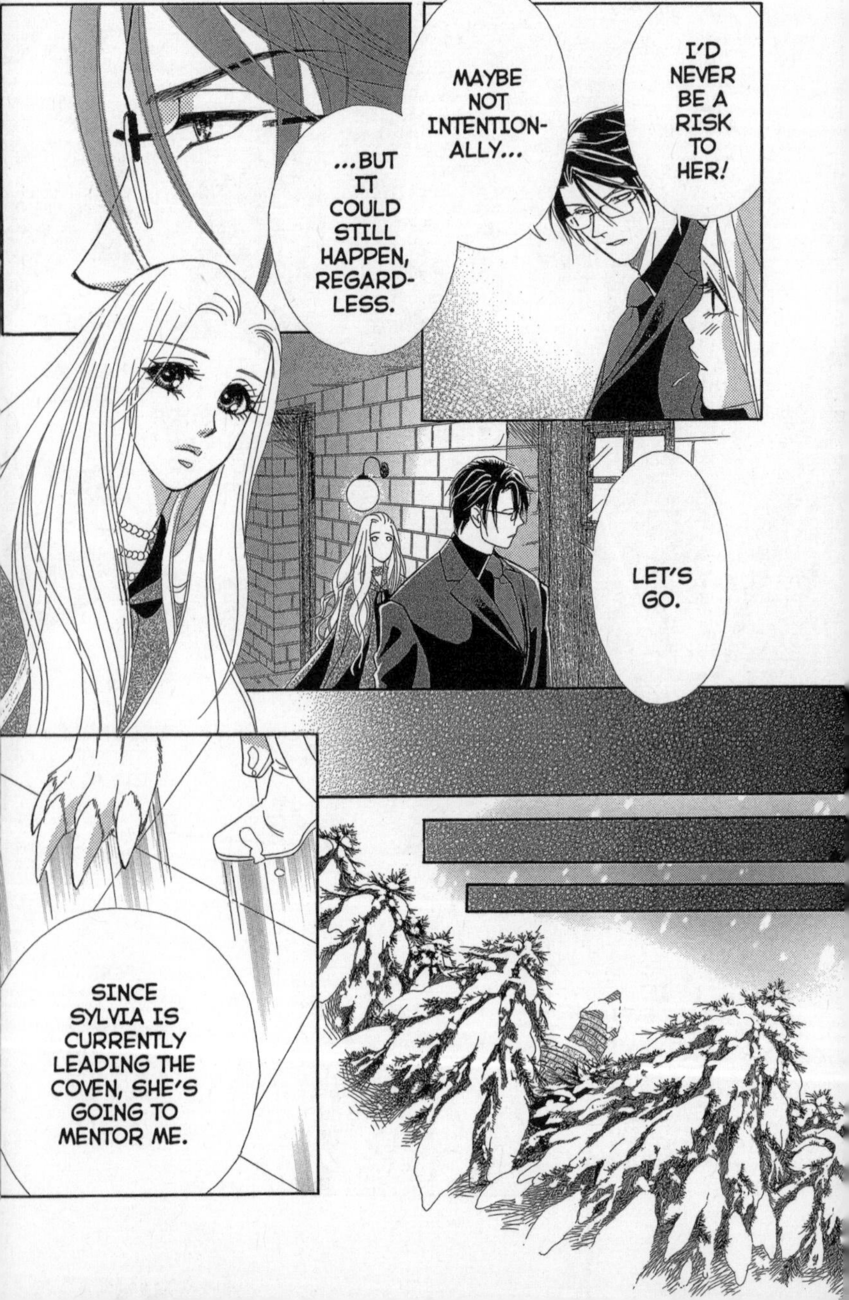
I'D NEVER BE A RISK TO HER!
MAYBE NOT INTENTION-ALLY...
...BUT IT COULD STILL HAPPEN, REGARD-LESS.
LET'S GO.
SINCE SYLVIA IS CURRENTLY LEADING THE COVEN, SHE'S GOING TO MENTOR ME.

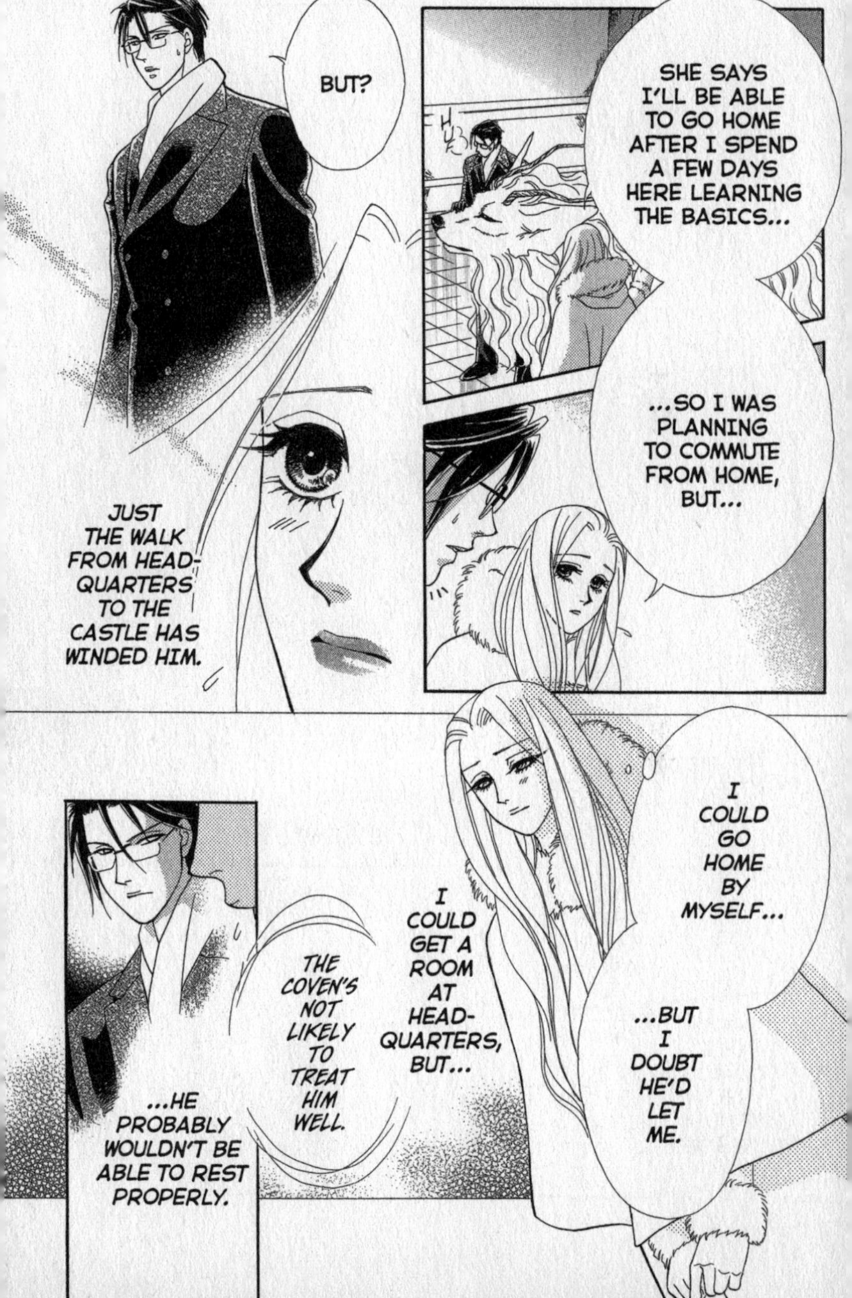
SHE SAYS I'LL BE ABLE TO GO HOME AFTER I SPEND A FEW DAYS HERE LEARNING THE BASICS...
...SO I WAS PLANNING TO COMMUTE FROM HOME, BUT...
BUT?
JUST THE WALK FROM HEAD-QUARTERS TO THE CASTLE HAS WINDED HIM.
I COULD GO HOME BY MYSELF...
...BUT I DOUBT HE'D LET ME.
I COULD GET A ROOM AT HEAD-QUARTERS, BUT...
THE COVEN'S NOT LIKELY TO TREAT HIM WELL.
...HE PROBABLY WOULDN'T BE ABLE TO REST PROPERLY.

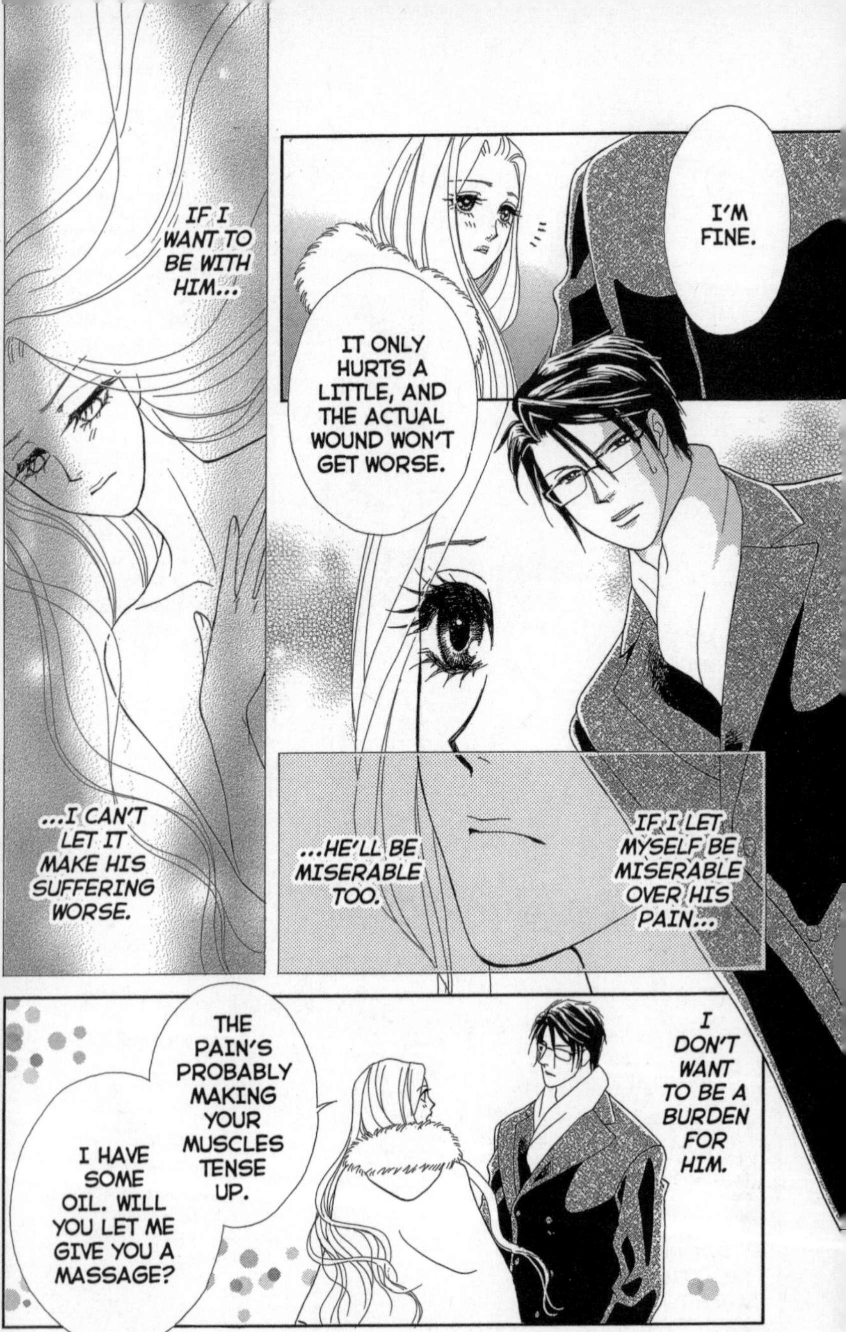
I'M FINE.
IT ONLY HURTS A LITTLE, AND THE ACTUAL WOUND WON'T GET WORSE.
IF I LET MYSELF BE MISERABLE OVER HIS PAIN...
...HE'LL BE MISERABLE TOO.
IF I WANT TO BE WITH HIM...
...I CAN'T LET IT MAKE HIS SUFFERING WORSE.
I DON'T WANT TO BE A BURDEN FOR HIM.
THE PAIN'S PROBABLY MAKING YOUR MUSCLES TENSE UP.
I HAVE SOME OIL. WILL YOU LET ME GIVE YOU A MASSAGE?

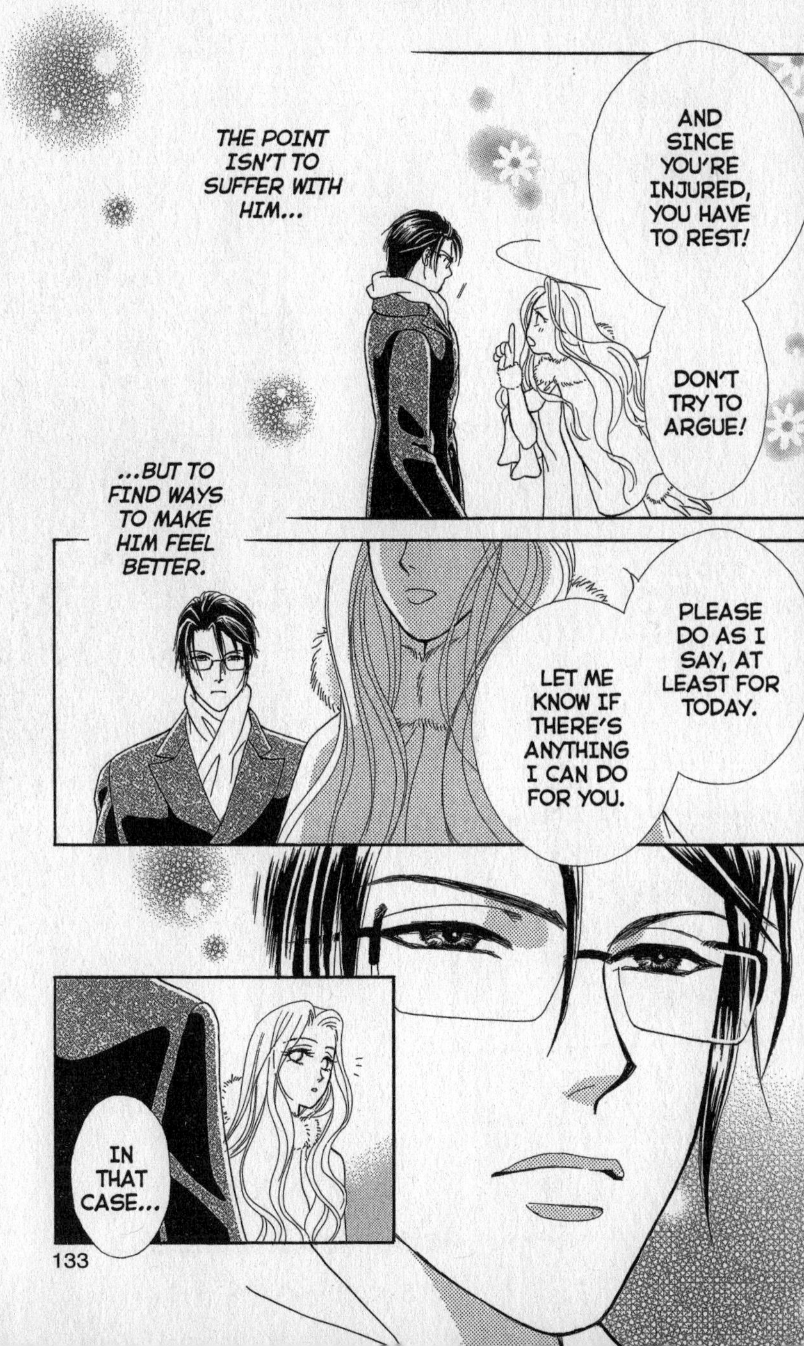
AND SINCE YOU'RE INJURED, YOU HAVE TO REST!
DON'T TRY TO ARGUE!
THE POINT ISN'T TO SUFFER WITH HIM...
PLEASE DO AS I SAY, AT LEAST FOR TODAY.
LET ME KNOW IF THERE'S ANYTHING I CAN DO FOR YOU.
...BUT TO FIND WAYS TO MAKE HIM FEEL BETTER.
IN THAT CASE...

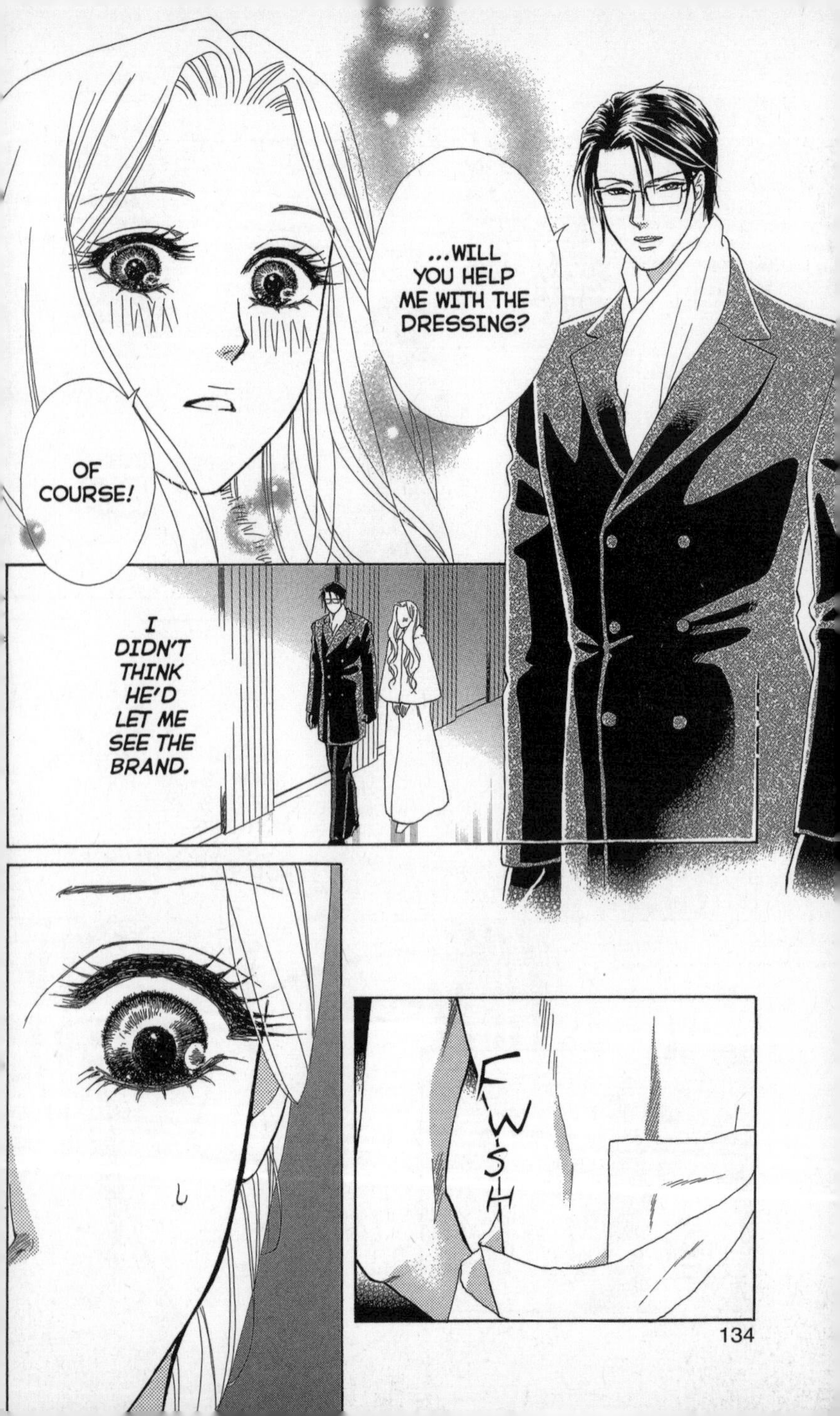
...WILL YOU HELP ME WITH THE DRESSING?
OF COURSE!
I DIDN'T THINK HE'D LET ME SEE THE BRAND.
FWSH

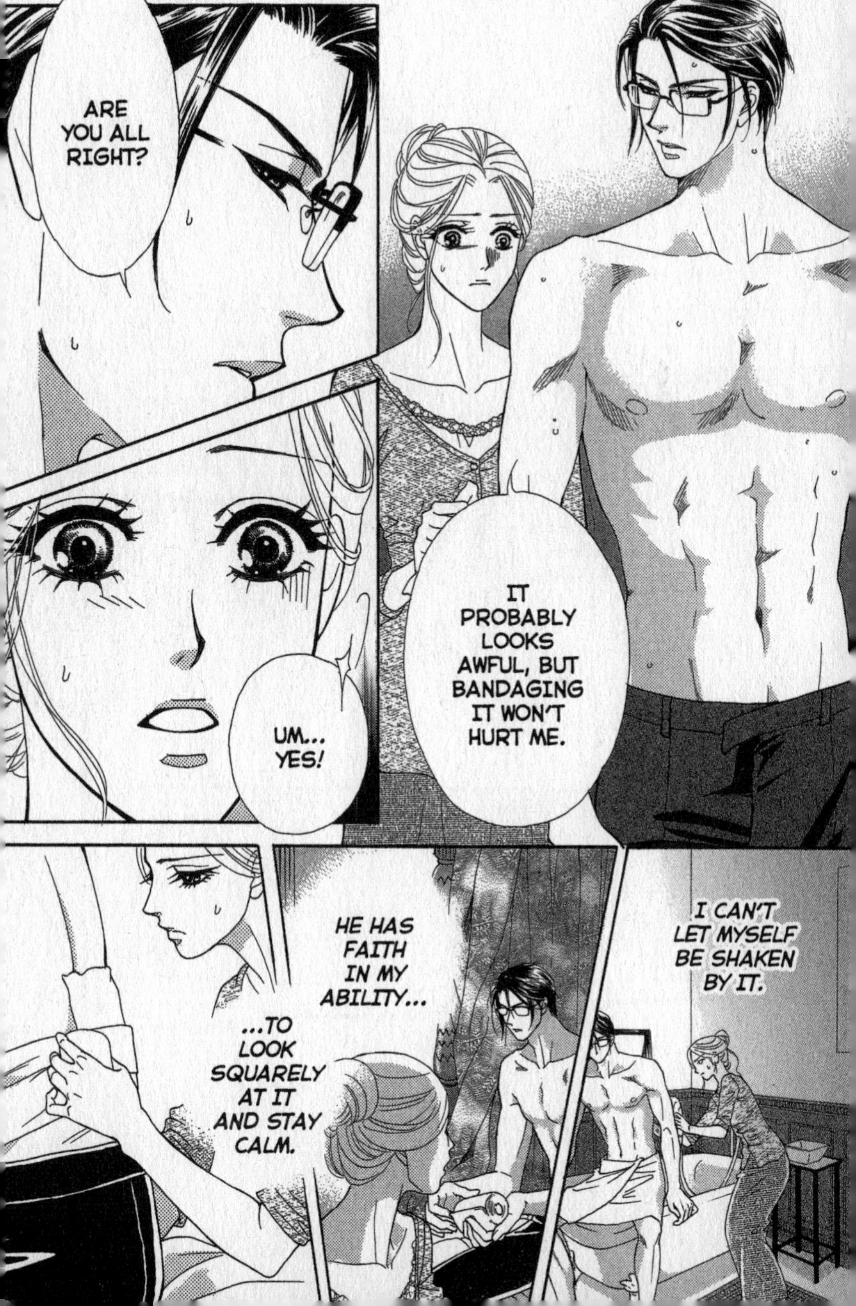
IT PROBABLY LOOKS AWFUL, BUT BANDAGING IT WON'T HURT ME.
ARE YOU ALL RIGHT?
UM... YES!
I CAN'T LET MYSELF BE SHAKEN BY IT.
HE HAS FAITH IN MY ABILITY...
...TO LOOK SQUARELY AT IT AND STAY CALM.

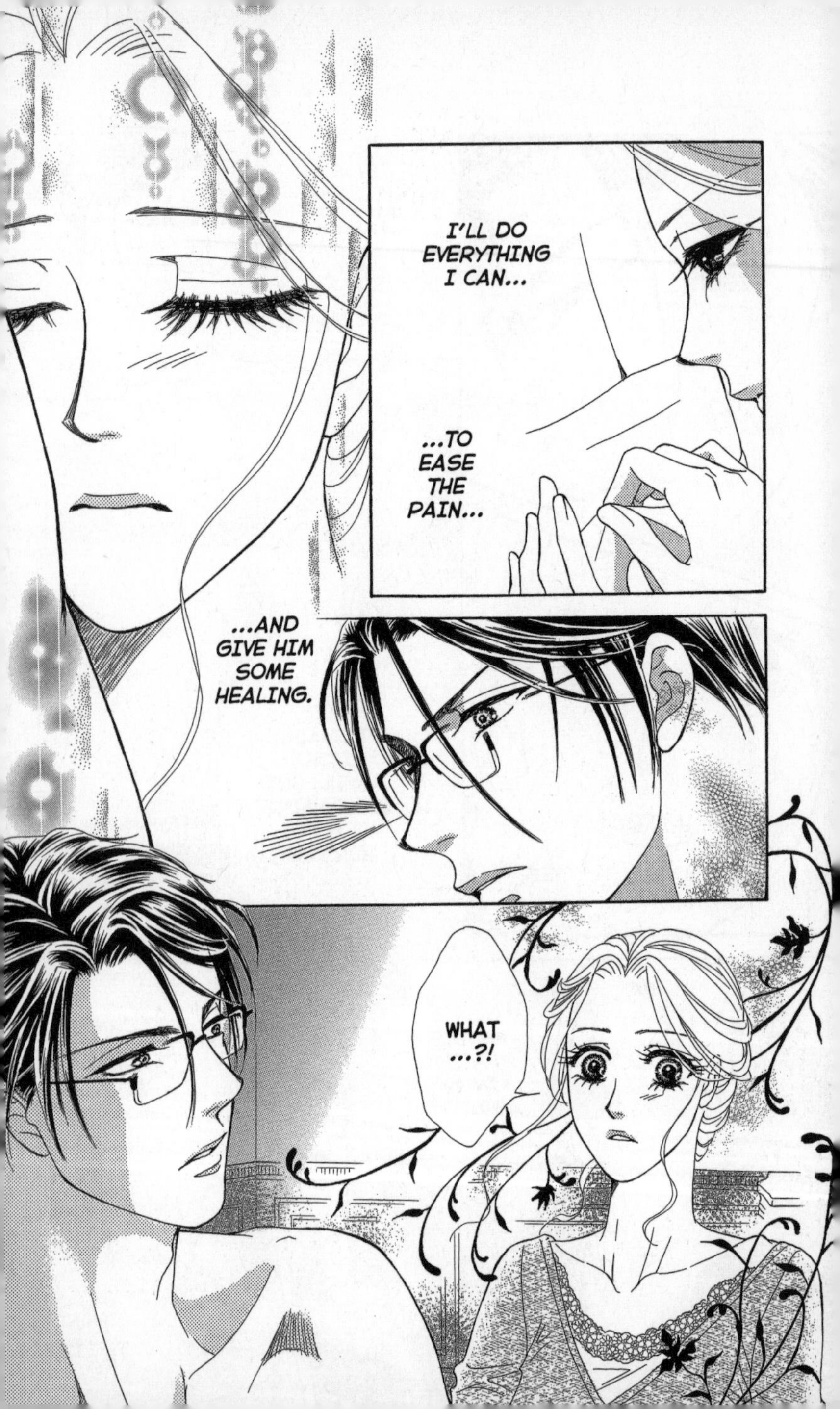
I'LL DO EVERYTHING I CAN...
...TO EASE THE PAIN...
...AND GIVE HIM SOME HEALING.
WHAT ...?!

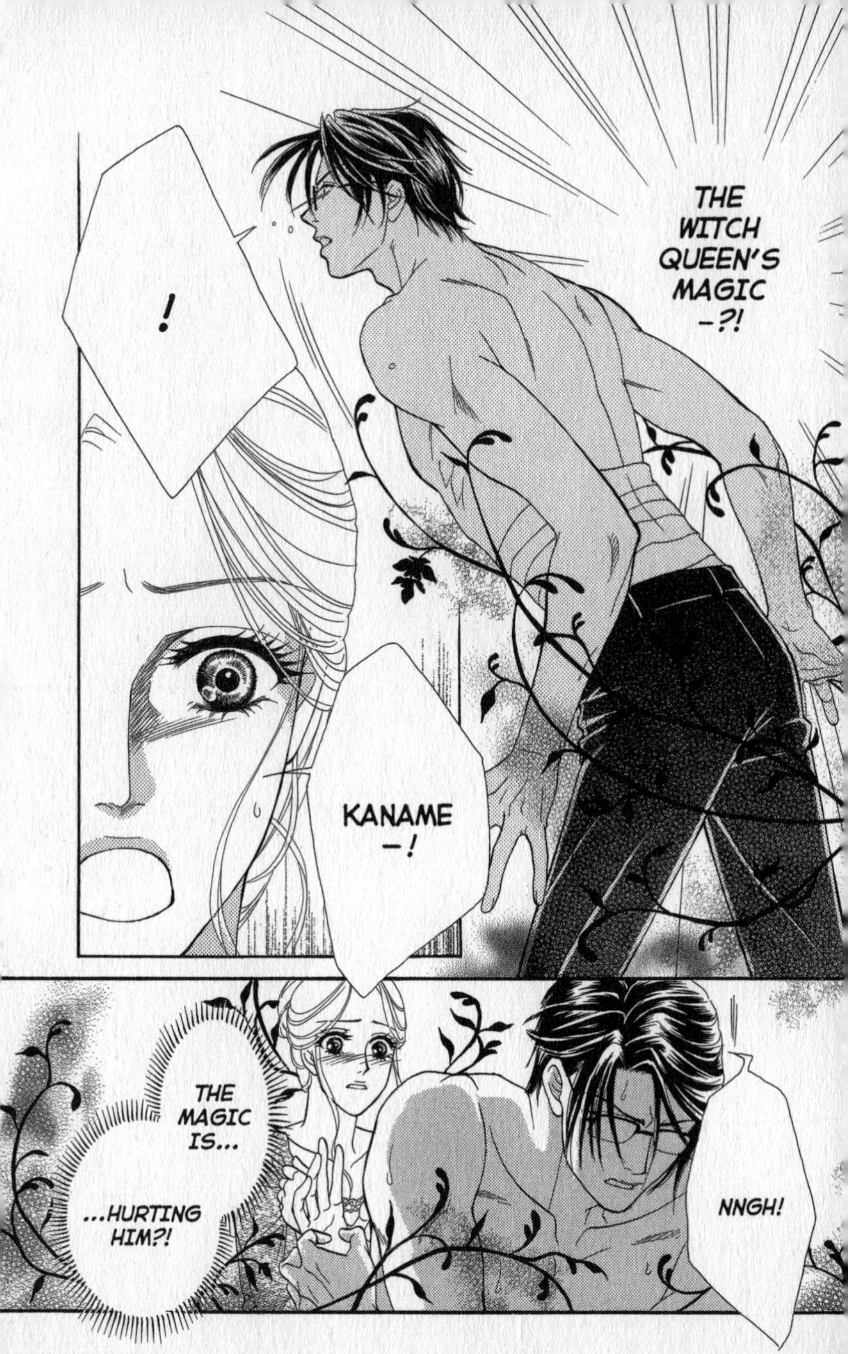
THE WITCH QUEEN'S MAGIC —?!
!
KANAME —!
NNGH!
THE MAGIC IS...
...HURTING HIM?!

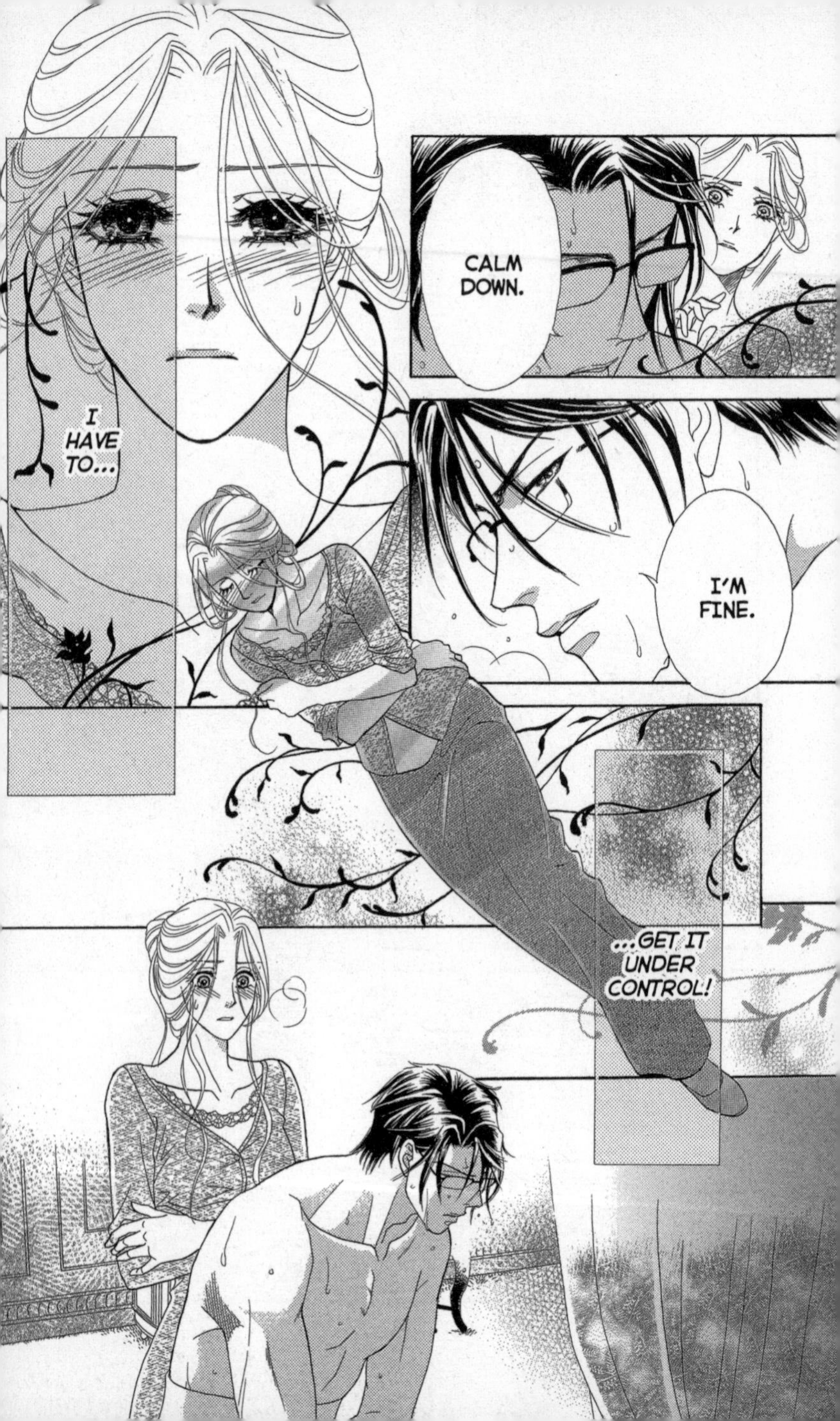
CALM DOWN.
I'M FINE.
I HAVE TO...
...GET IT UNDER CONTROL!

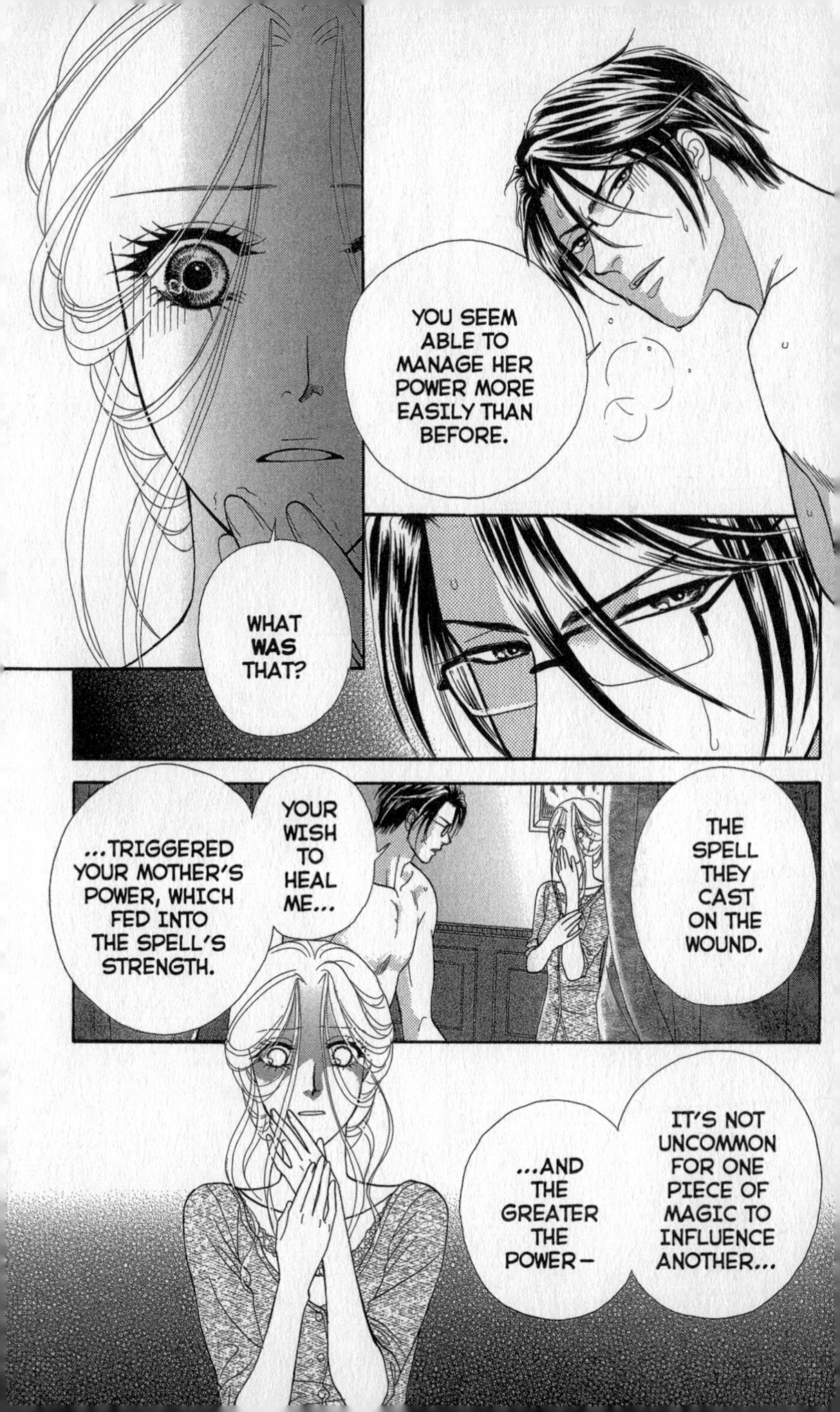
YOU SEEM ABLE TO MANAGE HER POWER MORE EASILY THAN BEFORE.
WHAT WAS THAT?
THE SPELL THEY CAST ON THE WOUND.
YOUR WISH TO HEAL ME...
...TRIGGERED YOUR MOTHER'S POWER, WHICH FED INTO THE SPELL'S STRENGTH.
IT'S NOT UNCOMMON FOR ONE PIECE OF MAGIC TO INFLUENCE ANOTHER...
...AND THE GREATER THE POWER—

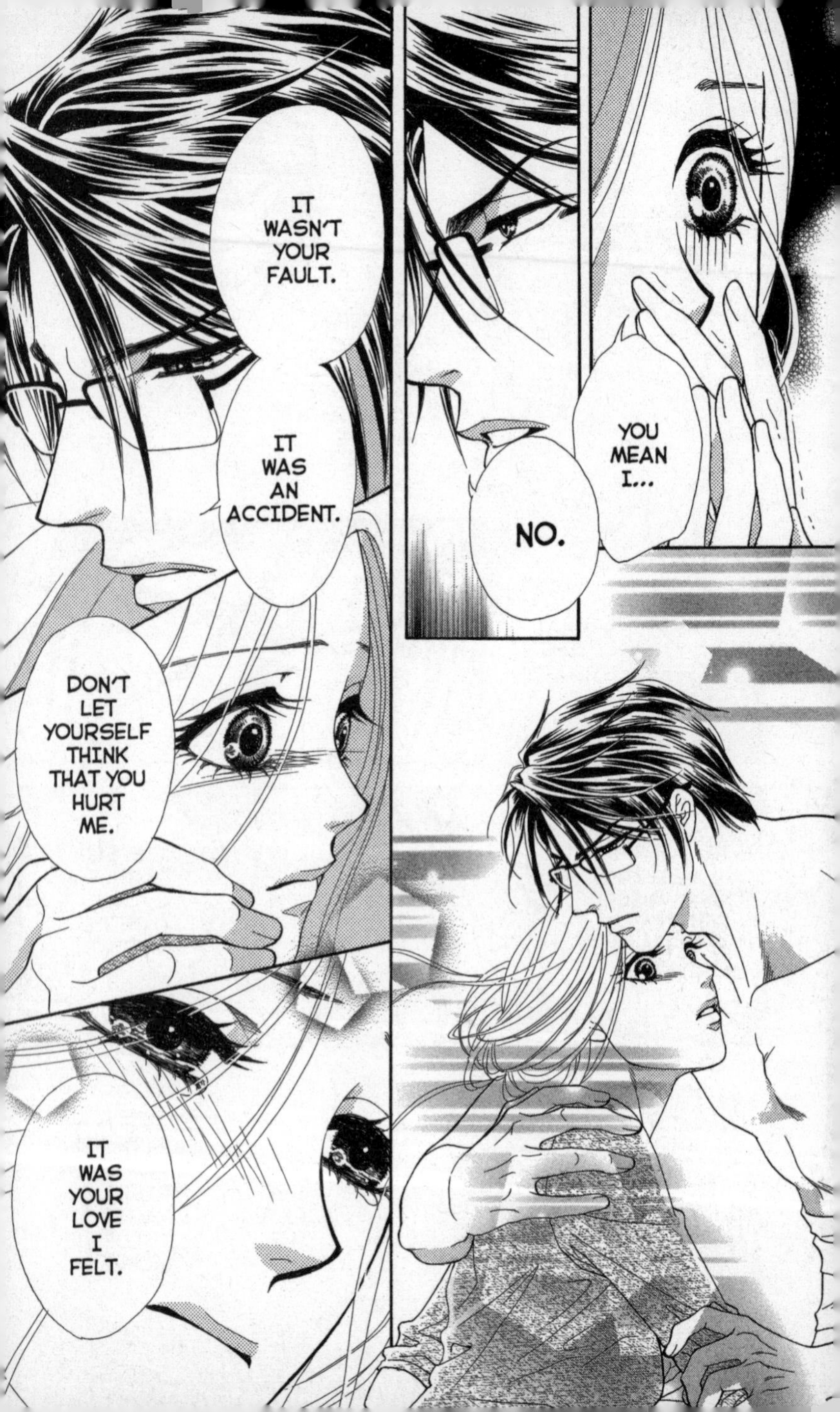

YOU MEAN I...
NO.
IT WASN'T YOUR FAULT.
IT WAS AN ACCIDENT.
DON'T LET YOURSELF THINK THAT YOU HURT ME.
IT WAS YOUR LOVE I FELT.

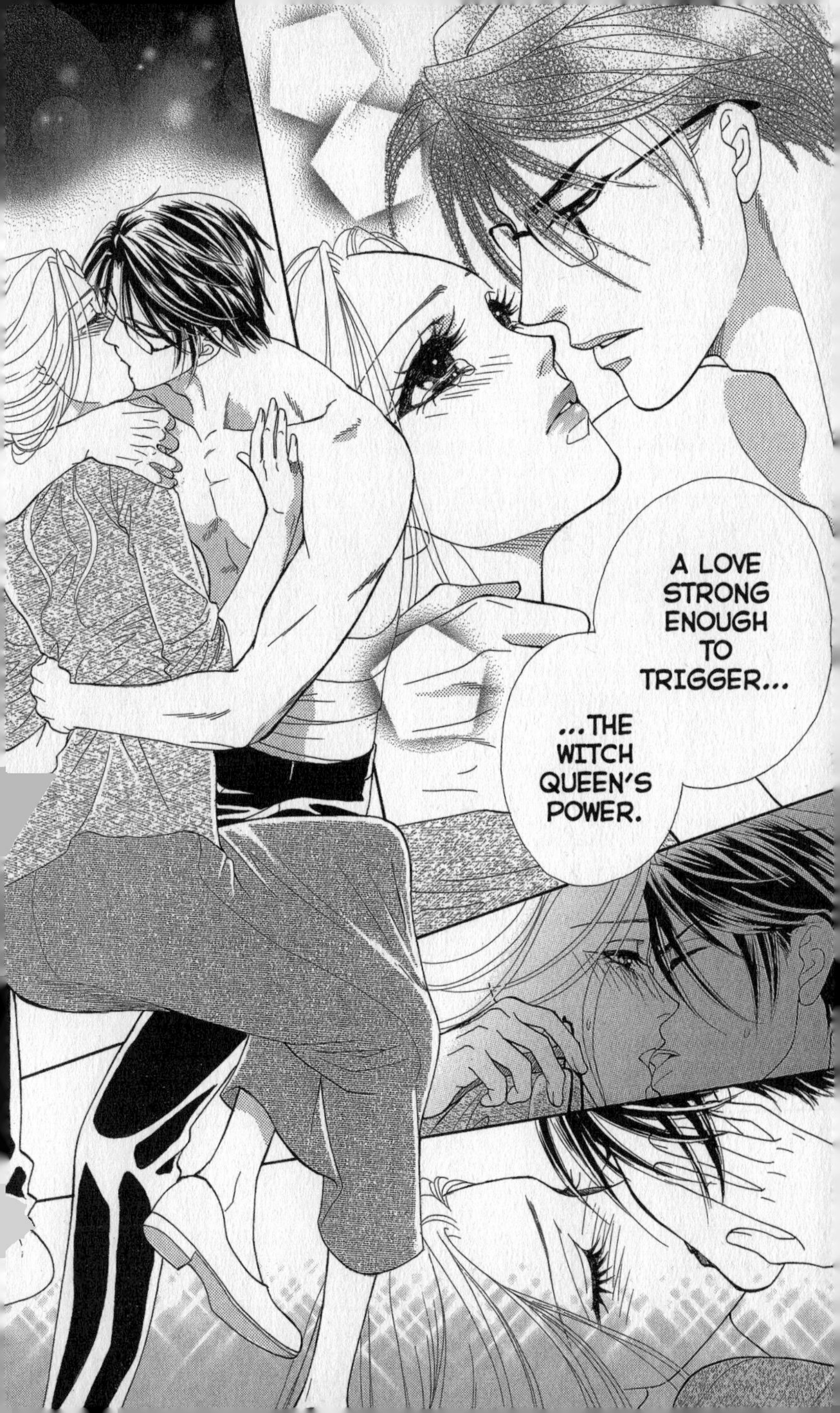
A LOVE STRONG ENOUGH TO TRIGGER...
...THE WITCH QUEEN'S POWER.

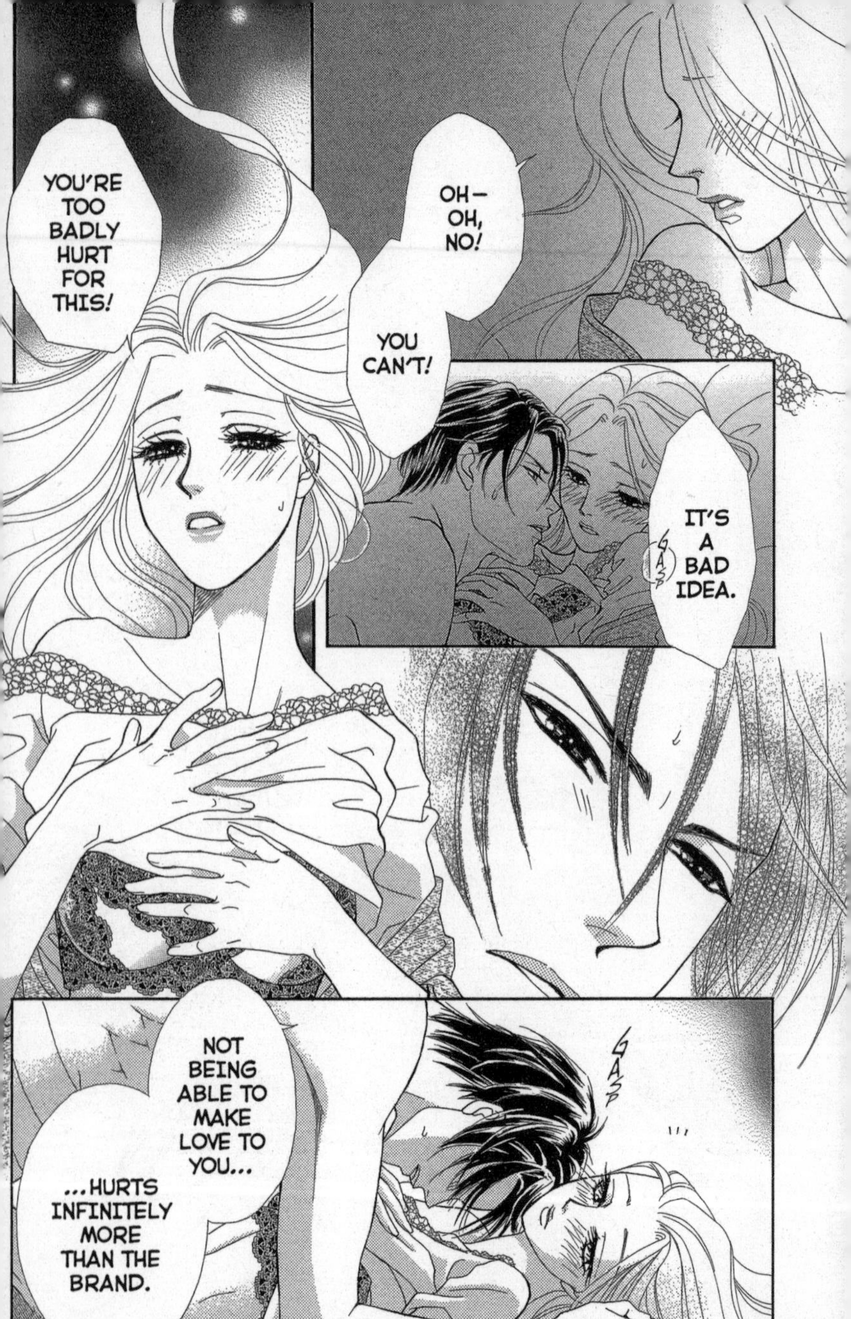
OH— OH, NO!
YOU CAN'T!
GASP
IT'S A BAD IDEA.
YOU'RE TOO BADLY HURT FOR THIS!
GASP
NOT BEING ABLE TO MAKE LOVE TO YOU...
...HURTS INFINITELY MORE THAN THE BRAND.

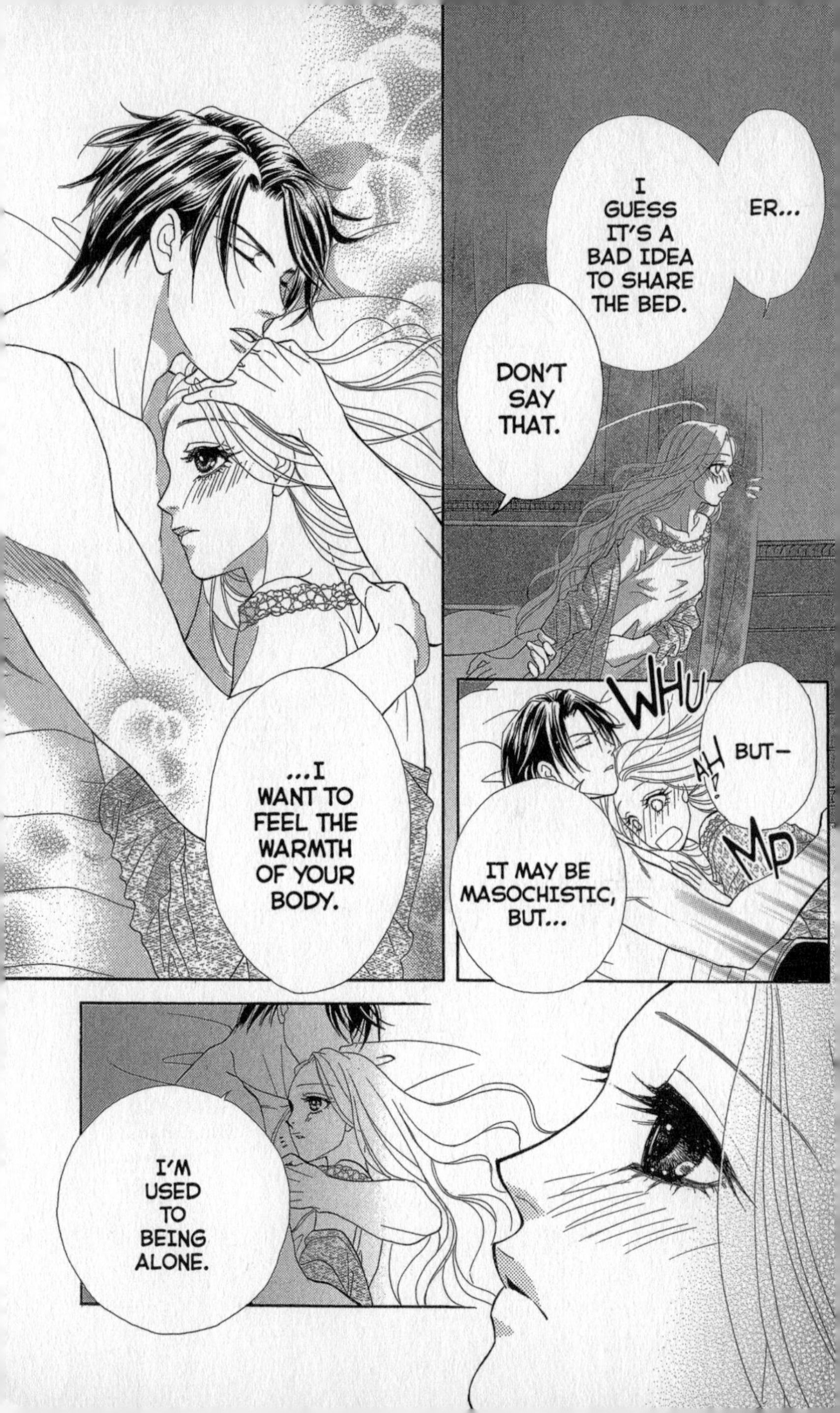
ER...
I GUESS IT'S A BAD IDEA TO SHARE THE BED.
DON'T SAY THAT.
BUT—
WHU
AH?!
MP
IT MAY BE MASOCHISTIC, BUT...
...I WANT TO FEEL THE WARMTH OF YOUR BODY.
I'M USED TO BEING ALONE.

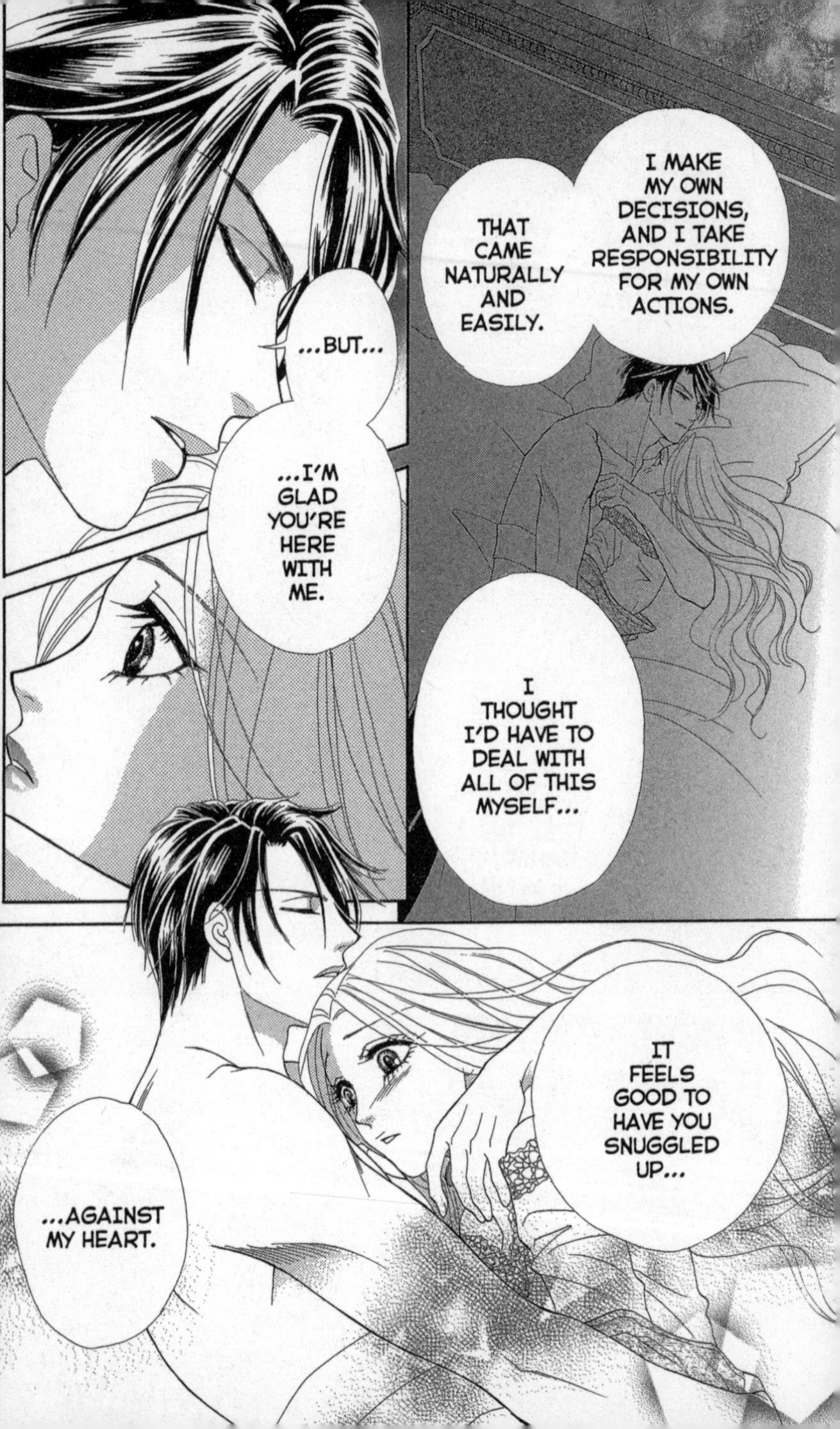
I MAKE MY OWN DECISIONS, AND I TAKE RESPONSIBILITY FOR MY OWN ACTIONS.
THAT CAME NATURALLY AND EASILY.
I THOUGHT I'D HAVE TO DEAL WITH ALL OF THIS MYSELF...
...BUT...
...I'M GLAD YOU'RE HERE WITH ME.
IT FEELS GOOD TO HAVE YOU SNUGGLED UP...
...AGAINST MY HEART.

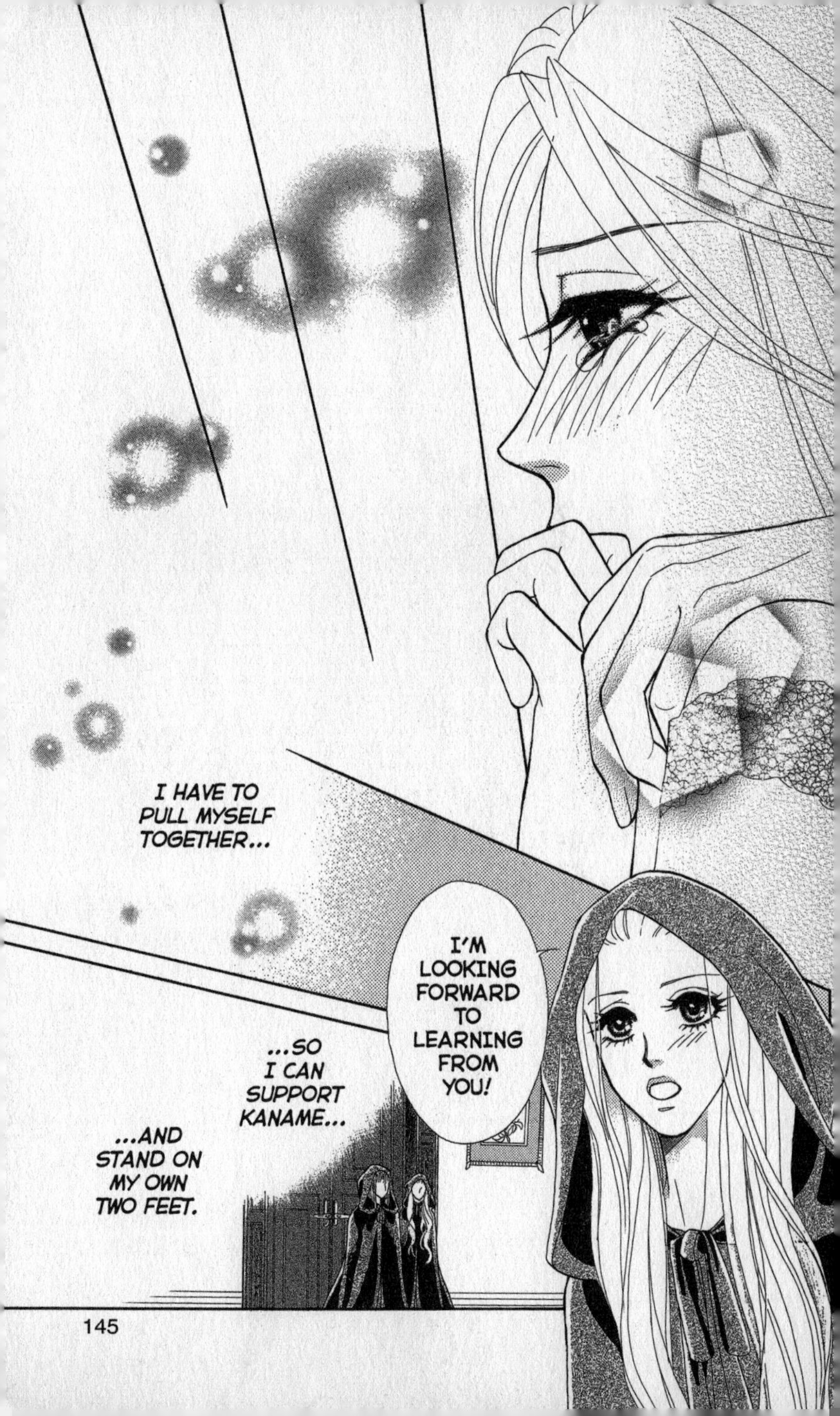
I HAVE TO PULL MYSELF TOGETHER...
I'M LOOKING FORWARD TO LEARNING FROM YOU!
...SO I CAN SUPPORT KANAME...
...AND STAND ON MY OWN TWO FEET.

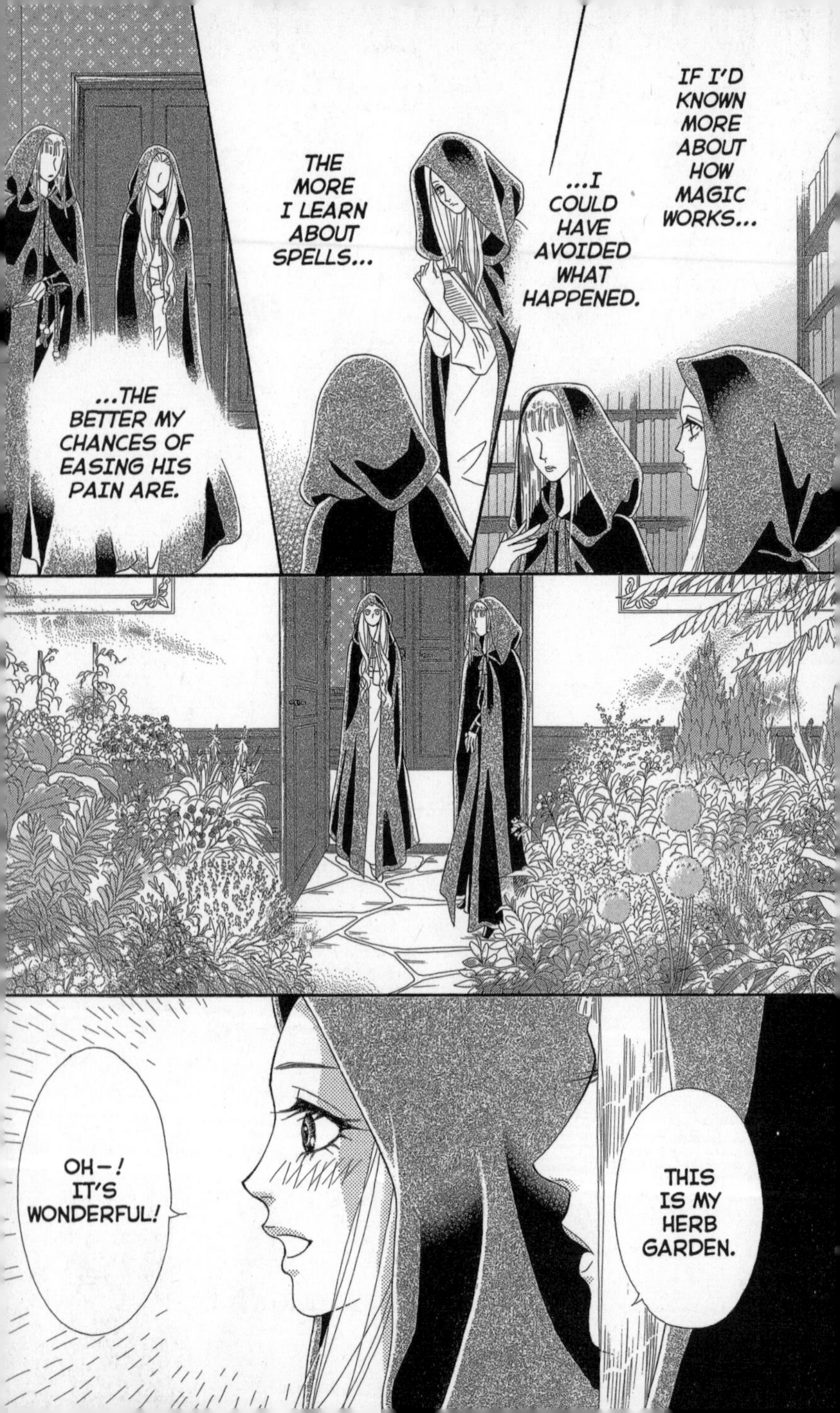
IF I'D KNOWN MORE ABOUT HOW MAGIC WORKS...
...I COULD HAVE AVOIDED WHAT HAPPENED.
THE MORE I LEARN ABOUT SPELLS...
...THE BETTER MY CHANCES OF EASING HIS PAIN ARE.
THIS IS MY HERB GARDEN.
OH—! IT'S WONDERFUL!

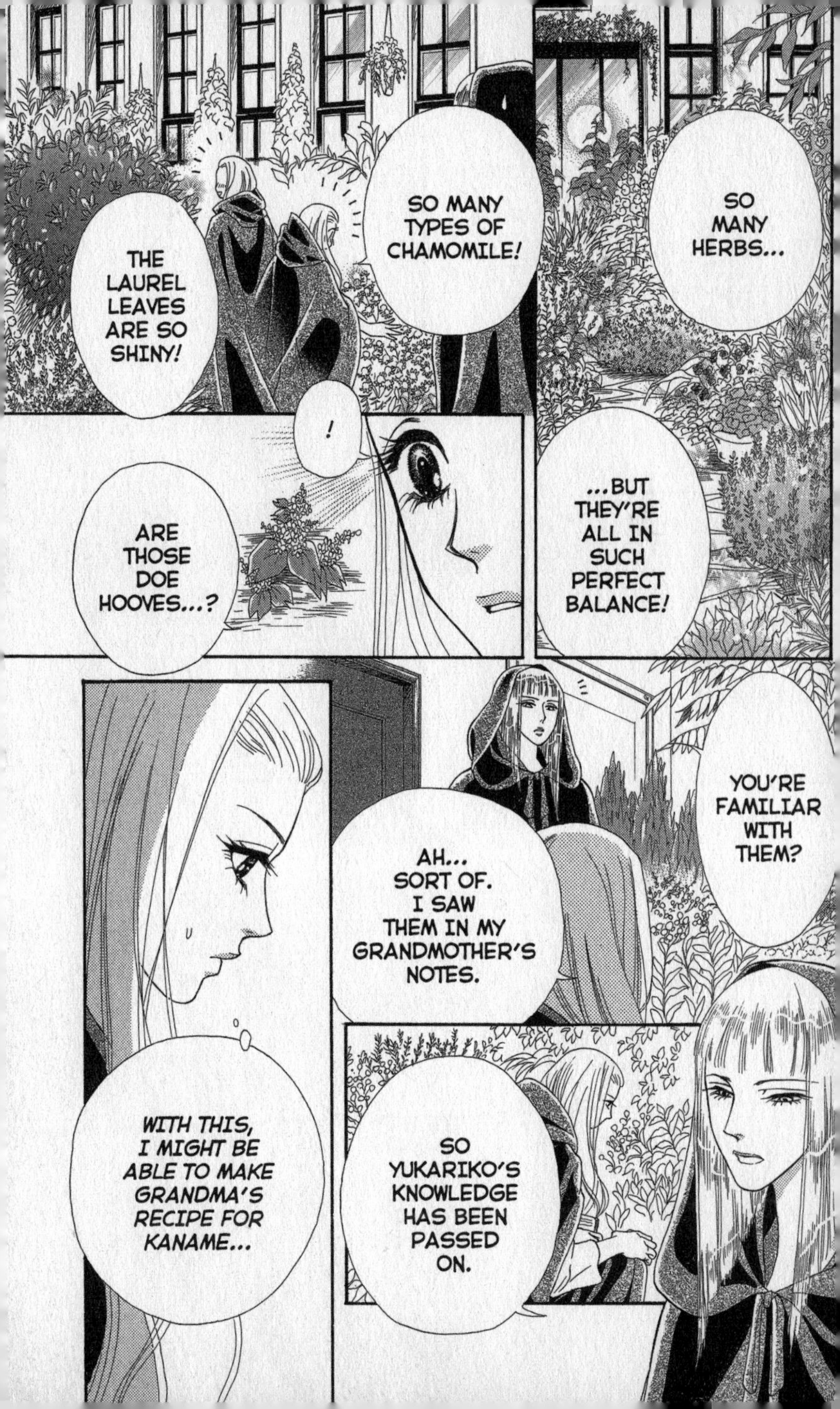
SO MANY HERBS...
...BUT THEY'RE ALL IN SUCH PERFECT BALANCE!
SO MANY TYPES OF CHAMOMILE!
THE LAUREL LEAVES ARE SO SHINY!
!
ARE THOSE DOE HOOVES...?
YOU'RE FAMILIAR WITH THEM?
AH... SORT OF. I SAW THEM IN MY GRANDMOTHER'S NOTES.
SO YUKARIKO'S KNOWLEDGE HAS BEEN PASSED ON.
WITH THIS, I MIGHT BE ABLE TO MAKE GRANDMA'S RECIPE FOR KANAME...

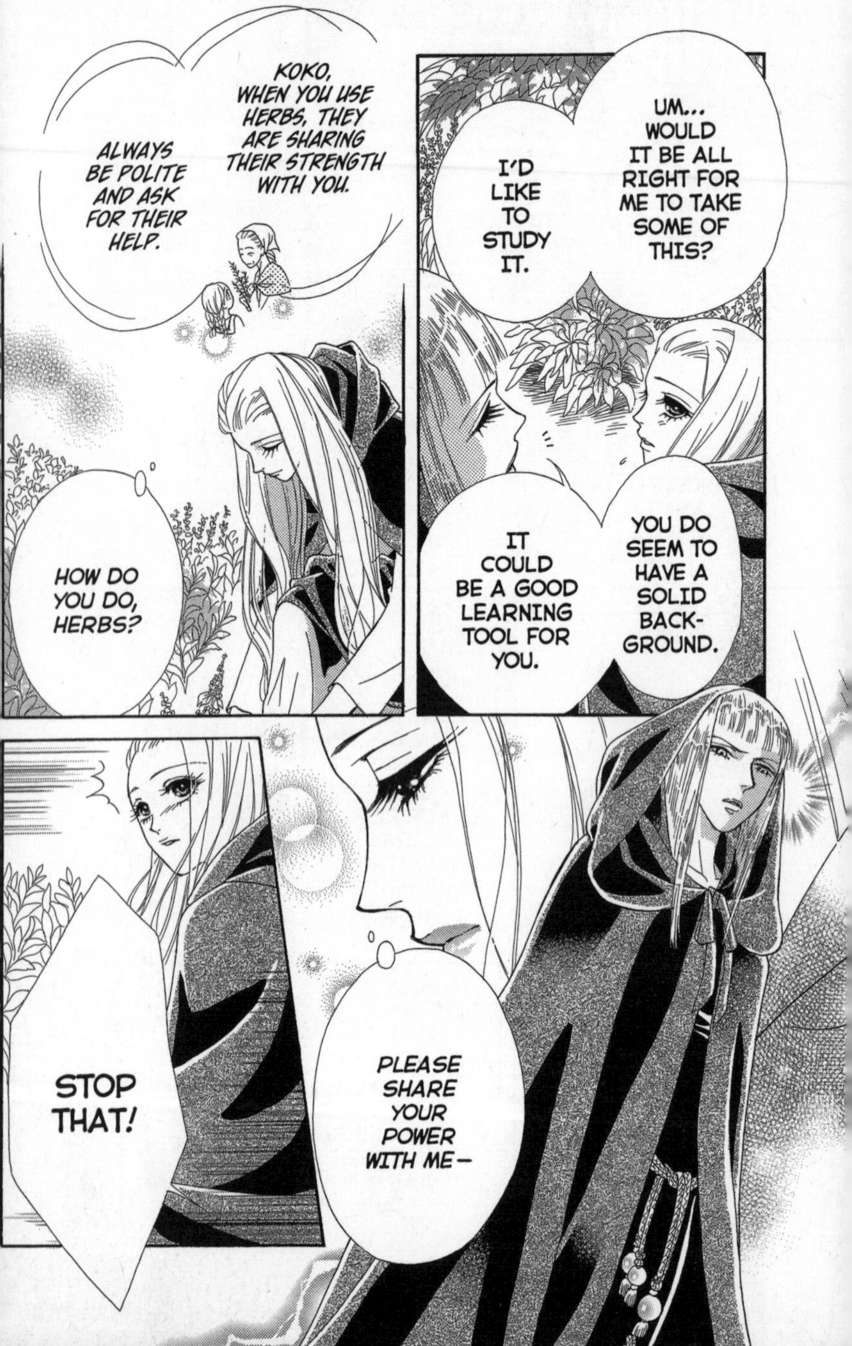
UM... WOULD IT BE ALL RIGHT FOR ME TO TAKE SOME OF THIS?
I'D LIKE TO STUDY IT.
YOU DO SEEM TO HAVE A SOLID BACK-GROUND.
IT COULD BE A GOOD LEARNING TOOL FOR YOU.
KOKO, WHEN YOU USE HERBS, THEY ARE SHARING THEIR STRENGTH WITH YOU.
ALWAYS BE POLITE AND ASK FOR THEIR HELP.
HOW DO YOU DO, HERBS?
PLEASE SHARE YOUR POWER WITH ME—
STOP THAT!

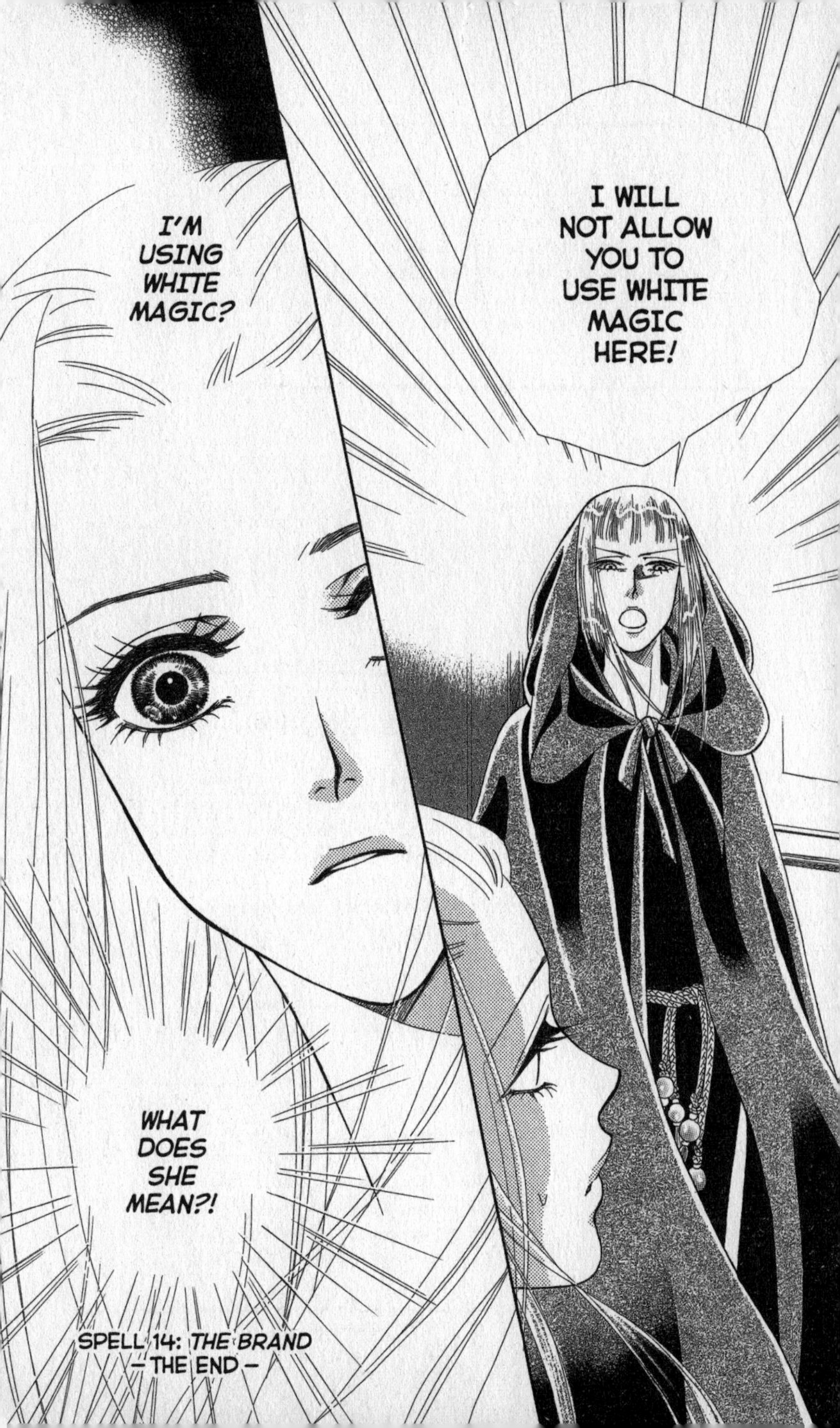
I WILL NOT ALLOW YOU TO USE WHITE MAGIC HERE!
I'M USING WHITE MAGIC?
WHAT DOES SHE MEAN?!
SPELL 14: THE BRAND
–THE END–

– THE BRAND –

The knights said that fallen knights are treated worse than animals, but my cat is treated like royalty. So even if you're getting worse treatment than a cat, you could still be pretty well off!

– CONTROL AND CHARM –

This was my vague plan: when Koko was still a virgin (a white witch), her skin would mostly be kept covered, and there'd be a sort of innocence and purity to her sexuality. When she lost her virginity and became a black witch, she'd become more overtly sexy and flaunt her gorgeous body.

I say the plan was "vague" because it turned out there were times when I just couldn't help myself. (Heh heh)

Until now, since I couldn't have sexiness in the actual story, it revealed itself in the title page art. Now that I can make her look sexier in the story, I still find myself doing things like a color drawing of a hand touching her butt or a close-up shot of a hand massaging her breast. I keep catching myself going overboard. (Heh heh)

HEY!

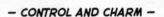

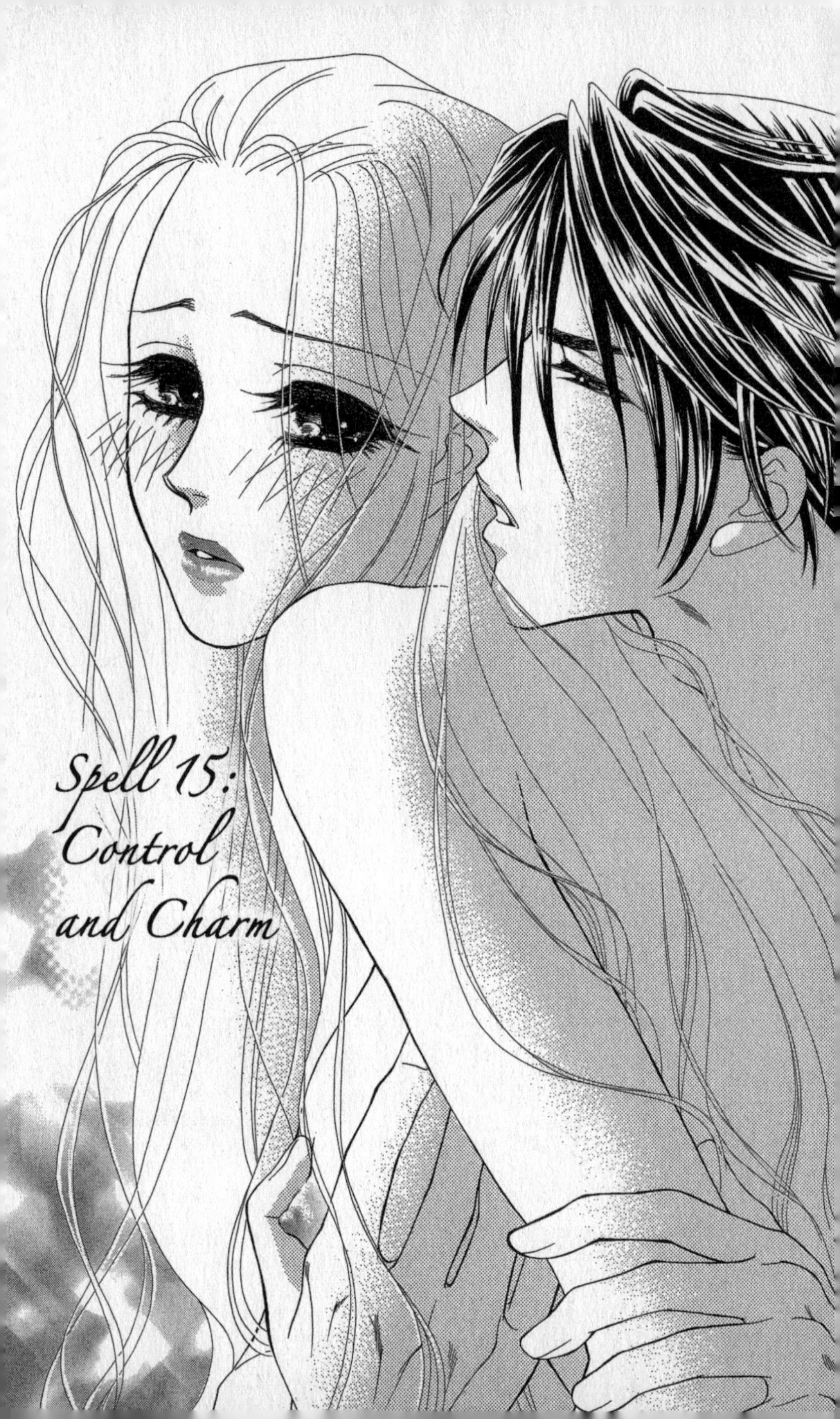
Spell 15:
Control
and Charm

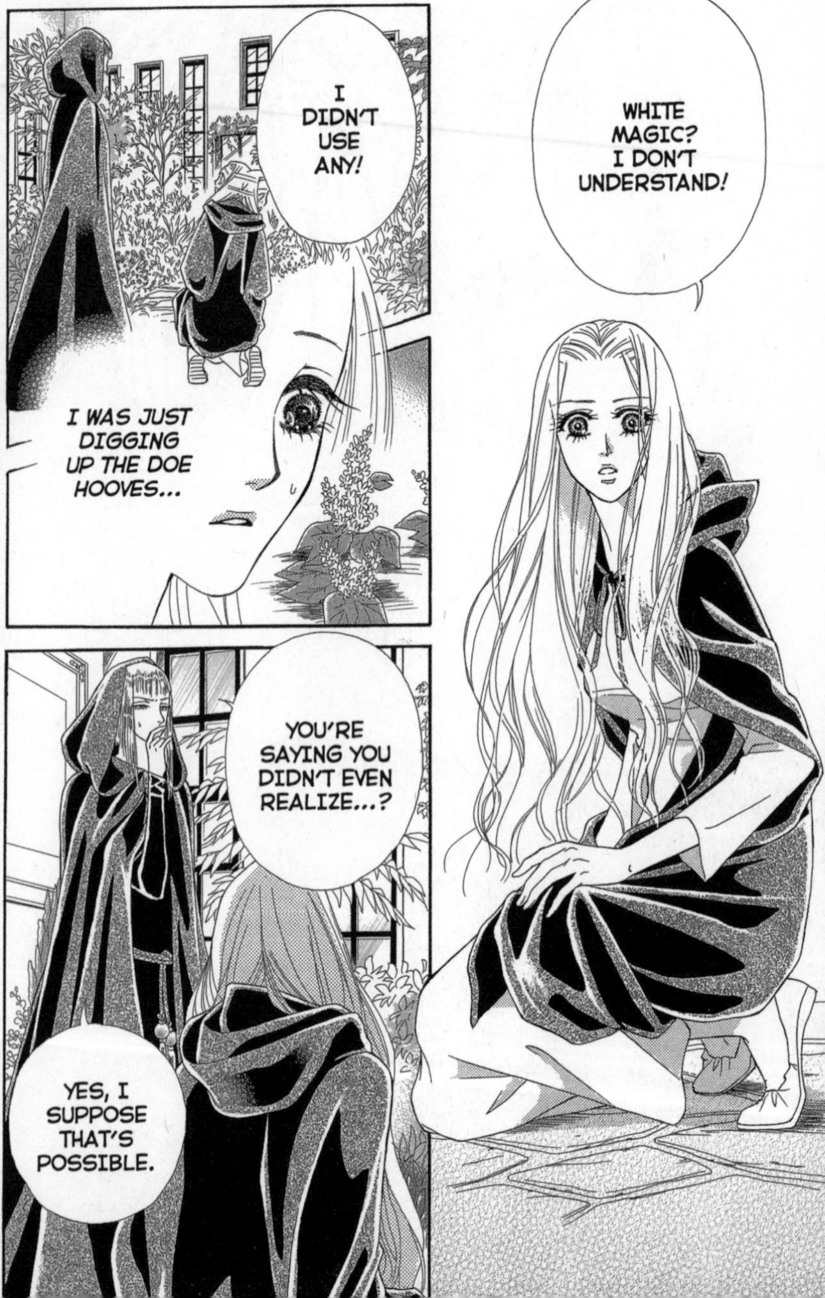
WHITE MAGIC? I DON'T UNDERSTAND!
I DIDN'T USE ANY!
I WAS JUST DIGGING UP THE DOE HOOVES...
YOU'RE SAYING YOU DIDN'T EVEN REALIZE...?
YES, I SUPPOSE THAT'S POSSIBLE.

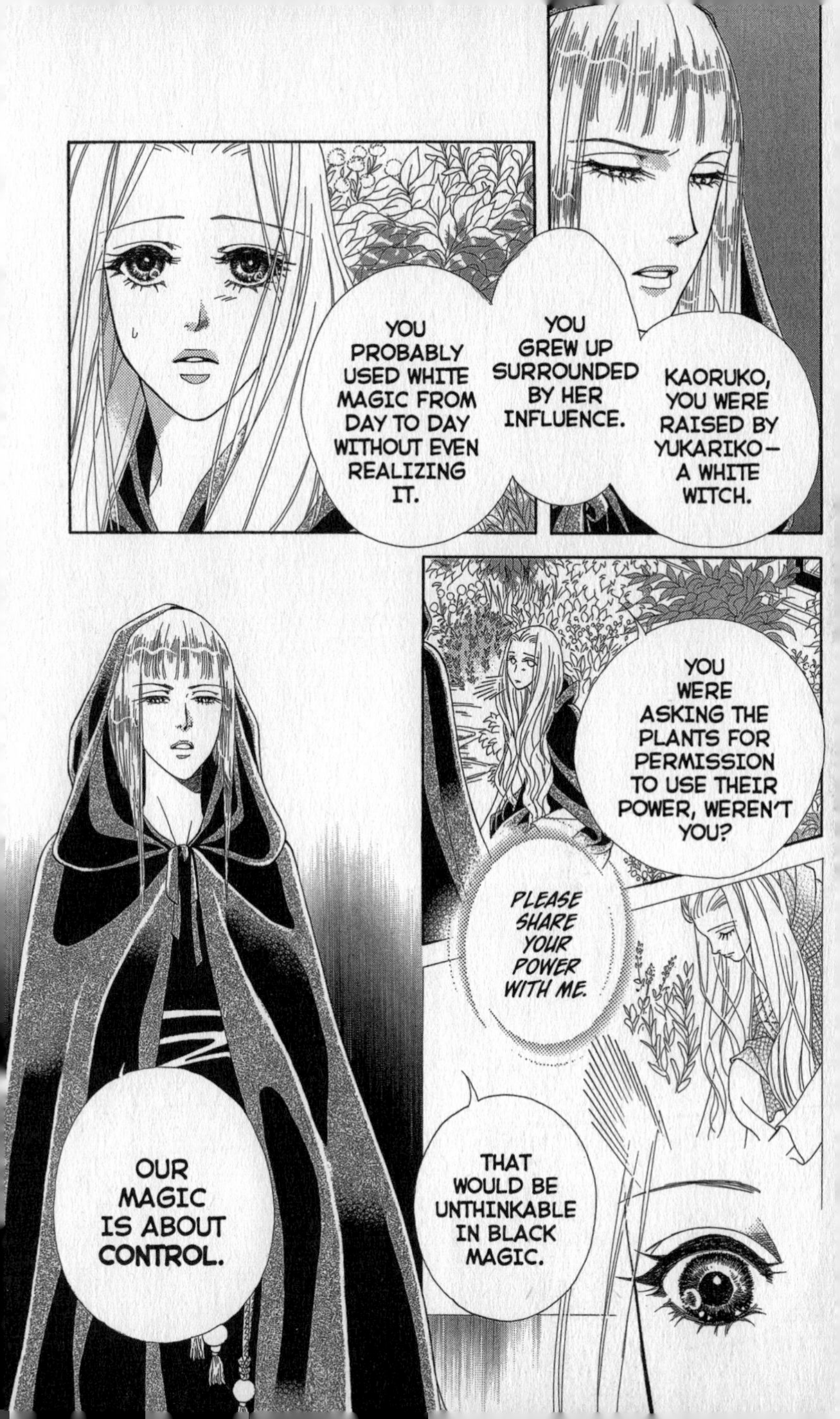
KAORUKO, YOU WERE RAISED BY YUKARIKO— A WHITE WITCH.
YOU GREW UP SURROUNDED BY HER INFLUENCE.
YOU PROBABLY USED WHITE MAGIC FROM DAY TO DAY WITHOUT EVEN REALIZING IT.
YOU WERE ASKING THE PLANTS FOR PERMISSION TO USE THEIR POWER, WEREN'T YOU?
PLEASE SHARE YOUR POWER WITH ME.
THAT WOULD BE UNTHINKABLE IN BLACK MAGIC.
OUR MAGIC IS ABOUT CONTROL.

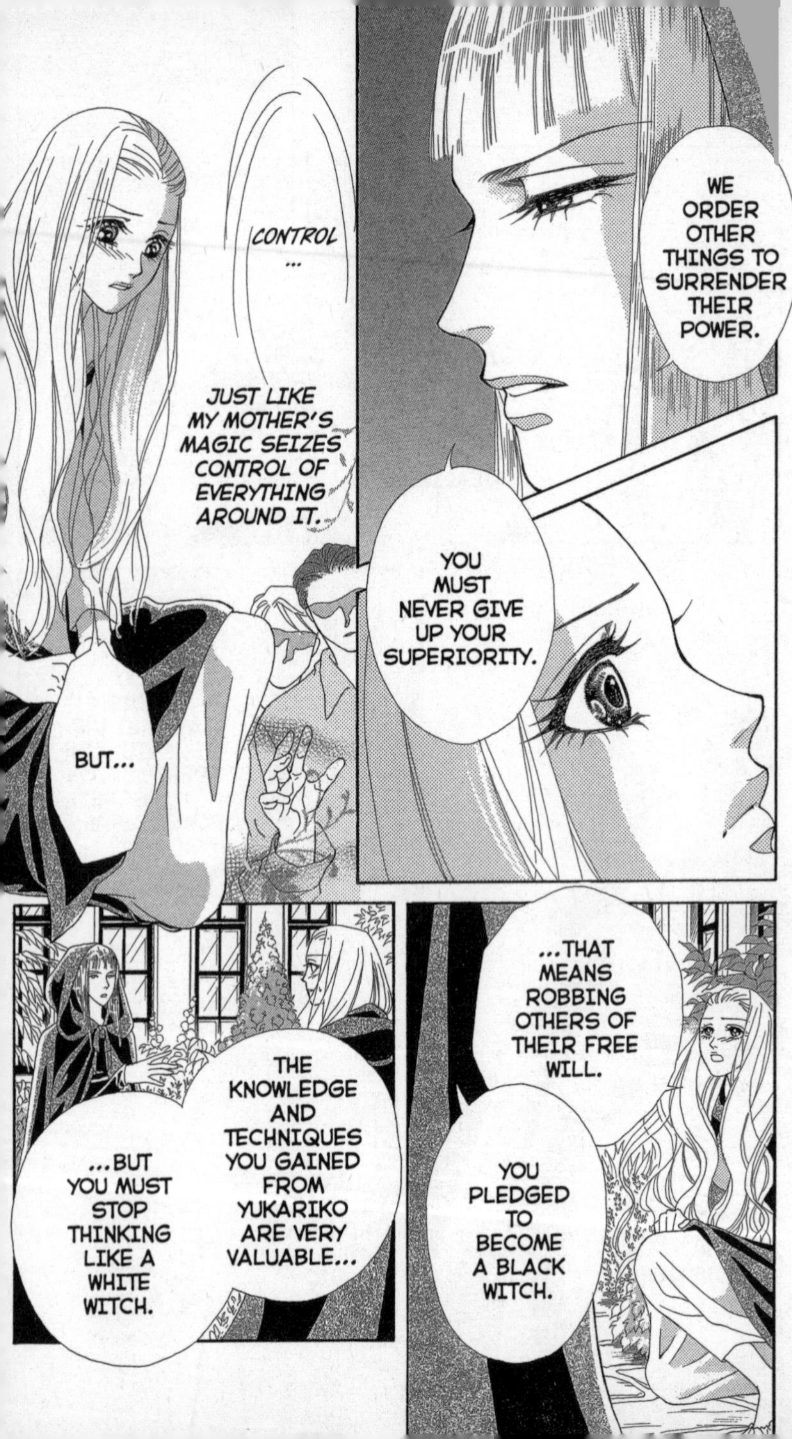
WE ORDER OTHER THINGS TO SURRENDER THEIR POWER.
YOU MUST NEVER GIVE UP YOUR SUPERIORITY.
CONTROL ...
JUST LIKE MY MOTHER'S MAGIC SEIZES CONTROL OF EVERYTHING AROUND IT.
BUT...
...THAT MEANS ROBBING OTHERS OF THEIR FREE WILL.
YOU PLEDGED TO BECOME A BLACK WITCH.
THE KNOWLEDGE AND TECHNIQUES YOU GAINED FROM YUKARIKO ARE VERY VALUABLE...
...BUT YOU MUST STOP THINKING LIKE A WHITE WITCH.

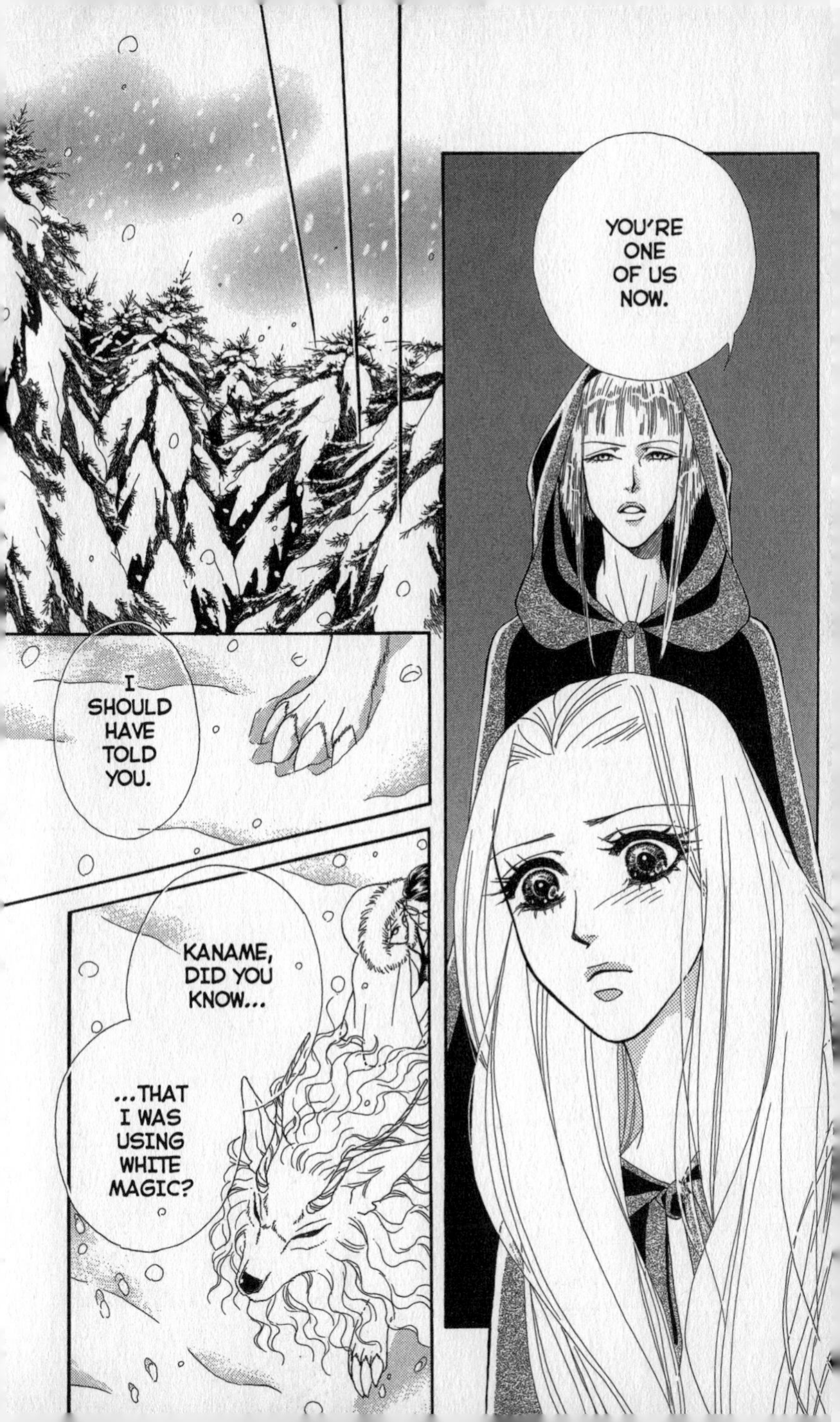
YOU'RE ONE OF US NOW.
I SHOULD HAVE TOLD YOU.
KANAME, DID YOU KNOW...
...THAT I WAS USING WHITE MAGIC?

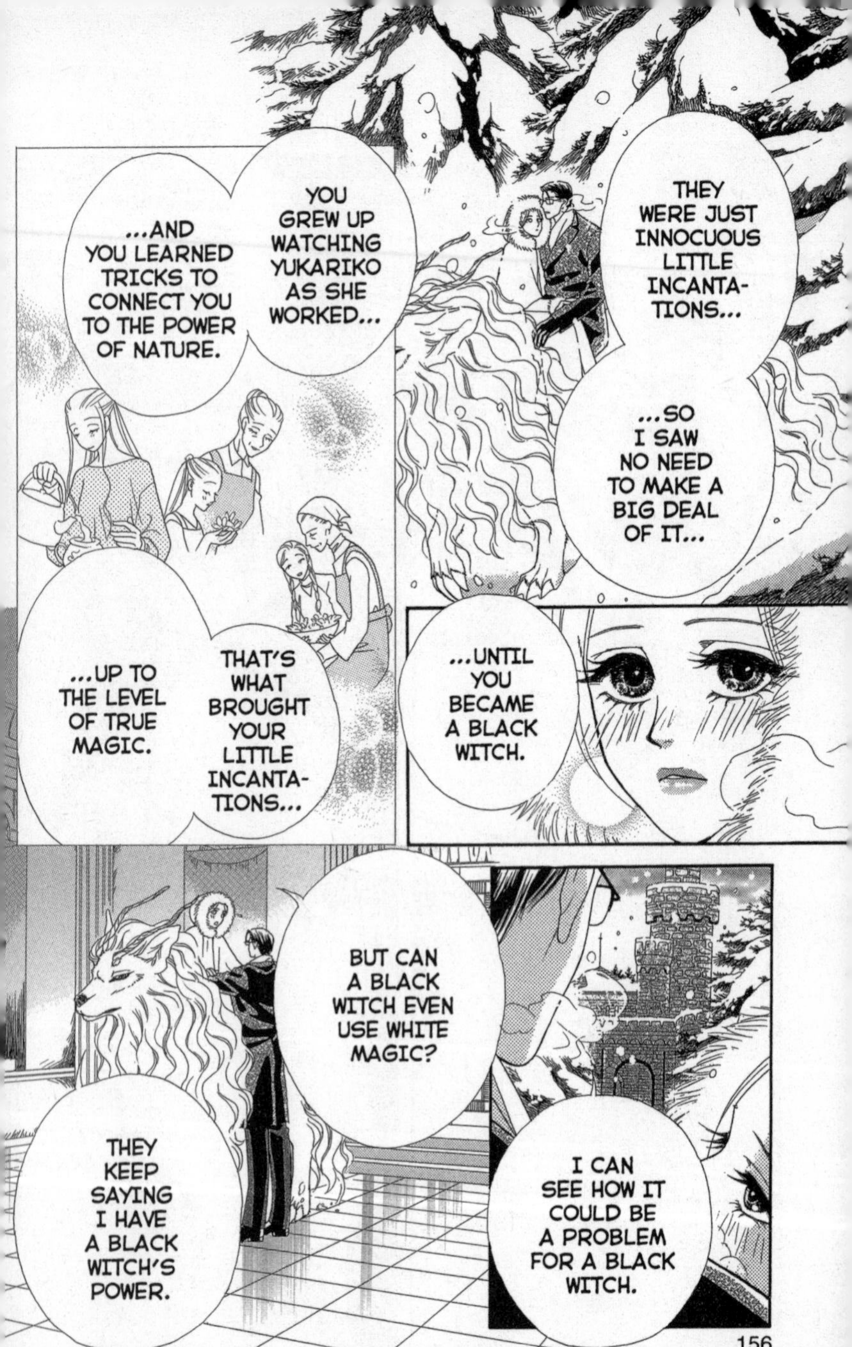
THEY WERE JUST INNOCUOUS LITTLE INCANTATIONS...
...SO I SAW NO NEED TO MAKE A BIG DEAL OF IT...
...UNTIL YOU BECAME A BLACK WITCH.
YOU GREW UP WATCHING YUKARIKO AS SHE WORKED...
...AND YOU LEARNED TRICKS TO CONNECT YOU TO THE POWER OF NATURE.
THAT'S WHAT BROUGHT YOUR LITTLE INCANTATIONS...
...UP TO THE LEVEL OF TRUE MAGIC.
I CAN SEE HOW IT COULD BE A PROBLEM FOR A BLACK WITCH.
BUT CAN A BLACK WITCH EVEN USE WHITE MAGIC?
THEY KEEP SAYING I HAVE A BLACK WITCH'S POWER.

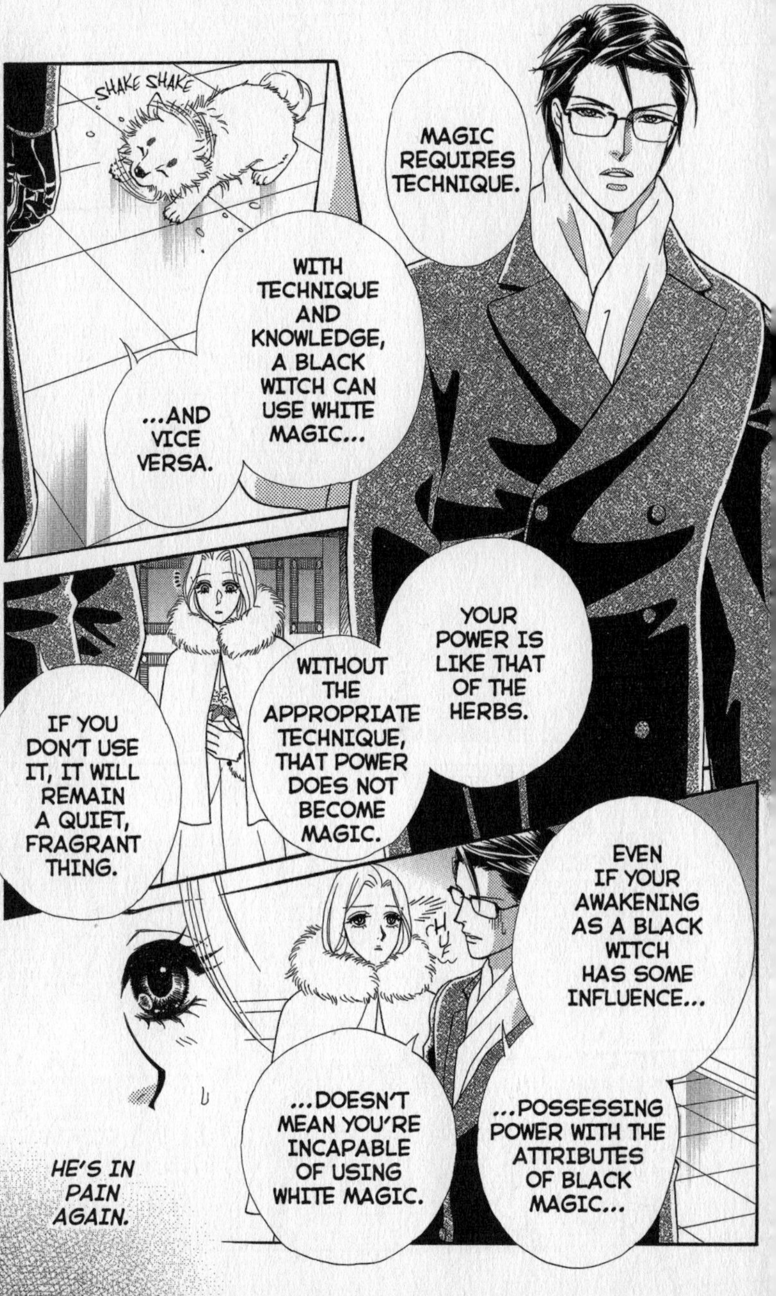
MAGIC REQUIRES TECHNIQUE.
WITH TECHNIQUE AND KNOWLEDGE, A BLACK WITCH CAN USE WHITE MAGIC...
...AND VICE VERSA.
SHAKE SHAKE
YOUR POWER IS LIKE THAT OF THE HERBS.
WITHOUT THE APPROPRIATE TECHNIQUE, THAT POWER DOES NOT BECOME MAGIC.
IF YOU DON'T USE IT, IT WILL REMAIN A QUIET, FRAGRANT THING.
EVEN IF YOUR AWAKENING AS A BLACK WITCH HAS SOME INFLUENCE...
...POSSESSING POWER WITH THE ATTRIBUTES OF BLACK MAGIC...
...DOESN'T MEAN YOU'RE INCAPABLE OF USING WHITE MAGIC.
HE'S IN PAIN AGAIN.

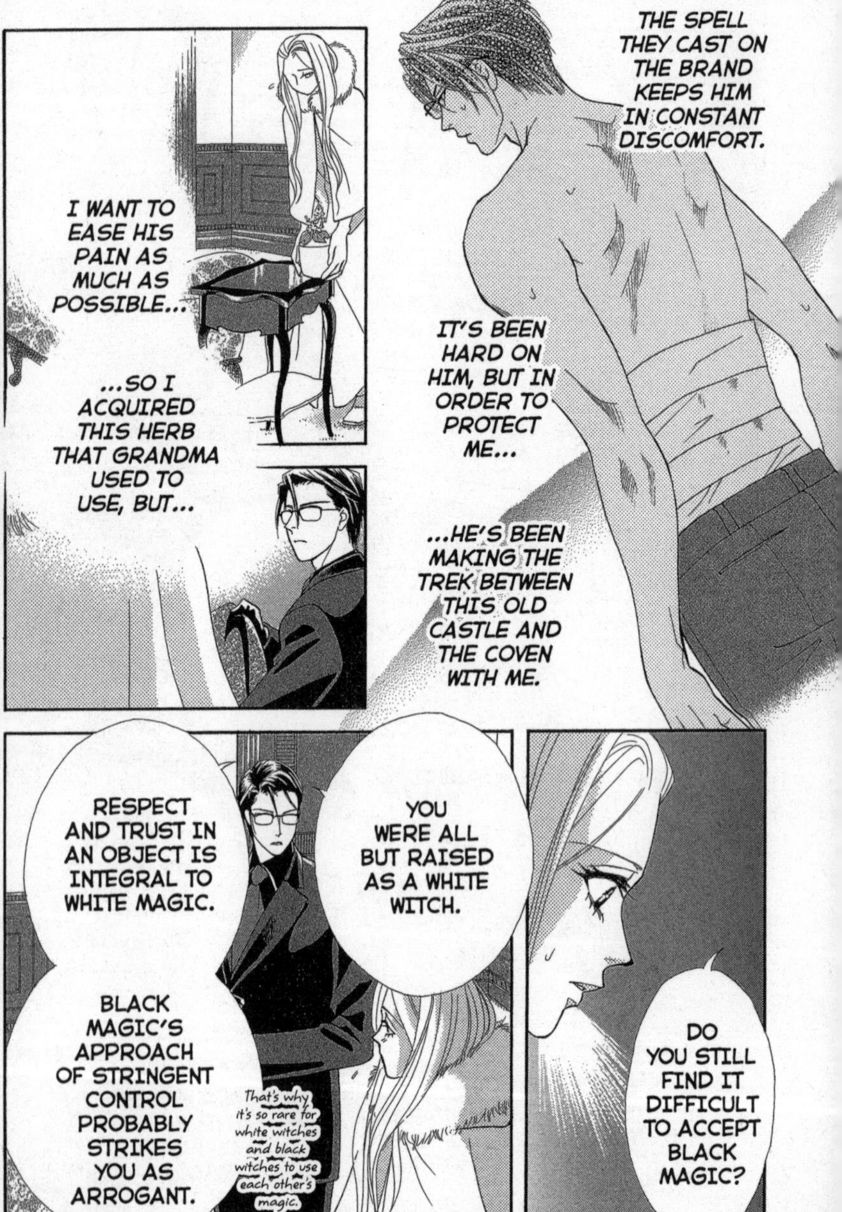
THE SPELL THEY CAST ON THE BRAND KEEPS HIM IN CONSTANT DISCOMFORT.
IT'S BEEN HARD ON HIM, BUT IN ORDER TO PROTECT ME...
...HE'S BEEN MAKING THE TREK BETWEEN THIS OLD CASTLE AND THE COVEN WITH ME.
I WANT TO EASE HIS PAIN AS MUCH AS POSSIBLE...
...SO I ACQUIRED THIS HERB THAT GRANDMA USED TO USE, BUT...
DO YOU STILL FIND IT DIFFICULT TO ACCEPT BLACK MAGIC?
YOU WERE ALL BUT RAISED AS A WHITE WITCH.
RESPECT AND TRUST IN AN OBJECT IS INTEGRAL TO WHITE MAGIC.
BLACK MAGIC'S APPROACH OF STRINGENT CONTROL PROBABLY STRIKES YOU AS ARROGANT.
That's why it's so rare for white witches and black witches to use each other's magic.

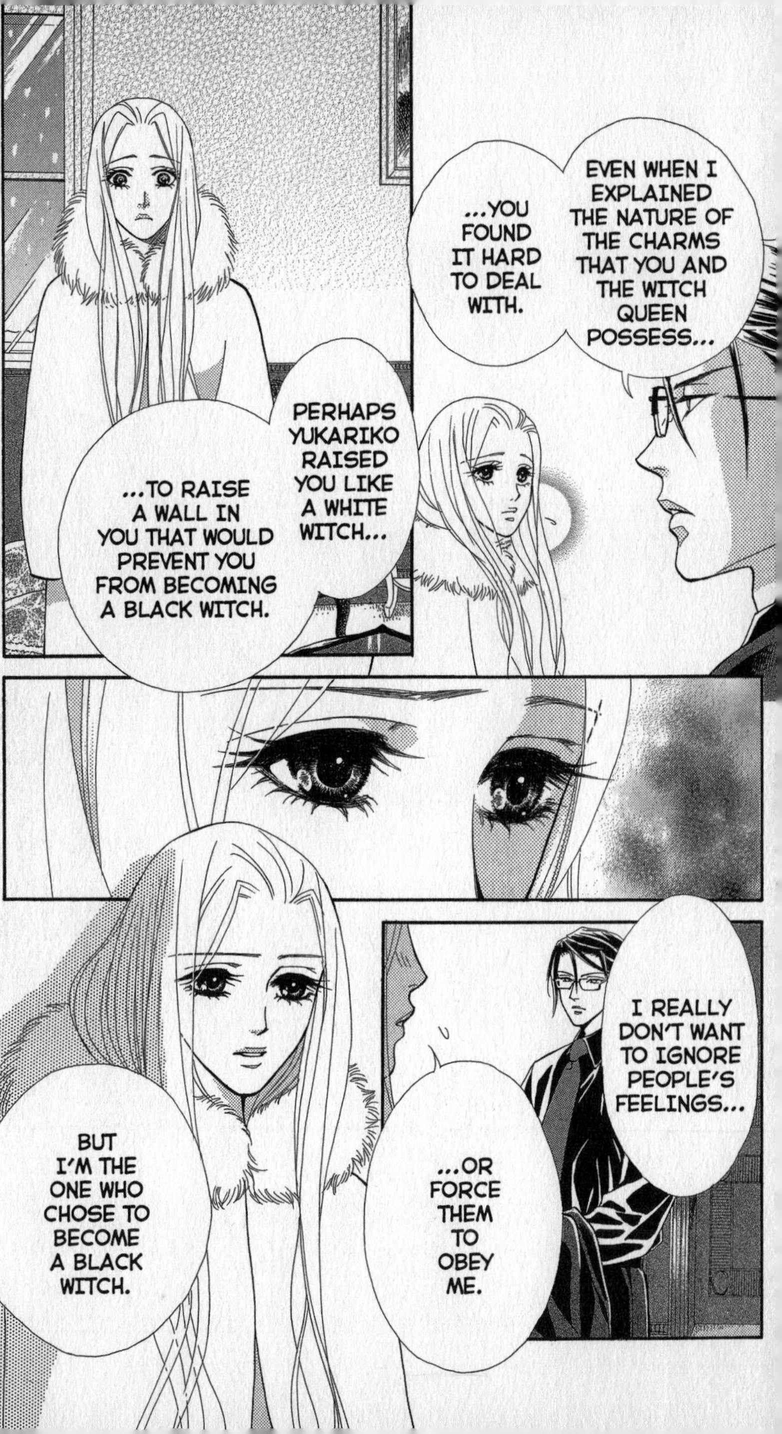
EVEN WHEN I EXPLAINED THE NATURE OF THE CHARMS THAT YOU AND THE WITCH QUEEN POSSESS...
...YOU FOUND IT HARD TO DEAL WITH.
PERHAPS YUKARIKO RAISED YOU LIKE A WHITE WITCH...
...TO RAISE A WALL IN YOU THAT WOULD PREVENT YOU FROM BECOMING A BLACK WITCH.
I REALLY DON'T WANT TO IGNORE PEOPLE'S FEELINGS...
...OR FORCE THEM TO OBEY ME.
BUT I'M THE ONE WHO CHOSE TO BECOME A BLACK WITCH.

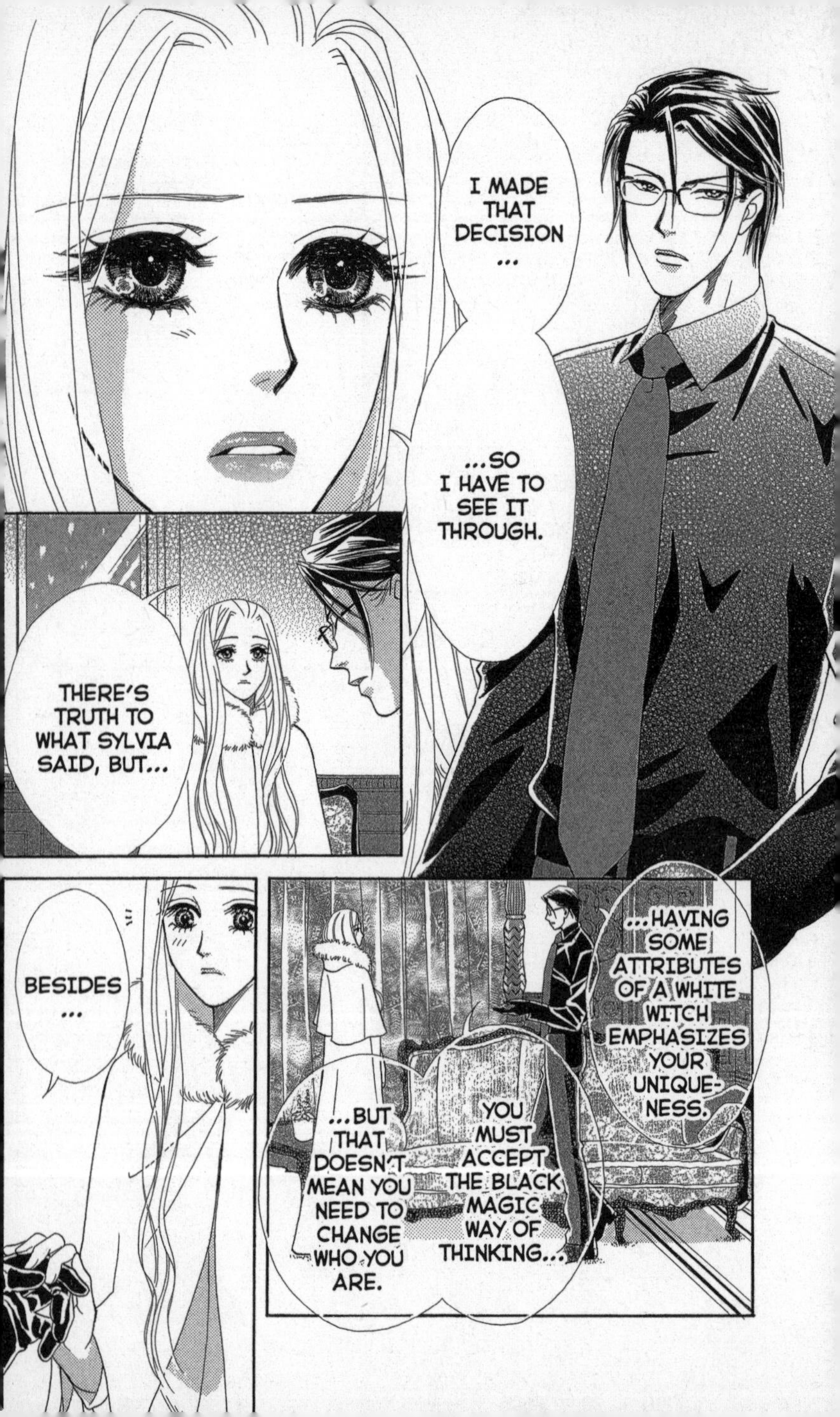
THERE'S TRUTH TO WHAT SYLVIA SAID, BUT...
I MADE THAT DECISION ...
...SO I HAVE TO SEE IT THROUGH.
BESIDES ...
...HAVING SOME ATTRIBUTES OF A WHITE WITCH EMPHASIZES YOUR UNIQUE-NESS.
YOU MUST ACCEPT THE BLACK MAGIC WAY OF THINKING...
...BUT THAT DOESN'T MEAN YOU NEED TO CHANGE WHO YOU ARE.

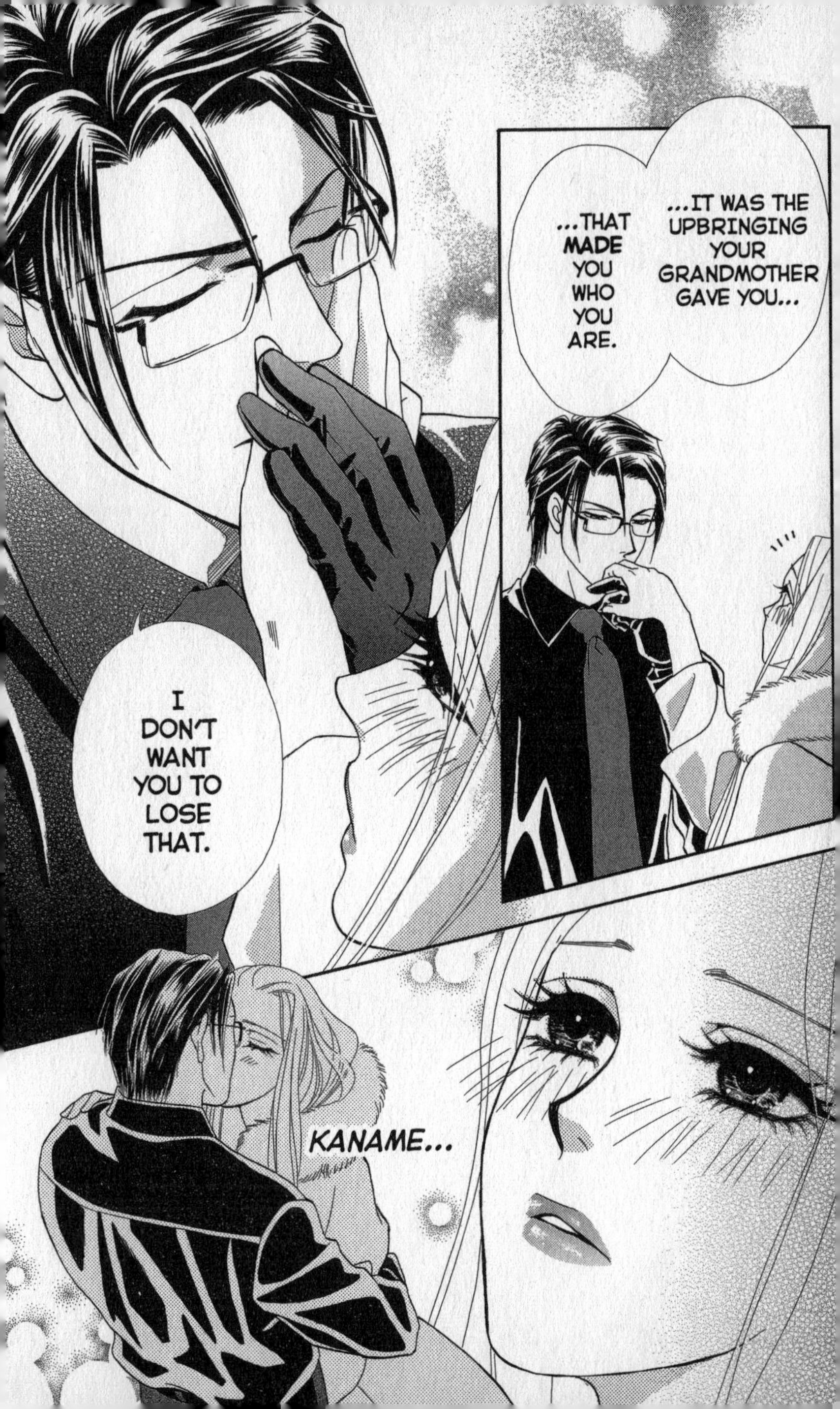
...IT WAS THE UPBRINGING YOUR GRANDMOTHER GAVE YOU...
...THAT MADE YOU WHO YOU ARE.
I DON'T WANT YOU TO LOSE THAT.
KANAME...

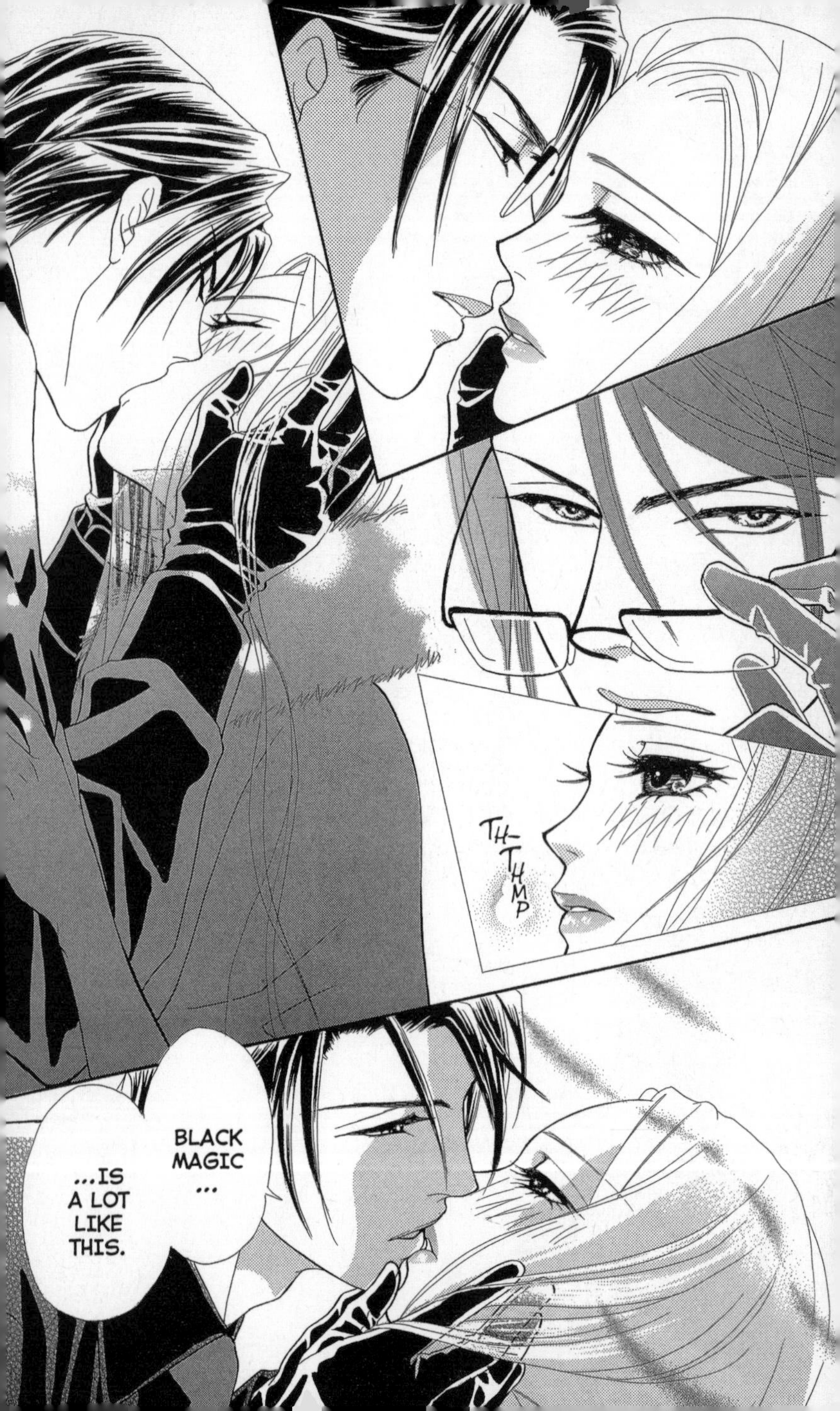
TH-THMP
BLACK MAGIC ...
...IS A LOT LIKE THIS.

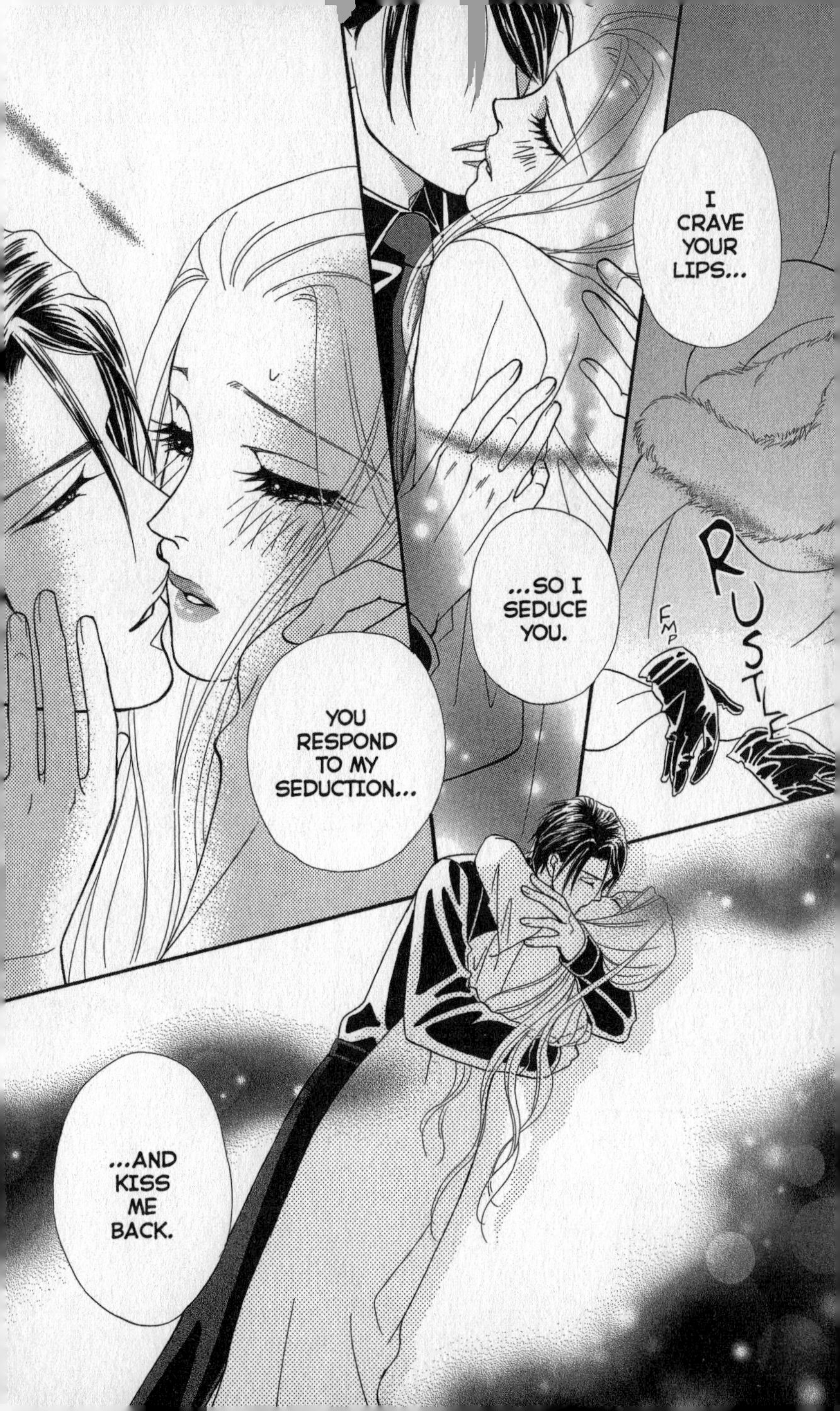
I CRAVE YOUR LIPS...
RUSTLE
FMP
...SO I SEDUCE YOU.
YOU RESPOND TO MY SEDUCTION...
...AND KISS ME BACK.

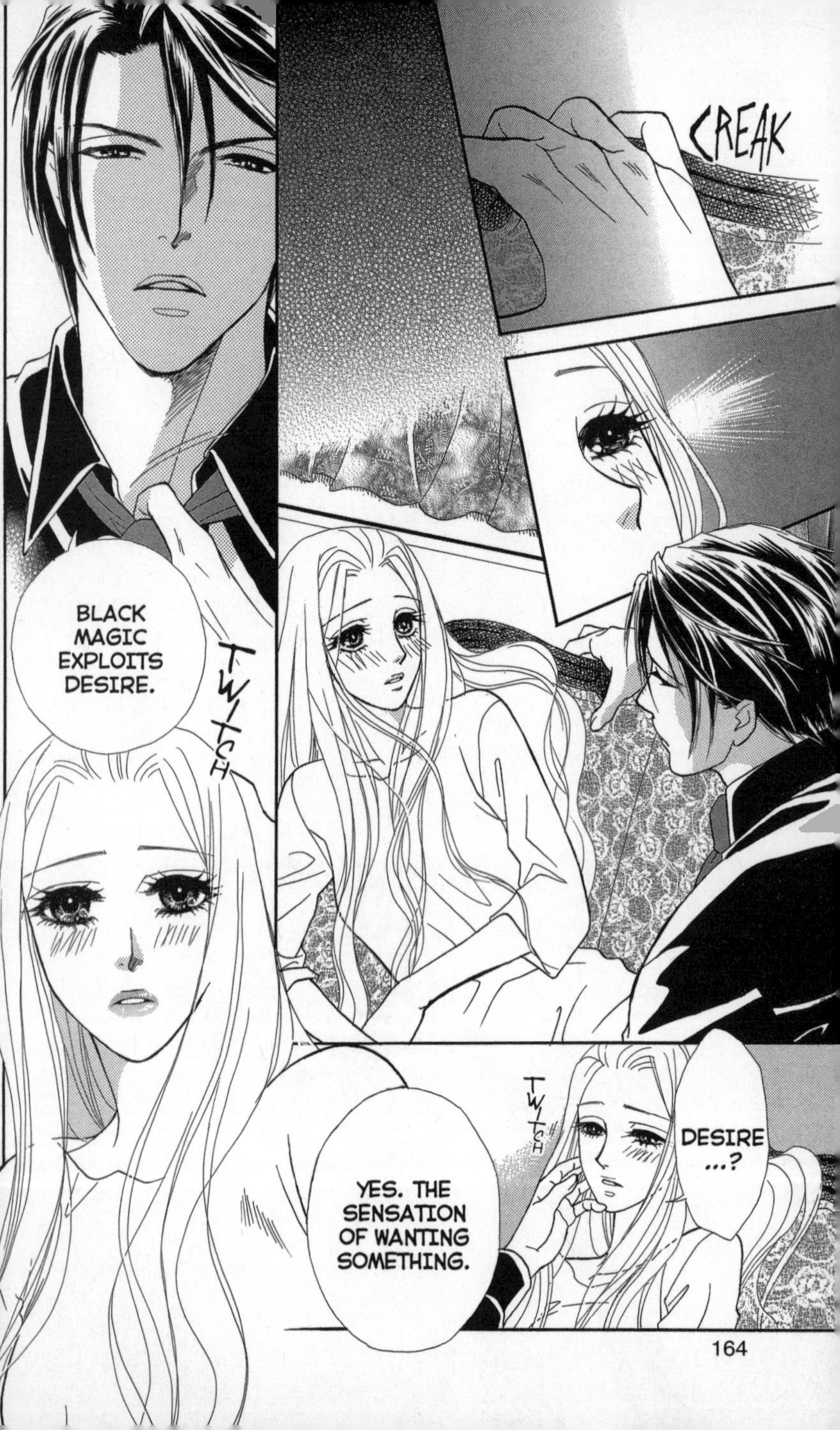
CREAK
BLACK MAGIC EXPLOITS DESIRE.
TWITCH
DESIRE ...?
TWITCH
YES. THE SENSATION OF WANTING SOMETHING.

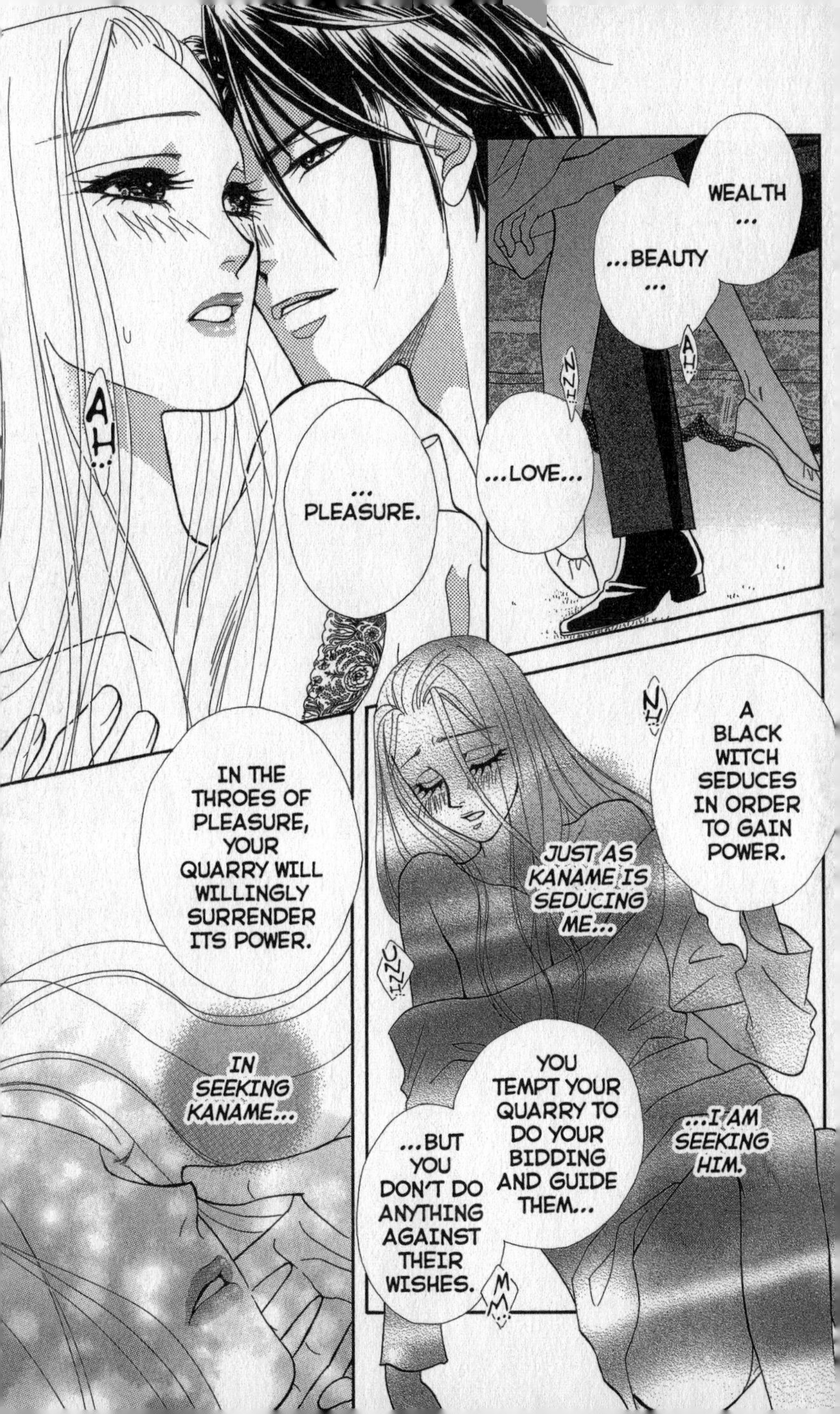

WEALTH...
...BEAUTY...
AH...
NN...
...LOVE...
... PLEASURE.
AH...
NH...
A BLACK WITCH SEDUCES IN ORDER TO GAIN POWER.
JUST AS KANAME IS SEDUCING ME...
NN...
...I AM SEEKING HIM.
YOU TEMPT YOUR QUARRY TO DO YOUR BIDDING AND GUIDE THEM...
...BUT YOU DON'T DO ANYTHING AGAINST THEIR WISHES.
MM...
IN THE THROES OF PLEASURE, YOUR QUARRY WILL WILLINGLY SURRENDER ITS POWER.
IN SEEKING KANAME...

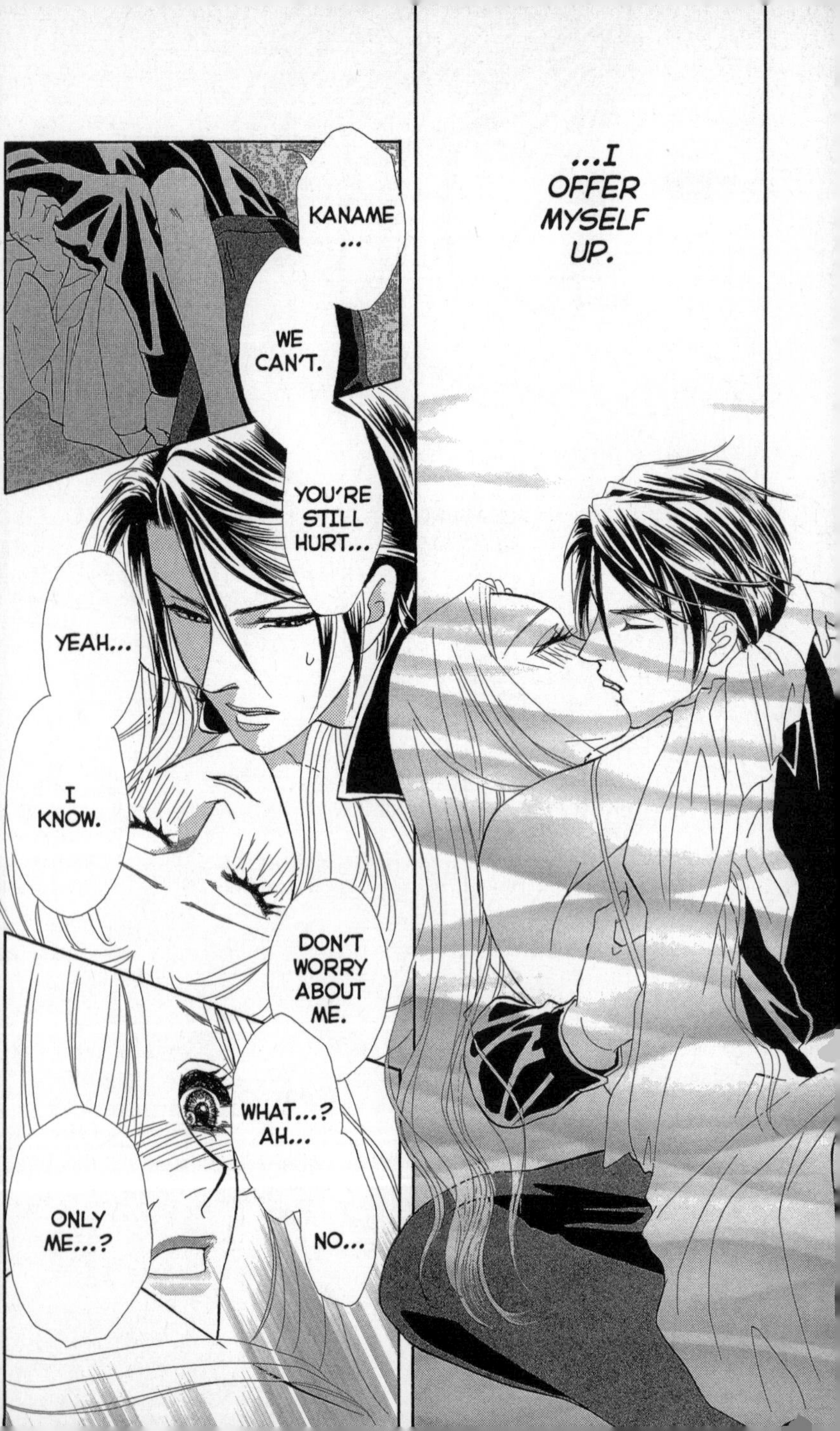
...I OFFER MYSELF UP.
KANAME ...
WE CAN'T.
YOU'RE STILL HURT...
YEAH...
I KNOW.
DON'T WORRY ABOUT ME.
WHAT...? AH...
NO...
ONLY ME...?

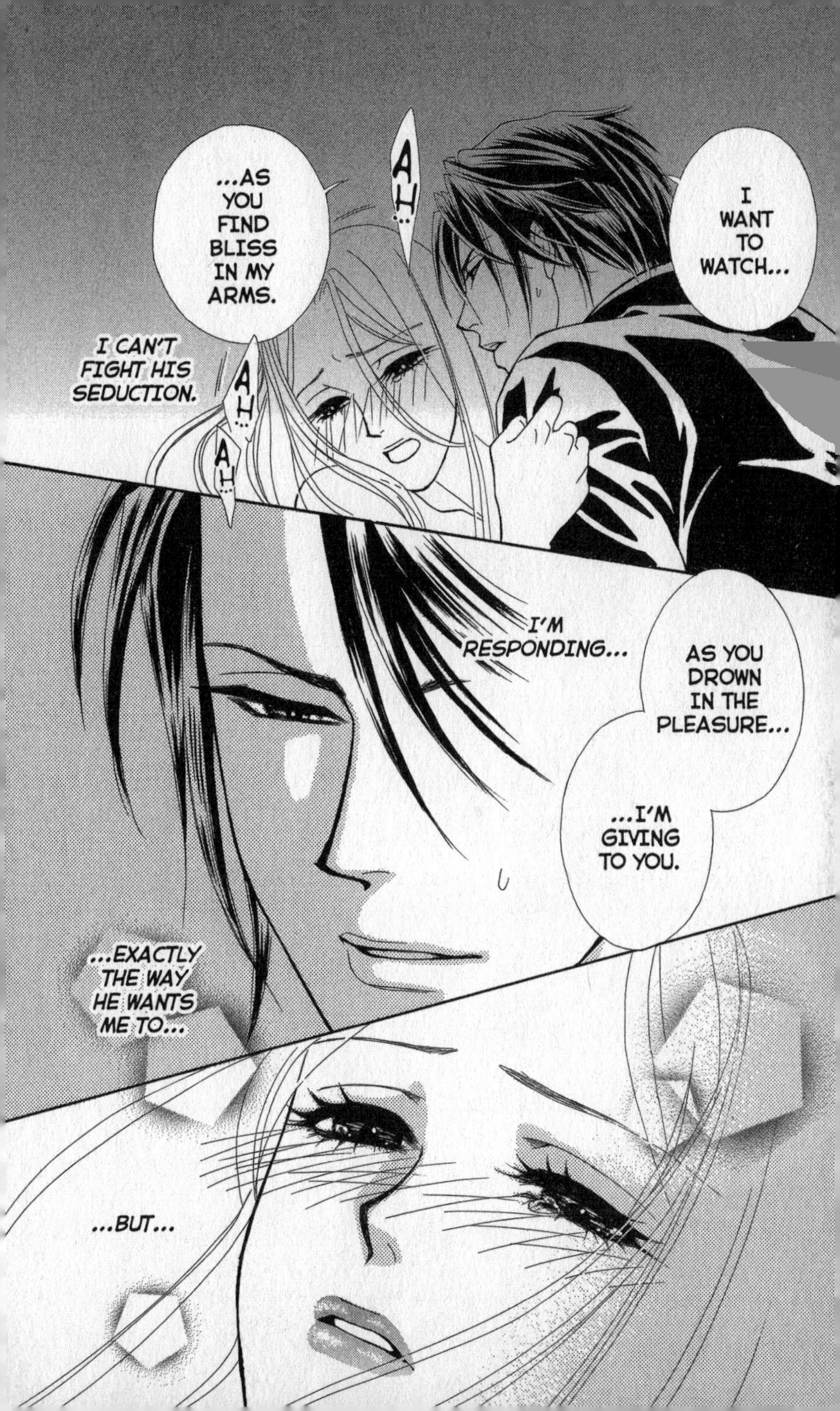
I WANT TO WATCH...
AH...
...AS YOU FIND BLISS IN MY ARMS.
I CAN'T FIGHT HIS SEDUCTION.
AH...
AH...
AS YOU DROWN IN THE PLEASURE...
...I'M GIVING TO YOU.
I'M RESPONDING...
...EXACTLY THE WAY HE WANTS ME TO...
...BUT...

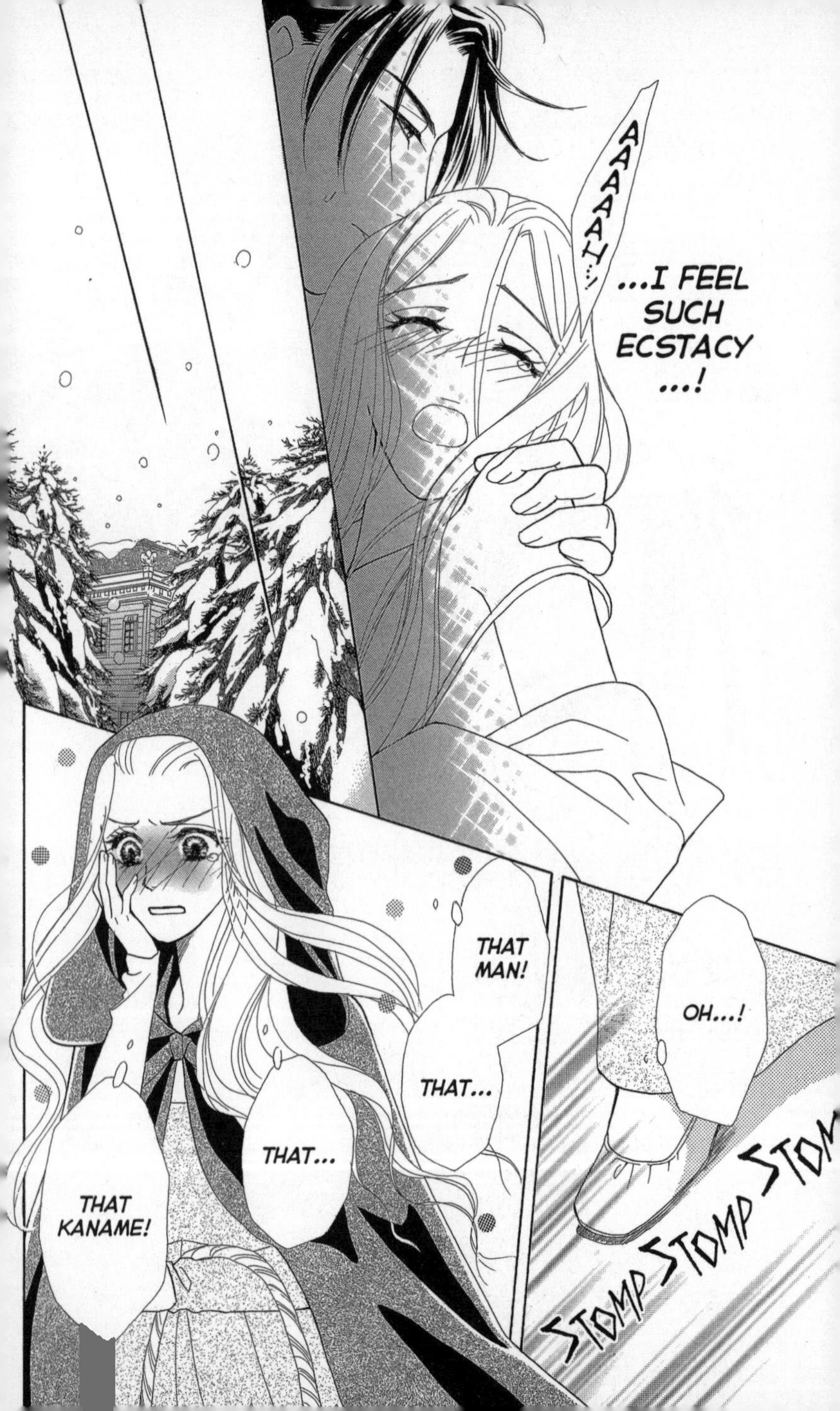
AAAAAH...!
...I FEEL SUCH ECSTACY...!
OH...!
STOMP STOMP STOM
THAT MAN!
THAT...
THAT...
THAT KANAME!

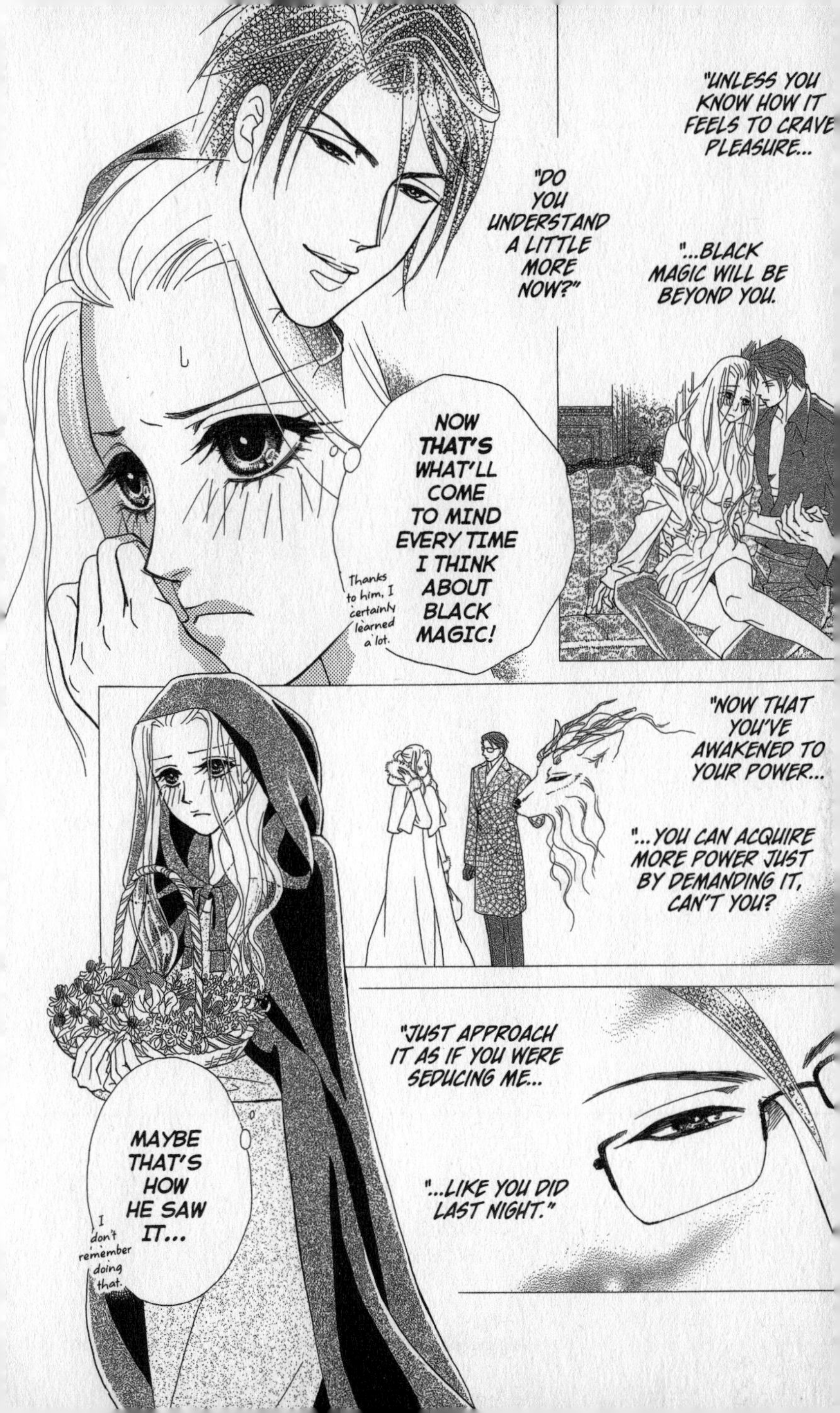
"UNLESS YOU KNOW HOW IT FEELS TO CRAVE PLEASURE...
"...BLACK MAGIC WILL BE BEYOND YOU.
"DO YOU UNDERSTAND A LITTLE MORE NOW?"
NOW THAT'S WHAT'LL COME TO MIND EVERY TIME I THINK ABOUT BLACK MAGIC!
Thanks to him, I certainly learned a lot.
"NOW THAT YOU'VE AWAKENED TO YOUR POWER...
"...YOU CAN ACQUIRE MORE POWER JUST BY DEMANDING IT, CAN'T YOU?
"JUST APPROACH IT AS IF YOU WERE SEDUCING ME...
"...LIKE YOU DID LAST NIGHT."
MAYBE THAT'S HOW HE SAW IT...
I don't remember doing that.

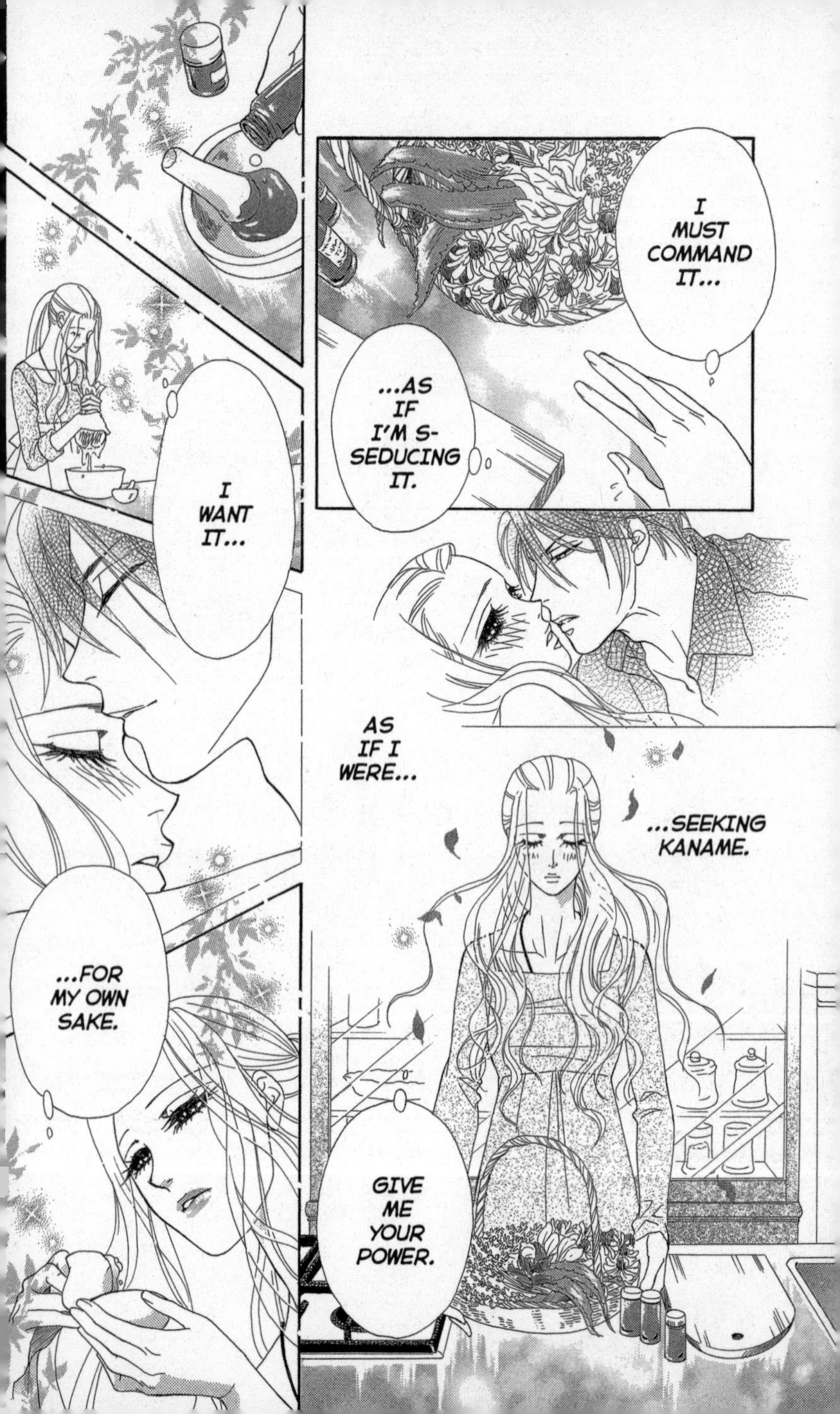
I MUST COMMAND IT...
...AS IF I'M S-SEDUCING IT.
AS IF I WERE...
...SEEKING KANAME.
GIVE ME YOUR POWER.
I WANT IT...
...FOR MY OWN SAKE.

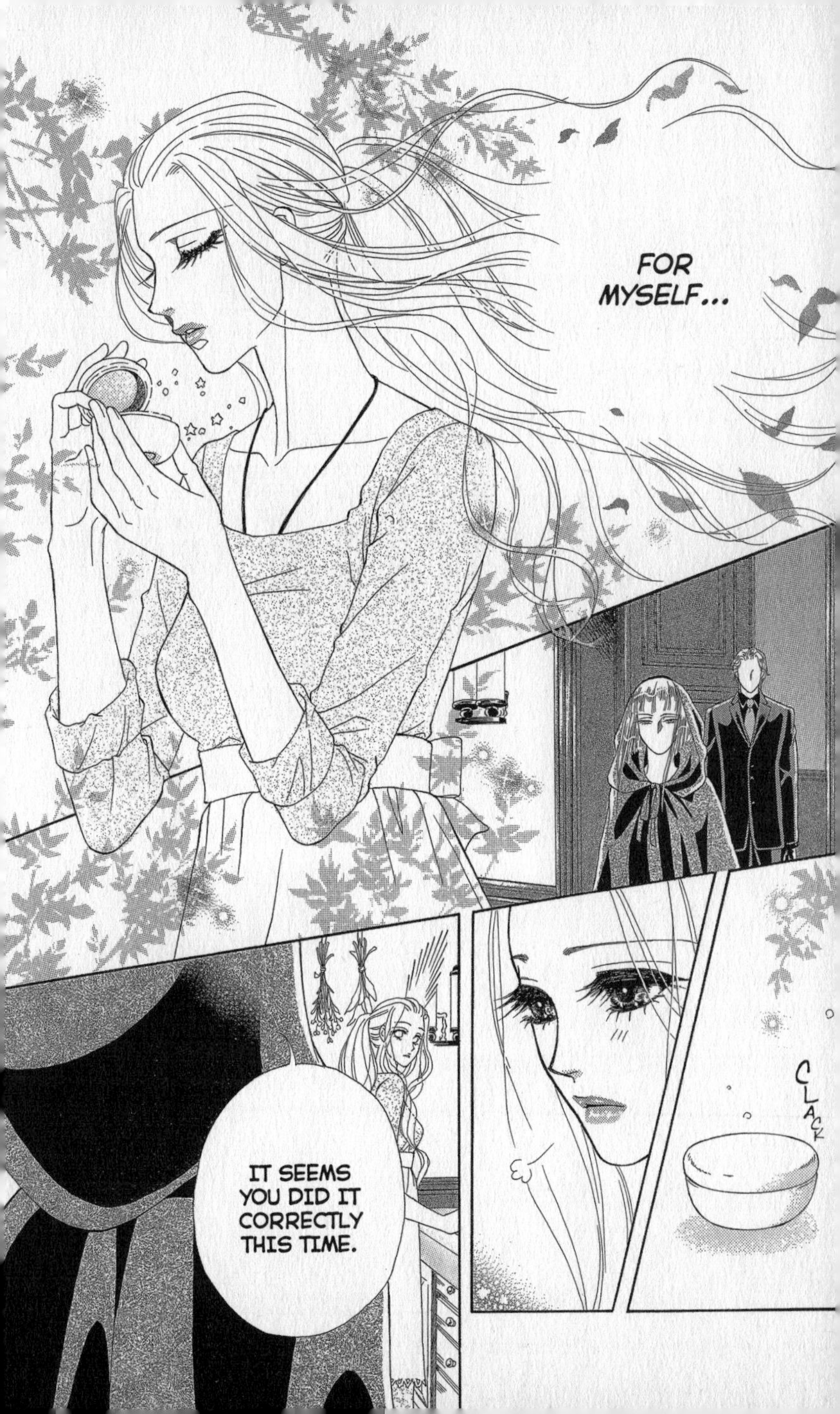
FOR MYSELF...
CLACK
IT SEEMS YOU DID IT CORRECTLY THIS TIME.

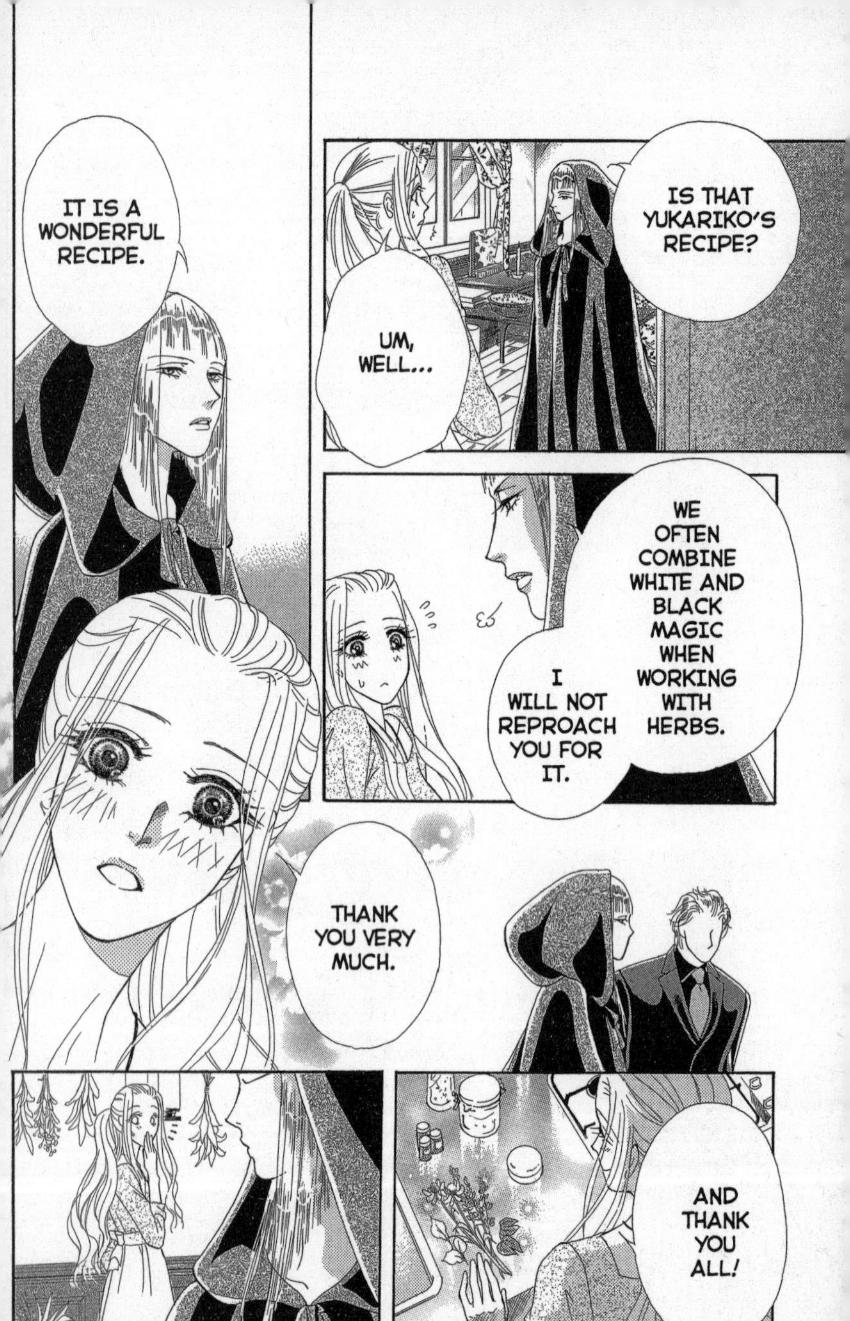
IS THAT YUKARIKO'S RECIPE?
UM, WELL...
WE OFTEN COMBINE WHITE AND BLACK MAGIC WHEN WORKING WITH HERBS.
I WILL NOT REPROACH YOU FOR IT.
IT IS A WONDERFUL RECIPE.
THANK YOU VERY MUCH.
AND THANK YOU ALL!

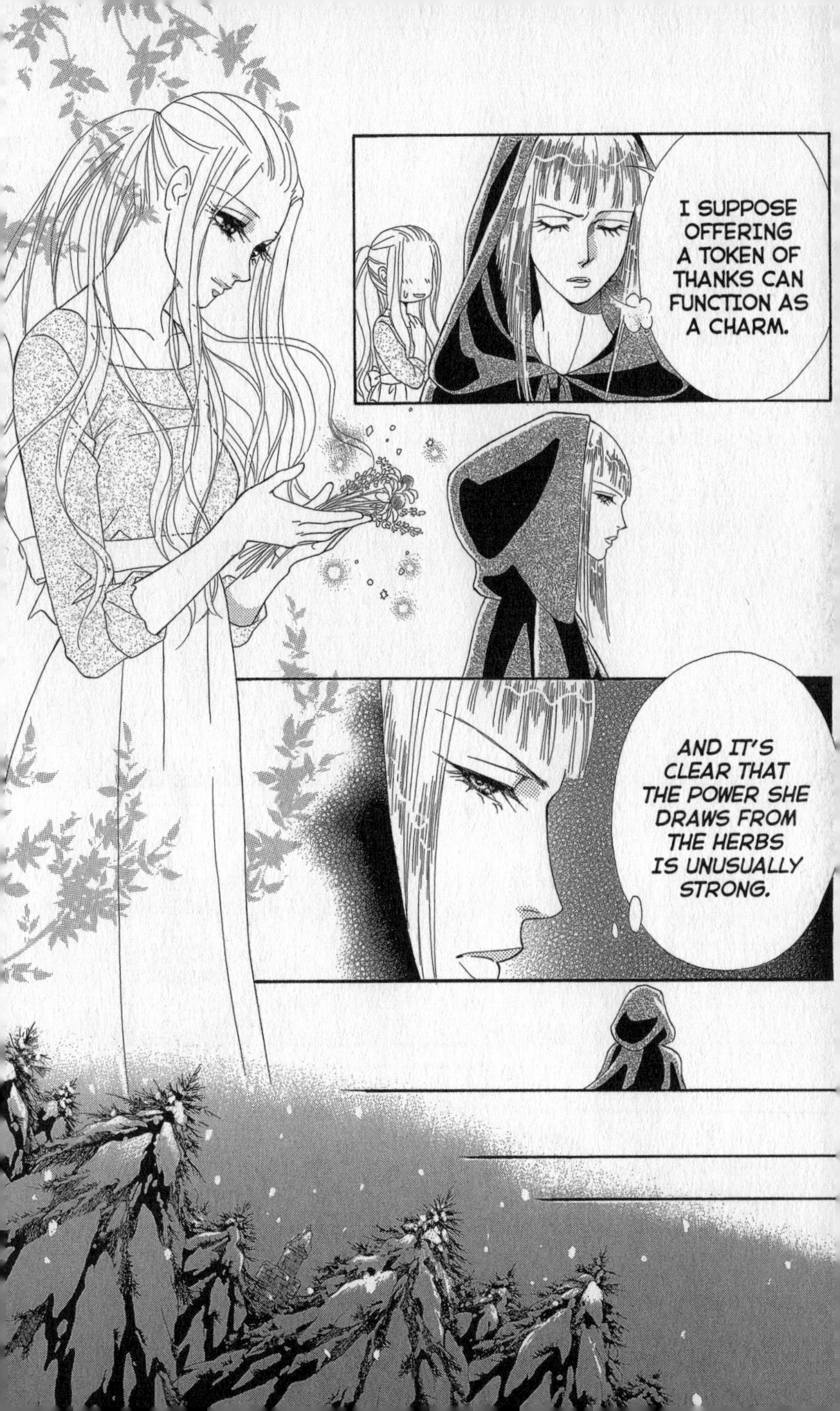
I SUPPOSE OFFERING A TOKEN OF THANKS CAN FUNCTION AS A CHARM.
AND IT'S CLEAR THAT THE POWER SHE DRAWS FROM THE HERBS IS UNUSUALLY STRONG.

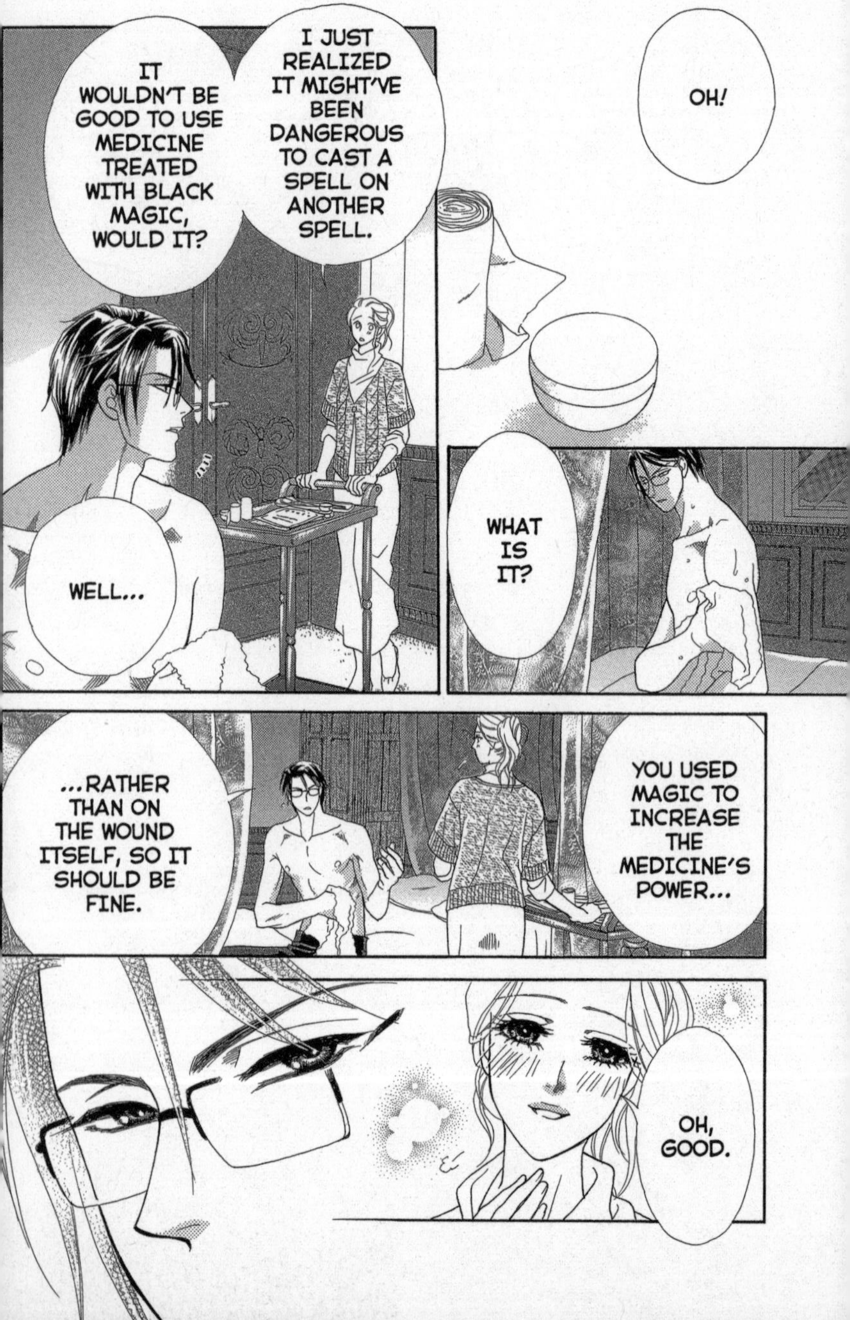
OH!
WHAT IS IT?
I JUST REALIZED IT MIGHT'VE BEEN DANGEROUS TO CAST A SPELL ON ANOTHER SPELL.
IT WOULDN'T BE GOOD TO USE MEDICINE TREATED WITH BLACK MAGIC, WOULD IT?
WELL...
YOU USED MAGIC TO INCREASE THE MEDICINE'S POWER...
...RATHER THAN ON THE WOUND ITSELF, SO IT SHOULD BE FINE.
OH, GOOD.

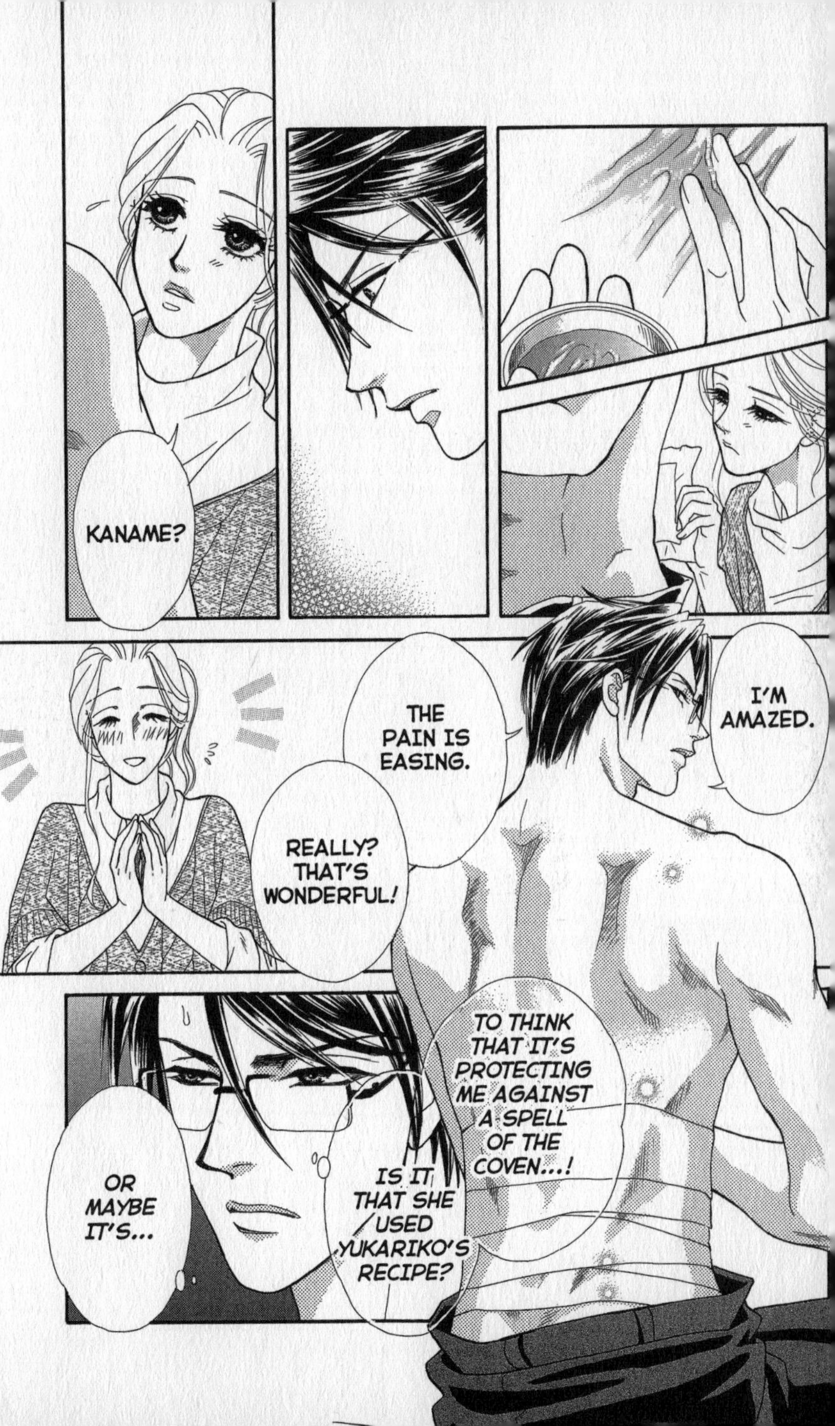
KANAME?
I'M AMAZED.
THE PAIN IS EASING.
REALLY? THAT'S WONDERFUL!
TO THINK THAT IT'S PROTECTING ME AGAINST A SPELL OF THE COVEN...!
IS IT THAT SHE USED YUKARIKO'S RECIPE?
OR MAYBE IT'S...

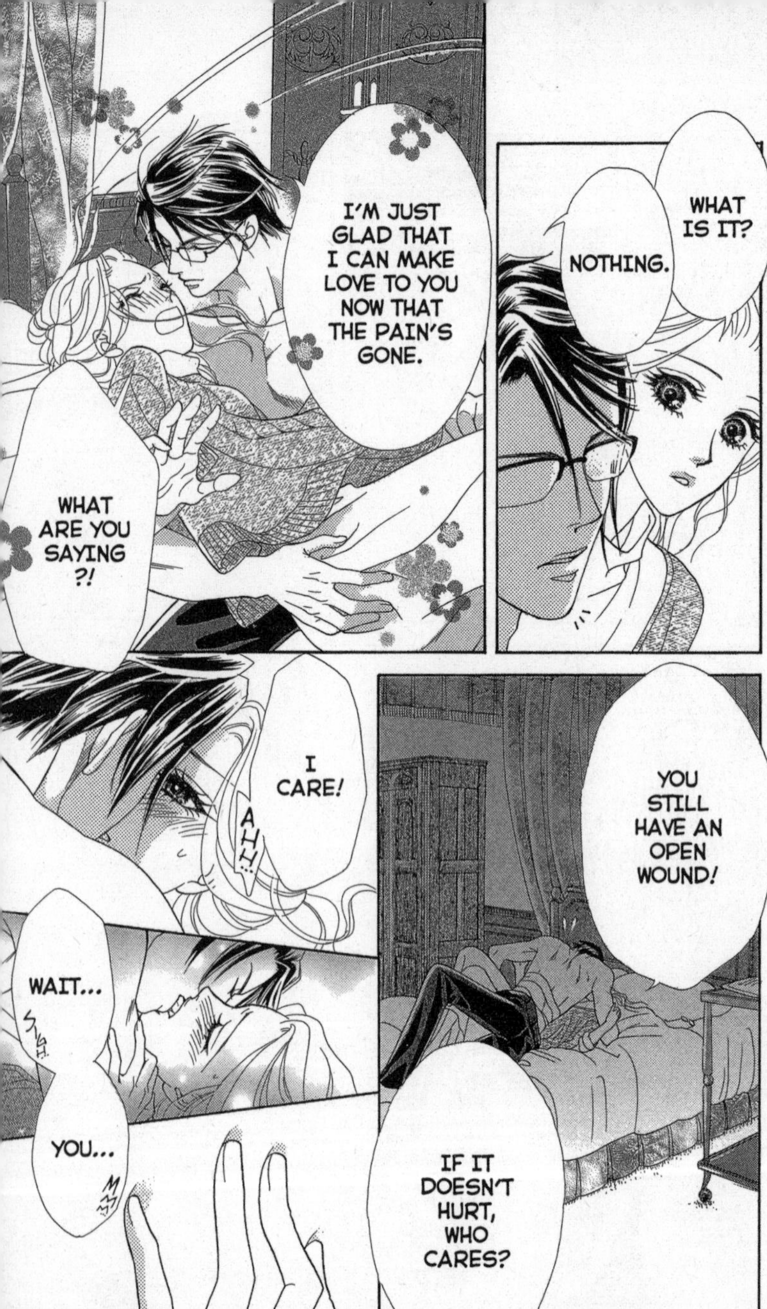
WHAT IS IT?
NOTHING.
I'M JUST GLAD THAT I CAN MAKE LOVE TO YOU NOW THAT THE PAIN'S GONE.
WHAT ARE YOU SAYING ?!
YOU STILL HAVE AN OPEN WOUND!
IF IT DOESN'T HURT, WHO CARES?
I CARE!
AHH...
WAIT...
SIGH
YOU...
MMM

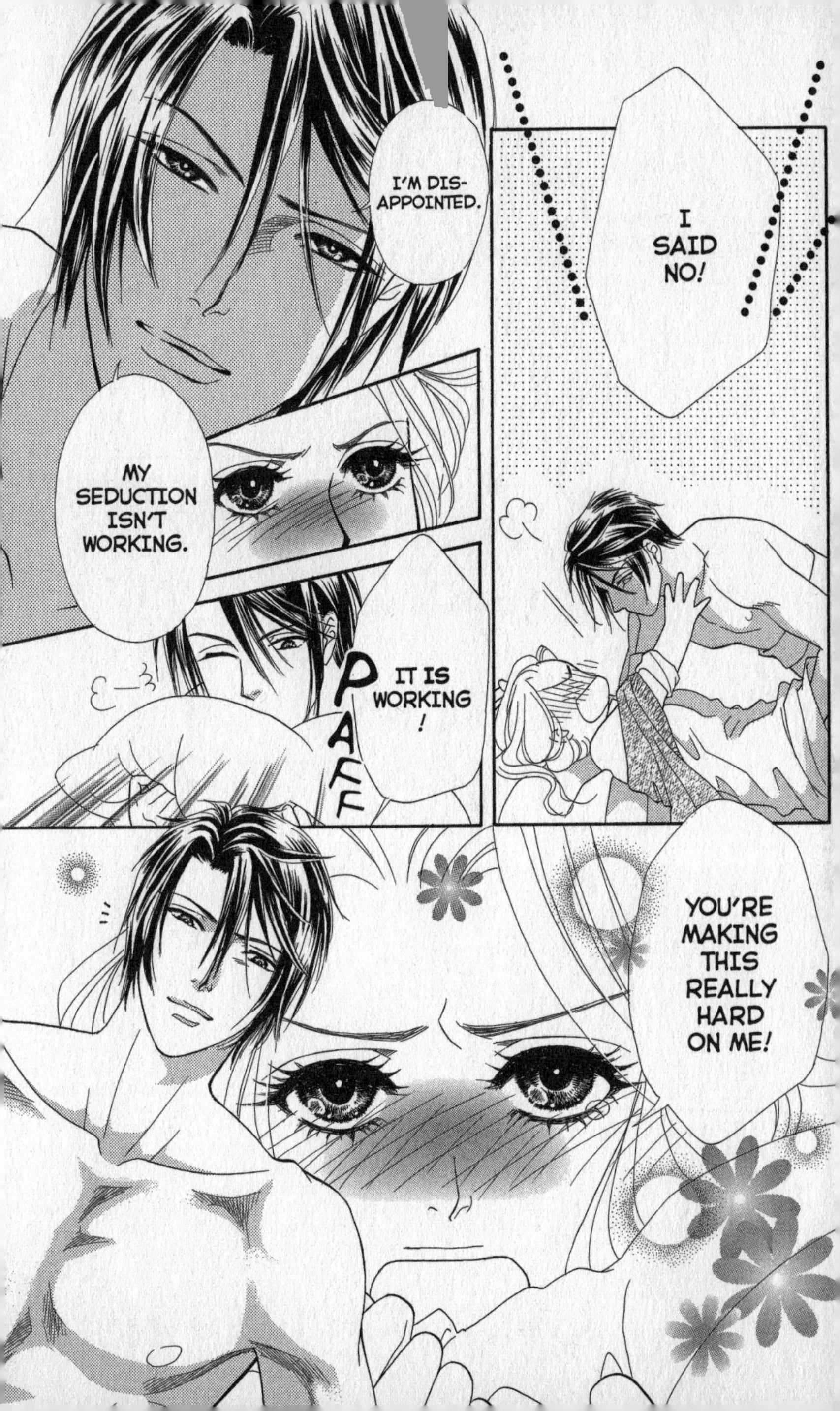
I SAID NO!
I'M DIS-APPOINTED.
MY SEDUCTION ISN'T WORKING.
IT IS WORKING!
PAFF
YOU'RE MAKING THIS REALLY HARD ON ME!

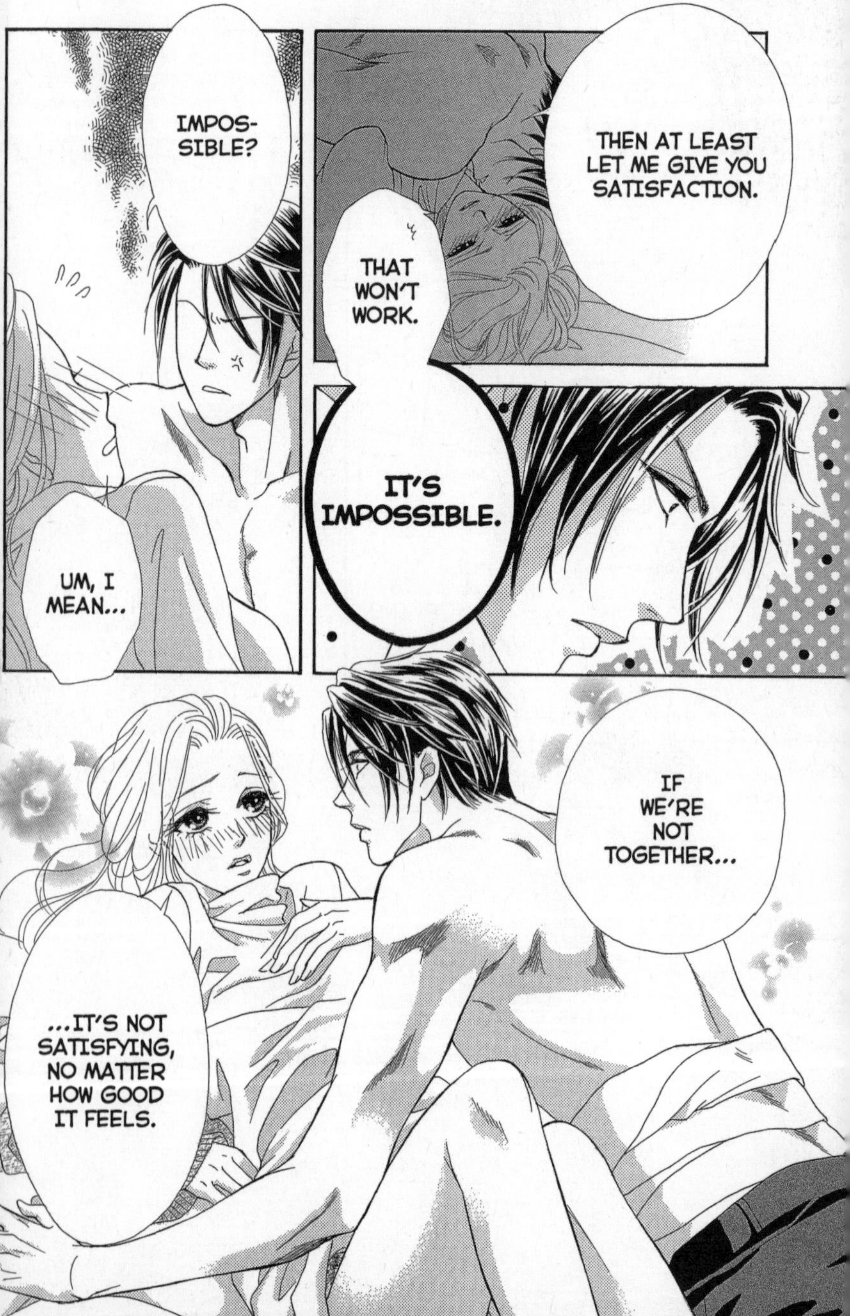
THEN AT LEAST LET ME GIVE YOU SATISFACTION.
THAT WON'T WORK.
IT'S IMPOSSIBLE.
IMPOS-SIBLE?
UM, I MEAN...
IF WE'RE NOT TOGETHER...
...IT'S NOT SATISFYING, NO MATTER HOW GOOD IT FEELS.

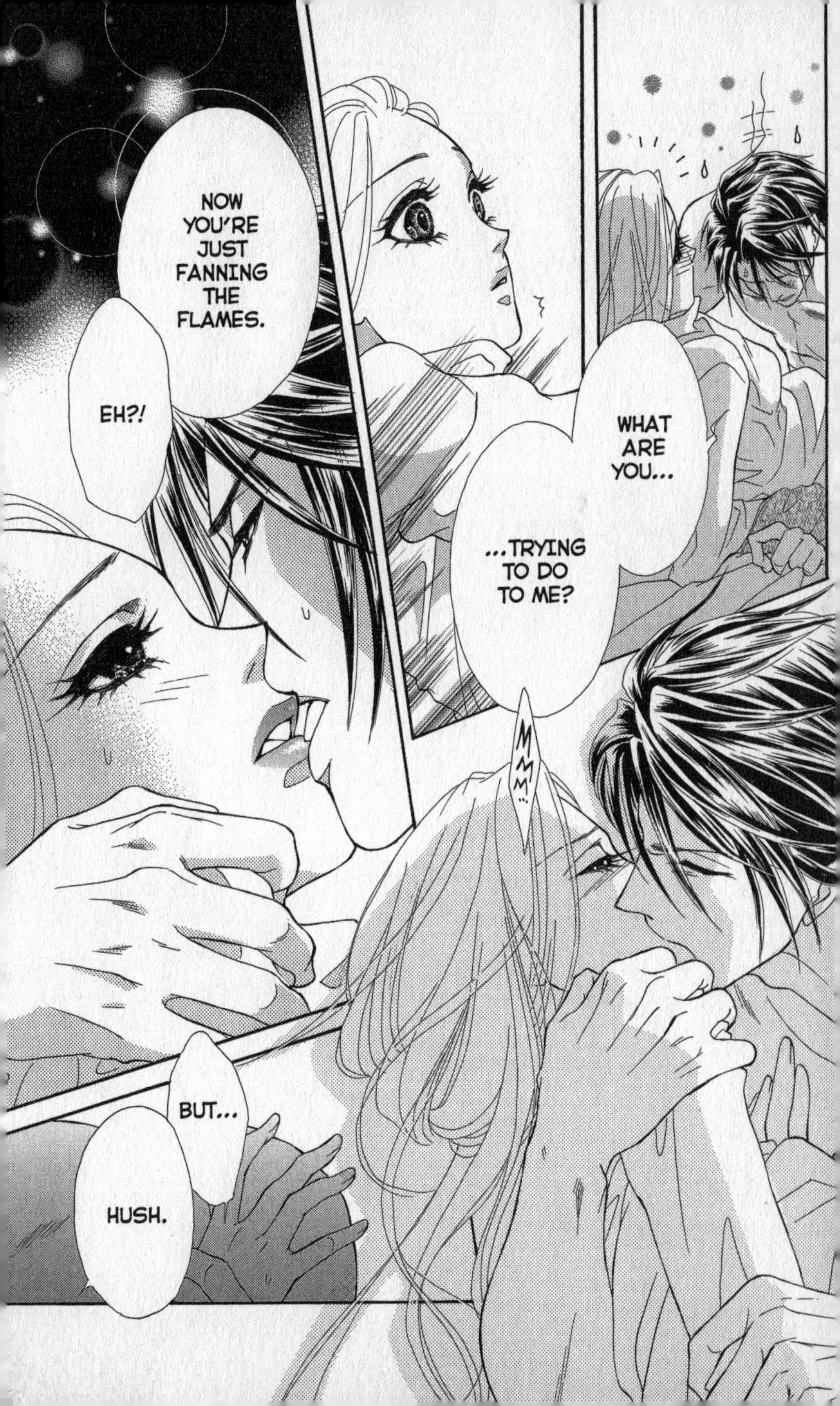
WHAT ARE YOU...
...TRYING TO DO TO ME?
NOW YOU'RE JUST FANNING THE FLAMES.
EH?!
MMM...
BUT...
HUSH.

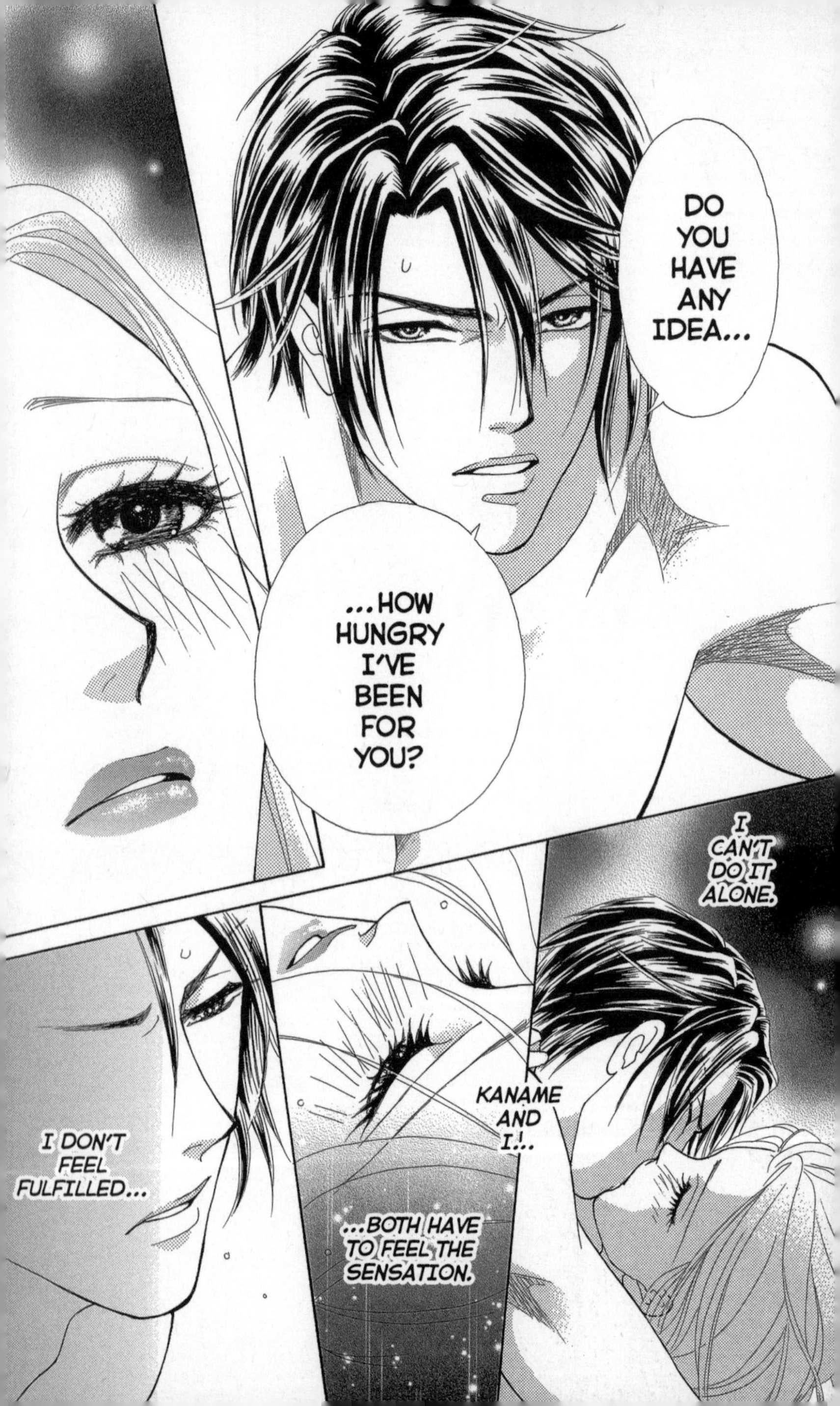
DO YOU HAVE ANY IDEA...
...HOW HUNGRY I'VE BEEN FOR YOU?
I CAN'T DO IT ALONE.
KANAME AND I!..
...BOTH HAVE TO FEEL THE SENSATION.
I DON'T FEEL FULFILLED...

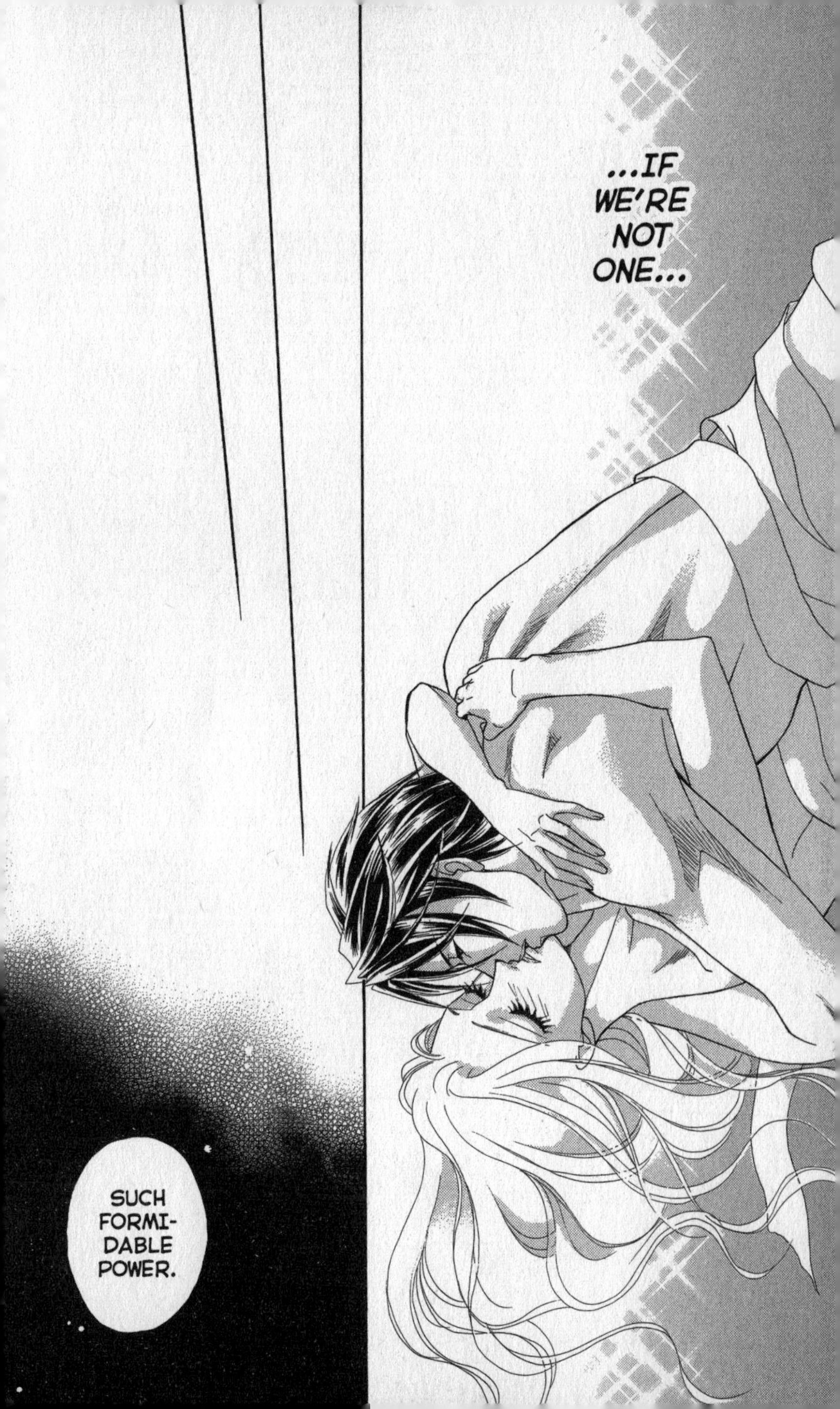
...IF WE'RE NOT ONE...
SUCH FORMI-DABLE POWER.

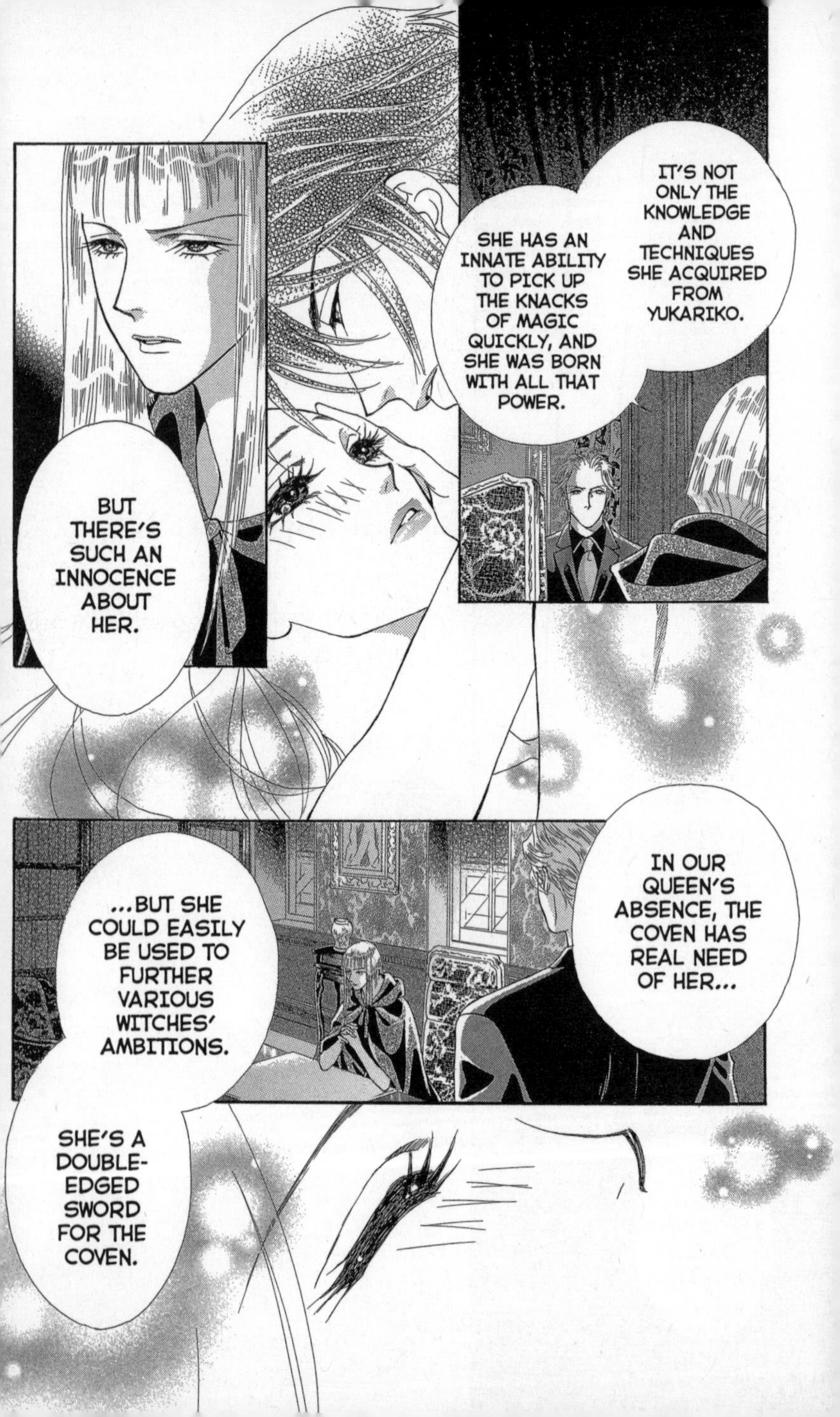
IT'S NOT ONLY THE KNOWLEDGE AND TECHNIQUES SHE ACQUIRED FROM YUKARIKO.
SHE HAS AN INNATE ABILITY TO PICK UP THE KNACKS OF MAGIC QUICKLY, AND SHE WAS BORN WITH ALL THAT POWER.
BUT THERE'S SUCH AN INNOCENCE ABOUT HER.
IN OUR QUEEN'S ABSENCE, THE COVEN HAS REAL NEED OF HER...
...BUT SHE COULD EASILY BE USED TO FURTHER VARIOUS WITCHES' AMBITIONS.
SHE'S A DOUBLE-EDGED SWORD FOR THE COVEN.

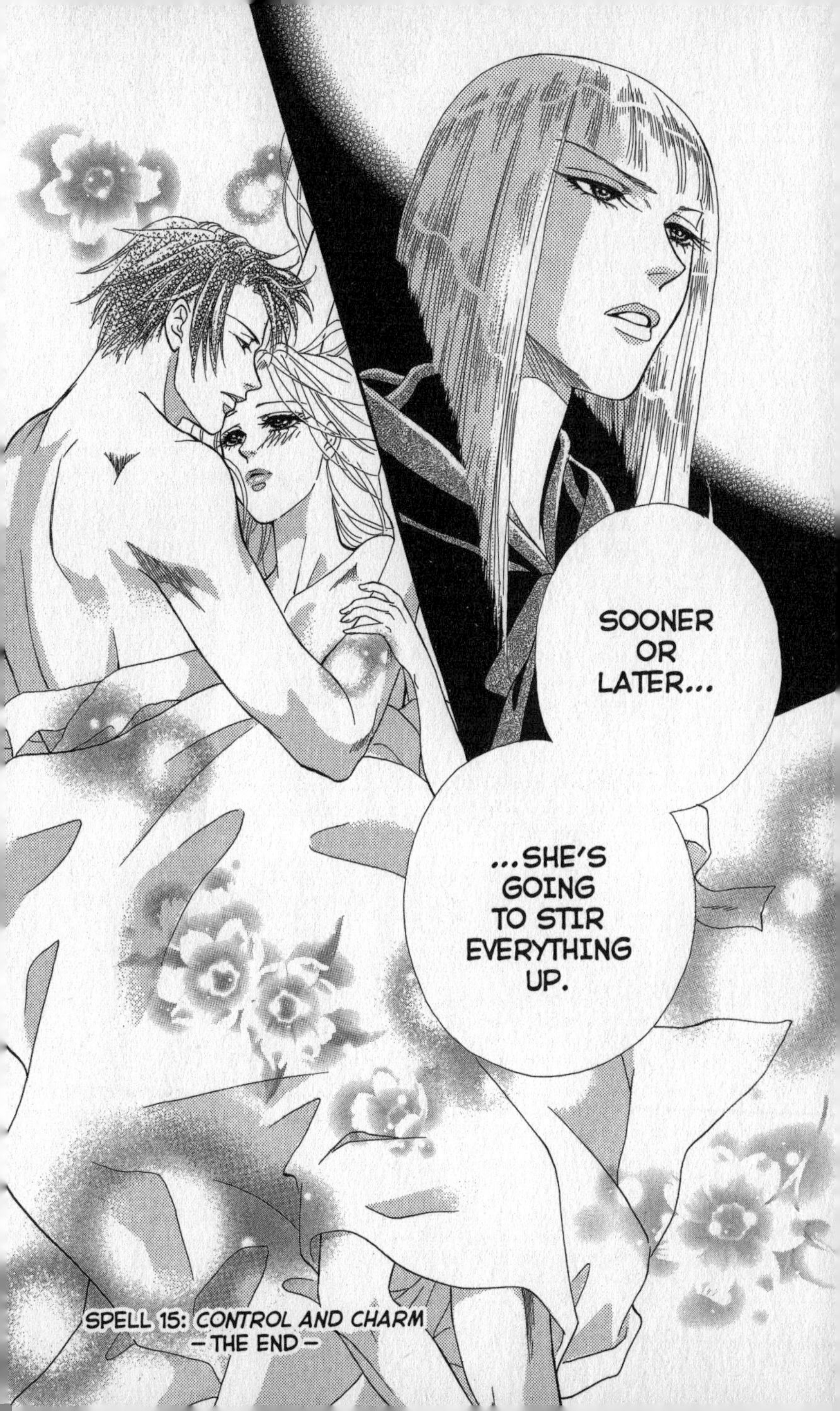
SOONER OR LATER...
...SHE'S GOING TO STIR EVERYTHING UP.
SPELL 15: CONTROL AND CHARM
– THE END –

AFTERWORD

Hello! This is Tomu Ohmi!

I'm so delighted that you've picked up my 30th volume!

Thirty books! Can you believe it?

I've been able to do so much work thanks to my editors and to all the people who've offered me guidance, but it's especially due to all of you who've been reading my work. I'm truly grateful! Thank you so much!

Now that Koko and Kaname have joined, body and soul, it's fun watching them making out and being so loving. But their future is still uncertain!

What will happen to these two? And what has become of Kitty? (*Laugh*) I hope you continue enjoying this story.

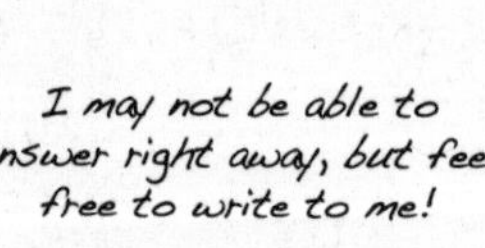

They're not home yet. ☼

I'm looking forward to seeing you again in *Petit Comic*!

Thanks to everyone who helped me with this manga and to all the readers.

I may not be able to answer right away, but feel free to write to me!

Tomu Ohmi
c/o Spell of Desire Editor
Viz Media
P.O. Box 77010
San Francisco, CA 94107

You can also email your thoughts to the *Petit Comic* web address. I shouldn't say this is in lieu of a reply, but I'd like to send you a New Year's greeting card, so please include your address.

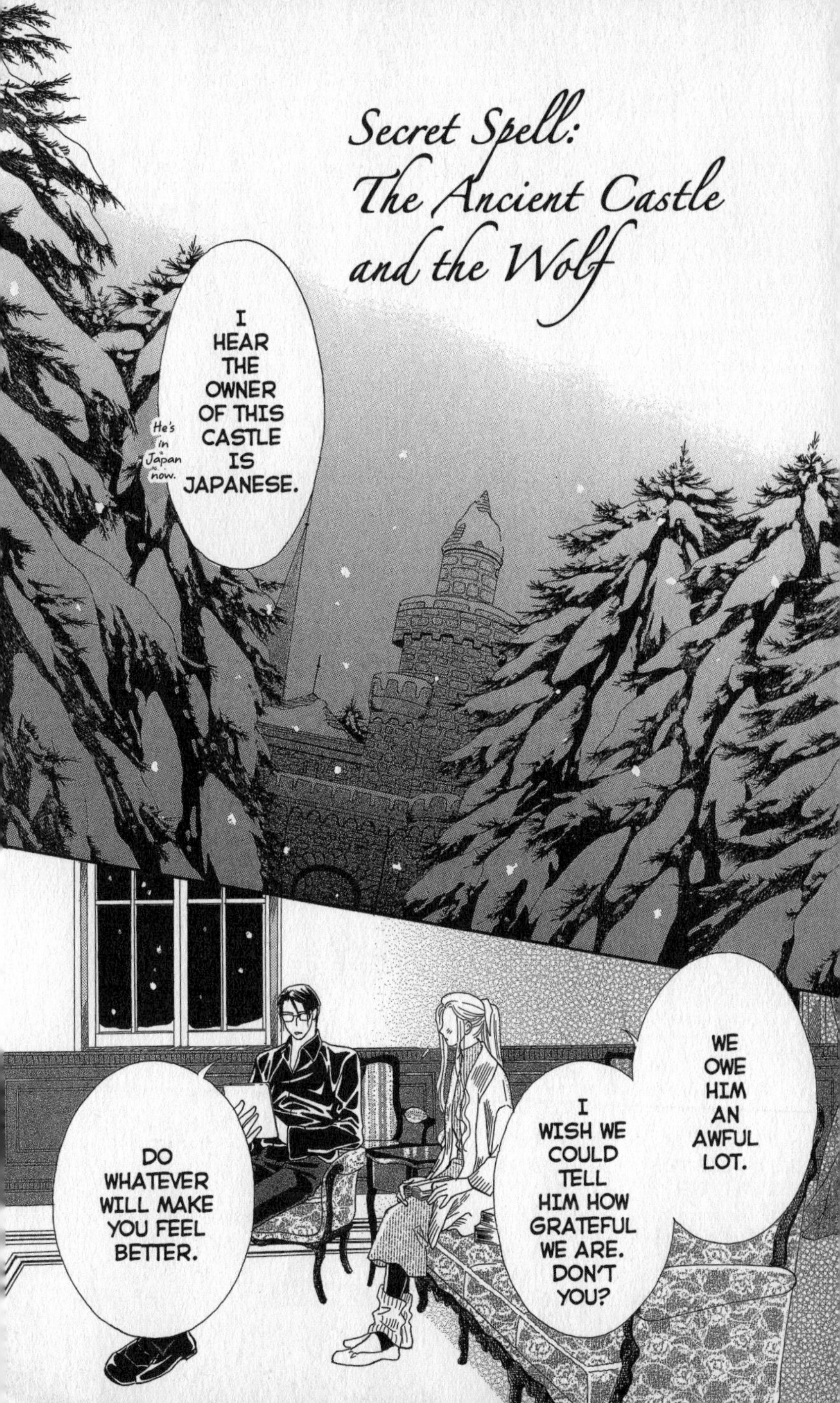
Secret Spell: The Ancient Castle and the Wolf
I HEAR THE OWNER OF THIS CASTLE IS JAPANESE.
He's in Japan now.
WE OWE HIM AN AWFUL LOT.
I WISH WE COULD TELL HIM HOW GRATEFUL WE ARE. DON'T YOU?
DO WHATEVER WILL MAKE YOU FEEL BETTER.

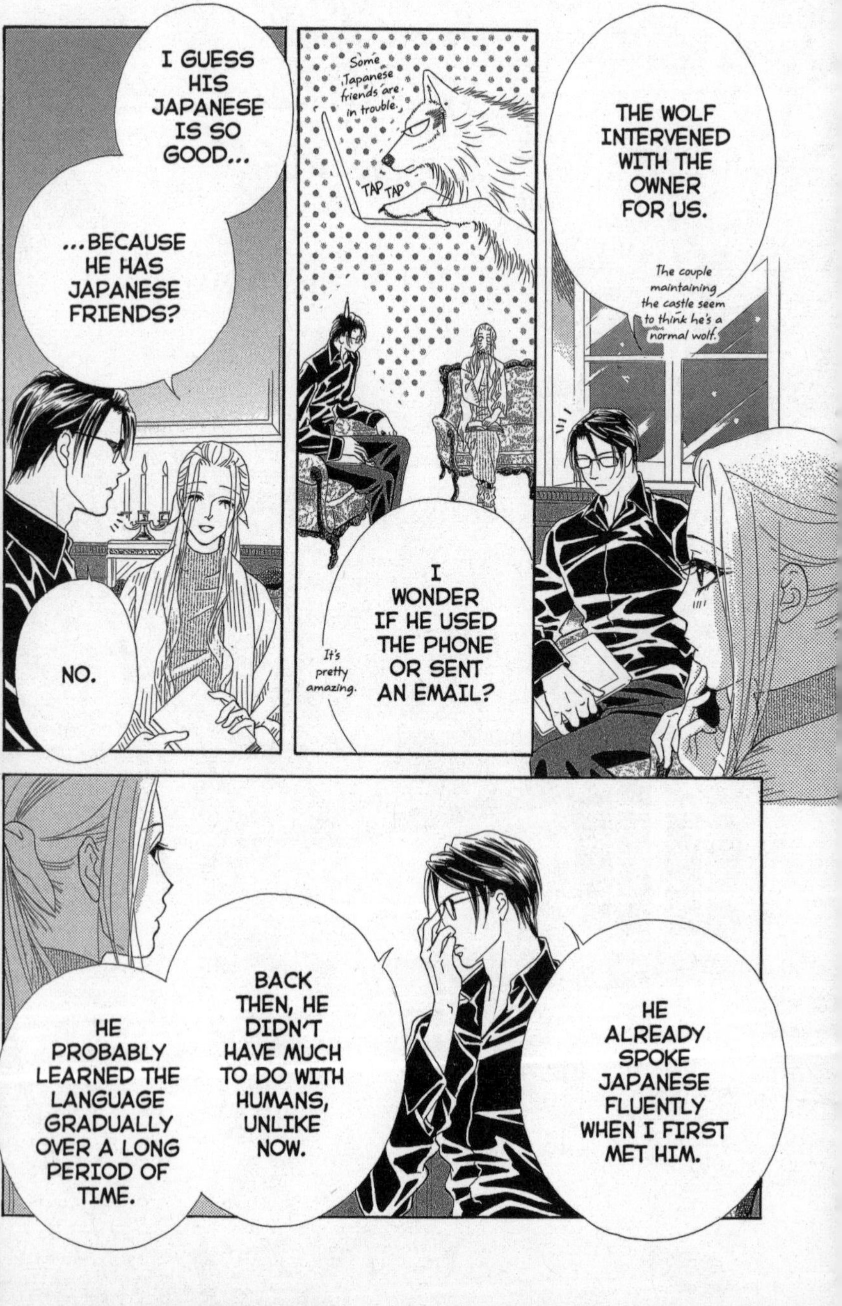
THE WOLF INTERVENED WITH THE OWNER FOR US.
The couple maintaining the castle seem to think he's a normal wolf.
Some Japanese friends are in trouble.
TAP TAP
I WONDER IF HE USED THE PHONE OR SENT AN EMAIL?
It's pretty amazing.
I GUESS HIS JAPANESE IS SO GOOD...
...BECAUSE HE HAS JAPANESE FRIENDS?
NO.
HE ALREADY SPOKE JAPANESE FLUENTLY WHEN I FIRST MET HIM.
BACK THEN, HE DIDN'T HAVE MUCH TO DO WITH HUMANS, UNLIKE NOW.
HE PROBABLY LEARNED THE LANGUAGE GRADUALLY OVER A LONG PERIOD OF TIME.

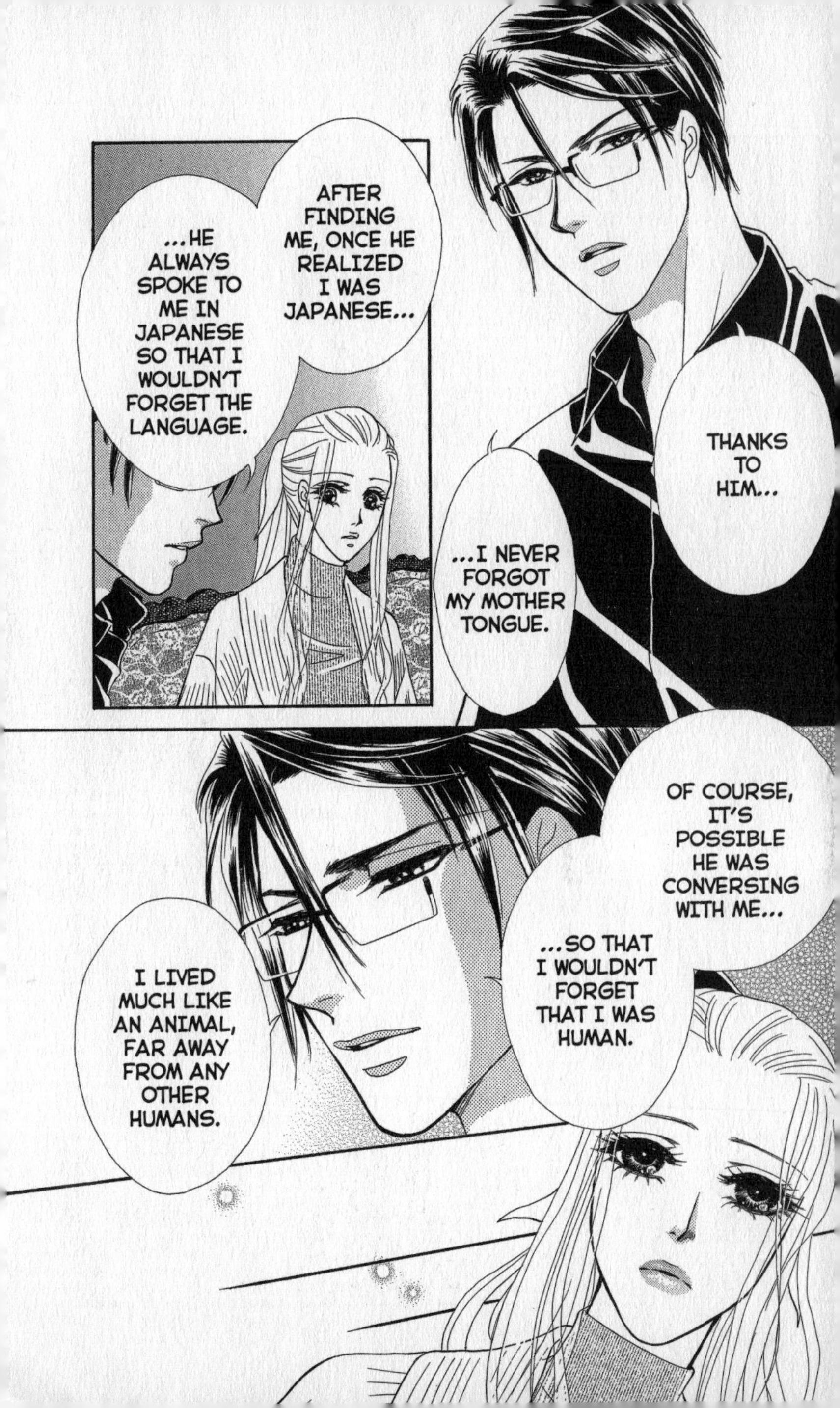
AFTER FINDING ME, ONCE HE REALIZED I WAS JAPANESE...
...HE ALWAYS SPOKE TO ME IN JAPANESE SO THAT I WOULDN'T FORGET THE LANGUAGE.
THANKS TO HIM...
...I NEVER FORGOT MY MOTHER TONGUE.
OF COURSE, IT'S POSSIBLE HE WAS CONVERSING WITH ME...
...SO THAT I WOULDN'T FORGET THAT I WAS HUMAN.
I LIVED MUCH LIKE AN ANIMAL, FAR AWAY FROM ANY OTHER HUMANS.

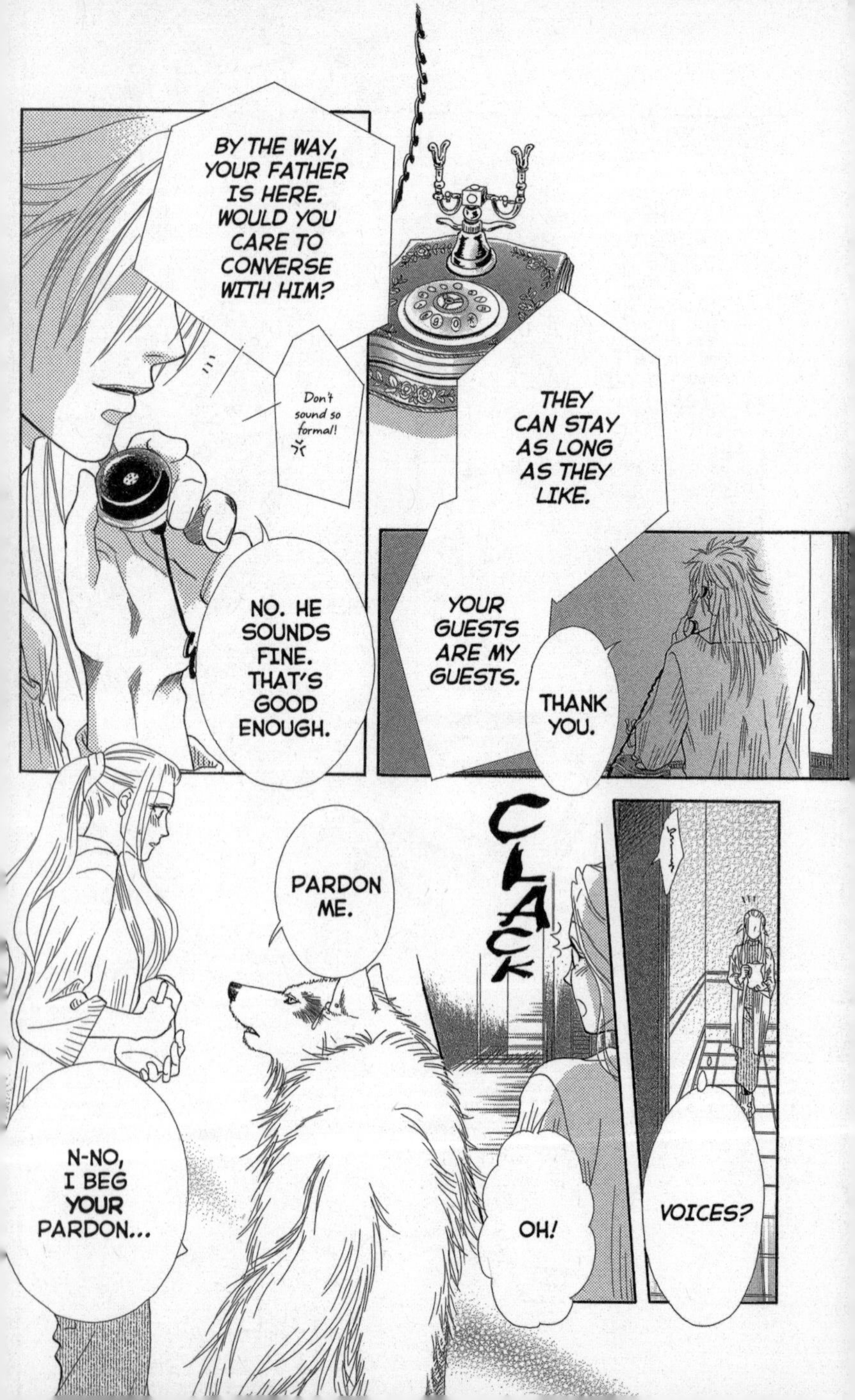
THEY CAN STAY AS LONG AS THEY LIKE.
YOUR GUESTS ARE MY GUESTS.
THANK YOU.
BY THE WAY, YOUR FATHER IS HERE. WOULD YOU CARE TO CONVERSE WITH HIM?
Don't sound so formal!
NO. HE SOUNDS FINE. THAT'S GOOD ENOUGH.
CLACK
VOICES?
OH!
PARDON ME.
N-NO, I BEG YOUR PARDON...

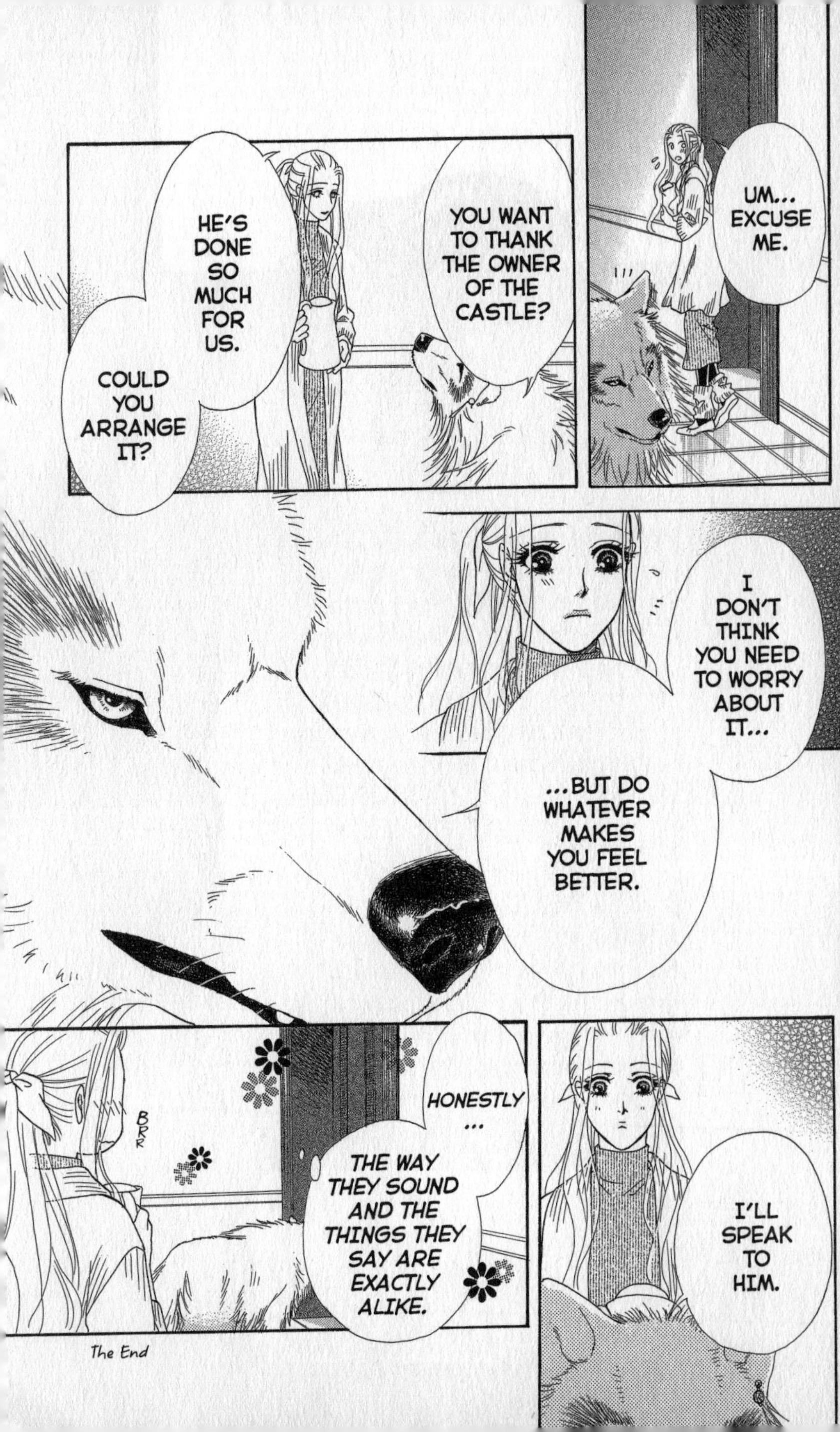
UM... EXCUSE ME.
YOU WANT TO THANK THE OWNER OF THE CASTLE?
HE'S DONE SO MUCH FOR US.
COULD YOU ARRANGE IT?
I DON'T THINK YOU NEED TO WORRY ABOUT IT...
...BUT DO WHATEVER MAKES YOU FEEL BETTER.
I'LL SPEAK TO HIM.
HONESTLY...
THE WAY THEY SOUND AND THE THINGS THEY SAY ARE EXACTLY ALIKE.
BRR
The End

A WITCH'S FAMILIAR...

...IS A BLACK CAT, OF COURSE!

Yay! ♥ This is my 30th book!! Thank you very much for picking this up! I'm amazed that this is my 30th book. Come to think of it, it's been over 10 years since I first began drawing for *Petit Comics*. It's thanks to all of you that I'm able to continue in this business. I feel so grateful!

–Tomu Ohmi

⮜◈◈◈ Author Bio ◈◈◈⮞

Born on May 25, Tomu Ohmi debuted with *Kindan no Koi wo Shiyoh* in 2000. She is presently working on *Petit Comic* projects like *Spell of Desire*. Her previous series, *Midnight Secretary*, is available from VIZ Media. Ohmi lives in Hokkaido, and she likes beasts, black tea and pretty women.

Spell of Desire

VOLUME 3
Shojo Beat Edition

STORY AND ART BY
TOMU OHMI

MAJO NO BIYAKU Vol. 3
by Tomu OHMI

Original Japanese edition published by SHOGAKUKAN.
English translation rights in the United States of America, Canada, the United Kingdom, Ireland, Australia and New Zealand arranged with SHOGAKUKAN.

English Adaptation/Ysabet Reinhardt MacFarlane
Translation/JN Productions
Touch-up Art & Lettering/Monalisa de Asis
Design/Izumi Evers
Editor/Amy Yu

Printed in the U.S.A.

Published by VIZ Media, LLC
P.O. Box 77010
San Francisco, CA 94107

10 9 8 7 6 5 4 3 2 1
First printing, February 2015

www.viz.com

PARENTAL ADVISORY
SPELL OF DESIRE is rated M for Mature and is recommended for ages 18 and up.
ratings.viz.com

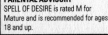

This is the last page.

In keeping with the original Japanese comic format, this book reads from right to left—so action, sound effects, and word balloons are completely reversed. This preserves the orientation of the original artwork—plus, it's fun! Check out the diagram shown here to get the hang of things, and then turn to the other side of the book to get started!